The Art of Warfare
in the Age of Marlborough

A TRAVELLER'S GUIDE TO THE BATTLEFIELDS OF EUROPE   2 Vols.

A GUIDE TO THE BATTLEFIELDS OF EUROPE

THE CAMPAIGNS OF NAPOLEON

PARKER & MERODE-WESTERLOO: THE MARLBOROUGH WARS

NAPOLEON

THE ILLUSTRATED NAPOLEON

MARLBOROUGH AS MILITARY COMMANDER

THE ART OF WARFARE ON LAND

A DICTIONARY OF THE NAPOLEONIC WARS

WATERLOO — THE HUNDRED DAYS

AN ATLAS OF MILITARY STRATEGY, 1618-1878

THE JOURNAL OF JOHN MARSHALL DEANE

SEDGEMOOR — AN ACCOUNT AND AN ANTHOLOGY

NAPOLEON'S MARSHALS

THE MILITARY MAXIMS OF NAPOLEON

THE DICTIONARY OF BATTLES

BATTLES AND BATTLESCENES OF WORLD WAR TWO

AUSTERLITZ, 1805

GREAT BRITISH BATTLES OF THE SANDHURST COMPANIES

R.M.A. SANDHURST — 250 YEARS

JENA, 1806

D-DAY ENCYLOPAEDIA

ESSAYS 'ON THE NAPOLEONIC WARS'

THE OXFORD ILLUSTRATED HISTORY OF THE BRITISH ARMY

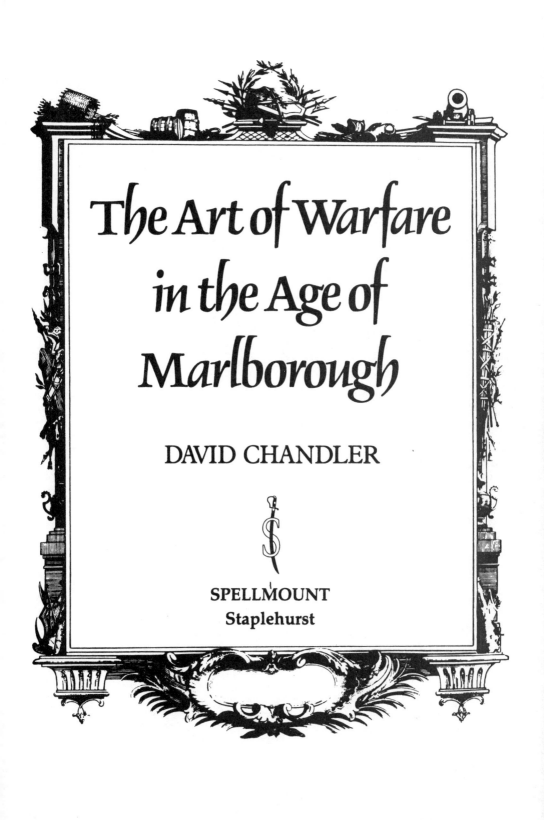

The Art of Warfare in the Age of Marlborough

DAVID CHANDLER

SPELLMOUNT
Staplehurst

British Library Cataloguing in Publication Data:
A catalogue record for this book is available
from the British Library

Copyright © David G Chandler 1976

ISBN 0-946771-42-1

First published in the UK in 1976 by Batsford Ltd

This edition published in the UK in 1990 by
Spellmount Limited
The Old Rectory
Staplehurst
Kent TN12 0AZ

Tel: 01580 893730
Fax: 01580 893731
E-mail: enquiries@spellmount.com
Website: www.spellmount.com

5 7 9 8 6 4

Printed in Great Britain by
Biddles Ltd, King's Lynn and Guildford

Contents

List of Illustrations

Diagrams

Acknowledgements

The Author and Publishers would like to thank the following for permission to reproduce illustrations: Courtauld Institute of Art (Witt Collection), Fig 3; Marquess of Anglesey and the Department of the Environment, Fig 2; Mary Evans Picture Library, Figs 4, 10 and 14; Musée de la Marine, Paris, Fig 11; Parker Gallery, Figs 1 and 9; Trustees of the National Army Museum, Figs 5 and 6; Victoria and Albert Museum, Figs 7, 8, 13 and 15. Figs 12, 16 and 17 are from the Publisher's collection. Dr D.R. Sellman is thanked for providing the drawing of the Eighteenth Century Fortification on page 238.

Foreword

'Every Art and Science has its peculiar terms, which are obscure to all who are not vers'd in it,' wrote the anonymous compiler of *A Military Dictionary*, published in London in 1702. 'The Art of War, like all the rest, has many words unknown, or at least not familiar to any but those whose profession and duty obliges to be masters of them. . . . These difficulties are generally pass'd by unregarded, as if not material for the understanding of what is read; and yet, in reality, they are as necessary and proper to be known as any other part of the relation, which without them becomes but a confus'd notion of something done or acted, without any distinct judicious knowledge of the methods, parts and circumstances of the action. . . .'

It is my hope that this volume will go some way towards dissipating a little of the 'fog of war' surrounding the military organization, training methods and tactical concepts of late seventeenth- and early eighteenth-century European armies. It is not a comprehensive study of the wars or leaders of the period, but rather a background analysis of certain martial aspects which are often taken for granted or dismissed in a few words by biographers and general historians. Those looking for strategic, logistical or sociological analyses will be disappointed – although some of these subjects are touched upon in the Introduction. This volume is devoted to a fairly full examination of how the regimental officer and soldier fought and manoeuvred, whether in the line of battle or siege trenches, and of the equipment, doctrine and training that enabled them to perform their duty. My purpose, therefore, is to provide a work of reference that may help the serious reader towards a fuller appreciation of the realities of eighteenth-century warfare. It is titled *The Art of Warfare in the Age of Marlborough* because the First Duke was probably the pre-eminent military figure in Western Europe between the eras of Turenne and Condé on the one hand and the period of the mature Frederick II of Prussia on the other. Although John Churchill did not appear decisively on the military scene until 1702, and died just 20 years later, his influence was pervasive, both directly and indirectly, for a generation after his death. But this study is really concerned with the fortunes of the men he led and those he defeated – the small cogs in the military scene without which nothing whatever would have been achieved.

Many friends and colleagues at both Sandhurst and several universities have given me the benefit of their knowledge and advice on various aspects of this study, and it would not be possible to mention them all. However, I would particularly like to thank Brigadier Peter Young, DSO, MC, MA, FSA, whose initial suggestion ten years ago led me to undertake this project, Miss P. C. McGlinchy, Mrs Denyse Marples and Mrs Margaret Ward who tackled most of the typing without flinching, and Mr Michael Stephenson of B. T. Batsford Ltd. who steered the volume to publication. I am grateful to the staffs of the Central Library at RMA Sandhurst and of the Ministry of Defence Library (Central and Army), for much assistance in tracing elusive books and for making numerous suggestions. I also owe a debt to the Trustees of the British Museum and the authorities of the Public Records Office for permission to cite manuscript material, and to the Historical Sections of the Danish, Swedish and Dutch General Staffs for copies of otherwise unavailable sources and other assistance. I also owe a great deal, as always, to my wife and family for their invaluable assistance with the tedious but important task of indexing.

The Royal Military Academy, Sandhurst

Introduction

The 60 years between 1688 and 1748 form a watershed in the history of the development of warfare. More scholarly attention has tended to be paid to the periods of the Thirty Years War and the earlier parts of the reign of Louis XIV on the one hand, and to the events of the main Frederickan era, the American War of Independence and the ensuing Revolutionary and Napoleonic Wars on the other, than to the intervening years. Of course the achievements of Marlborough, Prince Eugene and Marshal Saxe have been analysed and re-analysed in a number of recent notable works, and new attention has been drawn to the struggle in the Spanish Peninsula in the early eighteenth century, but few works have devoted more than a few pages or at best a chapter to a close examination of the development of the art of war in these generations. It is hoped that this book will go some small way towards remedying this deficiency, for it is extremely difficult to judge the great commanders of any age and the martial proclivities and fluctuations of the major European powers unless they can be set clearly against their military backgrounds. All too often these action-filled years are cursorily dismissed as being of little interest, or branded as a period of 'limited warfare', barren of significant developments – and yet in fact they saw the laying of important tactical foundations for succeeding generations.

Professor Nef declared over a quarter of a century ago that '. . . no Age is more in need of re-examination than the 100 years which began in England with the outbreak in 1642 of the Civil War and in France with the accession of the infant Louis XIV in 1643. These 100 years were of immense importance in the general history of Europe and of the European colonies. . . .' * The scope of this present volume does not exactly coincide with the century Nef referred to, and only attempts to deal with a very circumscribed aspect of even the military affairs of that period, but it does hope to contribute something to aid the comprehension of military events.

This study has been deliberately restricted to an examination of the tactical organisation and handling of the European 'teeth arms' of the late seventeenth

* J. U. Nef, *War and Human Progress* (Harvard, 1950, 2nd edition), p. 147.

and the first half of the eighteenth centuries. That is to say, its four main
sections deal with the Horse, the Foot, the Trains of Artillery and the Engineer
Services of the period, describing their representation, organization, equipment,
training and tactical employment. The treatment is not restricted to the
examination of a single army alone: most attention is devoted to the English and
French forces, which serve as controls, but comparisons are drawn with Dutch,
Swedish, Prussian, Austrian, Russian and Turkish practices on a more limited
scale to demonstrate regional differences and peculiarities. Thus it is hoped that
something of an over-view of European military practice at the tactical level will
emerge. Finally, a number of appendices have been added in which the more
important wars, and a selection of the battles and sieges of the period, are
comparatively analysed in outline form.

Perhaps it should be stressed at the outset that a number of vital military
subjects receive no treatment, except incidentally, in these pages. This book does
not set out to study the great generals in their own right – except insofar as they
were responsible for significant tactical or organizational developments.
Similarly, few strategic or grand tactical analyses will be found; nor do logistical
considerations figure large, and the sociological aspects of the armies of the time
receive only passing attention. This is in no way intended to imply that these
subjects deserve less attention than the organizational and operational aspects
treated below, but they have been deliberately excluded as being beyond the
scope of this study. Besides, a number of significant volumes have been devoted
to several of these subjects in recent years.*

However, in order to place in context the four main studies that follow, it is
necessary to establish a number of basic strategic considerations affecting the
conduct of military operations during the period under review. The century from
1650 to 1750 is often described as forming a period of 'limited' warfare, and of
military mediocrity. These concepts require a little examination, for they can be
misunderstood.

It is true that many of the wars that took place between 1650 and 1750 were
relatively 'limited' in the way they were conducted – that is to say, that concepts
of 'totality' were rejected as impracticable or inadvisable for one or more
pragmatic or ideological reasons. The notorious Thirty Years War (1618-48) had
been a 'total' struggle during the most devastating parts of its long course. It had
been an ideological struggle fought over bitter religious issues between Catholic
and Protestant populations; it had been a constitutional power struggle within
the Holy Roman Empire, in which the Emperor's authority had been challenged
by some of his princes; and it had become the scene of inter-dynastic rivalry, as
first Sweden, and then France, had intervened for various motives in the war
and broadened its scope to include a power-struggle by the Houses of Vasa and

---

* Including: R. E. Scouller, *The Armies of Queen Anne* (Oxford: 1964) – a full study of its
administrative and organizational aspects; G. Perjés, *Army Provisioning, Logistics and Strategy in
the Second Half of the Seventeenth Century*, (Budapest, 1970) an invaluable examination of the
relationship between food supply and military strategy; and A. Corvisier, *L'armée française de la
Fin du XVIIe Siècle au Ministère de Choiseul: (le soldat)* 2 vols, (Paris, 1964), basically a
sociological survey.

(later) Bourbon against the Austrian Habsburgs. This complex and prolonged war or series of wars had been conducted with a terrible and ruthless ferocity which had led to the depopulation of sizeable tracts of Southern and Central Germany. The loss of life proved grave, and in the years after the Peace of Westphalia there had developed an international reaction against such measures, and a demand for the avoidance in future conflicts of such extremes. This, then, was the basic psychological restraining factor behind the succeeding period of so-called 'limited' wars. However, there were notable exceptions. The ancient Habsburg-Ottoman struggle in South-East Europe continued to be waged spasmodically with most of its old religious animosity, and parts of the Great Northern War between Sweden, Poland and Russia were similarly waged with great ferocity. Even in Western Europe there were occasional barbaric episodes but at least they were rare enough to cause international outcries.

There were also important physical limitations on the conduct of war, which indubitably restrained the intensity of the waging of campaigns. The seasonal nature of campaigning was dictated by the appalling condition of European roads and waterways during some seven months in the year, and this in turn encouraged the prosecution of sieges or elaborate manoeuvres rather than attempts to achieve all-out victory. Mediocre generals preferred siege wars for a number of reasons. They were largely predictable – in terms of both course and likely outcome. They were economical in terms of movement and (they believed, often erroneously) in terms of casualties – and this was regarded as a practical as well as a humanitarian factor. And they offered something tangible (useful pawns for peace negotiations) in the event of success. Major engagements were unpopular for the opposite reasons: they were often hard to procure strategically; they were very expensive in terms of casualties – especially in view of certain developments in weaponry which will be examined at some length later in the volume; and they were rarely predictable.

But by far the most significant limitation on the fighting of wars was bound up with logistics. It has been convincingly demonstrated in recent years that the war *aims* of the major combattants were rarely limited. Perhaps they were not so 'total' as the concepts of 'unconditional surrender' demanded in the world wars of this century, but they were far-reaching enough in their demands for reallocation of frontiers and territories, and armies were steadily growing in size as governments increased their administrative organization. In one vital respect, however, the powers failed to rise to the challenges they set themselves: they never proved capable of solving the basic problem of supplying their armies effectively whilst in the field.

This was the factor that caused what Professor Perjés has termed 'the crisis in strategy'.* The development in the size of field armies will be treated in some detail below, but here it is sufficient to mention that whereas early-seventeenth century field forces had rarely exceeded 40,000 men, by the end of the first decade of the eighteenth century individual armies in excess of 100,000 men

---

* Perjés, *op. cit.*, p. 51. He also cites in support the views of H. Delbruck, *Geschichte der Kriegskunst*, vol. IV, Berlin 1920, p. 343.

were not unknown. Generals often argued in favour of smaller forces, for they became increasingly aware of the problems posed by the need to subsist the larger armies that the ambitions of their masters forced upon them as they strove to outbid the claims of rivals to hegemony in Europe and overseas. The period of so-called 'limited war', therefore, was dominated by much aggressiveness on the national level, only thinly disguised by a veneer of rationalism. Surprisingly, perhaps, there was no great upsurge in population sizes or agricultural productivity to underpin this military expansion, except in the cases of the United Provinces (of a short-lived nature) and of England. France's population was actually declining a little at the turn of the century, and the overall growth of Europe's peoples was only very slight. What had changed dramatically was the improvement in the means and methods of state administration – which made it possible to mobilize, equip and marshal more and more men in pursuit of national objectives. It did not, however, make it commensurately easier to feed them – and there lay the rub. As Guibert declared, the overall decline in the standards of the art of war during the eighteenth century in France was in large measure due to the imprudence with which Louis xiv and his minister, Louvois, had inflated the manpower of France's armies, which caused them to become clumsy and largely unmanageable masses.* The expansion in army sizes, therefore, was due far more to political causes than to social, economic or purely military factors. Political ambitions came to outstrip the means of production. Larger armies could be collected, but the means of supplying, transporting and commanding them remained inadequate to the challenge.

   The basic problem, simply stated, was that the quantities of food needed to feed these larger armies could not be obtained on the spot. Neither the populations nor the levels of agricultural productivity were large enough to maintain, even for a brief period, so vast an accretion of men and horses. Armies, their increased sizes notwithstanding, still functioned along single lines of operation. There was little idea of moving, and subsisting, in a number of widely separated columns in order to spread the burden over the roads and countryside more evenly, before concentrating to fight. Such concepts would hardly be encountered before the French Revolution and the Napoleonic *corps d'armée* system. Consequently, the only means of subsisting armies that marched, as well as fought, in concentration, was to collect huge quantities of food and fodder in magazines and depots before the opening of a campaign – and to pass forward the supplies to the moving armies by means of convoys operating in their rear. Armies had used convoys to some extent in every age, of course, but never on the scale now required – and neither the administrative machinery nor the logistical experience necessary to satisfy the new demands existed; nor did roads of a type suitable for the weight and volume of traffic now envisaged. Small wonder, therefore, that many campaigns were conducted with what seemed to be deadening slowness and lack of decisiveness. 'Now it is frequent to have armies of 50,000 men of a side standing at bay within sight of one another,' complained Daniel Defoe, 'and spend a whole campaign in dodging – or, as it is genteely

---

* H. de Guibert, *Essai Generale de Tactique*, Tomes I – II, London 1772 (II) p. 6.

termed – observing one another, and then march off into winter quarters.'* Only the very greatest commanders of the age – Luxembourg, Marlborough, Eugene, Villars, Saxe and Frederick – proved occasionally capable of transcending these logistical limitations, and thus returned something of pace, colour and decisiveness to the conduct of warfare.

It has been calculated that an area had to support a population of 35 people to the square kilometre to be able to provision an army which was operating without benefit of magazines. This calculation is based on the assumption that such areas were self-supporting, with locally-grown grain stocks available. A study of regional population distribution in the seventeenth and eighteenth centuries reveals that only five areas of Europe possessed such a population and the implicit agricultural yield, namely parts of France, the Spanish Netherlands, Westphalia, parts of the Rhineland area, and Lombardy. It comes as no surprise, therefore, to discover that these were pre-eminently the 'major seats of war' throughout our period.**

The sheer bulk of provisions required was staggering. Most armies tried to issue each man a kilogram of bread a day, but on account of extra-rations issued to officers, and the need to feed waggoners and expert craftsmen accompanying an army, a force of 60,000 men might require all of 90,000 rations a day; Puységur calculated that 120,000 soldiers required 180,000 bread rations – and Dupré d'Aulnay, perhaps the most skilled logistical expert of the mid-eighteenth century, laid down the principle that it was always necessary to allow rations on a scale one third greater than the nominal strength of an army,[†] just to allow for the surplus entitlements of the French officers and general staff. Thus for a six month campaign, an army of 60,000 men would require, in terms of bread alone, almost 43 million kilograms, and few indeed were the areas of Europe capable of bearing such a burden without facing utter local destitution, starvation and depopulation.

Professor Perjés has calculated every aspect of the problem of supplying an army with bread. On the basic assumption that 60,000 men required 900 quintals or hundredweight of bread a day (made from 675 quintals of grain or flour), at least 60 ovens operated by a staff of 240 bakers would be needed to undertake the baking of four days' rations. Armies habitually marched for three days and halted the fourth, which was needed for rest and re-supply. To build a single oven called for 500 two-kilogram bricks, so to supply the basic requirements for 60 ovens called for 60 carts of bricks, and it required several days' work to establish an efficient bakery and the necessary stores around it. The fuel problem was even more dramatic. To fire the 60 ovens seven times a month required all of 1400 waggon-loads of fuel (a single baking called for 200 loads). The milling of flour also presented daunting logistical problems: local mills were often targets for enemy interdictive action, so armies had to carry grinding equipment with them – still further enlarging the trains; on occasion

* D. Defoe, *An Essay upon Projects* (ed. London 1889), p. 135.

** Perjés, *op. cit*, pp. 4–6.

[†] Puységur, *op. cit*, Tome 2, p. 62; and D. d'Aulnay, *Traité generale des subsistances militaires*, Paris 1744, p. 116.

commanders are known to have issued small hand-mills to regiments – as did Marlborough in 1705.

Some idea of the basic problems involved in feeding an army on campaign in our period may be gained from consideration of statistics of this kind. Unless a force could build-up large quantities of milled flour at convenient points prior to entering on campaign, its operational freedom could be severely restricted. Only rarely were such resources available in advance – although most armies attempted to build up some reserves during the winter season (for example this formed a perennial duty for the French intendancies along the frontiers) – and this of course tended to restrict the scale and scope of operations. Although recourse was often had to wholesale requisitioning of supplies and transport in friendly or hostile areas alike – and many were the outcries of outrage that such actions provoked – the areas capable of supporting large numbers of men even if the local inhabitants went largely without were limited as we have already noted. Only in those rare instances of an army being in a position to pay its way was anything approaching local cooperation wholeheartedly given. One such case was Marlborough's march to the Danube theatre from the Netherlands in 1704 – when it was noted that the local people vied with one another to bring supplies to the collecting points, for the Duke's quartermasters were paying good English gold at fair prices. But this was regarded as a wonderful novelty: in most cases, local populations regarded the presence of *any* army, whether friend or foe, as an unmitigated disaster, and prayed with fervour for it to march away elsewhere.

Given these difficulties, Marlborough's proud claim that during his period of command, '... everything has been so organised, and there has been so little cause for complaint, that all know our army in Flanders has been regularly supplied with bread during the war ...' * proves of no little significance.

However, if reserves were to be built up in advance, much reliance had to be placed on civilian contractors. No country possessed a formal procurement executive as such until the mid-eighteenth century, so much recourse had to be made to civilian entrepreneurs. This system was open to abuses from both sides: contractors were occasionally fraudulent and corrupt – mixing sand with the grain and resorting to other nefarious practices; but at the same time many governments were extremely remiss in honouring their agreements to produce payment. The English army dealt with contractors through the agency of Commissioners of Supply and Transport, appointed by the government, and acting through field commissaries. The bulk bread contractors of the early eighteenth century in Flanders included such names as Solomon and Moses Medina, Mynheer Hecop, Vanderkaa and Machado, most of them Spanish or Dutch Jews. The last-named together with Solomon Abraham were amongst the less scrupulous, and had to be carefully watched. But if the English army in Flanders was generally well-supplied with necessaries, the same cannot be claimed for other armies – for example the English and Dutch forces serving in Portugal and Spain. Thus in 1704 King Pedro of Portugal was induced to replace Salvador Segundez – as chief contractor – by Messrs. Gomez. This

* Parliamentary History, Vol. 6, p. 1088.

achieved nothing, as Segundez had control of the sources of supply, both bread and meat, such as they were in that semi-barren land, and proceeded to hold his successors to ransom. After one month of the autumn campaign that year shortages steadily grew, and sometimes the army was three days without basic rations – which effectively immobilised General Fagel's forces.* Difficulties of this sort were common throughout Europe. Only when the French government came to rely upon the brilliant logistical skills of D'Aulnay did they begin to set their supply system in order. Prior to the mid-eighteenth century, they had placed reliance on the Intendants to find rations for the armies – but the development of central procurement – at least to a certain degree – proved an enormous advantage.

If feeding the troops posed enormous problems, that of finding fodder and forage for the horses – tens of thousands of which accompanied every army – was equally difficult. An army of 60,000 men would have at least 40,000 horses accompanying it. In the campaigning season – the exact length of which was dictated equally by the state of the roads and the availability, or otherwise, of fodder – such an army needed to find 10,000 quintals a day; in time of winter quarters, this dropped to about 5,000 quintals of solid feed – oats and straw. To convey such quantities called for some 1,000 carts in summer, and perhaps 500 in winter.

It was rarely attempted to convey such bulky quantities during the spring and summer, and all armies relied on local requisitioning – but local reserves of the period were once again not always equal to the task. Oats were only provided for the first and last months of a campaign, and for the period of winter quarters. At other times, continuous recourse was had to 'Grand Foragings', which might need anything from 4,000 to 10,000 troops to carry out at any one time. The best periods when the grass was lushest were first the main spring months and next the six or so weeks before the harvest. Less abundant supplies were available in early summer and late autumn. In spring it was estimated that horses needed two weeks of grazing to 'purify' themselves after the inadequate feeding of the winter months. In April 1710, the Hungarian patriot leader, Rakoczi, wrote that no operations could yet be undertaken '. . . before grass, for the army horses are depressed and look down upon the ground.' Thus another limitation on the waging of effective campaigns becomes apparent.[†] Foraging was as perennial a chore as baking.

'Grand Forages' were in any case elaborate affairs, calling for minute organisation and control – for it was during them that the ever-present danger of desertions reached its peak. Almost as many troops were therefore employed as guards and patrols as were involved in cutting the grass. On each occasion sufficient forage would be gathered for four or five days.

Few generals could break away from these deadening routines. Prince Eugene of Savoy, *pace* many historians, was insistent that his armies should operate from pre-stocked magazines. During his Italian campaigns of 1701 and 1702, he

---

* See D. Francis, *The First Peninsular War, 1702-13* (London 1975) pp. 99-100.
[†] *Archivum Rackoczianum*, vol. I, p. 229 cited by Perjés *op. cit.* p. 15 (fn).

was particularly insistent on the establishment of suitable depots in the Frioul and Tyrol; in 1707 it was partly dissatisfaction with the supply arrangements – and his unwillingness to rely on the British Fleet as a source of major supply – that led to the abandonment of the siege of Toulon; and next year, it was his 'conventional' concern for convoys and lines of communication that led him to oppose Marlborough's grandiose scheme, after Oudenarde, for an invasion of France along the coast (drawing supplies from the Fleet through Abbeville), and caused him to insist on the siege of Lille instead.

Some countries proved more adept than others at measuring up to these problems. The French, as the Earl of Orrery percipiently noted as early as 1676, '. . . with great prudence attack places in the beginning of the Spring, when there is no army to relieve them; and in the Summer, when the whole confederacy is in the field, they are usually on the defensive, and cover what they have took [*sic*]; and in my weak judgment they do at least as much by their always providing well to eat, and by their entrenched encamping, as by their good fighting, which questionless is the most hopeful and most solid way of making war.' * The French 'pounce' on Namur early in 1692 is a good example. Surprisingly, for in other respects the Ottoman Turk lagged in many of the martial skills and sciences, the strategy of the Porte was also realistic. Count Raimondo Montecuculi noted that they operated from well-filled magazines, and only when forage was available, seeking short, sharp wars and deliberately courting battle by invariably seizing the initiative and invading. His views were corroborated by de la Colonie, the seasoned Bavarian campaigner: 'The Turks in all preceding wars against the Empire had always given battle on the first opportunity,' he observed. 'If they lost the day, they immediately retired and made off to their homes. If victory declared itself in their favour, they would then make an extremely rapid advance, not employing themselves as is the custom in Europe in discussing camping grounds and strategy, for they believed the only way to make war upon the Christians was to strike a blow as rapidly as possible.' Although he considered most of their huge armies, the Janissary Corps and the *sipahis* apart, as 'a mob', . . . 'ignorant of all discipline . . .' and remarked cuttingly on the disorder of their encampments, he nevertheless admired the simplicity of the Tartar ration system. 'Each of these nations are fed in a different fashion. That of the Tartars, perhaps has the merit of at least being the most convenient in form, the only provisions carried by their soldiery being cheeses made of mares' milk . . . When required for use the Tartars scrape a little into a pannikin of water, stir it up with their finger, and swallow the mixture, which is as white as milk and constitutes their only nourishment. If we could all exist on such food, what a deal of trouble would be spared the world in general!'†

However, the 'Old Campaigner' believed in rather more elaborate self-help where supplies were concerned. Writing of the battle of Belgrade in 1717, he reveals he '. . . had taken the precaution of seeing my canteens were well filled

---

* The Earl of Orrery, *A Treatise on the Art of Warre* (London: 1677) p. 139.
† De la Colonie, *Chronicles of an Old Campaigner*, ed. W. C. Horsley, (London, 1908) pp. 414–418.

with provisions, including plenty of wine. . . . I have always taken care to do this, finding it to be of the greatest use on all occasions . . . but never more so than upon this day, for after the battle everyone suffered from hunger, and still more from thirst, and my officers of rank who had not shown the same forethought were much relieved to find that I had the wherewithal to minister to their needs.' *

Logistics, then, played a vital, even determinant, part in strategy. Some commanders, like Vendôme, tried to ignore the implications; that officer even ordered on one occasion that he was not under any circumstances to be troubled with matters pertaining to the supply of his men. Others became totally dominated by these problems – and achieved little in consequence. As in so many matters, it was Gustavus Adolphus of Sweden who had pioneered the seventeenth and eighteenth century system of logistics. Although his armies were smaller and therefore handier than their successors, he developed an integrated system of pre-stocked magazines, compact supply trains and well-organized services, and preached the advantages of orderly requisitioning over the traditional methods based upon indiscriminate looting and devastation. By the early eighteenth century, the formalized warfare of the day had become almost wholly based on an elaborate and ritualized system of logistics that sacrificed both range and mobility. This was the period of the 'rolling magazine', and of inter-related systems of fortified depots and defended lines of communication. Baggage and supply trains became ever larger as armies grew and as officers demanded the presence of more comforts in the field. Requisitioning became closely controlled, administered whenever possible through municipal and provincial authorities under terms often formally defined by treaty. Battles became rare; military movements sluggish and often aimed against hostile lines of communication and bases rather than armed forces *per se*. In other words, 'War became an appendage of logistics', and Frederick II of Prussia would be moved to remark that 'the masterpiece of a successful general is to starve the enemy.'

Thus there is justification in talking about a 'crisis of strategy' in the late seventeenth and for much of the eighteenth centuries. Wars became 'limited', but not really because the war aims were restricted; indeed, an examination of many of the struggles of the period reveals the opposite. In 1672, France set out, quite simply, to destroy the United Provinces. The Spanish overseas empire had fallen apart, and the Dutch and Swedes fell into major decline by the 1720s; France and Turkey forfeited much of their former paramountcy whilst new major powers – England, Russia and Austria – moved to the centre of the world stage. These were not matters of a few frontier adjustments here and there – they represented major shifts in the balance of power, and the wars that led to these adjustments were fought with the intention of imposing a solution on the enemy rather than in seeking an accommodation or compromise with him. Yet these wars were undoubtedly 'limited' in a very real sense – namely in the restricted ability of armed forces to carry out the grand strategic or political aims

* *Ibid.*, pp. 442-3.

ordered by their rulers and governments. Schemes of vast manoeuvre and rapid decision were beyond their scope. Campaigns and even wars were therefore largely controlled by logistical factors: an army was only operationally viable for areas over which it could carry its bread. Magazines of pre-stocked supplies were essential, but this reliance placed obstructions on the freedom of strategic movement. No army dared to advance more than a week's march from its latest magazines. Then it had to halt to establish a new depot, resite the ovens, and bake a fresh bread supply. And of course the likely presence of enemy fortresses in the vicinity still further impeded freedom of action. A general was ever aware of the vulnerability of his lines of communication – and these could be interdicted by enemy raiding parties unless all fortresses were either reduced by siege operations or at least carefully masked. Small wonder, then, that so many campaigns became dominated by formal siege warfare.

It has been calculated that the average campaigning season might last six months. But this period of time was never open for an uninterrupted advance, and unless a decisive battle could be forced at the very outset of a campaign (Ramillies in May 1706 is a rare case in point), there would be inadequate time for any truly effective follow-up or exploitation of the success gained. Normally a battle situation took several months to procure, and a victorious commander would be fortunate if he had 100 days left for pressing his advantage. But no less than 70 of these days would be taken up by basically administrative considerations. The 24 hour halt every four days for foraging and issuing bread used up some 25 days; the need for regular rest days accounts for a further 16 days; and when due allowance has been made for the resiting of magazines closer to the army, and the time taken in securing these moves, we find a mere 30 days left for true military advances. Few day's marches averaged above 10 or 12 miles, so the maximum operational range for a successful army, which had won a battle by mid-campaign and thus earned the initiative, works out at a probable distance of between 300 and 350 miles. This would not in fact be achievable, for it presupposes the absence of any enemy fortresses to impede the line of march or threaten the extending communications behind the advancing army and also the absence of continuing resistance by the defeated army. As a result, it was physically impossible for a victorious army to defeat its opponent's main force and then occupy a substantial area of hostile territory before the onset of the next season of Winter Quarters, during which the defeated foe could recover both his morale and his strength.* Small wonder that many wars became matters of elaborate manoeuvre.

Such then was the nature of the 'crisis in strategy'. The armies of the period were too preoccupied with problems of supply to be able to achieve a truly total victory. Even Marlborough's acclaimed march to the Danube in 1704 in fact covered little more than 250 miles – and all of the route was through friendly territory. The French could not intervene on the River Neckar to create a diversion because, the marshals declared, they could not operate there without first establishing magazines. After Ramillies the whole campaigning season lay

---

* See Perjés, *op. cit.* pp. 35-51 for a full analysis of this hypothesis.

ahead of the victorious Duke – and the result was the dramatic clearing of the French and their allies out of almost the whole area of the Spanish Netherlands. But opportunities of this sort were only rarely experienced. Limitations of space and time, and of manoeuvrability, hedged in even the most gifted of commanders with pressing and daunting difficulties – and this fact accounts for the indecisiveness of so many of the campaigns in our period. The situation had thus been reached in which decisive victory could only very rarely be won by the field armies of the day: they had become too large to be truly operationally viable. The results were long-drawn out wars of attrition until the processes of mutual exhaustion led to a pacification.

So much for this consideration of strategy in the early eighteenth century. As will be appreciated, this is a vast subject which deserves full examination in a volume on its own; all that we have had space for here, however, is the briefest sketch of some of its salient features, in order to place the studies of individual arms which make up the body of this study in some sort of strategic context, however inadequately treated.

To conclude this introduction, a few words may usefully be devoted to a consideration of Grand Strategy – or the use of war and peace as instruments of government policy between 1688 and 1745. Once again, this is a vast subject deserving far fuller treatment than is possible in these pages, but a few main points may be suggested.

There is no denying that our period was a bellicose one; a glance at Appendix One will show that wars of one sort or another filled an approximate total of 82 years (taking overlaps into account) between 1688 and 1745. No countries were of course involved in all these struggles, but France was involved in 30 years of conflict, and Austria in all of 63 to a greater or lesser extent. The contemporary writer, Casimir Freschot, could justly assert that 'Peace is not always the condition of the world, and is found, if truth be told, only infrequently; and when we have it we do not keep it for long.* But these long spans of near-perpetual war were interspersed with frequent periods of recourse to the conference table. As Professor Ragnhild Hatton has written: 'Negotiations for peace continued throughout the wars – sometimes sincerely meant, sometimes in the hope of breaking the cohesion of the powers ranged on the other side, sometimes for form's sake since it was generally accepted that not to listen to peace offers and a restoration of the *status quo ante bellum* rendered even a just war [i.e. one that the other side had started] unjust.'† As we have already seen, another motive for seeking a negotiated settlement was a tacit realisation that a dictated peace based upon an overwhelming military victory was out of the question, as the armies of the day could not achieve the necessary level of decisive success. This did not mean that pacifications were rapidly reached: long months and even years of negotiations all too often proved barren, and disputes over minor points of protocol or procedure could delay or even prevent the reaching of agreement. In the end, however, compromise settlements were

---

* C. Freschot, *Histoire du Congres et la Paix d'Utrecht* (Utrecht, 1716), p. 6.
† R. Hatton, *War and Peace, 1680-1720* (An Inaugural Lecture, LSE) London 1969, p. 6.

arrived at, for 'There comes a time when even Kings have to agree to peace.'*

Wars in our period may broadly be said to have been fought out for three principal and overriding reasons: for security, for power, and for *la gloire*. This third reason earned the approval of the French political thinker, Raymond Aron, 'because each of the three terms corresponds to a concretely defined attitude while it also expresses a specific notion.'** The search for national or sometimes international security underlay the great Alliances masterminded by William III in his ceaseless attempts to confine the ambitions of France and to maintain a workable basis for the European balance of power. National security was also a matter of great concern for the Habsburgs in their intermittent but bitter struggles with the Ottoman Turks. As for the lust for power, it was one strand of motivation behind Louis XIV's seemingly insatiable territorial ambitions, although it is notable that it was at his suggestion that England and France tried to avert the coming crisis that would be unleashed when Charles II of Spain died by negotiating the Partition Treaties of 1698 and 1699. The hope proved vain – but it was probably genuine enough at the time of its inception.

Frederick II of Prussia entered Silesia in 1740 with deliberate intent to increase the power of Prussia at the expense of its Austrian neighbour – but for part of the War of the Austrian Succession, and for almost all the Seven Years' War (which does not form part of this volume's scope) he fought with increasing desperation in the hope of obtaining a compromise peace when his foes came to appreciate that to beat him would take both vast effort and much time. In the latter struggle he had few illusions about Prussia's ability to conquer the Austro-Russian armies, but he determined to hold out until his opponents fell apart and until war-weariness could blunt both their reserves and morale.

Charles XII of Sweden's motives were largely aggressive. If the maintenance of the security of Sweden's homeland and South Baltic provinces might be invoked as a justifiable *casus belli* at the outset of the Great Northern War, it is not possible to interpret all his successive campaigns in this light. Here was a monarch who was a genuine 'war lord' in our period, whose dedication to the practice of the martial arts and sciences at times bordered on the near-insane.

The pursuit of *la gloire* was indubitably a major factor in the motivation of both the Baltic soldier-king and of *le roi soleil*. 'Louis XIV probably loved glory as much as power,' concludes Aron. 'He wanted to be recognised as first amongst monarchs, and he made use of his force in order to seize a city and fortify it, but this half-symbolic exploit was still a way of showing his force. He did not conceive of a disproportionately enlarged France, furnished with resources superior to those of her allied rivals. He dreamed that the names of Louis XIV and of France would be transfigured by the admiration of nations.'† War was also regarded as the legitimate expression of the 'last argument of kings', the ultimate tests for countries and dynasties alike. As Gustavus Adolphus had expressed this, at the time of the Thirty Years' War, 'I recognise no one above me, except God and the sword of the conqueror.'

* C. Freschot, *op. cit.*, preface.
** Raymond Aron, *Peace and War* (London, 1966) p. 73.
† *ibid.*, footnote 19.

It was not, however, an age devoid of hope. The majority of both the men of action and the men of letters had at least a measure of belief in the possibility of human progress. The pessimism disseminated earlier in the seventeenth century by the horrors of the Thirty Years' War – and so clearly reflected in the philosophical writings of Thomas Hobbes – gave place to the more positive ideals of John Locke. Scholars wrote of the rise and fall of successive empires instead of dwelling on the inevitable and rapid decline of hell-bent mankind. Belief in reason led to more optimistic concepts. Some monarchs genuinely attempted to introduce policies of domestic reform out of humanitarian as well as practical concern. Some equally genuinely attempted to avoid recourse to war and bloodshed with the intention of avoiding an increase in human misery and suffering. As Professor Hatton remarked of the period 1680-1720, 'Wars were in any case more controlled.' * Better discipline, better (if still rudimentary) ideas of hygiene had improved the lot of soldier and civilian alike, whilst the general absence of ideological warfare did achieve something to lessen 'some of the terror of war'. A code of conduct was shared between the armies of Europe. The intense indignation when the gentlemanly conventions were transgressed is illustrated by the furore when the Flemish governor of Monzon, the Chevalier de Mous, was ungallant enough to fire cannon at 11 o'clock at night on the house where the Archduke Charles was quartered in 1710.** Far more typical was the courtesy of the French gunners who sent a flag of truce to William III's camp to enquire the exact location of his quarters so that they might avoid aiming at them.†But such gentlemanly courtesies and niceties – and more will be recounted in the chapters devoted to siege warfare below – must not disguise the fact that the wars of the period still brought misery, famine and pestilence in their train when the mask slipped – as in the case of the Palatinate, twice ravaged by French armies, or of Bavaria (subjected to military execution by Marlborough and Baden in July 1704), or again the burning of Altona by the Swedes in 1712. Such happenings however enraged the conscience of the age, as the protests they evoked demonstrated.

In some respects, then, the conduct of war was less barbaric than it had been in the recent past, and by no means so extensive and total as it was to become in the future. The period between 1688 and 1745 was therefore in the main a period of military transition and general mediocrity, enlivened by only a few commanders of genius; but, as the chapters that follow will show, it also held the seeds of many future developments and refinements in equipment and tactics, and although all armies could be charged with committing the occasional atrocity, the period proved that the prosecution of war and the profession of arms could still be both honourable and relatively civilised.

---

* Hatton, *op. cit.*, p. 11.
** Francis, *op. cit.*, p. 309.
† N. A. Robb, *William of Orange* (London 1966) Vol. II, pp. 61-2.

Part I

The Horse

1

Cavalry roles and representation

Throughout the seventeenth and eighteenth centuries, as in any period of military history prior to the invention of the internal combustion engine, all armies were inevitably dependent upon their cavalry for a number of indispensable functions, both in and out of action. As one of Napoleon's marshals, Gouvion St. Cyr, was aptly to describe it, 'The cavalry represent the legs and the eyes of an army; the infantry and artillery are its body and arms.'[1]

When an army was on the march, the horse and dragoons reconnoitred ahead, seeking indications of the enemy, or served to guard the flanks and rear of the lengthy columns of foot, cannons and baggage against the possibility of surprise attack. When the army camped, vedettes of horsemen watched over the security of the lines of tents and campfires, ceaselessly patrolling roads and countryside in the vicinity of the encampment, while other parties performed the equally vital services of supervising foraging forays, escorting convoys and generals on their journeys, or raiding distant villages and townships to secure supplies by means of contract, contribution or bare-faced looting according to circumstances. Further detachments would hover as near to the enemy's position as they dared, watching hawk-eyed for signs of impending movement or reinforcement. Still others would lie quietly concealed in wood or lane, watchful for any fleeting opportunity to intercept important personages or ambush a slow-moving convoy of provisions or munitions.

On the day of battle, the mounted soldier, whether cuirassier, dragoon or light horseman, would really come into his own. The squadrons wheeled and manoeuvred over the plain, supporting the foot and guns with carbine, pistol, sword and sabre, clashing with the hostile horse, charging and re-forming, until the cohesion and morale of one army or the other deteriorated under the combined impact of cannonade, musketry and cold steel, to the point where its commander was prepared to concede the honours of the day. Thereupon, in the event of victory, it was often the particular duty of the cavalryman and dragoon to head the pursuit and exploit success, harrying the enemy's rearguard, cutting down or rounding up fugitives and deserters, and affording the retiring foe as scant an opportunity as possible to recover his balance or prepare his fortified towns and strong places for proper defence. On certain occasions, large numbers of horsemen would penetrate deep into the enemy's countryside, carrying fire and the sword, rapine and destruction. If, on the other hand, the fortunes of the day proved contrary, the cavalry's duty was to cover the retreat of their discomfited fellows, delaying the enemy's pursuit and distracting his attention from the vulnerable swarms of disorganized, disheartened and weary infantrymen. They might on occasion render assistance also by taking their wounded or exhausted comrades on to their horses. As Napoleon – the destroyer of the relics of eighteenth century warfare – was to write almost a century later, 'Cavalry is useful before, during and after the battle',[2] and there is no reason for supposing that his martial predecessors were not equally aware of the contribution made by *l'arme blanche* to the prosecution of their campaigns, although with certain rare exceptions – Marlborough, Charles XII and de Saxe amongst them – they often failed to appreciate the full significance of the all-out pursuit as the crowning act of victory, and as such forming part and parcel of the science and art of fighting and winning battles.

This widespread recognition of the value of the mounted arm of the service enabled the cavalry to retain much of its ancient prestige, both military and social, but at the same time there are indications that the mounted soldier's importance on the battlefield was, in certain respects, beginning to wane. One probable reason for this was the considerable improvement taking place, especially in the earlier part of our period, in infantry firearms and tactics. The cavalryman became increasingly vulnerable to the new combination of flintlock musket and socket bayonet, and the later eighteenth century introduction of the iron ramrod further increased the efficiency of infantry firepower. The full implications of this technological revolution will be considered later but where the cavalry on the battlefield was concerned it involved an increase in the casualties habitually sustained and a gradual decline in its tactical importance. At least until the late-seventeenth century, the cavalry had often been the battle-winning arm, but by the mid-eighteenth century this predominance was slowly but surely passing to the infantry. 'Firearms and not cold steel,' wrote Puysegur in the 1740s, 'now decide battles.'[3] Nevertheless, the cavalry still represented 'the offensive element' in many armies well into the first quarter of the eighteenth century.

In former times the use of matchlocks and pikes had tended to restrict the manoeuvrability of infantry on the battlefield; not only were both weapons bulky and heavy, but the matchlocks' proneness to misfires and the time they took to reload also encouraged the adoption of massive phalanx-like formations. Under such conditions, the cavalry had been expected to perform most of the decisive manoeuvres. With the change of weapons the relative importance of the infantry *vis-à-vis* the cavalry began to increase, and in due course the latter's monopoly of tactical mobility and shock-power largely disappeared, but *'l'arme blanche'* still habitually gave the *coup de grâce* in many an engagement, as all Marlborough's four great victories illustrated. However this trend would later be reintroduced by the Prussian Seydlitz and, in due course, by the Frenchman Murat, although the cavalry would never regain its former numerical strength.

A second reason for the gradual decline in the significance and numbers of the horse – and probably the decisive factor – was the question of cost. Somewhat paradoxically, the general increase in the size of armies over the period encouraged a proportionate reduction in the mounted arm, for most of the new troops raised in time of war were infantry. The cavalry was undoubtedly the more expensive arm. A horseman was expensive to train, equip, pay and maintain. A suitable cavalry charger for the English Army cost between £12 and £15 during the quarter century from 1688 to 1713 (although in the first instance the majority of troopers were expected to provide their own mounts on enlistment); a dragoon's mount cost £5 (in Ireland), a Spanish jade £9, but by George II's reign an average price for a dragoon's 'Yorkshire troop-horse' (1728), when almost all horses were provided from government funds, was about £15.[4] Similarly, the cheapest remount available to the Dutch and Imperial service in 1693 cost all of 90 *patagons*.[5] Inevitably the trooper's pay and subsistence money was higher than that of the *fantassin* (or common soldier) as he had to feed and care for his mount as well as himself – and it clearly took longer to train a raw recruit into an acceptable cavalryman than to teach the new foot soldier the rudiments of drill and musketry. Taking these considerations all together, the Marquis de Santa-Cruz estimated in the 1730s that 'the maintenance of 1,000 cavalry costs as much as the maintenance of 2,500 infantry.'*[6] This seems if anything a modest estimate. Governments were consequently unlikely to raise new regiments of horse without very good reason. They often reached a compromise by settling for a larger number of somewhat cheaper dragoons.

In this connection the following analysis of the proportions of cavalry to other arms, based on the researches of the German scholar, Professor G. Bodard, is relevant. To some extent, of course, all statistical information is liable to distortion and misrepresentation, and the generalized sets of figures that follow do not reveal the seasonal fluctuations, and consequently should only be regarded as an approximate guide.

This table would seem to reveal a dramatic drop in proportionate cavalry representation over the 200 years dividing the Thirty Years' War from Waterloo. The period roughly within the scope of this present volume (the central two columns refer) shows indications of an overall decrease of a more gradual nature – indeed the cavalry of England, Russia and Turkey hold their ground – and it is clear that the great reduction came after 1780. Nevertheless it is revealing *inter alia* that the French mounted arm shrinks from a proportion of about one cavalryman to every two foot soldiers under Louis XIV to one in five by the general period of the Seven Years' War, and that Austria's native and imperial cavalry shrinks from a third to a quarter – a decline shared by the Spanish army.[7]

Bodart's figures are fairly borne out by the eighteenth century military writers. *Maréchal de* Puységur, for instance, states (of the first decade) that 'one commonly finds two-thirds infantry to one-third cavalry'.[8] The Chevalier de Folard, writing in 1730, avows that regular cavalry should make up one quarter

---

*The French practice of including a double allocation of officers in each cavalry troop – half holding commands, half serving as *'reformés'* or reserves in the roles of ordinary troopers, served still further to raise the cost of a cavalry unit in terms of pay.

The Horse

PERCENTAGES OF CAVALRY IN ARMIES BY NATIONALITIES (alphabetical order)

Country	1618 – 48 %	1648 – 1715 %	1740 – 80	1805 – 15 %
Austria	33	30	27	16
Denmark	50	40	–	–
England	37	27	27	12.5
France	35	30	21	16.5
German states	33	30	27	–
Italian states	–	27	15	–
Poland	60	60	–	30
Prussia	–	40	30	17.5
Russia	–	25	25	22
Spain	36	30	25	11.5
Sweden	40	45	–	–
Turkey	–	45	45	30

of an army's strength, while the Spaniard Santa-Cruz claims that between a fourth and a fifth is acceptable, except for mountain warfare where only a sixth is justifiable, but goes on to suggest that an additional number of light cavalry can be extremely useful. *Maréchal de* Saxe, on the other hand, required more cavalry than any of these other contemporary 'experts', but drew a clear distinction between the cuirassier and dragoon contingents. For an army of 40–50,000 men he advised a 'heavy' cavalry of merely 40 squadrons (or 6,000 troopers), but to this he added 80 squadrons of dragoons (or about 12,000) – thus reaching a figure of 18,000 horsemen, or a proportion of two-fifths of the army.[9] The estimates of General Weygand also lend some support. According to this authority, in 1668 the overall French army comprised some 70,000 infantry and 35,000 cavalry; by 1693, its gross strength had risen to 440,000 men, but of these only 60,000 were 'regular' cavalry (the General probably discounted dragoons in this case); then, after a sharp dip between 1697 and 1702, French strength recovered by 1713 to a figure of some 300,000 troops, including a cavalry proportion of about one-quarter. By 1727 it would seem that there were 35,300 horsemen (including the 'augmentation') to 120,940 foot (exclusive of militia and 'free' companies totalling some 73,000 more) in Louis xv's forces.*[10]

Inevitably, local conditions were often responsible for causing variations in the numbers of cavalry a country employed. Such powers as Russia or Turkey had far greater need for large numbers of horsemen with which to control the vast plains of the steppes or Asia Minor than other countries further west. At its peak, Peter the Great's cavalry comprised no less than 84,000 horsemen[11]

---

*In time of peace, however, considerable cuts were implemented. Thus by 1738, the French Army in pay numbered only 100,000 foot and 20,000 horse – or one cavalryman to five infantrymen (Add Mss. 19,036 f.l). Ten years later the proportion seems to have shrunk still further, although the French army was greatly expanded for the War of the Austrian Succession: out of 474,000 officers and men serving in 1748, only 64,000 belonged to the mounted arm. (Add Mss. 35,893 f.148 – Br. Mus.)

including Cossacks and similar irregulars, and in 1720 his *regular* army consisted of 57,956 infantry and 36,333 cavalry according to Ivanhoff's estimates. By way of contrast, on his accession to the Prussian throne in 1740, Frederick the Great inherited a mounted force of 20 regiments (114 squadrons), comprising 12 regiments of cuirassiers (60 squadrons), six of dragoons (45 squadrons) and two corps of hussars (9 squadrons), or some 17,000 troopers out of an army of 39,000 men.[12]

A study of the number of cavalry present at a selection of battles is also revealing – though again it would be imprudent to place absolute reliance on the accuracy of available information. Furthermore, account has to be taken of other reasons besides those of deliberate national policies of cavalry reduction to explain the general decrease in the numbers of horsemen. Clearly considerations of local terrain, availability of forage and, even more decisively, of operational necessity are equally relevant.

Battle	Year	Modern Region	Total Cavalry Present	Percentage of force Present
Fleurus	1690	Belgium	19,000 (out of 88,000)	21.6%
Steenkirk	1692	Belgium	27,000 (out of 120,000)	22.5%
Landen	1693	Belgium	49,000 (out of 130,000)	37.7%
Zenta	1697	Yugoslavia	56,000 (out of 150,000)	37.3%
Blenheim	1704	W. Germany	35,000 (out of 108,000)	32.4%
Ramillies	1706	Belgium	33,000 (out of 122,000)	27%
Oudenarde	1708	Belgium	41,000 (out of 170,000)	24.1%
Malplaquet	1709	Franco-Belgian Frontier	50,000 (out of 183,000)	27.3%
Poltava	1709	Russia	17,000 (out of 80,000)	19%
Belgrade	1717	Hungary	100,000 (out of 200,000)	50%
Parma	1734	Italy	22,000 (out of 90,000)	24.5%
Chotusitz	1742	Germany	15,000 (out of 56,000)	28%
Dettingen	1743	W. Germany	12,000 (out of 61,000)	19.6%
Fontenoy	1745	Belgium	25,000 (out of 110,000)	22.7%
Laufeldt	1747	Holland	40,000 (out of 180,000)	22%

Poltava's percentage was exceptionally low, largely on account of the extreme rigours of the previous winter which destroyed much of the Swedish cavalry; Belgrade's, on the other hand, was unusually high, partly due to the participation of the Turkish army which always enjoyed a higher proportion of horsemen than the European powers. Nevertheless, after allowing for such discrepancies, the broad impression left by this selective survey would seem to support the thesis that the numbers of cavalry incorporated within the field armies of the late seventeenth and the first half of the eighteenth century reflected a slight general overall decrease in the representation of the mounted arm in the armed forces as a whole. This does not necessarily indicate a great diminution in the importance of the cavalry as a whole – perhaps its greatest days lay ahead in the 1760s and early 1800s – but during the period covered by this volume there are signs of at least a temporary recession in its fortunes *vis-à-vis* the infantry.

2

Types of cavalry and equipment

Most armies employed two main varieties of mounted soldier; several also included a third. The two standard types were 'the horse' and the dragoons, but these were supplemented by various types of light cavalry in the armies of Austria, Russia, France, Poland and those of the Turk. It is proposed to examine each kind in turn, and attempt an estimate of their various contributions to armies in the field.

The horse

The 'horse' is a generic term that covers several kinds of cavalry, including the *corps d'élite* of the various monarchies, the cuirassiers, the carabineers and the large number of ordinary cavalry regiments that made up the numbers of men who fought on horseback. The organization of their various formations will be analysed in more detail in the next chapter, but here it will suffice to say that the great majority were gathered into regiments of horse, sub-divided into a number of troops, which in action were combined in twos and threes to form *ad hoc* squadrons. The great exception to this general rule concerns the Household or *élite* cavalry, who are never referred to as serving in regiments but always in special troops – or companies – of an enlarged variety, which in fact approximated in numbers to a squadron or even a weak regiment.

The Household Cavalry of most armies trace their origins to the personal bodyguards of mediaeval sovereigns. In the case of England (from 1660 onwards) there were at different times between three and four troops of Life Guards, regimented with one or two troops of Horse Grenadier Guards. The mounted elements of the French *Maison du Roi* were rather more numerous, including one *Compagnie des Grenadiers à Cheval*, the *Gardes du Corps* (up to four companies), the *Compagnie des Gendarmes de la Garde* (not to be confused with the *Gendarmerie* which will be described later), the *Compagnie des Chevaux-Légers* (or Light Horse), and finally the two Companies of Musqueteers (commonly called *Mousquetaires gris* and *Mousquetaires noirs* on account of the colour of their Horses).[13] Similar formations existed in almost all armies – for instance the Dutch Horseguards, the King of Sweden's *Drabants*, or the Austrian Emperor's *Trabans*. Service within these privileged units carried special pay, conditions and ranks (some of these will be described later), as well as uniforms of better material than ordinary, and in the French *Maison* at least the Captaincies were usually reserved for Princes of the Blood or Marshals of France.

These crack formations were often brigaded with the most important regiments of horse when serving in the field. Thus the English Life Guards built up close ties with the Royal Regiment of Horse Guards ('The Blues'), and the French *Maison* frequently served alongside the *Gendarmerie* – the famous corps which Francis I once described as 'the arm that carries my sceptre'.[14] King Louis XIV was Captain of the first four companies of the *Gendarmerie*, and in due course it comprised some 16 troops; the cavaliers bore the name *Maîtres* to distinguish them from the troopers of the line cavalry, while the troopers of the English Life Guards and the Blues were all termed 'gentlemen'.

The 'horse' also included a further large number of cavalry types. There were the cuirassiers, or heavy cavalry, who were reserved for shock action on the field of battle. There were the carabineers, who despite their name, carried musketoons – a type of blunderbuss, holding several musket balls – rather than carbines. They were usually recruited by selection from the cavalry regiments. After various experiments, Louis XIV saw fit to create a *Corps de Carabiniers* some 100 companies strong, divided into four brigades, all of which bore the proud royal motto, *'Nec Pluribus Impar'*. The English army recruited a regiment of this type in 1691 when the Sixth Dragoon Guards were retitled 'The King's Carabineers'.[15] Then there were a large number of units simply designated 'Regiments of Horse', many of which were raised at the outbreak of war and often disbanded at the peace. Somewhat confusingly, the French military experts insisted on terming the bulk of their regular cavalry *Chevaux-Légers* in order to distinguish them from the *Maison* and the *Gendarmerie*, and this can cause confusion to the unwary. There was no connection whatsoever with the light cavalry, properly so-called, whose introduction on a regular footing was one feature of the period. Both the *Cuirassiers-Royals* and the *Carabiniers* were technically parts of the 24 regiments of the so-called 'light' cavalry of Louis XIV's army. But this is not the end of the difficulties, snares and delusions, caused by the use of this term, for, as M. de la Chesnaye pointed out in his *Dictionaire Militaire* published during the reign of Louis XV, 'this name should not be confused with the corps of Light Horse of the Ordonnance' (i.e. the *Chevaux-Légers* of the *Maison du Roi*) – so it would seem that no less than *three* different interpretations have to be allowed for.[16]

The equipment and armament issued to the horse varied enormously from war to war and unit to unit. The 'heavies' retained varying amounts of body armour, although the tendency was for this to diminish rapidly as the period wore on. In both the Austrian and the French services, the cuirassier wore the traditional 'back and breast' besides long iron gauntlets reaching to the elbow, on top of a thick leather coat – but only the Habsburg and Bavarian troopers retained the iron lobster-helmet into the early eighteenth century.[17] Marshal Villars issued only the *démi-cuirass* (presumably to discourage any unnecessary retreats), but under the great de Saxe the formations of French heavy cavalry were re-equipped with a lighter cuirass of under 30 lbs weight and a form of helmet. Details of equipment remained subject to local variations, vagaries of fortune and mere regimental whims to a remarkable degree. The English Royal Horse Guards, for instance, abandoned their breast-plates in 1688 on the order of James II, who ordered them to expedite their march from Winchester to Salisbury, ready to intercept William of Orange's march on London.[18] Many other regiments returned their cuirasses to the Ordnance in 1699, but in 1707 Marlborough ordered the re-adoption of the breast-plate which was to be worn *beneath* the red coat. Charles XII of Sweden, on the other hand, banned all forms of personal armour from the start of his reign.

The breast-plate remained standard equipment for cavalry officers of many nations, and Louis XIV was insistent that all members of the *Maison* and many regiments of his so-called light horse should also wear it. As late as 1735 we find Louis XV ordaining that all cavalry (save only hussars) should wear cuirasses for reviews, exercises and marches. As a rule, however, the use of body-armour gradually grew out of favour, and by the 1740s it had all but disappeared save for cuirassiers and the purely symbolic officers' gorgets. By the mid-century all cavalry were wearing long cloth coats of varied hue with distinguishing linings and facings.

Cavalry headgear went through a period of transition. The armoured helmet soon disappeared from most armies, but there was at first little agreement as to how the hat should be worn. After a period of experimentation in folding the cloth in different fashions, the well-known if rather impracticable tricorne hat made its appearance, and soon became almost universal for all arms of the service except grenadiers. Although the prudent continued to wear a metal pot within the crown, the main drawback of this headgear lay in its instability, particularly when the fashionable dictates of the day made huge periwigs *de rigueur* for officers. Even when wigs had gone out of fashion the celebrated fate of the Marquis of Granby at the Battle of Warburg, 1760, who lost his hat in the heat of the moment and charged the foe with bald pate gleaming in the sunlight, amply demonstrates the basic instability of the military headgear, although in this instance the accident afforded the gallant officer an immortal place in his country's legendary history, as many a public-house sign testifies to this day, and the even rarer distinction of adding a phrase to the language.*

For the rest, all cavalry wore heavy thigh-boots of leather with the tops turned down to produce a double-thickness at the knee, a portion of the cavalryman's anatomy that was particularly exposed to damage in the confusion and press of a mounted charge or scrimmage. The Count of Mérode-Westerloo had particular reason to be thankful for his boot's protection at the Battle of Blenheim: 'My knee had swollen to the size of a man's head,' he recalled in his *Mémoires* '[but] ... although a bullet had been fired at me at point-blank range, it had failed to penetrate thanks to my strong thigh-boots with thick flaps down to the knees ...

*To go 'bald-headed' – or impetuously.

The bullet had got as far as my stocking but had penetrated no further.'[19]

As for weapons, it is again almost impossible to give an accurate list. Armament varied from unit to unit within the same army, let alone between different nationalities. It would be tedious to list the many variations, so suffice it here to say that most of the horse were armed with the straight sword, a pair of pistols, and often a carbine or musketoon apiece.* Other equipment included cartridge boxes, sword and carbine belts. Saxe later wished to re-introduce a long lance but this was never implemented in his day.

The dragoons

Passing on to consider the dragoons, we find that most contemporaries were unwilling to consider them cavalry, but classified them as mere mounted infantry well into the eighteenth century – indeed until as late as 1784 in the case of the French army. It is convenient, however, to describe them in this present chapter as constituting part of the mounted arm, and indeed as the period progressed they come to be employed more and more in their mounted capacity in battle; as a result the dragoons became barely distinguishable from the regular horse in terms of role.

The regiments of dragoons were the 'handymen' of late seventeenth and eighteenth century armies. Their adaptability is reflected in the description accorded them in the *Military Dictionary* published in 1702:

> Musketeers mounted, who serve sometimes a-foot, and sometimes a-horseback, being always ready upon anything that requires expedition, as being able to keep pace with the horse, and do the service of foot. In battle, or upon attacks, they are commonly the *Enfans Perdus*, or Forlorn [hope], being the first that fall on. In the field they encamp either at the Head of the army, or on the wings, to cover the others, and be the first at their arms.[20]

Commonly armed with a carbine, a bayonet and hatchet as well as broad-sword and pistols (although these last were withdrawn from English dragoons as early as 1697), the dragoon never wore armour, but sported the long cloth coat, tricorne hat, heavy boots and the distinguishing broad cross-belts supporting his sword, bayonet and ammunition pouch. Grenade pouches had disappeared by 1697.

The prejudice that denied the dragoon regiment a formal place alongside the horse is reflected in Montecuculi's statement that 'dragoons are still infantry to whom horses have been given to enable them to move more rapidly'.[21] Nevertheless, every army placed great reliance on them for multifarious duties. Besides their dual role in battle, they were expected to carry out reconnaissances and escort duties, and were, on occasion, relied upon to bridge streams or fill ditches with fascines of brushwood or trusses of hay to expedite the advance of the main army (as at the storm of the Schellenberg Heights in 1704 and the

---

* See Chapter Six below for a discussion of the characteristics of these weapons.

passage of the Lines of Brabant the following year), and sometimes were called upon to build or raze field fortifications. It is clear that this consideration was very much in the mind of Peter the Great when he ordained that a fifth of his blue-coated Russian dragoons should carry axes in addition to their normal equipment, whilst a further tenth were to carry shovels and as many more sharpened spades.[22] Certain governments found a further, rather less honourable, role for their dragoons by using them to persecute unpopular elements of the population through compulsory billeting, permitting the men complete licence short of actual murder. Louis xiv's ruthless employment of the *dragonnades* against the Huguenots and later against the *Camisards* is perhaps the most notorious example. However the Hanoverians were not above applying similar measures on a more limited scale in the disaffected Highlands of Scotland after both the '15 and the '45.

In the last years of the seventeenth century, dragoon regiments tended to be outnumbered by regiments of horse in most armies. Thus the English army's establishment for 1691 (including Dutch and Allied units in pay) listed only seven regiments of dragoons as compared to 31 of horse, although the larger size of the average dragoon unit slightly redressed the balance; thus there were 3,440 dragoons in some 52 troops in William III's army, as compared to 8,702 horse (144 troops).[23] In the same way, Marshal Soubise's French army serving in Flanders in 1692 fielded 20 squadrons of dragoons as opposed to 48 squadrons of cavalry and a further two of light horse.[24] Taken as a whole, however, Louis xiv's forces included as many as 43 dragoon regiments in 1690, although by 1704 this number had shrunk to 30. Nevertheless, in 1668 there had only been 14 to 66 of regular cavalry.

As the new century progressed, however, there are many signs of a rapid increase in the numbers of dragoons maintained by the powers. Perhaps the most dramatic case of expansion in this respect was the army of Tsar Peter. On his accession in 1700 he found his regular mounted arm contained precisely two dragoon regiments, and he immediately set himself to amend this situation. In 1701 he made a start by raising eight new regiments, and over the next ten years added a further fourteen. By 1711, the Russian regular cavalry totalled 30 regiments, almost five-sixths of them of the dragoon variety.[25] Although no other country ever rivalled Russia in this respect, by the 1730s we find the great Marshal Saxe advocating a proportion of two dragoons to every heavy cavalryman.[26] And even earlier, the British army lists between 1707 and 1714 contain the names of some 11 regiments of native horse to 18 of dragoons, the preponderant proportion of the later being largely due to the peculiar requirements of the Spanish front which Napoleon was to rediscover a century later.

Notwithstanding this increase in repute and representation, the dragoon never enjoyed the full social standing of the regular horseman – at least in the English army. This is reflected by his considerably lower rates of pay and subsistence. In the English army of Queen Anne, for example, the differentiation was clear throughout the regimental hierarchy. Whereas a Colonel of Horse received a total of 41s a day, his opposite number in the dragoons was paid only 35s, although his responsibility in terms of men and horse was frequently one-third larger. Similarly a Captain of Horse received 21s 6d to a Dragoon Captain's 15s 6d, while the cavalry trooper's half-crown a day pay and 14s weekly subsistence money contrasted most markedly with the humble dragoon's daily 1s 6d supplemented by a meagre 8s 2d weekly subsistence rate.[27] There is need for care in not confusing the proper regiments of dragoons with the six regiments of so-called English 'Dragoon Guards', which were from the earliest days part of the horse, and consequently deemed themselves of superior caste. Their titles, however, enabled cheese-paring governments to avoid paying them at full cavalry rates. This fact notwithstanding, the Queen's Dragoons (also variously known as the Tangier Horse or Royal Dragoons) were the senior mounted regiment in the English army after the Life Guards and the Blues.[28]

The social position of the dragoon officer was substantially different in France. Many famous families served as dragoons, the Brissacs, la Fertés and Boufflers amongst them, and it was deemed an especial honour to be promoted 'Captain of Dragoons and *Chevalier* of St Louis'. This close association with the noble houses of France survived into the 1780s.[29]

Light horse

Thirdly in this survey of the mounted arm, we must turn to a description of the Light Cavalry – which during the years we are considering was something of a novelty in the majority of armies. This type of cavalryman had its true origins in the irregular formations of Eastern Europe. The Russian prototype was, of course, the Cossack (or *Khasak* – literally 'free' or 'freebooter') – who had played a notable part in his country's affairs since at least the fifteenth century. The Cossack peoples were mainly of Tartar origin, and had settled in the Caucasus, Black Sea and Caspian regions; perhaps the most famous came from the vicinity of the River Don. In return for tax exemptions and the right to hold land, every Cossack male was liable for service with the Tsar's armies. Coming from a hardy, warlike and wiry race of skilled horsemen, the Cossacks under their *Hetman* or leader were well suited for reconnaissance, outpost and raiding work. On the other hand, their notorious indiscipline and treacherous tendencies largely precluded their suitability for inclusion in the formal line of battle. By the late seventeenth century their armament included sabres, lances, pistols and carbines, while their 'uniform' comprised fur caps, voluminous cloth or animal-skin coats, baggy breeches and soft leather boots. Each *sotnia* or band of these vaunted irregular horsemen possessed its own *chorigoy* or standard, and often rode to the sound of drum and other musical accompaniment.

Peter the Great appreciated the value that could be obtained from raising disciplined regiments of light horsemen for full time service. Recalling the notorious unreliability of some of the Cossack tribes – it will be remembered that Charles XII of Sweden hoped, though vainly, to inspire a revolt amongst Mazeppa's Cossacks in 1709 – the Tsar raised an experimental formation of 300 light horsemen in 1707, recruiting it mainly from Magyars, Serbians and the inhabitants of Moldavia and Wallachia. Within three years this small nucleus had been expanded to include eight regiments, but this total was subsequently reduced. However, in 1723 Peter re-raised a corps of hussars under conditions of service, pay and organization that closely resembled the Austrian pattern, and in 1740 a further large number were added to the Russian military establishment. [30]

The rulers of Austria had employed irregular light cavalry for even longer than the Russian Tsars. As early as 1445, light horsemen of Magyar origin had distinguished themselves in the battles of Matthias Corvinus, but it was not until the early seventeenth century that the Emperor raised a number of Hungarian regiments on a quasi-permanent basis. The first truly regular regiments of hussars* were only raised as late as 1688. From the first the hussar uniform was closely patterned on the dress of the Hungarian irregulars, not only in the Austrian service but also in the armies of all other countries that eventually followed the Habsburg lead. Every last detail was reproduced, and often exaggerated – the fur caps, the tight breeches, bright tunics with horizontal frogging across the breast, even the fur-trimmed jacket slung carelessly over the left shoulder. By the mid-eighteenth century hussar uniforms were the most splendid, and costly, of any in use, and their wearers earned the reputation of being the darlings of the ladies. Their weapons included the curved sabre, pistols, and a carbine.

The French army soon followed the Austrian example. Since 1620 the *élite Maison du Roi* had included a company of *Chevaux-Légers* as already described, but this unit had generally patterned itself upon the Musketeers, and consequently did not provide the model for the new Light Cavalry, properly so-called. The first genuine French hussar regiment was recruited in 1692 from Imperialist deserters,[†] but the splendid uniforms were soon all the rage at Versailles. Generals tended to recruit their own semi-regular hussar units to serve alongside their regular formations, but Marshal Luxembourg collected these small groups into larger companies and employed them for reconnaissance tasks, reporting well of their performance. By 1701 there were four regiments, one being raised on the instigation of Villars, another being donated to Louis xiv by the Elector of Bavaria. Between 1719 and 1745 several more were added to the establishment, including the famous *Régiment d'Esterhazy* (1734) and the *Hussards de Ferrari* (1745). In 1745 there were seven hussar regiments in French pay, three of Hungarian origin, four recruited from Germans and Liègeois, and three years later they totalled 6,133 officers and troopers, forming about one-tenth of the mounted arm.

Besides their uniforms, hussar units inherited other tendencies from their Hungarian forebears. 'The Hussar companies were somewhat democratic,' states Ambert, 'for in Hungary and even in France, until the reign of Louis xv, the captain was expected to take the advice of his troopers before attacking the

*The term hussar derives from the Hungarian word *Husz* – meaning '20' – reflecting the fifteenth century practice of conscripting one man in every twenty for service in this mounted militia.

†Richelieu had raised a small unit in 1635 called the 'Hungarian Cavalry', and this might properly be deemed the introduction of the hussar-type horsemen into the French army.

enemy – and they would discuss and represent their views forcefully.'[31]

The description of the mid-eighteenth century French hussar given by the celebrated *Père* Daniel is worth quoting:

> The arms of the hussars are a large curved sabre, or a straight-bladed and even larger variety ... it is for sabering right and left, and for striking from high to low. Some, in addition to the sabre, carry a long thin sword which they do not carry at their sides but rather place it along the sides of their horses from the breast to the crupper ... (these) they use to spit the enemy; ... when they employ them, they rest the butt against the knee. They also carry a carbine and pistols, besides very large '*gibicières*' (powder containers) on a bandolier, in the form of a haversack ... Their discipline is strict, their subordination admirable, and their punishments rough; the most usual is the bastinado of a fixed number of strokes applied to the back or buttocks. Good use is made of this militia in small parties for carrying out reconnaissances, for forming the advance and rear guards, for covering forage-parties or for raiding because they are very light and mobile. However they cannot stand up against squadrons in full order of battle.[32]

Frederick William II raised two hussar corps (totalling nine squadrons) for his Prussian army, and by the mid-century they were a standard feature of most European armies. Great Britain employed regiments of light dragoons in this capacity, but only changed their names to hussars at a later period.

These light cavalry were not universally admired by their contemporaries in other arms of the service, at least during the earlier part of the eighteenth century. If the cavalryman tended to scorn the dragoons, both affected to despise the hussar, and this attitude was not restricted to the mounted arm. Colonel de la Colonie, a French infantry soldier serving in the Bavarian army, described hussars as 'properly speaking, little more than bandits on horseback'.[33] His view is repeated in more dramatic form in the evidence of Marlborough's Quartermaster-General, William Cadogan, who evidently believed himself most fortunate to have avoided the attentions of French hussars when he was made a prisoner of war in 1706:

> I was thrust by a crowd that I endeavoured to stop into a ditch [he wrote in a letter to Lord Raby]. With great difficulty I got out of it, and with greater good fortune escaped falling into the [French] hussars' hands, who first came up with me. A little resistance I persuaded some few of the dragoons I had before made alright, and who could not get to their horses, saved them and me, since it made me fall to the share of the French carabines [*sic*] who followed their hussars and dragoons, from whom I met with quarter and civility, saving their taking my watch and money.[34]

It would seem from such evidence that the hussars enjoyed a somewhat barbarous reputation.

The Turkish mounted arm

Light Horse of varying sorts also existed in the Polish* and Turkish forces. The former included a large number of irregular lancers. In the latter, parts of the *Seratculi* cavalry carried out functions approximating to those of hussars in the Christian armies. No mention has yet been made of Turkish cavalry in this chapter, for it retained the organization and nomenclature of an earlier age, but it will be convenient to close this section with a brief analysis of the variety of horsemen employed by the Porte in the practically ceaseless wars against the Habsburg power in south-eastern Europe.

There were four main categories of Turkish cavalry, several of which contained a variety of types. The major divisions were derived from methods of recruitment rather than from considerations of operational role. The senior Moslem mounted formations were termed the *Capiculi* cavalry (*Kapi Kullari* or 'Slaves of the Porte'). These horsemen formed the *élite* of the Sultan's army, and many of the rank and file spahis (or *sipahis*) were of important family. The *Capiculi* formed a major part of the Sultan's bodyguard, and in battle were generally kept in reserve for the masterstroke. There were two types – the *Ulefelys* (or Right Wing of senior spahis serving in sections of 20 under a *Boluk Basi*, who between campaigns also served to collect exactions and taxes from the Sultan's subjects), and the *Chiaous* (or Left Wing, the junior spahis). The former were distinguished by a red standard; the latter by one of yellow. The *Capiculi* or regular cavalry was commanded as a whole by the *Selictar Aga* (or General of Horse), and in the first half of the eighteenth century numbered some 15,500 troopers.[35] Secondly there were the *Topracly* cavalry, raised provincially, which contained four types of horsemen: the *Beglars, Beglerbeys, Zaims* (usually employed on garrison duties) and the *Timariots*.

In the third place there were the *Seratculi* cavalry (*Serhadd Kullari* – 'Slaves of the Frontier') – the descendants of the old feudal host – originally concerned as their name suggests with the defence of the limits of the Turkish Empire, but by the 1700s being increasingly raised by provincial governors in general out of the proceeds of tax-farms and by forced levies. This variety included *Gonullus* (or heavy cavalry), the *Beshlis* (or light horsemen) and the *Delis* (who served as scouts).

Lastly there was the Tributary cavalry, comprising contingents of Crimeans, Wallachians, Moldavians and Transylvanians and including contingents of the feared Tartars, supplied by conquered areas as a form of tribute to the Sultan.

Taken altogether, these different types of provincial and tributary forces added between 50,000 and 100,000 horsemen to the 15,000 regular cavalry. As might be expected, details of equipment varied enormously as regards both type and quality. The Sultan's *élite* were armed with superb weapons, scimitars, carbines and pistols of modern type, many of them inlaid with jewels and precious metals. The bulk of the provincial horsemen, however, continued to

---

* These included the famous 'winged lancers' who aided John Sobieski in his relief of Vienna from the Turks in 1683.

display the weapons of a bygone age, amongst them lances, *coupies,* ancient matchlocks and bows and arrows. De la Colonie, who served with Prince Eugene in the famous Belgrade campaign of 1717, commented upon the general dearth of pistols amongst the Turkish horsemen, but speaks highly of their skill with the sabre.[36]

We have now completed this survey of the types of mounted troops employed by the armies of the late seventeenth and first half of the eighteenth century. Next we must turn to consider in rather more detail the organization of mounted formations, and describe the training that was undertaken to prepare them for operations in the field.

3

Organization and basic training

Establishments of the cavalry, dragoons and light horse inevitably varied enormously in their detail, but it is possible to describe certain broad principles of organization common to most armies in our period. The largest formation of the mounted arm was still the brigade of between eight and 12 squadrons, and when contemporaries refer, for example, to the 'corps of hussars' in the French service they are not describing a tactical or administrative unit but simply a loose association. There were not even divisions of horse at the time about which we write, although Charles XII conducted some experiments in this direction during the later years of his reign, and Marshal Saxe advocated the attachment of what he termed a 'half-century' of light cavalry to each of his 'legions', thus approximating to the all-arm organization of the Roman Legions of antiquity, and in some ways anticipating the creation of the self-contained divisions and *corps d'armée* of the French Revolutionary and Empire periods. However, as we have had occasion to mention elsewhere, a sort of rudimentary higher organization of large numbers of troops for battle, march or camp existed in the subdivision of armies into the usual two 'lines', and sometimes an additional 'reserve' for action, and 'wings' for marches, each of which contain a 'General of Horse'. All these minutely regulated formations invariably included a varying proportion of cavalry, although dragoons and hussars rarely figured in the main lines of battle, usually taking post in the rear on days of conflict, or performing special duties along the picquet line such as bridging obstacles to the fore of the army, as at Blenheim in 1704.

Brigades of horse, like the 'lines' or 'wings' to which they were attached, were essentially temporary, *ad hoc* formations, created by drawing together two or three regiments of cavalry, or of dragoons, for a particular campaign or service. Almost invariably such formations were disbanded at the end of each campaign, and always at the conclusion of peace. The Brigadier-General (who was usually also a Colonel of a regiment) was assisted by a Brigade-Major – the equivalent of the Adjutant-General at army level – and might also have the services of a 'guidon' or pennant-bearer, and aide-de-camp, and sometimes, a trumpeter, but such staffs were hardly official, and apart from the Brigade-Major there appears to have been no regular establishment for them. Indeed, as late as

Frederick the Great the Prussian cavalry had no formation higher than the regiment.

The regiment of horse, dragoons or light cavalry, was therefore the largest permanent cavalry formation. Each regiment was sub-divided into a number of troops which fluctuated enormously in both quantity and strenght, but each nation provided a fairly constant hierarchy of officers and NCOs for these units, though nomenclature and details of inclusions clearly varied from nation to nation. It is hard to find a formal establishment for the squadron in the first half of our period, though cavalry usually adopted such formations for battle and many documents and contemporary accounts mention them as such. As one eighteenth century authority described it, 'A squadron is a number of combattants mounted on horseback, drawn up in several ranks, armed and organized so as to fight together.'[37] It would seem that they were formed by grouping two or three (sometimes four) troops under the control of the senior troop commander. Thus a cavalry regiment in the field would often comprise two or three *ad hoc* squadrons, whilst a dragoon regiment would normally consist of three, four or more companies.

A regimental headquarters – whether of horse or dragoons – included a colonel (frequently an officer holding higher, army rank and thus likely to be an absentee from his unit) who was often the owner of the formation as well as its titular head, a lieutenant-colonel, and a major; beneath these field officers clustered a number of lesser lights – usually an adjutant, a chaplain, surgeon and a kettle-drummer (or, alternatively in a dragoon regiment, a gunsmith and his servant – at least in time of war). Similar basic hierarchies existed throughout Europe, although additions of further personnel, such as secretaries, *étapiers*, aides and provosts are to be found.

Formations of Household cavalry inevitably possessed their own special rank structures. Usually organized only in troops or companies, the English Life Guards were commanded by a captain-and-colonel (per troop), assisted by two 'lieutenants-and-lieutenant-colonels,' one 'cornet-and-captain', and four 'exempts-and-captains'; other ranks included four brigadiers,* as many sub-brigadiers, a kettle-drummer, and four trumpeters. The Troops of Horse Grenadiers, however, enjoyed a slightly different structure, including only one 'lieutenant-and-lieutenant-colonel', but adding two 'lieutenants-and-captains', a major, and a guidon instead of a cornet, and two sub-lieutenants instead of exempts; similarly, the unit possessed an adjutant, surgeon and chaplain, whilst the NCOs comprised six sergeants and as many corporals, and the musicians included four drummers and as many hautbois. We might add at this point that a troop of Life Guards contained an average of 156 'private gentlemen', and one of Horse Grenadier Guards some 145 'private men' or 'grenadiers'.[†38] As might

---

*This rank is apt to be confused with the junior grade of general officer. In the Household Cavalry the role was equivalent to that of a Sergeant of Infantry or Corporal of Horse, but the bearer was a commissioned officer.

† There were considerable variations. WO 24/12 reveals that in 1689 the Second Troop, for example, comprised 200 'Private Gentlemen' and 25 officers and staff. The same source puts the strength of the mounted grenadiers at only 70 (including officers and staff).

be surmised from the curious 'double' ranks of their officers, Household troops received higher rates of pay than their line cavalry colleagues. Thus a 'captain-and-colonel' of Life Guards received a total of 46s a day, to the line cavalry colonel's 41s in 1709, whilst at the other end of he scale the gentleman-trooper received a basic 4s a day to the ordinary trooper's half-a-crown.

The French *Gardes du Corps* were even more privileged. Louis xv's *Ordonnance* of 1719 laid it down that both the Lieutenants and Ensigns should simultaneously hold 'army rank' as full colonels of cavalry, a privilege shared by the *aydes-major* (approximately Quartermasters), whilst the Exempts were considered Captains of Horse, and the *brigadiers, sous-brigadiers* and *porte-etendart* held equivalent rank to Lieutenants of Horse. The higher ranks of the *gardes* were not mentioned in the *Ordonnance,* for it was the invariable practice for the captains and majors to be marshals or lieutenant-generals before appointment. Similarly, the gentlemen-guards received no definite equivalent rank, but it was the practice to appoint them to cavalry troops when they quitted the Guards as lieutenants with seniority calculated from the date of their entry into the *Maison.* The same seniority rule applied for Guards officers transferring to the line cavalry – that is to say their seniority as Colonels of Horse was calculated from the date of their commissions as Ensigns, etc in the Guards. [39] The pay of the *Gardes du Corps* was fixed by Article XXXII of the *Ordonnance* of 20 April 1702, ranging from six livres (30 francs) a day and eight rations* for a lieutenant to 33 *sols* and $1\frac{1}{2}$ rations for each Guard, trumpeter and kettle-drummer, who incidentally received 13 *sols* more than the humble surgeon.[40] (The English Lifeguards clearly esteemed their medical services rather more highly, paying their surgeons 8s a day including a forage allowance.) Officers of the French Guards were allowed to carry ivory-tipped ebony staffs as symbols of their status.

Each company of the *Gardes du Corps* had an establishment of one captain, 3 lieutenants, as many Exempts, 12 brigadiers and sous-brigadiers. half-a-dozen standard bearers, seven trumpeters and one kettle-drummer, and up to 400 Guards. Each company was habitually sub-divided into six *'brigades'.* The Company of Horse Grenadiers – which was recruited from the line regiments, each recruit having to be 'tall, strong, brave, wise and wearing moustaches'[41] – was somewhat smaller, numbering only 128 NCOs and Grenadiers in 1725; their officers received much the same emoluments as the *Gardes du Corps,* but the grenadier received only 20 *sols* a day basic pay.

Similar details could be produced for the many other *élite* formations serving the various monarchies of Europe, but there is not space for them here. Instead, we must pass on to consider the troop or company organization of the ordinary line cavalry and dragoon regiments.

The average troop of horse was commanded by a Captain, aided by one

---

* The French 'ration' for much of the period officially comprised two 24-ounce loaves and two pints of wine, 'measure of Paris', or in lieu two pints of cider or beer. Guiscard, *L'Ecole de Mars* (Paris: 1725) p. 424.

lieutenant, a cornet, and a quartermaster (or *marechal-des-logis*). Many French troops contained a double allocation of officers in time of peace, 're-formed' officers serving in the ranks on slightly reduced rates of remuneration. The NCOs included two or three corporals of horse according to the size of the troop, and one or two trumpeters. Most dragoon units had an identical officer structure, but contained one or two sergeants (in lieu of corporals of horse) besides two or three corporals of dragoons; the musician representation was also different, comprising one or two kettle-drummers and as many hautbois instead of trumpeters.

The numbers of troopers included in such formations varied enormously from country to country, regiment to regiment, and of course peace-time establishments were far lower than those of war-time. Nevertheless, as a *very* general guide it might be suggested that a troop consisted of approximately 50 officers and troopers; thus an 'average' squadron may be said to have consisted of 150 horsemen, and a 'typical' cavalry regiment from 300 to 450 men. The dragoon regiments were frequently larger, containing rather more troops and companies.

It must be stressed, however, that these generalizations are extremely tenuous and unsatisfactory, and the paragraphs that follow will amply show that there were many exceptions and anomalies.

According to the venerated Puységur, many of the French cavalry regiments (both 'Light' and *Gendarmerie*) comprised 12 companies, each of 50 troopers and four officers, at the time of the Nine Years' War. By the outbreak of the Spanish Succession struggle in 1701, however, most companies had shrunk to 36 troopers apiece, though the number of companies to a squadron had been increased from three to four. By 1744, all cavalry regiments were sharing a common establishment of four squadrons (dragoons had five), each containing 12 officers (including four quartermasters), besides a number of reserve officers serving in the ranks and 120 troopers or dragoons. Thus in the case of a single country, France, the official strength of a squadron swung between 120 and 160 horsemen in the course of half a century.[42] Some of these figures are substantially confirmed by documents in the British Museum. One (dated 1706) places French squadron strength at about 152 officers and men – or four companies of 3 or 4 officers and 35 cavalrymen apiece – at the opening of a campaign, but goes on to estimate that 140 was a more realistic total for units actually in the field. Another describes a squadron of French hussars as 200 troopers. A third reveals that a squadron at full war establishment in 1738 totalled 210.[43] However, as Leblond testifies, soon after the Peace of Aix-la-Chapelle (1748) the French Cavalry was drastically reduced to a peacetime establishment, according to which all French Horse and Dragoon regiments were reduced to two squadrons apiece (apart from the Colonel-General's Regiment and the *Carabiniers* which retained three and ten respectively), while the strength of the individual companies shrank to three officers and 30 men. But this was an improvement on the prevalent situation 10 years earlier, when a troop on peace establishment had numbered 25 troopers, of whom only 15 were actually mounted.[44]

Austrian practice would seem to have been somewhat different. For much of the period 1688–1713, the Habsburg cuirassier and dragoon regiments commonly contained a dozen companies (perhaps 1,000 cavalrymen or dragoons in all), which were normally paired to form operational squadrons.* By 1711, moreover, each formation had come to include a company *d'élite* – namely a company of carabineers in each cuirassier regiment and a mounted grenadier company in the dragoons. At the same period, we might add, the Austrian hussar regiments generally sported a dozen companies until 1710, when the number of squadrons were reduced to five (or 10 troops) during the general reordering of the Imperial cavalry arm inspired by Prince Eugene.

Swedish cavalry organization broadly paralleled the Austrian pattern. By the time of Charles XII, regiments comprised two tactical squadrons, each of two troops – although sometimes only of one. It is apparent, however, that at certain periods Swedish cavalry and dragoon regiments were considerably larger than most of their European contemporaries. For the invasion of Russia in 1707, Charles' army included a total of 16,000 dragoons divided between 12 regiments (or an average of some 1,330 dragoons apiece), whilst his 8 cavalry regiments (exclusive of the *Drabants* and *Valacks*) totalled 8,450 troopers (or almost 1,060 each).[45]

As might be expected, English practice remained an unpredicatable as ever. The 'official' strength of English mounted regiments in the reign of William III, as revealed in the annual estimates of forces presented to Parliament by the Secretary-at-War for the purpose of obtaining supply, varied between 300 (six troops) in the case of line cavalry regiments and 480 (up to eight troops) in that of dragoons – but most units were of the smaller order.[48] The general run of cavalry troops would seem to have held some 52–58 officers, men and musicians at this time.[47] Some dragoon troops, on the other hand, seem to have risen from about 60 dragoons in 1690 to almost 70 in 1693[48] – exclusive of officers. These estimates, however, are only partly supported by the 'Fighting Chaplain' of the 1st Foot Guards, whose annual 'Histories' form one of the best contemporary accounts of the Nine Years' War in Flanders as experienced by the English army. He calculates a squadron of horse at 130 troopers (which accords well enough with our other source) but places only 100 men in a squadron of dragoons.[49] Similar fluctuations are to be found in the following reign. In 1705, some cavalry troops had a strength of 67 officers and men, but in 1713, when the reduction was clearly operative after the withdrawal of British forces from the war the previous year, the total was down to 43. The strength of dragoon troops similarly drops from 67 to 47 over the same years.[50] Many other anomalies and fluctuations could be cited for there is no end to them.

The numbers of men in the cavalry formations of other countries show the same trends. The Dutch cavalry, for example, placed 72 men in a cavalry troop in 1689, reduced them to 48 in 1688, and by 1702 restored the number to 65.

---

*In 1706, a force of 3,800 Imperialist cavalry were divided between 23 squadrons – which would suggest an average of about 165 per squadron. Davenant Mss, Vol. VIII (Add Mss 4747, f.14, Br. Mus.)

The figures for their dragoons in the same years read 80, 50 and 80 respectively.[51] Information for other Allies is difficult to find, but the figures available in the British Museum for 1703 at least give an indication of national variations at that date. Thus Danish Cavalry troops contained an average of 60 men apiece, their dragoons some 89; Hessian cavalry number about 50 per troop, their dragoons 68; whilst Prussian cavalry show a strength of 55 men in a troop, a figure that contrasts markedly with the showing of Hanover, which seems to have been only able to muster 40.[52] Under the 'drill-master of Europe' and his gifted son, the Prussian horse was organized in cuirassier and dragoon regiments of between five and 10 squadrons each, and hussar units of between three and six. Most contained six officers, 12 NCOs and 130 troopers in four troops by 1740.

There we must leave this tantalisingly uncertain and inconsistent subject of cavalry and dragoon strengths. In conclusion, however, it is important to repeat that all figures are approximate; the English practice, for instance, of allowing one or two 'widow's men'* to appear on the official establishments reflected corresponding practices in other armies, and makes accurate computation virtually impossible. Different authorities similarly paint very different pictures of the situation.

The training of cavalrymen was often a long and laborious process, although the majority of recruits knew at least the rudiments of horsemanship on joining their regiments, indeed in several armies they were expected to bring their own horses with them. Although General Kane speaks as an infantryman – and only devotes a bare page of his *Discipline for a Regiment of Foot upon action, also the most essential discipline of the Cavalry* (1745) to the mounted arm – his opinion is worth quoting:

> It is sufficient for them [the horse] to ride well, to have their horses well managed, and train'd up to stand fire; that they take particular notice what part of the squadron they are in, their right and left-hand men, and file-leaders, that they may, when they happen to break, readily know [how] to form. Breaking their squadrons ought to be practised in their common discipline. That they march and wheel with a grace, and handle their swords well, which is the only weapon our British Horse makes use of when they charge the enemy; more than this is superfluous . . .
>
> . . . [Dragoons] should be well instructed in the use of fire-arms, having often occasion to make use of them on foot; but when on horseback, they are to fight as the horse do.[53]

Here are the bare essentials of cavalry training in all armies of our period, although it should be noted that several continental armies would challenge Kane's insistence on cold steel as constituting the only suitable weapon for the cavalry – an English tradition going back to the days of Rupert and Cromwell, who in their turn drew inspiration from Gustavus Adolphus. This important

---

*'Widow's men' were unfilled vacancies in a unit, which nevertheless the government allowed the regimental agents to draw pay for; the motive was the humane one of providing a fund for the relief of the dependants of men killed on active service. Such monies were, however, often misapplied.

matter, however, relates more to tactics than to drill, and will be discussed in the final chapter of this section.

As the cavalry invariably fought in squadrons of two to four troops in strength, they often exercised in this formation, being drawn up in three ranks with their officers to the front (although Marlborough reputedly favoured exercising – and fighting – in two ranks). Every unit would first be made proficient in the 'doublings' – the ability to close up and open out the ranks and files. The normal 'open order' distance between each horse (both rank and file) was six feet; and in the 'close order' these distances were reduced to three feet; and in what was rather clumsily termed the 'close order from close order', the troopers would place themselves knee to knee in ranks, and their horses head to crupper in the files. Other types of 'doubling' exercises were designed to reduce the ranks from three to two, and sometimes only one – *'se ranger en haie'*, or 'draw up in Hay' [*sic*] – with minimum confusion and expenditure of time.

According to the *Orders and Regulations for the Horse* published at the Hague in 1691, the basic movements required of cavalry were four – namely the 'facings, doublings, countermarches and wheelings'.[54] Great stress was laid on the pivot men standing fast during the wheelings in the English service, but in certain other armies the pivot men gave ground to their left and rear – thereby increasing the likelihood of confusion. Writing almost a century later, M. Le Blond also listed four essential movements as forming the basis of French cavalry training: the ability to close and open ranks and files; proficiency in making a half turn to right or left; skill at the 'conversion' or *caracole* (whereby a complete troop or squadron could be turned through 180 degrees without changing its ground); and lastly the skills needed to form to left or right of the squadron front by divisions.[55]

Cavalrymen and dragoons were also trained to perform the 'postures' – or exercise of arms. Details again vary from country to country, but the broad principles were the same. The words of command for the basic exercise were the following:

> Take Heed – Lay yr. right hands on your swords – Draw yr. swords – put yr. swords in yr. bridle hands – Lay your hands on your pistols – Draw your pistols – Cock your pistols – Hold up your hands (i.e. present) – Give fire – Return your pistols – (followed by identical practice with the second pistol) – Lay your hand on your carabines – Cock your carabines – Present – Fire – Let fall your carabines – Take your swords from your bridle-hands – Return your swords.[56]

There was also sword drill, the sweeping cut to left or right being practised by troops armed with sabres, the point or edge being stressed for those equipped with the broad sword. Most cavalrymen were taught to slash at their opponents' bridle headstalls, thus causing their horses' bits to fall from the mouths – making control impossible. In the time of Frederick William II, the Prussian cavalry performed mounted drill twice a week and dismounted drill once.

As for dragoons, they were put through cavalry and infantry drills, both in three ranks. The former exercise was almost identical with that of the horse, but the latter also included bayonet drill and was closely linked with the Exercise for the Foot, with one colourful addition; at the end of the evolution, the dragoons would ground their firearms, seize their swords, and charge outwards with a huzzah. During the foot exercise, as during dismounted action, the horses would be tethered together by their bridles in a fashion that made quick release feasible. Horse-handlers were told off by troops, two or three apiece.

The details of how mounted formations were variously employed in action will appear below, but to close this discourse on cavalry training it is interesting to quote parts of a passage from Marshal Saxe's writings, which reflects the 'best' French practice towards the middle-years of the eighteenth century.

The movements should be simple and solid; it [the cavalry] should be taught nothing but speed and lightness; the chief point is to show the cavalry how to fight together, and not to split up ... the only moves that need be learnt are the *caracole*, turns to right and left by half and quarter ranks, and how to open order. *That is all.* In this way you can march left or right to take up a position when you could not have done it as a squadron ... But observe one fundamental principle —↘ *never* halt during the *caracole* to improve the dressing; this is a point of infinite consequence ... It is above all necessary to teach cavalry to gallop long distances. A squadron that cannot charge at full stretch for 2,000 paces without breaking order is only fit to be placed in the rear.[57]

4

The mounted arm in battle and on campaign

The basic duty of the cavalry on the field of battle was to engage and defeat the enemy's horse; thereafter, if all was going well, the mounted arm would be directed to fall upon the foe's infantry, guns and trains in order to destroy them or at least induce the rival commander to abandon the engagement. Most seventeenth and eighteenth century experts reiterated this order of priorities, but on the question of actual cavalry tactics there were considerable differences of both opinion and practice. No account of the roles of the mounted arm in our period would be complete without an evaluation of the variation of method employed.

At the beginning of the War of the League of Augsburg the reputation of the French cavalry was still at its height as a battle-winning weapon, and many countries not unnaturally tended to model their military methods on those of the strongest power in Europe. By this date, however, French cavalry tactics were already based on a doctrinal compromise, and in the end this was a factor which contributed to their delcine.

On the one hand there was a strong desire to make the utmost use of the cavalry as an instrument of sophisticated fire-power; on the other there was a wish to employ shock-action and cold steel to the full. For most of the first half of the seventeenth century, the advocates of fire-action had carried the day. Cavalry usually moved to the attack, two squadrons at a time, on the frontage of a single *compagnie*, the remaining five troops advancing one after another behind the leader. Moving forward at a slow trot to within carbine or pistol range, each troop would in turn rein in, discharge their fire-arms, and then trot to the rear of their six-troop-deep formation to reload; meanwhile the second troop moved up into the newly vacated space to fire in their turn.

This type of *'perpetuum mobile'*, however impressive on the parade ground, sacrificed practically all the advantages of shock-action. The examples of Gustavus Adolphus of Sweden, and to a lesser extent of Prince Rupert and Oliver Cromwell, who all advocated and practised *'la charge sauvage'*, eventually caused a considerable shift in French military opinion. As a result, in the days of Turenne and the Great Condé, much of the French cavalry reverted to a more dramatic and forceful battle role. However, as the years passed, many of their precepts began to be misapplied by lesser commanders, and towards the end of the century a compromise between the 'fire' and 'shock' schools of thought was becoming increasingly the fashion. The French cavalry – usually massed on the flanks of the infantry and guns – still advanced at the trot to fire, but this it now gave in three ranks all at once. Following the discharge of pistol and carbine, the squadrons spurred through the smoke to engage in the *mêlée*, swords in hand.[58] There was, however, relatively little attempt to press home the attack with the ruthless vigour of a Gustavus or a Cromwell.

In much the same way, hussar tactics – as practised by both France and Austria – remained somewhat undeveloped – though flexible. This was no doubt largely due to the prejudice which excluded these barely 'respectable' formations from the main lines of battle. As *Père* Daniel described it in 1721:

> Their usual method of fighting is to envelop an enemy squadron, and to scare it by their cries and varied movements. As they are very adept at managing their horses, which are of small height, they have very short stirrups, and keep their spurs close to the horse's flanks, thereby forcing them to move faster than the heavy cavalry; they rise up in their saddles and are dangerous, above all, to fugitives. They rally easily, and can pass a defile with plenty of speed ... However, [he concludes] they cannot hold their own against a squadron in full battle order.'[59]*

Despite its deficiencies, the French cavalry remained predominant for another generation. At times they were handled with considerable imagination and success, particularly for raids deep into enemy territory with the intention of unsettling a supposedly 'safe' province or of needling an unwary opponent who allowed himself to be caught napping in winter quarters. Pre-eminent amongst cavalry commanders for this sort of activity – known as *courses* – was the French Marquis de Feuquières, whose raid on Savigliano in the winter of 1691 forms a classic example:

> I was commanding at Pignerol that winter; the Duke of Savoy had billeted four squadrons of his Gendarmes in Savigliano as part of his winter quarter arrangements, though the town was only guarded by citizen militiamen. I knew the place as I had visited it several times the previous year, and I was aware that there was an earthen bastion, hard by the Carmagnole Gate, adjoining the town wall, near which there was a wicket-gate that was merely locked at night but not guarded.
>
> On the basis of this information I resolved to capture the Gendarmes – so idle were they about their security. I chose a time of hard frost as it would be

---

*De la Colonie corroborates this impression in his description of Austrian hussars in 1717; '... it is impossible to fight them [hussars] formally, for although they may, when attacking, present a solid front, the next moment they scatter themselves at full gallop, and at the very time when they might be thought to be entirely routed and dispersed, they will reappear, formed up as before.' J. C. Horsley *Tales of the Old Campaigner* (London 1909) p. 159.

Nevertheless, Austrian hussars had their moments of triumph, as in 1740 when they surprised a regiment of Prussian dragoons, captured its standard, and almost took Frederick the Great prisoner.

necessary to pass over the bastion's ditch, which was full of water. I introduced a trusty spy into Savigliano, who, on the night appointed for the plan's execution, was to draw out the nails securing the gate bolt with pincers . . .

I made good speed with 800 cavalry carrying 500 infantry on their cruppers, and arrived outside the bastion two hours before dawn. After reconnoitring the bastion and the gate in the wall to ensure my spy had done his work, I passed my infantry over the frozen ditch, drew them up in battle-order in the square, seized the guards at the main gate, opened up for my cavalry, and rounded up the four troops of Gendarmes without opposition – all of whom I led back to Pignerol; had I been suspected or discovered, the Duke of Savoy could have fallen on me with four times my number of horsemen.[60]

Two years before this exploit, Brigadier General Feuquières had carried out a 35-day raid between the Neckar and the Danube, levying contributions as he went. Covering over 800 kilometres, he occupied Wurzburg, Nuremberg, Ulm, Augsburg and Pforzheim in turn, always eluding the clumsy attempts of his foes to catch up with him, and in due course returned to Montclar's army laden with four million *livres* of loot and contributions.

The Habsburg cavalry, largely conditioned by the precepts of the famous Montecuculi, who was not, however, a great cavalry commander, applied techniques of the French type with rather less success (except in certain crucial engagements against the Turks which will be discussed later). Similarly William III's Dutch and English regiments made little impression on their French opponents. Shorly after the battle of Fleurus (1690), Marshal Luxembourg, while paying compliments to the sturdy Dutch infantry, was moved to remark that 'the Prince of Waldeck has good reason to resent his cavalry for ever.'[61] A year later, the same French commander rubbed home the point at the Combat of Leuze. Learning that Waldeck (who had just taken over the Allied command from William III) was passing his army over the river La Catoir without taking proper precautions prior to entering winter quarters, confident that the French were too far distant to be able to interfere, Luxembourg determined to end the campaign on a high note by bearding his opponent. He conducted a secret forced march from Espierre over 17 kilometres under cover of a convenient mist at the head of 28 squadrons of horse and dragoons (many of them belonging to the *Maison du Roi* and including in their number the youthful Villars) and fell upon the 75 squadrons and five battalions of the Allied rearguard on 19 September 1691. Surprise was almost complete. Leaving two regiments of dragoons to engage the Allied foot near Caparelle, Luxembourg attacked the disordered horse – who had only managed to form a single line – and proceeded to administer a sound drubbing. But for a heroic counter-charge by the English Life Guards – one of whose guardsmen fought his way through the French ranks to engage the Marshal in personal combat – the defeat might have been even more humiliating for William's forces, but as it was the Allies lost 1,500 casualties and 40 standards before being able to extricate themselves to the further bank of the river.[62] So pleased was Louis XIV at the outcome that he ordered a commemorative medal to be struck, and awarded a special standard to the troop of Horse Grenadiers of the *Maison* which had particularly distinguished itself in the action.

Throughout the War of the League of Augsburg, indeed, there seems to have been no stopping the French cavalry, and at Landen (1693) they again demonstrated their superiority by storming William III's earthworks at the fourth attempt, a feat which enabled them to capture Neerwinden village from the rear.

The days of unquestioned French cavalry ascendancy, however, were numbered. Soon after the turn of the century, her horsemen began to lose some of their old standards, and it soon became clear that superiority had passed to the Anglo-Dutch camp for a generation. As early as the engagement of Eckeren in 1703, a single troop of 40 Dutch cavaliers led by Major-General Hompesch routed 1,500 cavalrymen drawn from the best French and Spanish regiments in a tough dyke-top encounter, and 'pursued them closely for almost a mile'.[63]

Much of the improvement in Allied cavalry methods that this feat reflected stems directly or indirectly from the reforms in training and tactical method encouraged by their Captain-General, John Churchill, First Duke of Marlborough. Unlike many of his easy-going and complacent opponents, he placed great personal stress on good equipment, well cared-for-horses and continuous training. In late June 1704 Prince Eugene was particularly impressed by the fine bearing and good equipment of the English cavalry when they were well on their way to completing the arduous 250-mile march from the United Provinces to the Danube:

'My Lord', said Eugene, 'I never saw better horses, better clothes, finer belts and accoutrements; but money, which you don't want [lack] in England, will buy clothes and fine horses, but it can't buy that lively air I see in every one of these trooper's faces.'[64]

Marlborough's record in this respect contrasts forcibly with that of Tallard's army making the far shorter march from Strasbourg to Augsburg during which almost a third of his cavalry horses died in an epidemic of glanders.

Unlike most French and Imperial generals, 'Corporal John' had no time for cavalry using firearms. 'The Duke of Marlborough would allow the horse but three charges of powder and ball to each man for a campaign,' recalled General Kane, 'and that only for guarding their horses when at grass, and not to be made use of in action.'[65] Instead the Anglo-Dutch cavalry were trained to base their fighting on twin-squadron charges delivered at a fast trot, each squadron drawn up in two lines, using cold steel. At the grand tactical level Marlborough was unconventional in the amount of cavalry he retained in reserve for the *coup de grace;* this enabled him to produce superior numbers of fresh horsemen at the critical moment in a battle – as happened at Blenheim, Ramillies and Malplaquet in turn. He was also a past master at supporting his cavalry with guns and foot, and thus greatly increased the tactical effectiveness of his mounted attacks.

The Battle of Blenheim (1704) '. . . was decided almost altogether by the judicious use of the cavalry of the Allied army', wrote Denison.[66] Two specific incidents stand out, one relatively small, the other larger. The first was the rout of eight squadrons of the vaunted French *Gendarmerie* by merely five English squadrons commanded by Colonel Palmes. Robert Parker describes this stirring achievement:

> When the commanding officer of these squadrons [the *Gendarmerie*] had got clear of their lines, he ordered the squadron on his right and that on his left to edge outward, and then march down till they came on a line with Palmes [*sic*]; at which time they were to wheel inward, and fall upon his flanks, while he charged him in front. Palmes perceiving this, ordered Major Oldfield,* who commanded the squadron on his right, and Major Creed, who commanded that on his left, to wheel outward, and charge those squadrons that were coming down on them; and he, not in the least doubting but they would beat them, ordered them when they had done that, to wheel in upon the flanks of the other squadrons that were coming upon him, while he charged in front; and everything succeeded accordingly. This was a great surprise to Tallard, . . .[67]

The French commander-in-chief was indeed surprised, and when he came some time later to list the reasons for his defeat, he wrote: 'First, because the *Gendarmerie* were not able to break the five English squadrons.'[68]

The climax of the battle was equally impressive. After passing over the Nebel and its marshes, Marlborough's 80 fresh squadrons, closely supported by 23 battalions of infantry and Colonel Blood's guns, survived and drove off a desperate attack by the 60 French squadrons holding Tallard's centre, and then began an inexorable advance against the blown and disordered remnant. The first surge forward was checked, but the second proved irresistible, and nine exposed French battalions were overwhelmed whilst Tallard's exhausted squadrons, after vainly trying to stem the red tide with their pistols and carbines, broke and fled, many of them to drown in the Danube or be crushed to death on its banks – a fate that the Count of Mérode-Westerloo almost shared:

> So tight was the press that my horse was carried along some three hundred paces without putting hoof to ground – right to the edge of a deep ravine: down we plunged a good twenty feet into a swampy meadow; my horse stumbled and fell. A moment later several more men and horses fell on top of me as the remains of my cavalry swept by all intermingled with the hotly pursuing foes. I spent several minutes trapped beneath my horse.[69]

The Allied cavalry never lost its superiority for the rest of the war. There were of course several setbacks – especially in Spain, where at Almanza (1707) the Portuguese cavalry broke on the Allied right, precipitating disaster for Galway's

*Creed was Major of the Duke of Schomberg's Regt of Horse (later the 7th Dragoon Guards); he was killed in his unit's third charge at Blenheim. (See Dalton, *op.cit.*, v pt. II p. 223 f.n.2). Major Oldfield belonged to General Wood's Regt of Horse (later the 3rd Dragoon Guards). He left the Army in 1707 with the rank of Lt. Colonel. (Dalton, *ibid.*, p.17 f.n.2).

army, whilst at Brihuega (1710) four regiments of English horse and dragoons were forced to surrender to Vendôme's superior forces. Nevertheless, it would be possible to cite a dozen examples of the Allied horse carrying off the palm in the years after 1704: the use of cavalry to head the columns – and bridge the streams – in Marlborough's passage of the Lines of Brabant in 1705 – and their subsequent charges at Elixem, led by their Captain-General in person; his handling of the cavalry the next year at Ramillies to procure a decisive superiority on his left centre, cunningly transferring units from his right behind a concealing ridge – and the subsequent pursuit and exploitation which led to the conquest of almost all the Spanish Netherlands; the unleashing of Orange's and Overkirk's squadrons from the cover of the Boser Couter at Oudenarde (1708) to take Vendôme's wing of the French army in the rear whilst Natzmer and Eugene fell upon the further flank; the massive cavalry clash at Malplaquet (1709) when the reserved Allied squadrons swept through the French redoubts, newly taken by Orkney's infantry – to meet Villars' massed horsemen in a combat involving all of 30,000 cavalrymen – 'one of the greatest cavalry actions of history' as Sir Winston Churchill rightly described it; the staunch performance of the outnumbered English cavalry in bringing off victory at Almenara in 1710 or the use of fast-moving cavalry and dragoon squadrons to outwit the same Villars in 1711 in the celebrated *Non Plus Ultra* Lines episode. These, and many more, are examples of English skill at handling cavalry in battle and on campaign.

Yet even Marlborough's fine record with cavalry and his careful supervision of its training and equipment should not conceal the reverse of the medal. In many ways, the Allied cavalry of 1701–13 were almost as conservative as their opponents. There were still no hell-for-leather charges delivered at the gallop; for fear of disordering the sacred line, a fast trot was alone countenanced – in other words Marlborough relied more on numbers and weight than upon speed and impact. True, it was important that his guns and foot should be capable of keeping pace with the advance of the horse, but this over-rigid insistence continued to rob the cavalry of its fullest expression, whilst the retention – indeed reissue – of breastplates on Marlborough's express orders obviously helped to some degree to reduce their capacity for speed. And at the same period, we find many Prussian, Danish and Habsburg cavalry formations in Marlborough's, Eugene's and Baden's armies continuing to place undue reliance on cavalry firearms as zealously as the French, Bavarians and Spaniards.

In addition to the routine tasks of the mounted arm, at times of great emergency they could also be called upon to perform special services as in the famous *'affaire des poudres'*, 1708, when the Duke of Burgundy attempted to pass a quantity of sorely-needed gunpowder through the Allied lines into beleaguered Lille. This dramatic incident deserves further description from contemporary writings. Captain Robert Parker, for instance, describes how *Lieutenant-Général* le Chevalier de Luxembourg (son of the famous *'Tapissier de Notre-Dame'*) undertook this desperate task:

His method was this. He took about 2,000 choice horse, each of which carried behind him a bag of powder, containing about 100 [pounds] weight. These put green boughs in their hats, and marched with the Duke in great order from Douai. About the dusk of the evening they came up to the outer barrier of our circumvallation line, and pretending to be a party of German horse, that had been out on an expedition, and were returned with some prisoners, the officer opened the barrier and let them in: from thence they rode on gently to the next officer's guard, where there was no barrier, and he asking some questions which the Duke did not like, they clapped spurs to their horses, and rode in a full gallop through the intervals of our camp towards the town, but the officer ordering his guard to fire, it gave the alarm, and the Quarter-Guards turning out, and the soldiers of the camp running to their arms, all fired upon them.[70]

For the predictable and gory outcome of this discovered attempt, let us turn to the Memoirs of another eye-witness, the Count of Mérode-Westerloo:

Our men seized their arms and opened fire; this made several sparks set fire to some of the enemy's powder-bags; in an instant several hundred of them were hurled into the air amidst a terrifying explosion which shook the earth. As it turned out between six and seven hundred of the men in the centre and van of the column reached the city, but those in the rear turned about and made for Douai. As their powder-bags were made of linen and not of leather, several sprung leaks, leaving a trail of powder along the road behind them. As they rode their horseshoes made the sparks fly which set fire to the powder-trail and this in turn ignited the sacks, blowing up a number of men and horses with an infernal din. It was a horrible spectacle to see the remains of men and horses, whose legs, arms and torsoes even had been flung into the trees.[71]

The true *beau sabreur* of cavalry warfare of the period up to 1722 was Marlborough's esteemed contemporary, the King of Sweden. This soldier-monarch was the very embodiment of the cavalry qualities of martial courage, dash, energy and determination, and if his dedication to *élan* encouraged a lack of caution and sound judgement which in the end led him to failure, he was nevertheless the greatest cavalry leader of his day. Like Marlborough, he paid close attention to his mounted arm's equipment and administration; like him, he had no time for cavalry carbine or pistol fire, going so far as to forbid their use completely except in the dragoons. The long, straight sword was universally employed, the thrust being enjoined rather than the sweeping cut. Unlike Marlborough, however, Charles repeatedly stressed speed as the most important factor in a cavalry attack, and to this end the Swedish troopers were forbidden any form of personal armour. Charles' cavalry was expected to baulk at no obstacle whatsoever, and under his personal supervision was trained to manoeuvre with a rapidity hitherto unknown amongst disciplined European armies. The most skilled rider was hard put to keep up with the dynamic leader, and at a single review in 1707 Charles is known to have ridden two steeds to death.

Until Poltava – where the miserable remnants of the once-imposing Swedish army, ruined by exposure, went down before Peter the Great's superior numbers and his cunning use of earthen redoubts to support his horse and foot – Charles and his horsemen never found their match. Poles, Saxons and Russians went down before the ferocious yet disciplined blue-coated horsemen. Thus at Klizow (19 July 1702), 21 Swedish squadrons won the day with cold steel, routing 34 Saxon squadrons employing pistols. For battle charges, Charles devised an arrow-shaped formation for his squadrons. Instead of riding 'knee by knee' in approximately straight lines, Swedish troopers spurred 'knee behind knee', their cornet riding at the apex of the formation with two long flanks of horsemen stretching away in echelon to left and right. This formation conferred considerable tactical advantages – especially against static targets, [72] although it was probably rather expensive in cornets.

Charles XII's second great innovation was a deliberate doctrine of pursuit after victory. Although Marlborough's conquest of the Spanish Netherlands after Ramillies was a splendid achievement, it was rare for most contemporaries to follow through their successes to the uttermost, owing to a combination of practical difficulty and mental disinclination. But what Napoleon later termed *'la poursuite à l'outrance'* was common practice in Charles' armies, and a routed foe was allowed no respite. After the retreat of Marshal Schulenburg's Saxons in 1704 the Swedish cavalry pursued their discomfited foes for nine days without once unsaddling, and eventually overtook them at Sanitz. Without hesitation, two regiments of unsupported Swedish cavalry charged 10,000 Saxons. Riding down the infantry, they proceeded to rout the Saxon horse, and then returned to cut down the gunners and remaining foot. Nightfall saved the relics of Schulenburg's army, but his escape over the frontier was only bought at the price of all his guns.

Small wonder that Denison was moved to write that the Swedish cavalry was 'the natural outcome of his [Charles'] daring and chivalrous spirit'. [73]

The only mounted arm of our period that may be said to have rivalled the dash of Charles XII's Swedes – though not its discipline – was that of the Ottoman Turk. The wiry Arab horses on which many Moslem horsemen were mounted were fleet of foot and easy to manoeuvre at speed. Their tactics, like their discipline, remained rudimentary – a series of loosely-coordinated hell-for-leather rushes which were designed to unnerve all but the steadiest adversaries – for to obtain success the Turk usually relied on inducing the foe to break up his formations. The mounted Ottoman warrior fought essentially as an individual rather than as a member of a team, and in so far as manoeuvres were laid down at all they deserve to be called 'horde tactics', seeking to demoralize and overwhelm rather than to out-think. Strong tendencies towards indiscipline, particularly amongst the semi-trained levies that invariably made up a sizeable part of the Porte's armies in the field, often prepared the way for heavy defeat if the opponent remained calm and compact in the teeth of the fury of a 'Turkish storm'. This lesson was soon learnt by the Habsburg forces, horse and foot alike, and it became the practice for them to weather out the Turkish attack from within a barricade of portable *chevaux de frise*, before counter-charging once the enemy's energy had begun to flag. Even then great care had to be exercised lest the advancing forces should become over-extended in the desire to reach the rich booty of the Ottoman encampments, for on many occasions premature and ill-conducted pursuits came to grief when the supposedly-routed Turks turned unexpectedly at bay.

As de la Colonie observed at first hand, the individual Turk was often a superb horseman, capable of riding at breakneck speed and yet still able to fire his short musket from the saddle with fair accuracy, whilst his skill with sabre and scimitar was often legendary.[74] For such tasks as rounding-up stragglers or massacring a fleeing army, the Turkish cavalry – both regular and irregular – had few peers, but against cool adversaries such as Baden or Eugene, their rampant indiscipline and a fatal tendency to ignore the support obtainable from their cannon and foot soldiers, often proved their undoing. One notable example of this occurred at Mohacs in August 1687 when Piccolomini charged with the second line of imperial cavalry at exactly the right moment, flinging the jaded Turkish horsemen back on to their infantry, who broke under the combined impact, and subsequently induced them to abandon their two lines of field entrenchments to the jubiliant troops of the Duke of Lorraine and his ally, Max Emmanuel, Elector of Bavaria. Although the celebrated Comte de Bonneval tried to introduce much needed reforms and modernization during the 1730s, his efforts met a storm of conservative opposition and at best proved transitory.

As the eighteenth century progressed, however, it was the French cavalry – formerly the outclassed squadrons of Blenheim or Merida – who re-emerged as the most influential mounted force in Europe. The lessons of their defeats were slowly assimilated, and under such great martial figures as Marshals Villars and de Saxe a new spirit began to enthuse the mounted cavaliers of Louis xv. Although de Saxe's *Rêveries* were of a somewhat wishful nature – as their title suggests – his opinions on the correct handling of the ideal cavalry force are of interest as revealing his innermost thoughts on the subject. Most of it is hard common sense bred from experience.

> When the cavalry charges the enemy, one cannot impress on it enough the need to keep closed up together, and not to pursue in a scatter . . . One should set off at a slow trot for a hundred paces; speed it up as the distance narrows – and finally gallop. Spurs should not be used until the last 20–30 paces, and their application should be signalled by the commanding officer crying *'A moi!'* It is necessary to instill this into cavalry, and to practise it well so that it becomes very familiar; it should be carried out like a flash of lightning.[75]

Saxe was very much a thinker as well as a fighter, and saw the need for reform. He saw the requirement for light arms and equipment if cavalry was to perform its full role, and was instrumental in re-establishing the lance as a cavalry weapon, thus founding the modern *Uhlan*. As we have seen he introduced helmets and a lighter breastplate, insisting on their being worn – despite obvious draw-backs to overall mobility – on the grounds that their use would encourage the enemy cavalry to rely on firearms to bring the French horsemen down – a circumstance that would prepare the way for their defeat when the well-delivered French charge crashed home. Similarly, he forbade his cuirassiers to carry pistols, planning to arm the front rank with 12-ft lances (weighing six pounds), which doubled as tent-poles when the day of action was past.[76] He agitated for the issue of breech-loading carbines and four foot swords, and was insistent that all mounted formations – whether 'heavies' or dragoons – should fight in three ranks. He called for clear distinction between the cuirassier elements (who were to be reserved for important engagements) and the dragoons, who were to perform all minor tasks – including active skirmishing, during which their third ranks would operate in open order. He laid down minimum heights for the two categories of troopers (5ft 6ins and 5ft 1in respectively) and specified the types of horses required. He devised dismounted drills for dragoons, and insisted on unpopular exercising of the horses in winter together with accustoming them to gunfire and smoke. Continual practice was enjoined to make both men and horses hardy, enabling them to endure fatigue, maintain speed and cover large distances. Every aspect of cavalry organization and employment thus attracted the Saxon adventurer's careful attention.

Experimental reforms of this nature – though some were never adopted – did much to refurbish the French cavalry arm, and regained it much of the old lustre. Although many contemporary writers on the military art display a rather unhealthy fascination for the conservative methods of the 1700s, Saxe was able to implement at least some of his more advanced ideas, and the hard-won victory of Fontenoy – where the French horse sacrificed themselves to enable their foot to re-form – was the outcome. He increased the number of light cavalry in the Army of Flanders, and made of them *la longue-vue du général en chef*.[77]

The years that saw the fame of Saxe reach its zenith also witnessed the emergence of the great commander of the next generation – Frederick of Prussia. Under his father and Prince Leopold von Anhalt-Dessau – 'The Old Dessauer' – the cavalry arm had tended to be ignored in favour of the infantry. Frederick William I had enjoined that charges were only to be delivered at the trot; musketry and pistol practice had been encouraged, and 13 years of peace had done much to dull the zeal of the Prussian horse. 'My father left me a bad cavalry,' wrote Frederick long after; 'hardly an officer who knew his duty. The men were afraid of their horses and hardly ever mounted them; they only knew how to drill on foot.' Or again, 'They were giants on elephants, and could neither manoeuvre nor fight. There was never a parade at which some of them did not fall off . . .', and his impression of their battle unworthiness was borne out at Mollwitz (10 April, 1741), where the slow and unimaginative Prussian cavalry were swept from the field. 'The cavalry are so bad that it isn't worth the devil's while to take them away; they can drill with the precision of grenadiers, but are equally slow,' was Frederick's verdict after this abysmal occasion.[78]

Frederick was not remiss in implementing drastic reforms within months of Mollwitz. His 'Instruction for Cavalry in Battle', issued in March 1742, enjoined the charge at the gallop, forbade the use of carbines or pistols in mounted attacks, and stressed the all-importance of the squadron commander using his initiative. Two months later the Prussian cavalry showed considerably better form at Chotusitz – although it was again ultimately defeated. Following the Peace of Breslau, the reforming work continued. The lessons of Chotusitz were absorbed: the interval between squadrons was reduced; a third line of squadrons was added. The Second Silesian War proved the effectiveness of these efforts, and the battles of Hohenfriedberg, Soor, Hennersdorf and Kesseldorf all redounded to the credit of the Prussian cavalry, although the main Prussian strength continued to reside in its superb infantry.

The succeeding eleven years of peace (1745–56), saw the completion of the transformation of the Prussian cavalry. Frederick's main ideas may usefully be summarized here as they were already formulated to a large degree by 1745. His cavalry was trained to form in three lines on one or both flanks of the infantry. The first comprised the 'heavies', placed at close intervals, charged with the task of riding down the foe. Three hundred yards back stood the second line, consisting of squadrons placed with wide intervals, their line consequently overlapping the one to the front by some 150 yards. The task of these units – mostly dragoons – was to supplement the efforts of the cuirassiers, filling gaps and tackling any enemy breakthrough. Finally, 200 yards to the rear, was placed the third line of hussars, serving as a general reserve with the duties of re-establishing the fight if necessary, of protecting the rear and flanks of the lines to their front. Frederick was insistent that a proportion of this reserve must be kept in hand for pursuit – which was only to be undertaken when the foe's infantry began to leave the field. As has been well said, Frederick's mounted attacks were based on three principles: the simultaneous action of his whole force pursuing one common object; the combination of frontal with flank attack – giving the latter the emphasis whenever possible; and the use of surprise (especially the deployment of cavalry under cover) to ensure the gaining of the initiative. These methods came to their perfection at Prague (1757). In the words of Hamley, 'He (Frederick) walked round the Austrians like a cooper round a tub.'[79] The French were to fare little better.

But the years of true Prussian cavalry greatness under the inspiration of Seydlitz still lay ahead in 1745, and the French retained their superiority as the *doyen* of the mounted forces of Europe. This is not, however, to belittle the fighting qualities of the cavalry of Great Britain. Although the Dutch Cavalry broke and fled at Fontenoy, the British and Imperialist horse had enjoyed a glorious day at Dettingen two years earlier; the Third Dragoons, for example, met a nine-squadron French charge with but two weak squadrons in hand, yet headed for the heart of them and hacked their way through – though at no little cost – whilst at a later stage the British and Austrian cavalry clinched the day by decisively routing the *Maison du Roi*. And the famous instance at Fontenoy when 15 squadrons of English horse patiently bore the concentrated fire of the French artillery for a whole hour at the halt until their General Campbell lost a leg – they were then withdrawn – would seem to show that the proverbial coolness and gallantry of the English cavalryman were still undimmed with the passage of the years, however inept the orders of their higher commanders.

It would, of course, be possible to cite a great many anecdotes relating to the gallantry of cavalrymen of many nations during our period; the wars of the day were rich with inspiring incidents. Here one single tale of courage must represent all the rest. It concerns Trooper Thomas Brown of the Third Dragoons at the battle of Dettingen in 1743. During ferocious fighting, his unit lost almost all its officers – and spying his Regiment's standard lying unheeded on the ground, Trooper Brown prepared to leap down from his horse to recover the precious emblem. At that moment, a French horseman slashed at him with his sword, severing two fingers of his bridle-hand. His horse bolted straight into the rear of the French lines, and there Brown espied the standard being borne off in triumph by a French trooper. Forgetting his painful wound, he galloped after the horseman, killed him, and regained the standard. Wedging the staff between leg and saddle, he turned to fight his way single-handed through the enemy army to regain his own lines. This he managed to do, but with three bullets through his hat and seven wounds in his face and body. His feat did not go unrecognized or unrewarded. At the close of the day, King George II saw fit to mark his victory by dubbing a number of knights banneret in the field, and amongst them was Dragoon Thomas Brown.

Here we must leave our studies of the mounted soldier – cuirassier, dragoon and light horsemen – and turn to other aspects of eighteenth century warfare. It is hoped that enough has been said to demonstrate that the annals of the armies of Europe at this period are packed with incidents redounding to the credit of *l'arme blanche,* sword or sabre.

Part II

The Foot

5

Representation and types of infantry

As in practically every age, the infantry soldier formed the backbone of almost all armies. Between 1688 and 1745 there took place a considerable increase in both the military esteem and the numerical representation of 'the poor Foot' most particularly in time of war, although the reductions implemented at the conclusion of each peace inevitably hit the infantry hardest. In 1688, for example, the French army numbered some 150,000 men, two-thirds of whom were foot soldiers, but by the middle years of the War of the League of Augsburg these 100,000 infantry had been expanded to more than three times that number divided into 246 regiments each of several battalions.[1] Such a huge force could not be sustained for long, and after 1697 many regiments were disbanded. At the outbreak of the Spanish Succession War, Louis XIV possessed a nucleus of 150,000 infantry, and subsequently expanded his army, horse and foot, to between 250,000 and 300,000 men (1705), and by the end of the war there were 350 Regiments in existence including 270 of infantry, but from 1714 there was a further substantial reduction. Thus in 1727, Louis XV could deploy only 120,940 infantry (178 battalions − exclusive of militia, veterans and invalids), and 11 years later there were barely 100,000 foot in service (besides 60,000 militia under arms). In 1740 there were 98 regiments (155 battalions) or 85,000 officers and men on the peacetime establishment, but with the declaration of war this soon rose to 175,000 in 227 battalions. The climax of the War of the Austrian Succession, however, saw far larger French armies take the field, and by 1748 it is estimated that there were over 236,000 French regular infantry on the muster rolls besides some 95,000 militia and garrison troops.[2] After the peace of Aix-la-Chappelle, however, 53 battalions were immediately disbanded.

England's armies were considerably smaller than those of France. Though James II had worked hard to expand his army, William III inherited no more than 25,186 infantry from his predecessor, but by 1696 he was asking Parliament to sanction an army of 87,440 men, including almost 70,000 foot.[3] Within two years, however, this imposing array had shrunk to a bare 18,000 men of all types, only one-thrid of them being permitted to be kept in England and Scotland on the peacetime establishment. The exigencies of the Spanish War soon reversed this trend, and by the year of Malplaquet Queen Anne could call on the services – on paper at least – of 58,235 English infantry, perhaps 75 battalions in all, besides large numbers of foreign troops in British pay.[4] In the more peaceful decades that followed the Hanoverian ministers rapidly dismantled this imposing array of native infantry, for many years the total barely rose over 26,000 men and even at the height of the Jacobite Rebellion of the '45 (with an expeditionary force in Flanders), the British foot totalled only 33,000 (out of an army of some 40,000).

Such fluctuations in the size of the infantry arm were inevitably paralleled in the armies of other European powers. Between 1689 and 1702, for instance, the Dutch infantry fluctuated between a strength of 59,504 (out of 73,000 troops) and 78,905, dropping during the inter-war years to 40,289.[5] The Habsburgs had some 105,000 infantry under arms out of a total army of 140,000 men in 1710, and 17 years later they were still in a position to field 92,600. Austria's perennial opponent, Turkey, maintained a field force of 59,000 *élite* Janissaries and 100,000 'regular' *capiculi* infantry during the early years of the century, besides further huge numbers of irregulars, but it is difficult to discover reliable comparative figures.* Peter the Great only laid the foundations of a modern army in 1699, when 29 new infantry regiments were raised to replace part of the ancient *strelsi* and feudal levies. By 1705, all Russian forces numbered 168,000 men, of whom 130,000 were foot.

In terms of rapid military growth, however, two centuries shared Europe's astounded attention. On the accession of Frederick William II in 1713, Brandenburg-Prussia possessed an army of barely 40,000 men, but by that monarch's death in 1740 this number had risen to 89,000,† (of whom some two-thirds were infantry) – a very substantial force for a nation of merely $2\frac{1}{2}$ million and an annual revenue of little over £1,000,000 sterling.[6] At the height of the Great Northern War, on the other hand, Charles XII's army included 65,000 Swedish infantry (out of 110,000 of all arms) – although his country's population numbered less than a million. He mounted his invasion of Russia in 1707 at the head of 43,650 men, of which half were infantry in 14 line regiments and three battalions of Guards. Such a disproportionate military effort – which had to be maintained year after year – placed an almost impossible strain on Sweden's resources, and inevitably hastened her decline, dating from the disaster of Poltava in 1709.

These selected figures give some indication of the general representation of the infantry arm during our period, both within specific armies and between countries. It is clear that one reason for the increasing importance of infantry in the wars of the time was the comparative cheapness of recruiting, paying and equipping a foot-soldier; a mounted man was far more expensive. This economic motive was reinforced by a general improvement in the effectiveness of infantry

---

*To cite two examples, the army mobilized against Russia in 1710 numbered 118,400 men, 96,000 of which can be deemed infantry; at their great victory at the Pruth (1711), the Turks reputedly fielded 260,000 men, including 140,000 infantry.

†Some sources place the maximum figure for 1740 at 99,450 – probably including militia. See O. Groehler, *Die Kriege Friedrichs* II, (Berlin 1966) p. 22.

weapons, although tactical method remained essentially stereotyped and unimaginative in the great majority of armies.

Between the years 1688 and 1745, there were considerable changes in the types of infantry employed in the various armies. These variations were largely influenced by developments in infantry weapons (see next chapter), but here we will describe the evolution of the foot soldier and distinguish broadly the roles of the various types.

The pikeman

In the last decades of the seventeenth century, most European armies contained four distinct types of infantry soldier, and by the second quarter of the eighteenth a further type was fast emerging. First there was the pikeman, doomed to disappear from the military scene by about 1703. In the days of Montecuculi (1609–1681) there had commonly been a proportion of one pikeman to every two musketeers in each *terçio* or regiment. The same proportion was usual in the English Civil War (1642–46). In that generation the prime quality for the foot was considered to be solidity rather than manoeuvrability, especially in those forces habitually faced with the mass-attacks of numerically superior and fast moving Turkish hordes. 'Without the pike', Montecuculi wrote in 1674, 'which is the queen of foot arms, an infantry force attacked by a squadron, or by a battalion with pikes, cannot remain entire nor proffer a long resistance.'[7] By 1688, however, the proportion of pikemen to musketeers had dropped to one in five, largely due to the improvements in firearms. Despite this diminution the pikeman was still considered in many quarters an *élite* soldier, it being regarded as more gentlemanly to 'trail a pike' than to handle powder and shot. The 'ancient and puissant pike' – which commonly measured between 16 and 18 feet and weighed about 17lbs – had many champions including *Maréchal* d'Artagnan, who strenuously opposed Vauban's advocacy of the weapon's replacement by the musket in the French army, and it is interesting to note that several mid-eighteenth century soldiers and theorists – including de Saxe and Folard – argued for the weapon's reintroduction, albeit in vain. The pike's critics eventually won the day, basing their case on the weapon's unhandiness and above all on the waste of valuable fire-power its use involved. The development of an effective socket-bayonet, which enabled every musketeer to defend himself in close-quarter combat, without having to lay aside his firearms, destroyed the chief *raison d'être* for the pike's retention, and the advocates of fire-power triumphed. Indeed it is extraordinary that a man as intelligent as Saxe should have been as reactionary as to wish to employ it after this period.

The changeover took place by gradual stages over a period of some 20 years. In 1689, the Emperor ordered his armies fighting the Turk to substitute the boar-spear. The next year, at the battle of Fleurus, it was widely noted that several German battalions using firearms alone had proved capable of repulsing French cavalry more effectively than others armed with the conventional

number of pikes, and before the year was out the French Marshal Catinat had
ordered his men to abandon the weapon before undertaking his campaign in the
Alps. The Swedes had begun to reduce their numbers of pikemen as early as the
days of the great Gustavus Adolphus – but the weapon did not entirely disappear
from amongst their Russian rivals until about 1709. The French abandoned
their last pikes during late 1703 – although the Drill Manual issued in that year
still included '*l'exercise à la pique et au mousquet*,' and it is clear that Spanish
regiments were still equipped with a number at the battle of Eckeren: for we read
in Mérode-Westerloo's memoirs that his men were 'all in desperate confusion,
pikemen picking up muskets and musketeers laying hold of pikes'.[8]

The English forces were not so forward in discarding the 'Queen of Weapons',
as some authorities have claimed. On 20 June 1702 we find the commanding
officers of six regiments currently under marching orders for Ireland being
advised as follows by the Secretary at War:

> . . . Her Majesty's pleasure is that all pikes already issued to the Regiment of
> Foot under your command be returned into the Stores of Ordnance, in lieu of
> a sufficient number of muskets which you are first to receive out of the said
> stores.

A postscript went on to state, however, that this was '. . . not to hinder your
carrying your pikes to Ireland in case muskets be not time enough delivered to
you'.[9] The process of replacement seems to have been largely completed by
1704, although many English regiments retained a picquet or colour guard of a
dozen pikemen – mainly for regimental security duties – for a further number of
years. The very last time that pikes were issued to British fighting formations in
sizeable numbers may have been as recently as 1940, when for want of rifles Sir
Henry Page-Croft recommended their issue to part of the Local Defence
Volunteers (later the Home Guard).

The grenadier

The remaining types of infantryman were all equipped with fire-arms of various
kinds besides swords and, in most cases, bayonets. Foremost amongst them were
the grenadiers. These were hand-picked men, chosen from the line companies of
every battalion and generally organized into a special unit which took the place
of honour on the right of the battalion line. They were selected on the grounds of
being 'valorous, strong, robust and well *injambré*'[10], were commonly above the
average height, and usually mature in years. According to de Guiscard, it was
rare for a French grenadier to be allowed to serve beyond the age of 45 years, but
practice clearly varied from army to army.

The *Military Dictionary of 1702* describes 'granadiers' [*sic*] as 'soldiers armed
with a good Sword, a Hatchet, a firelock slung and a Pouch full of
hand-Granadoes . . . they have often been found very serviceable.' The addition
of hatchets and hand-grenades to the musket, bayonet and sword, reflects the
special tasks these chosen troops were expected to perform. Besides being an

example in coolness, discipline and courage to the rest of the battalion in the linear fire-fight, the grenadier was called upon to form the nucleus of every 'forlorn-hope' storming party and every last-ditch garrison. 'One celebrated operation by a picked group of grenadiers took place at the siege of Lille (1708), when Sgt. Littler succeeded in crossing the moat and hacking through the chains of a drawbridge immediately prior to a major assault.

Such operations were reflected in the famous song, 'The British Grenadiers'

> *'When'er we are commanded to storm the palisades,*
> *Our leaders march with fuses [fusils], and we with hand grenades;*
> *We throw them from the glacis, about the enemies' ears,*
> *Sing, tow, row, row, row, row, row, row, for the British Grenadiers.'*

The hatchet was intended for hewing an entry through hostile gates and palisades, whilst grenades (usually three per man carried in a leather pouch) were for destroying or at least demoralizing foes sheltering behind fortifications or within buildings, or alternatively for preventing the enemy scrambling into one's own positions. The hatchet was fast disappearing from English grenadier companies by 1697, but in other armies it remained standard equipment for many more years: writing in the 1780s, Le Blond reveals that the French still issued ten hatchets to each grenadier company. The grenade also remained on widespread issue, although its use was restricted to siege operations.

The origins of this type of *élite* infantry probably go back to the mid-seventeenth century. De Guiscard claims that the first 'modern' grenadiers were selected on a basis of four men from each of the 20 companies of the *Régiment du Roi* in 1667. By 1670 the practice of grouping these men into special companies was gaining ground amongst the 30 'Old Regiments',[11] and eight years later we find the diarist John Evelyn referring to English grenadiers as 'a new kind of Soldier,' which gives a good indication of when they first appeared in England. Other powers were not slow in following the French example, and from 1711 each Habsburg infantry battalion of 10 companies included two of grenadiers.

Some armies raised whole regiments of grenadiers. The Russian Tsars recruited several, but the most famous – indeed notorious – formation of this kind was King Frederick William II of Prussia's 'Great Grenadiers' (or 'Potsdam Giants'). The organization of this special corps will be outlined later. The main criterion for entry into this corps was inches rather than military expertise; the minimum acceptable height (without boots) was six feet, and Müller, 'the German Giant', is reputed to have been all of nine! These troops became world-famous for their smart appearance, precise drill and strict discipline, but were destined never to hear a shot fired in anger, for on his accession to the throne Frederick the Great, perhaps to annoy the shade of his detested father, ordered their disbandment. This notwithstanding, the Prussian army contained a number of crack grenadier battalions from this time on, although many were strictly composite formations of regimental grenadier companies.

The British Army never raised specific regiments of grenadiers in our period. The so-called 'Grenadier Guards' (at this time the 1st Foot Guards) only received this title after 1815 in recognition of their part in defeating the Imperial

Guard at Waterloo. However the practice of gathering together the regimental grenadier companies into *ad hoc* formations for special operations – such as the storming of the Schellenberg Heights on 2 July 1704 or the proposed attack on the fortified hill of Wavrechin at the seige of Bouchain seven years later – was often resorted to by British and other European commanders, including Frederick the Great. This tendency continued throughout the century and was to be particularly prevalent during the American War of Independence.

The fusilier

The third type of infantryman was the fusilier. This soldier derived his name from the fusil firearm he carried – a weapon somewhat lighter than the standard musket of the late seventeenth century and further equipped with a sling to enable its owner to assist in the handling of the artillery. The specific tasks of the original fusilier regiments were to provide close infantry support for the preoccupied gunners and to lend a hand in heaving the ponderous field guns into position. 'Fuziliers' [*sic*] says the compiler of the *Military Dictionary,* are 'Foot soldiers armed with Firelocks, which are generally slung. There is a Regiment of Fuziliers for the Guard of the Artillery.' As early as the English Civil Wars, companies of firelocks had been employed to guard the Train of Artillery.

The first regiment of fusiliers were raised for the French army in 1671, and 13 years later a second was added, the *Régiment Royal des Bombardiers.* Other armies were not slow in following suit. In England, Charles II raised the North British Fusiliers in 1678, and in 1685 James II added the Royal Fusiliers to the army establishment, following this up with the creation of the Royal Welch Fusiliers in 1688.

The special association between the fusiliers and the artillery did not long survive the turn of the century, at least in the English service. As more and more line regiments were re-equipped with the flintlock musket – a weapon very similar to the fusil – the distinction rapidly faded, and the fusilier regiments spent most of their active service in Flanders and Spain in a normal infantry capacity. The artillery and trains still required guards, of course, but the practice grew up of requiring every regiment to detail companies for this task by roster. Many officers and men of the infantry regarded this as an unpleasant duty, preferring to remain with their regiments in the line. In France, on the other hand, this trend was reversed. Thus the *Fusiliers and Bombardiers* were assimilated into the *Régiment Royale d'Artillerie* in 1720 and lost all connection with the Infantry.

The line infantryman

In the fourth category of foot soldiers was the ordinary musketeer of the line companies' rank and file, the arch-typical regimental soldier or *fantassin* who made up with his fellows the great bulk of the armies of the day. Usually of peasant stock, as often as not tricked, bullied or 'shanghaied' into joining the colours, the ordinary musketeer's martial competence, and his devotion to his profession, varied enormously even within a regiment. Originally equipped with the bulky matchlock musket, and later with the improved flintlock version, together with sword and bayonet, the line infantryman bore the brunt of the casualties in action, performed a thousand and one duties and fatigues at other times, and received the lowest rate of pay – 8d a day (including 6d subsistence) before stoppages. The best of them bore the vagaries of military life with a stoicism, steady courage and sense of humour; the worst were terrorized into obedience by the fear of the NCO's staves or the prospect of being flogged, hung or shot for grave misdemeanours. Some, like Sergeant John Millner of the Royal Regiment of Ireland, Corporal Bishop of The 8th of Foot (later the King's Regiment), Private Deane of the Foot Guards, or Corporal Todd of a later generation, were true soldiers endowed with a pride in their profession and additional gifts – rare at their level of society – for recording the details of their experiences on paper.[12] Others, like Peter Drake,* were prepared to desert from regiment after regiment, and even to drift from army to army, risking dire penalties if apprehended, in search of an easier billet or improved prospects of loot. A few were out-and-out rogues and criminals, the sweepings of the streets and the periodic jail-deliveries, who were often beyond hope of reform. Yet this somewhat unpromising material, in the right hands, could be induced to achieve marvels of valour and endurance, some of which will be briefly described in the final chapter of this section. Such then, were the main characteristics of the line infantry during the last years of the seventeenth century and the early years of the eighteenth.

Their immediate successors were not very different in character but broadly speaking the infantry types narrowed down to two from the original four. The disappearance of the pikeman and the gradual transformation of the fusilier into an ordinary infantry soldier (or in some countries his complete absorption into the artillery) accounted for this diminution. The result was an infantry arm almost wholly made up of general-purpose soldiery with a sprinkling of *élite* grenadiers and special formations of Guards and *corps d'élite*. But as the eighteenth century wore on a further distinct type of infantry soldier began to emerge – namely the light infantryman.

The light infantry soldier

It would be more accurate to say that the light infantryman re-emerged or was reintroduced, for troops of this type had existed in earlier armies, and had only suffered eclipse as recently as the mid-seventeenth century. Both the great Condé and the young Turenne had made considerable use of light troops in their earlier campaigns, but after the Battle of the Dunes in 1650 their employment began to

*Peter Drake served successively in three different armies during the War of the Spanish Succession, apparently changing employment with impunity. See *The Pen and the Sword*.

lapse. One reason for this retrograde development was, no doubt, the passion for military formalism and the mathematical perfection of linear battle formations which came to grip most military experts as the fire-power potential of armies increased. The norm became the delivery of massed volleys by serried lines at a range of little more than 50 yards – the 'elephantiasis of fire-tactics' as General Fuller has described it.[13] It was widely felt that the presence of deployed skirmishers would only serve to obstruct the main fields of fire, whilst the manpower thus employed (as in the case of the pikemen) was jealously coveted to increase the weight of the battalion, company or platoon volleys. And so the light infantryman virtually disappeared from the armies of Europe for at least two generations, although the supposedly conservative Turk continued to use his *Arnauts* in a skirmishing or sniping role, and a handful of sharp-shooters were occasionally employed by the British forces serving in Spain – but that was all.

The first military power to recognize the potential value of lightly-armed infantry was not, for once, France, but Austria. The continuous contact with the armies of the Porte was probably one reason for this, but it should be stressed that the first Imperial light infantry were irregular levies, particularly Croats (who could hardly be used as line infantry) – only later did formally constituted regiments appear in the Austrian army list. This pattern, as we shall see, was repeated by most of the powers of western Europe.

Guibert claimed that Maria Theresa first raised bands of irregular sharpshooters in 1740, but their use probably goes back at least another two generations. To ward off the irritating attentions of the sniping *Arnauts,* imperial commanders had long had recourse to recruiting irregulars from the Slavs, Serbs and Croats of the Habsburg *militärgrenze.* The notorious Baron Trenck, 'a born plunderer, hard, cold, unfeeling, totally without mercy and preferring pillage to war'[14] was one of their earliest commanders of note, but he was in due course surpassed by his sometime lieutenant, the brilliant Loudon. Of the bands themselves the Pandours bore the best reputation. Their value for outpost, reconnaissance and security duties became widely appreciated as, in Fortescue's colourful words, 'within a circle of these ruffians, the troops of the line marched in dignified security,' safe from the Turkish marksmen.

The first of these bands to be employed against western opponents was probably the 'Tirailleurs of the Tyrol' during the War of the Polish Succession. Marshal de Saxe was one of the first French commanders (since Turenne) to appreciate the value of such troops, and in his *Rêveries* (written in 1732), he called for the raising of disciplined bodies of a similar nature. After various experiments with handfuls of irregulars, he raised Grassin's Legion in 1744. This formation, some 900 strong, was made up of 600 light infantrymen and 300 light cavalry,[15] and was in fact the ancestor of the French rifle regiments, and one of the first eighteenth century units of regular light infantry. The formation served with distinction at Fontenoy (1745) where it tenaciously defended copses, woods and enclosures against Cumberland's massive attacks. By 1748 there were 16 'corps' of Light Infantry in the French army, totalling about 10,000 men, clear evidence of how highly the services of such forces were valued.

Grassin's Legion was soon widely copied. The year 1744 also saw the raising of the Prussian *Jägerskorps* of 300 men divided between two companies (some smaller units of skirmishers had in fact been used in 1740) and over the following years the Franco-Spanish army serving in Italy raised two battalions of mountain fusiliers – *los Mignones* or the Miquelets – and the King of Sardinia soon raised bands of Barbets to perform similar rôles.

In the British army, the first signs of the reintroduction of light infantry can be traced to 1710, although none saw service in Flanders under Marlborough. In that year the first independent companies of Highlanders were raised in Scotland in an attempt to suppress brigandage, but these were disbanded in 1717, being suspected of Jacobite sympathies. Eight years later four new companies of 300 men apiece were recruited to assist in the suppression of discontent in the Highlands, and in 1739 the addition of a further four companies led to the raising of the 43rd Regiment (later the 42nd Royal Highlanders or Black Watch), in 1740.

> They were principally intended to put a final period to the insurrection of the clans, and to secure their country from any attempts that might be made in the Jacobite interest. It was thought requisite to preserve their ancient habit that they might be more able to pursue any of these offenders into their fastnesses.[15]

Like the Pandours, they wore light shoes, and were armed with 'fusil, broadsword, dirk or dagger and a Highland pistol all of steel,' retaining their kilts and plaids.

Such, then, were the early stages of the reintroduction of light infantrymen into the armies of Europe. Their numbers were destined to increase rapidly towards the end of the century, and their training and operational employment would in due course become the standard pattern for all infantry formations.

The infantry of Turkey

To conclude this survey of infantry types, space must be devoted to a rapid description of the Turkish troops who were organized on very different lines, the main criteria being racial as much as military. The *élite* Janissaries were armed with reliable muskets besides scimitars and pistols, and performed battle roles roughly analagous to those of grenadiers; out of action, however, the Sultan's bodyguard was expected to perform many administrative duties including tax collection. The nearest equivalent to the fusiliers were the *Isarelys,* originally frontier guards commanded by artillery officers, who were responsible for handling small cannon. The mass of the rank and file of the Porte's *seratculi,* or irregular infantry was made up of *Azzars* (small corps named after their nation or region of origin), *Semenys* (peasant militia) usually organized into unreliable temporary formations, often unpaid, and lastly the *Musellims* or tributary Christians, always mistrusted by their Moslem masters and consequently never allowed to carry firearms. They usually bore axes into battle, and were regarded as a pioneer force or as expendable cannon-fodder. A fair proportion of the other varieties were armed with good muskets – especially the *Arnauts* or the *Azzars* who wielded their long-barrelled flintlocks with a high degree of skill – but the remainder of the Ottoman foot, according to de la Colonie, were 'a mob' carrying very rudimentary arms belonging to an earlier age including bows and arrows, scimitars, half-pikes, *coupies* (a kind of spear) and lances. But for all their antiquated weapons and organizations, the Turk remained a doughty opponent, if only on account of the size of his forces and the fury of his initial attacks, earning the grudging admiration of his Austrian and Russian foes. Thus the army mobilized to overawe Peter the Great in 1710 contained 20,000 Janissaries, 3,000 Egyptian Janissaries, 20,000 local infantry and 36,500 irregular foot, besides 20,400 *sipahi* cavalry, 10,000 ammunition carriers, 7,000 cannoneers and 1,500 craftsmen – or 118,400 in all. There were practically *twice* as many present next year at the battle of the River Pruth.

At the period progressed, the quality of even the Janissaries tended to decline through the admission of too many recruits and over-close association with civilian authorities and political intrigue, whilst the hereditable system of office did not tend to ensure efficiency. By the 1720s such phrases as 'the Janissaries were only terrible to their own Sultans' were coming into vogue, and Marsigli states that 'the Janissaries were renowned for their good eyes and limbs – the former to keep an eye on the unreliable cavalry who were prone to take flight, the latter to enable them to follow.'[16]

6

Infantry weapons and equipment

The development of military weapons is a highly specialized subject, and it is more dangerous than usual to make generalizations. Nevertheless it can be fairly stated that the period 1688–1745 saw the development of two main trends where infantry weapons were concerned – namely the replacement of the matchlock with the flintlock musket (and subsequent refinements) and the supersession of the pike by the bayonet of various types.

From matchlock to flintlock

In the last quarter of the seventeenth century there were numerous varieties of military firearms in use, but most of the infantry of all nations were equipped with versions of the matchlock musket.

This weapon had been in common use for over a century, and considerable improvements had been incorporated over the years. In the 1660s the standard version had been so bulky and heavy that some musketeers required a forked rest to support the ponderous weight of the piece when standing at the present. By the 1690s, however, considerably lighter versions were on issue, and the rests had disappeared. Nevertheless, the matchlock still remained an awkward weapon with grave drawbacks.* It was both inaccurate and unreliable. Misfires and other misadventures could account for one shot out of every two, the main contributory factors being the effects of dampness and of general mishandling by inexperienced troops. As one chronicler of William III's campaign in Ireland (1689) noted:

> ... A great many of the new men who had matchlocks had so little skill in placing of their matchlocks true and that scarce one in four could fire their pieces off, and those that did thought they had done a great feat if the gun fired, not minding what they shot at.[17]

Perhaps the greatest drawback was the time the matchlock took to reload. An

*See table of weapon specifications on p. 137.

average of one shot a minute was considered good, but even this rate of fire became difficult to maintain as the barrel became increasingly fouled with use. According to the *Exercise of the Foot* (1690), reloading drill required 44 separate movements, and a simplified sequence was as follows: first the musketeer had to rest his arms, and pour priming powder from powder-horn into the pan. Next, after blowing away 'loose corns', the musketeer 'cast about to charge', ordering arms ready to load the barrel. Taking a charger from his bandolier (in the days before pre-packaged cartridges), he would prise open its lid with his teeth and pour the gun-powder within down the muzzle. Fumbling in his ball-pouch for a bullet, and taking a wad of paper or cloth from his hat, he would place them in turn in the muzzle, and then draw his wooden ramrod or 'scourer' (very liable to break) and ram both ball and wad down upon the powder. If all these processes had been successfully carried out (and dampness had not affected his powder), the musketeer would now be ready to take the length of slow-match dangling from his wrist, blow one of its smouldering ends into a spark, present his piece in the direction of the target, and by pressing the smouldering match manually against the touch-hole in the pan (or pulling the trigger in later versions where the match was attached to a hammer) discharge his piece.

Effective range was in the order of 250 yards, but even rudimentary accuracy over 60 was exceptional. The butt of the matchlock was often not pressed into the shoulder but tucked under the armpit to avoid the elephantine kick of the weapon, and this practice did nothing to improve accuracy of aim; nor did the knowledge that flashbacks through the touch-hole were quite common occurencies encourage the close alignment of eye, barrel and target (although in due course a small vertical screen was added to protect the marksman's eye from such flashes).

Slow-match was usually soaked in a solution of potassium nitrate and then thoroughly dried-out. Most varieties burnt at about an inch in 15 minutes (quick-match, by contrast, burnt at a foot a minute), but a slower rate could be obtained by diluting the nitrate solution at a risk of reducing its combustible qualities. The French artillery expert, St. Rémy, gave a detailed specification for match:

> A good match should be made of flax or hemp tow. It must be spun into three strands of medium width, and each covered separately with pure hair ... it must be washed, well-glazed and well-tightened ... It must burn well, so that one piece, four or five inches in length, lasts one hour if possible ... It must make a good, hard coal which finishes in a point, which can stand up to being pressed against something.[18]

Slow-match had its own disadvantages. In night operations, the glowing matches could give away a formation's position, as happened to Dumbarton's Regiment at Sedgemoor (1685) despite the dense mist.[19] Furthermore it was a bulky commodity to carry into the field in sufficient quantities to supply both foot and guns. These drawbacks reinforced the many snags already inherent in the matchlock.

Despite the fact that far superior weapons were in widespread use for game-shooting by the mid-seventeenth century,* it was more than 50 years before even the majority of European armies had completely replaced the matchlock. Snaphances had been available since 1615 in France and even earlier in Holland. These weapons lit their powder-charges with a spark produced by striking flint on steel, and took their name from the Dutch words *schnapp-hahn*, literally 'pecking-cock', a nickname bestowed upon the decorated hammer and spring-activated cock which held the flint. Subsequently the term came to be loosely employed to describe any firearm fired according to this principle, including the French *fusil* and *fusée*, the Spanish *miquelet*, and Austrian *flinte*, not to forget the English flintlock which became the ancestor of 'Brown-Bess' and the Tower musket. Adaptations appeared for cavalry – the musketoon and carbine, which had shorter barrels than their infantry counterparts, some of them rifled. One rather peculiar line of firearms borrowing features from both the match- and flintlock was the *fusil-mousquet* or 'combination-lock', popular in the French, Imperialists and Swedish forces well into the first decade of the eighteenth century.

The advantages conferred by the flintlock musket were individually small but cumulatively important. Many versions were slightly lighter than the matchlock, and it was in several ways a more reliable weapon. An average misfire rate of only four shots out of 12 was a marked advance on earlier performances, this improvement being largely due to the superior reliability of flints over the rapidly-consumed and bulky slow-match. Even more important, the processes of reloading proved capable of simplification to only 26 evolutions, with the result that the rate of fire doubled. Closely associated with this improvement was the introduction of the pre-packaged cartridge made of greased paper, containing both powder and ball. It would seem, however, that these were not on universal issue to French troops until as late as 1738.

The musketeer now bit the end off each cartridge when loading, retained the ball in his mouth, and tipped the powder into the muzzle. He then spat the ball after the powder and folded up the paper to serve as the wàd, before ramming down as before. Calibres were also reduced in many cases; most matchlocks fired 16 balls to the pound, but the French *fusil* fired 24. This saving in weight was not universally applauded, however, and the British musket in general use in 1709 still fired one-ounce balls. One contemporary authority claimed that the 'considerable difference to the execution' caused by the heavier ball was one important reason for the superiority of British battalions in firefights against the French but the validity of this claim is dubious to say the least. [20]

In other respects there was little to choose between matchlock and flintlock. Range and general accuracy improved but little, and the retention of the wooden ram-rod until the 1720s remained a potential weakness. The new weapon also had special drawbacks of its own. In some models the flints tended to fall out with disconcerting ease, and in any case needed changing after 10 to 12 shots. A

---

*At the siege of Sherborne Castle (1645) Royalist gamekeepers were used as 'snipers', picking off Parliamentarian officers from the towers. In 1642 the Western Cavaliers armed their dragoons with fowling pieces.

long flint would snap off; a short one produce no spark.* It was also claimed that
the lighter ball of the French *fusil* and many similar weapons had less
penetrating power, probably justly.

These disadvantages largely account for the slowness in replacing the ancient
matchlock. On the one hand they strengthened the arguments of military
conservatism which tended to look askance at any new development; on the
other they reinforced the unwillingness of economy-minded governments to
provide the large sums required to implement such a radical changeover in
weapons. The French proved more hesitant in these respects than most powers.
In 1693 Louis xiv even decreed that soliders should abandon the flintlock on
pain of death as 'great inconveniences are being caused and notable losses may
result.' The French authorities retreated only slowly from this point of view. Of
course Fusilier regiments received firelocks with slings from their date of raising,
and faced by a growing body of military opinion, in 1670 it was decreed that
four men might carry *fusils* in every infantry company. This number later rose
to eight (1687) then abruptly to 21 in 1692. By that date a French infantry
company comprised some 52 soldiers, including 10 pikemen, so at least the *fusil*
had attained equality with the matchlock. One reason for this abrupt increase
was Marshal Luxembourg's report from the field of Steenkirk, where he had
seen his victorious men flinging away their matchlocks to take up the superior
flintlock weapons of the defeated Allies.[21] Thereafter the process of re-equipment
was practically completed within the next decade except in the case of militia
units, the last matchlocks being withdrawn from first-line French toops in 1708.
French fusilier regiments, of course, had the *fusil* from their dates of raising on
full issue.

Considering the admiration of the French troops for the abandoned firearms
of the English and Dutch battalions at Steenkirk, it might be supposed that the
English forces were well-equipped at that time, but any such deduction would be
an over-simplification. Before 1685 only the North British Fusiliers, raised in
1678, had been exclusively armed with flintlocks, although from 1679 all line
grenadier companies received a version with a 38-inch barrel. Thereafter the
rate of replacement slightly increased, and in 1685 we find James ii ordering 'the
adoption of flintlock muskets with all dispatch possible within the confines of the
appropriated funds'.[22] In the final phrase, however, there lay the rub. No matter
how attractive the superior weapon's advantages might be, these did not go far
to outweigh the grave financial difficulties of the day, so the older weapon was
retained with minor improvements incorporated in the interests of economy and
the avoidance of avoidable expenditure. When Dutch William took over the
English throne and set about a rapid expansion of the army, he was horrified at
the out-datedness and short supply of weapons in the arsenals. The troops
serving in Ireland in 1690, for instance, were only equipped with fusils or a
half-regimental basis. Attempts to remedy the deficiencies by buying up surplus
continental stores resulted in much unloading of still more defective firearms

*As de Goya wrote in *Arms and Engines of War* (1678), 'firelocks are apter to misgive than
muskets through the defect of the flints and springs.'

onto the hapless English battalions. 'The firelocks received from Holland and those parts do far exceed ours here,' ran one report of 1690 to the Board of Ordnance, 'the stocks being very rotten; if the locks chance to take wett (which cannot always be avoided) they are no more fitt for service.'[23] Another result of haphazard purchases and the absence of standardization was a proliferation in the types of firearms on issue. The *Summary of Arms, 1687–1691* reveals no less than 14 varieties, including three types of matchlock ('ordinary', 'with pan-covers' and 'for Dragoons straight') and four kinds of snaphances ('ordinary', 'extraordinary for sea service', 'with walnut stocks' and 'for dragoons') besides carbines of various types, musketoons, blunderbusses and pistols.[24]

From 1691, however, a degree of control began to be imposed. The native arms industry was put on an organized footing – particularly around Birmingham – and from 1692 Sir Richard Newdigate (to cite one example) was empowered to supply 2,400 muskets (embellished with 'walnut trees and ash stocks') a year for 17s apiece. The length of barrel was fixed at 46 inches, and this soon became the standard for many years to come, and in a very short time 'King William's Musket' was earning a deserved reputation as one of the soundest firearms in Europe. Even then, the rate of replacement remained slow and uneven, and in 1697 two soldiers still retained the matchlock for every three armed with the new musket. As late as 1704 the 4th of Foot (the 'King's Own') were reporting that their firearms were all of '24 years old' and thus presumably matchlocks. The whims of individual colonels also entered into a very complicated situation which the parsimonious nature of the Board of Ordnance did nothing to simplify. Thus we read of Irwin's Regiment (16th Foot) in March 1716/17, having to take private action in London to secure new muskets, 'the report from the Board of Ordnance being so much against us'. Richard Worthington, the colonel's agent, found a gun-smith in the Minories who had a pattern for a flintlock 'but 3 foot 9 inches of the barrell, but is very well finished and a good muzzle, which exclusive of the bayonet they will not make (at) under £1.7.6 ... But the worst of it is they'll not engage to make 100 under two months, the main reason is that ... there's not a hundred barrells fitt for ye Armey Service in the Citty of London, they comeing all from Birmingham.' (Temple Newsam Papers PO 2 cvf. 89, Leeds) Clearly as late as 1717 demand still tended to outrun supply.

Other armies adopted the flintlock musket at various dates. The processes of re-equipment may have been completed in Denmark by 1690, and in the Dutch native forces by 1692. That same year the Swedish authorities approved the pattern for a flintlock musket, although distribution did not commence for four more years, an interesting illustration of the difficulty of organizing re-armament even in those relatively unsophisticated days. The Habsburg forces and their German imitators continued to favour the combination-lock weapon, and this was not completely superseded by the *flinte* until 1710. Only in the huge but primitive Russian and Turkish forces did the matchlock remain on large-scale issue after the turn of the century, but the *élite* Janissaries handled more refined firearms as early as the 1670s. As Montecuculi wrote:

Turkish muskets are longer than our own and of smaller calibre; their
musketeers have neither bandoliers nor furnishings, and therefore require
some time to reload; but the quality of the iron is excellent, and they can
charge them with powder equal to the weight of the ball; they carry further
and to better effect than our own.[25]

The point about the quality of metal is important: as late as the 1690s the
largest charge that the average European musket could take without risking a
burst barrel was between half and two-thirds the weight of the ball. Early
eighteenth century improvements in casting and proving techniques, however,
eventually enabled larger powder charges to be used with safety.

It is clearly impossible here to detail all the many developments in European
muskets or the many modifications and improvements that were incorporated.
Space must be found, however, for a brief account of the development of the
'Brown Bess' firearm in the British service. 'King William's Musket' was the
direct ancestor of this famous weapon, but it is erroneous to claim that
Marlborough's armies were equipped with the 'Brown Bess', properly so-called,
because it only came into widespread use after 1715, and it was not until 1730
that a truly standardized firearm of this name came into universal issue for all
British infantry regiments.

How the weapon earned its sobriquet is uncertain, though explanations
abound. One attractive theory claims that it commemorates a bevy of beauteous
Spanish camp-followers of swarthy complexion and volatile temperament who
followed the drum during the long campaigns in the Peninsula between 1705 and
1712. A less attractive but more probable explanation is that it referred to the
practice of 'pickling' or browning the musket barrels to protect them from rust
and to eliminate tell-tale glare. Whatever the antecedents of the term, there can
be no doubt that *la besse brune* or *die braune liesl* was held in healthy respect by
the enemies of the British army.

The first prototypes were probably submitted to Marlborough and the Board
of Ordnance in the early 1700s, and it is considered that the very first, limited,
issue was made in 1703, but it was not until after 1715 that anything like
widespread issues of the weapon were made. Alternative names for the weapon
were 'Her Majesty's musket' or the 'Tower musket' — reflecting the growth of
governmental control over the maufacturers. Over the years several important
modifications were made. The 1710 version with the slightly-tapering barrel, for
example, was eventually shortened from 46 to 42 inches, with walnut stock,
brass mountings and a .76 calibre. Further improvements included a superior
bridle lock, reducing the incidence of misfires by ensuring a good spark, and
from 1715 musket-balls of .71 diameter were made the standard ammunition.
What this 'windage' of .05 sacrificed by way of range and accuracy it more than
made up for by speedier reloading, and it was held to be theoretically possible for
2,000 men to fire 10,000 shots in 60 seconds. Another important development
was the adoption of the iron ram-rod in place of the wooden, an improvement
first introduced in Prussia by the Prince of Anhalt-Dessau in about 1720, but
rapidly copied elsewhere.

In its perfected '1730' form, the 'Brown Bess' constituted a truly formidable firearm, probably the best available on general issue in Europe. It survived in various modified forms for 130 more years, and it is estimated that over this period some 7,800,000 were manufactured for distribution all over the globe,[26] thus greatly facilitating the use of violence from Calcutta to Quebec.

In conclusion, a word must be devoted to the hand-grenade. These existed in a profusion of types in our period as the *Military Dictionary* already cited reveals:

> Grenadoes [*sic*] are small shells, concave Globes or hollow Balls, some made of Iron, some of Tin, others of Wood, and even of Pasteboard; but most commonly of Iron, because the splinters of it do most Execution. This globe or Hollow is fill'd with Fine Powder, and into the touch-hole of it is stuck a Fuze, full of powder, beaten and tempered with charcoal dust, that it may not flash, but burn gently till it comes to the Charge. These are thrown by hand into places where Men stand thick, and particularly into Trenches and Lodgments the enemy make, and are of good use.

The fuses were generally lit from a length of smouldering slow-match dangling from the grenadier's wrist. Their usefulness in open battle was discouraged for they were capable of killing or maiming as many friends as foes, but for siege or trench work, as the passage indicates, they could be of 'good use'. A grenadier habitually carried three of these bombs in a leather pouch.

Weapons of cold steel: sword, pike and bayonet

Almost all infantry, of whatever nationality, continued to carry a sword in addition to their musket and bayonet. Every army issued swords of many different designs, and it is beyond the scope of this book to attempt any catalogue of their specifications and differences. A few suggested titles for those who wish to study these weapons are included in the Bibliography. Most infantry swords were made up of the usual blade, grip and guard, and scabbards were generally of black leather with brass or steel mountings. The greater number had straight blades of between 26 and 31 inches in length, to which must be added a further seven inches for the hilt and pommel. Some were slightly curved — as for instance the 'hanger' issued to some English troops; or the German falchion, a weapon used by Saxon troops in the eighteenth century, is described as an 'infantry sabre', measuring 70cms overall (blade 58.7cms long by 2.9cms broad) and weighing 0.785kgs, or about 1½lbs[27] whilst French grenadiers carried sabres with 31-inch blades. Officers naturally sported rather more sophisticated swords than their men, some highly practical, others merely ceremonial and decorative. The rapier was still very much in fashion.

The pike was a long and often bulky weapon. Pikes varied between 13 and 18 feet in length; in weight they fluctuated between a mere 4lbs and 20lbs according to size and type, but we have the testimony of de Saxe that 'ordinary pikes weigh about 17 pounds and are extremely unwieldy.'[28] The top 9–18 inches comprised the pike-head, a steel shaft tapering to a sharp point, either flat or triangular in section, held in place by long metal cheeks running for anything up to three feet down the pike-shaft (to ward off enemy sword blows). The wood for the shafts varied, but spruce and ash were often employed, sometimes covered in parchment. Some pikes were embellished with a velvet handgrip, and the heel was invariably reinforced with a metal cap and sometimes a blunt point.

The pike's *raison d'être* was to provide protection for the musketeer, especially when engaged in the lengthy task of reloading the matchlock. The pikemen normally formed up in a phalanx in the centre of the regimental array, with wings of musketeers on either side. Like the remainder of the men, they drew up some five ranks deep in close, half-distance or open order, and by forming square and lowering their pike-heads they could form a hedge of points which would cause the bravest cavalry horse to baulk and swerve away. The individual pikeman stood with his left shoulder towards the foe, legs apart, resting the often iron-shod butt against the right instep and grasping the shaft with his left hand, his arm being fully extended. With his right hand he grasped his sword. For many years the pikeman's equipment included a helmet besides back and breast plates, but towards the end of the seventeenth century this armour tended to be replaced by a stout leather coat and long gauntlets. The pikemen's function in action was not wholly static and defensive. On many occasions they would be ordered to advance and even charge with levelled weapons when the situation called for 'push of pike', but the sheer unwieldiness of their weapons often tended to hinder tactical mobility of the infantry in the field. As has already been mentioned the weapon had virtually disappeared by 1704, and even Maurice de Saxe's firm advocacy of its reintroduction in a modified form as secondary armament for half the infantry in his proposed 'centuries' availed nothing.

Certain staff weapons (closely-related to the pike) were, however, retained for a good many years. These were generally reserved for the use of officers and NCOs. The former often carried the spontoon (or *spontone*) – a weapon about eight feet long; the latter carried halberds ($6\frac{1}{2}$-foot) or half-pikes – *kurzgewehr* – (some as much as 12 feet long). These proved useful for correcting the alignment of the musket barrels at the present, and the half-pike was still being borne by British infantry sergeants as late as Waterloo.

The development of an effective replacement for the pike was a somewhat haphazard affair taking place over a considerable number of years, and it was not until the 1690s that a really satisfactory socket-bayonet evolved. The problem was to devise a weapon that would enable a musketeer to switch from fire-action to self-defence in close-quarter fighting without seriously diminishing his rate of fire. It would seem that the bayonet takes its name from the city of Bayonne, where, possibly, the first experiments in the manufacture of such a weapon were conducted. Early attempts to tie a knife onto the muzzle of a musket proved unsatisfactory, but eventually the 'plug' bayonet was invented:

> A Broad Dagger without any guard, generally made with a round taper handle to stick it in the mussle of a musket, in which manner it serves instead of a pike to receive the Charge of Horse, all the men having first the advantage of their Shot, and then as many as there is occasion for with their

Bayonettes thus in their Muskets, cover the rest of the Musketeers. (*New Military Dictionary of 1702*).

The adoption of this weapon soon spread to all European countries. An early version was being used by some French troops as early as 1647; another with a foot-long blade and a nine-inch handle was on issue to the English garrison of Tangier in 1663, and over the next 20 years every army carried at least a proportion of them. The favourite French versions, Puységur tells us, were 'straight, double-edged blades a foot long with tapering handles also a foot long',[29] and from 1671 they were carried by all French fusiliers and guardsmen besides many dragoons. (English dragoons followed suit from 1672). By 1680 the handle had been shortened to eight inches, the blade being an inch in width.

The main disadvantages of this weapon are clear. Either part of a Regiment had to fix bayonets and then stand idly by while the rest fired protected by their comrades, or everybody fired and then hastily resorted to fixing their secondary weapons. In any case, the plug bayonet was a clumsy weapon and took time to fix properly and even more to unfix. Sufficient time was not always forthcoming, as was General Mackay's unfortunate experience at Killiekrankie (1689). Reporting his defeat he wrote:

> The Highlanders are of such quick motion that if a Battalion keep up his fire until they be near to make sure of (hitting) them, they are upon it before our men can come to the second defence, which is the bayonet in the musle of the musket.[30]

After sundry experiments with boar-spear and *schweinsfeders*, (which were driven into the ground before the soldiers), particularly in the Imperial service, the ring bayonet made its appearance. Attached to the handle of the bayonet were a series of loose rings, which supposedly slipped over the muzzle, thus making it theoretically possible for a musketeer to fire his piece with bayonet fixed. Although this was a step in the right direction it proved unsatisfactory. French experiments conducted in 1678 revealed that as often as not such bayonets would fall off in the heat of action or be pushed back along the barrel.

At length, about 1687, the solution was found – the socket bayonet. In this the base of the bayonet's blade was drawn out into a metal sleeve with a recessed slot down one side. A metal lug was added to the musket near its muzzle. Thus once the bayonet sleeve had been drawn over the muzzle and the lug, a half-turn was all that was required to fix the bayonet firmly into position.

Different authorities attribute this invention to both General Hugh Mackay and the great Vauban; possibly it appeared simultaneously in both England and France. Some French units may have received the weapon in 1689, and there is evidence of Louvois's rather dubious interest the previous year.* There is no

---

*Writing to Vauban on 21 December 1688, Louvois asked:
'I beg you to explain to me how you envisage a bayonet at the end of a musket which will hinder neither firing nor reloading, and also the dimensions of such a proposed bayonet '. (cited by Favé, *op.cit*. p. 18).

question, however, that both armies possessed a large number of socket bayonets by 1698. Although details frequently differed, the most popular design had a 16-inch blade of triangular cross-section, though from 1710 a 17-inch length became widely used in the British army.

Of course the change-over was not effected suddenly or smoothly. In 1706, for instance, we find the Board of Ordnance rejecting Lord Kerr's request for a set of socket bayonets for his regiment at national expense as follows:

> All regiments raised since the disuse of pikes have provided bayonets as they do swords and belts at their own charge ... Few of the officers agree on the sort of bayonet fitt to be used, or on the manner of fitting them to the muskets, as may appear by the various sorts that there are of them in ye Army.[31]

The French, for their part, clung for a number of years to a fixing method whereby the bayonet fitted on *top* of the musket barrel, thus completely interrupting the line of aim (the British fitted to the side or below). It was also noted that overlong socket bayonets tended to transfix the musketeer's hand whilst ramming down his charge.

Other nations quickly took up the new bayonet, and by the early 1700s every army had a proportion. Regional variations inevitably crept in; the Austrian and Germanic model, for example, was shorter and squatter than its English or French counterparts. The Spanish authorities experimented with sliding-rod and spring-engaged bayonets, whereby the bayonet formed a permanent part of the musket, being brought into the fixed position when required after the fashion of the flick-knife. But the old plug-bayonet, like the pike before it, still had a number of champions well into the eighteenth century. De Saxe, for instance, would have re-equipped all soldiers with it. So disillusioned was he about the reliance placed in massed volleys discharged at random that he considered it would be a definite advantage if the troops found themselves unable to fire because of their bayonets until the correct place and time.[32] Such sentiments, however, were not widely held, and the socket bayonet became the infantryman's main defensive weapon, the French version in use in 1740, for example, measuring 49 centimetres and weighing eight ounces.

Uniform and equipment

Since the days of Gustavus Adolphus there had been a trend towards the adoption of distinctive regimental and national uniforms. Four main reasons underlay this development. First, the assistance a uniform theoretically gave in distinguishing friend from foe on the battlefield. Second, the psychological *esprit de corps* provided by a smart uniform; this was also considered an aid to recruiting. Thirdly, economy, since it proved cheaper to buy cloth in bulk – a point much appreciated by the colonels of regiments who were normally responsible (with varying degrees of financial assistance) for the clothing of their men. Lastly, the abandonment of body armour for the infantry (the last pikemen's corselets seem to have disappeared in 1697) encouraged the desire for achieving uniformity of appearance throughout the regiments.

One of the first armies to adopt a standardized uniform was that of Sweden, which by the 1630s favoured blue coats and blue breeches – and retained this combination well into the mid-eighteenth century. From 1660, the scarlet cloth coat (a colour originally selected, it is said, on account of the cheapness of the dyeing process) became increasingly accepted as the standard uniform of the English foot, although it should be noted that as late at 1695 some regiments were wearing grey coats as pictures by Marcellus Larson and others confirm. A contract of 1693 in the British Museum between Lord Castleton and Mr Francis Molineaux, a clothier, is of additional interest in that it reveals the prices of uniform items at that period – and an attempt (duly foiled by watchful regimental officers) by the supplier to make an excessive profit of the deal. Under 'Private Sentinell' we read:

	'Prices charged in the contract	Prices allowed
Grey coat and breeches	1–12–0	1–5–0
Hat	6–6	5–0
Shoes	4–0	4–0
Shirt	3–6	3–0
Neckcloth	1–0	10
Stockings	2–0	1–8
	2–9–0	1–19–6 '

The same document shows that a sergeant's coat of superior material cost an allowed sum of £3–12–0, whilst a grenadier sergeant's cap cost 14s (to the ordinary grenadier's 8s); each drummer was provided with a 'purple coat and grey breeches' at £3 apiece.[33*]

From the days of William III's and Marlborough's campaigns (if not of Cromwell's New Model Army), however, the red-coat became well established as the standard uniform, although details of quality, cut and embellishment varied enormously until standardizing regulations were enforced.

In France, under the stern supervision of successive Secretaries of State for War, Louis XIV's forces gradually assumed a measure of standardized appearance, the Bourbon white coat eventually replacing those of buff or grey-brown in the great majority of native line regiments. Some formations, however, including the *élite* troops and the *étrangère* regiments continued to wear coats of red, blue or green. For example the *Régiment des Gardes Françaises* wore blue coats with red linings and facings, whilst the Swiss Guards and Irish in the French service wore red uniforms with blue or other coloured trimmings. The forces of Austria mostly sported uniforms of pearl-grey, but the states of the Holy Roman Empire displayed a colourful degree of individuality. The Bavarian army adopted a uniform of light blue (with red stockings); Saxons

---

*Prices do not seem to have changed very much over half a century. In 1744, a private's coat and breeches cost £1–5–0, a sergeant's £3–10–0 and a drummer's £2–10–0. (Grosse II, p. 27–8).

wore basically red from 1695; the soldiers of Prussia paraded in dark blue coats with white breeches and black leggings; whilst those of Hesse and Hanover in due course copied the British scarlet. The Dutch authorities clothed their men in iron-grey until the 1730s, when blue was adopted in lieu. After a period of variegated uniform colourings, Russia eventually chose coats of dark green and red breeches from 1720. The only power wholly insensible to the spreading cult of national dress was Turkey, whose motley hordes continued to dress according to the whims of individual pashas, only the Janissaries boasting anything approaching a uniform.[34]

The cut of most of these uniforms was much the same from country to country though details differed. Until the 1720s the coats were generally full skirted to knee-length and of loose fit, with turned back cuffs, deep pockets, and were sometimes worn with lace ruffles at the neck and wrists. As the eighteenth century progressed, however, two main changes took place. In the first place, jackets became somewhat shorter and increasingly tailored to a snug fit with cut-away tails. The ministers of Louis xv, for instance, insisted that the tails should be one foot from the ground when a soldier knelt. Secondly, certain powers became increasingly averse to undue ostentation of uniform – most particularly England and France – whilst the degree of governmental supervision over the whole subject of military dress increased rapidly. Thus the lace-ruffle was soon replaced by the cravat, wound twice round the neck.

In the early years of our period the majority of governments were mostly concerned in varying degrees to see that cloth of sufficient quality was employed, both in the interests of military effectiveness and in those of the rank and file (who frequently repaid their colonels for their uniforms through pay deductions). Numerous French *ordonnances* related to such matters, whilst the English Board of General Officers included clothing and equipment supervision amongst its multifarious duties, and such instruments as the Royal Warrant of 1707 were specifically designed to impose close control and reduce the number of improper practices. The dress of officers remained broadly outside this type of control, however, and individual tastes were widely tolerated. Later in the eighteenth century, however, government intervention became more rigid and all-embracing. Uniform patterns had to be deposited and registered; officers of many armies were compelled to wear more or less the same uniform as their men (although of better material), and the addition of unauthorized lace or trimmings was sternly forbidden. In 1740 these restrictions became applicable even to senior generals in the French service. Details of regimental facings remained largely within the province of individual colonels, but a measure of uniformity was gradually imposed. In certain countries, central control was completely dictatorial. Frederick William ii of Prussia, for instance, minutely controlled every detail of the dress issued to the unfortunate 'Potsdam Giants', and highly impractical and uncomfortable – if ornamental on the parade ground – were the results.

Governments showed as much interest in their troops' headgear as in their coats and breeches. Many troops wore variations of the tricorne, or three-cornered hat made of black felt or other cloth. Originally this hat had been of a normal civilian type with crown and wide brim, but from the mid-seventeenth century it became increasingly the practice to fold up one or more sides to achieve a more dashing appearance. By the 1700s this process of experimentation had more or less stablized in the three-cornered fashion, and an edging of gold or silver lace was frequently added.

However there were several other versions of military headgear to be seen. From the first, grenadiers of all nations, for instance, found the tricorne or brimmed hat of any pattern completely unservicable, for as they slung their muskets and threw their grenades – or rather bowled them (over, or under-arm) with the right arm – they almost invariably knocked them off. In consequence, a different type of cap was adopted in lieu. At first this comprised a simple peasant's or fisherman's cap made of woollen cloth, with a tasselled bag hanging down behind. Some early English examples had edgings of fur. Later a copper or brass plate was added at the front, frequently engraved with the regimental badge or number. Finally, towards the end of the reign of Queen Anne in the case of the British army, the bag was also stiffened to make it stand upright, thus forming the famous mitred shape that gave this form of headgear its name. Some formations of grenadiers – including French, Austro-Hungarian and Russian – favoured caps of fur to those of cloth, but the general effect of all the various types was to give a grenadier the impression of extra height and martial splendour. The diarist Evelyn claims that the inspiration for this type of headgear originated from the towering conical caps of the Turkish Janissaries, but this is doubtful.

Another variant of military headgear much favoured by the Russians was a snug circular hat of fur or cloth with a three-quarter brim. This was either worn turned upwards all the way round to make a double-thickness, or could be pulled down to cover the ears and the back of the neck. Regiments of other nations originally raised as irregulars often retained local headgear; thus the High-landers wore bonnets, and Pandours their fur caps.

Eventually governments imposed increasing numbers of restrictions on ornamentation. With the exception of the grenadiers' mitre caps which became ever more splendid, the general trend was to reduce and formalize decoration. Plumes and feathers were soon discarded for infantrymen, and in their place came the cockade of folded cloth, often resembling the shape of the butterfly. Some countries eventually used these as badges of rank and also as national distinguishing marks. Thus the Count of Mérode-Westerloo, desirous of escaping from the victorious Allied army at Blenheim, 'removed the white cockade from my hat' before riding off unnoticed through their ranks.[35]

The authorities eventually became obsessed with military smartness. Further edicts by many administrations compelled their troops to wear their hair in a pigtail, and in the British service the so-called 'Ramillies-tie' (a black bow or ribbon worn near the top) became *de rigueur*. By the 1720s the practice of larding the hair and sprinkling it with white powder made of flour became widely established, coinciding with the gradual disappearance of the cumbersome shoulder-length wig which had been virtually compulsory wear for officers in the days of Luxembourg and Marlborough.

The amount as well as the quality of clothing issued to infantry obviously varied enormously from army to army, but the following list taken from the 'Regulations for clothing His Majesty's forces in time of peace', dated 20 November 1729, must stand as a single, albeit fairly typical, example.

FOR A FOOT SOLDIER

A good full bodied cloth coat, well lined, which may serve for the waistcoat the
  second year,
A waistcoat,
A pair of good Kersey breeches,
A pair of good strong stockings,
A pair of good strong shoes,
Two good shirts, and two good neckcloths,
A good strong hat well laced.

FOR THE SECOND YEAR

A good cloth coat well lined, as the first year,
A waistcoat made of the former year's coat,
A pair of new Kersey breeches,
A pair of good strong stockings,
A pair of good strong shoes,
A good shirt and a neckcloth,
A good strong hat well laced.

For the fusilier regiments, caps once in two years.
The new waistcoat, in the first year, is only given to regiments new raised, and to
  additional men: who are likewise to be furnished with two pair of stockings
  and two shirts.[36]

The two-year clothing cycle, issued on a regimental basis, was a standard feature in the British army from the early eighteenth century, but the last sentence in the 1729 regulations incorporates better terms for 'additional men' who happened to be recruited during the second year. In Marlborough's day, such unfortunates had to wait until the next 'first year' before receiving their full entitlement of waistcoat and second shirt. The prevalence of desertion amongst the new recruits was sometimes attributed to slowness in providing them with uniforms. Thus on 14 April 1717, an officer reported to Lord Irwin as follows: 'Your Lordship will finde yt. we loose men every day, and I cannot find any way to prevent their desartion [sic]; since we have no Ridecotes (red-coats) to give ye recrutes, if your LdShip thinke fit to order cloth to make Wast cotes [sic] for ye men yt. have none Ridecotes; probably yt might prevent their disartion.' Alternatively, the officer went on to point out, 'they might be ye sooner taken' by wearing such distinctive clothing. (Temple Newsam Papers, PO 2 cvf 104 a. Leeds).

Towards the mid-eighteenth century, it is interesting to note the scale of cloth provided by the French authorities for their infantry soliders. The unit of measurement was the *'aune'* (1metre 19cms). The king provided $\frac{1}{4}$ *aune* of grey-white cloth and $\frac{1}{8}$ *aune* of coloured cloth (for regimental facings), together with $4\frac{2}{3}$ *aunes* of serge for linings, for each new uniform. Quantities on this scale were delivered to the Major, who distributed the cloth to the Captains. They in turn handed it on to the company tailor for making up. However, such official provision only went part of the way towards clothing the soldier. A sergeant's uniform, for instance, comprising coat, waistcoat and breeches, required between $2\frac{2}{3}$ and $3\frac{3}{4}$ *aunes* of top cloth (according to corps) besides $\frac{1}{4}$ *aune* of facings and $5\frac{1}{2}$ more of serge for linings. The balance had to be purchased from regimental funds, subsequently deducted by instalments from the pitifully small pay of the individual *fantassins*.[37]

Other forms of military equipment issued to the rank and file soon became standardized in general type. Officers invariably wore sword-belts or *ceinturons*, the ancient baldricks and *baudriers* disappearing in most countries by the turn of the century. Most soldiers also came to wear white cross-belts supporting leather cartridge boxes (the French version of 1740 held 19 rounds) or grenade pouches on the right side, and bayonet and sword on the left. Bandoliers lingered on in many armies for a time – comprising a broad belt, sometimes of calf-skin, with eight or twelve dangling powder-charges (sometimes called 'the Twelve Apostles') of metal or leather, but these generally disappeared from the English service after 1697, to cite a single example, as cartridges became widely available, and were eventually followed out by powder-horns. Soldiers also carried a knapsack on active service. This was slung over one shoulder for most of our period, but by the 1740s some French grenadier companies were beginning to wear a version fastened securely to the back by two straps.* For the rest, campaign equipment often included a cloak, a rolled blanket, and a cooking pot. All foot soldiers were habitually issued with 24 rounds of powder and shot at the outset of a campaign (and three grenades for each grenadier), besides a few spare flints, and a proportion were at times expected to carry spades, mattocks or picks (receiving extra pay for this inconvenience in the French service from 1706), although these were often conveyed by the Artillery Trains and regimental transport. In all, including musket, it is estimated that the average foot soldier was expected to carry approximately 50 pounds of equipment.

All in all, therefore, infantry regiments in full dress could make a brave show on parade or review. Such finery rarely survived many days of real soldiering, however. In an attempt to preserve their men's bright coats, many armies ordered them to wear them inside-out for marches or fatigues, reserving the better side for days of battle or other important occasions. Even then, the ravages inflicted by wind, mud and rain soon affected the hues of red and blue, so all too often imperfect was the quality of cloth and dyeing, whilst the pipeclay from cross-belts would soon run and stain the clothing. So much for the romantic conception of martial splendour conveyed by many a historical

---

*The French haversack of *c.*1740 measured 18 inches square by 4 inches deep, and had an outer covering of cloth and a lining of skin. It held two shirts, one handkerchief, a cravat, a pair of pants, another of shoes, one pair of gaiters and toilet articles.

painting! The battle of Ramillies possibly formed an exception as it took place very early in the campaign of 1706, a fact that inspired one participant, de la Colonie, to recall of the French that 'the army had but just entered on the campaign; weather and fatigue had hardly yet the time to dim its brilliancy.'

The same source also casts doubt on the efficacy of national uniforms as a means of identification on the field of battle. The Bourbon white and Imperialist pearl-grey were notoriously difficult to differentiate amidst the clouds of battle-smoke. At the battle of the Schellenberg Heights (1704), Colonel de la Colonie

> became aware of several lines of infantry in greyish-white uniforms on our left flank. I verily believed reinforcement had reached us ... So, in the error I laboured under I shouted to my men that they were Frenchmen and friends. Having, however, made a closer inspection, I discovered bunches of straw attached to their standards, badges the enemy are in the custom of wearing in battle, but at that very moment was struck in the jaw by a ball that stupified me.[38]

Such confusions were frequently met with, and the fact that many armies dressed their *élite* formations in uniforms of different hues from those of most of their line regiments did nothing to ease the problem.

In conclusion, a brief word must be added about badges of rank. These were still in the process of evolution, and many variations were consequently to be met with. Where officers were concerned, the following distinguishing marks were commonly to be found – either singly or in combination. First, the decoration of the hat (and, until about 1714, the wearing of full-bottomed wigs) tended to be one indication of officer status; feather decoration, lacings or type of cockade were generally more sumptuous for officers than for rank and file – and so, too, were the quality and embellishment of the coat. Secondly, there was the question of armament. The carrying of the spontoon was usually reserved for officers. These were often of relatively junior grade, ensigns and lieutenants, but in some formations, including the French Guards, this weapon was born by all officers on foot. Thirdly, there was a growing reliance on different patterns of gorget. This, the last formalized manifestation of body-armour, was hung around the neck by a short chain. Distinguishing between infantry officers of various grades was often possible by noticing the appearance of the gorget. In England, for instance, the Royal Warrant of 1684 laid it down that Captains should wear 'corslets' of gold, lieutenants ones of black 'studded with gold', and ensigns ones of silver or polished steel. However, in the following decades regiments tended to sport their own varieties following the tastes of their colonels, and it is notable that gorgets were never worn by officers of dragoons or horse. Nevertheless, the gorget was widely used throughout Europe as a badge of officer rank although they were apparently late appearing in Prussia, where the only formal badge of rank for long remained a hat-plume of white ostrich feathers for general officers. Other indications of rank were the officer's sash (the French Guards wore one of black and gold), and from 1730 the shoulder-knot became increasingly popular, particularly for cavalry officers. This decoration – the ancestor of the epaulette –

consisted of a plaited cord of gold or silver bullion with tassels.

Rank badges for sergeants and corporals were also rapidly emerging. Besides slightly better clothing than the private soldiers' uniforms, sergeants were often distinguishable by their weapons, particularly the halberd and half-pike. Sleeve chevrons as understood today did not appear until about 1795, but an NCO was often permitted to wear gold lace above or upon his cuffs and also on his pocket flaps and collar. Most NCOs also bore different kinds of half-pikes or staves with which to belabour their charges, and these too constituted a kind of badge of office.

7

The organization and training of infantry

In all countries maintaining military establishments, the infantry regiments were graded according to some system of seniority and further sub-divided into a number of major categories. To cite one example, the French army organized its infantry arm as follows. First in seniority were the regiments of the Guards or *Maison du Roi* – including the French and the Swiss, to which we shall return in due course. Next came the famous *'vieux'* and *'petits-vieux'* formations, some 12 in all* – basically the long-established provincial regiments of France. Third there were the *Régiments Étrangères,* units of foreign origin but on the full-time establishment, including Germans, Irish and more Swiss. Fourth there were the 'newly-raised' regiments, usually brought into existence for a specific war and disbanded immediately after its close; thus in 1714 no less than 138 regiments ceased to exist on demobilization. Fifth came a number of detached companies on independent establishments, usually garrisons of distant colonies which did not merit a full regiment. And lastly there was the provincial militia, completely reorganized in 1688, entrusted with the tasks of local garrisoning and coastal protection, and increasingly required (from 1701) to supply drafts for the depleted line regiments in times of crisis. The means of recruiting these troops have been described elsewhere, but it is relevant to note here that the French militia eventually provided a total of 250,000 soldiers for service during the Spanish Succession War, mostly serving either as live replacements or as members of the 70 battalions organized to support the single-battalion regiments in the French service.

The English infantry was organized along broadly similar lines. Until 1707 their classification is made all the more difficult by the constitutional requirement that the troops serving in England, Scotland and Ireland were deemed to be serving on separate establishments, although regiments proceeding

*The 'oldest' (dates of creation in parenthesis) were Picardy, Piedmont, Navarre and Champagne (all raised between 1562 and 1575), which took precedence in turn. The remaining 'old' were the Regiments of Normandy (1616) of the Marines (1626), of Richelieu (1595), Bourbonnais (reformed 1660), Auvergne (1606), Tallard (1615), Boufflers-Rémiancourt (1610) and lastly the *Régiment du Roi* (formerly the Regiment of Beaumont but bought by Louis xiv in 1662).

abroad on active service almost always came on to the English establishment. Officially the only troops allowed to reside within England in time of peace were the 'Guards and Garrisons', but this term was in practice stretched to include other regiments as well. From 1707, however, the English and Scots military forces came under the same jurisdiction, slightly simplifying a very complex situation. But as Mr Samuel Lynn – a functionary in the Secretary at War's office – despairingly wrote in response to a demand from the House of Commons in 1710 for an accurate account of the disposition of the troops, 'I am sure I may puzzle my brains to pieces, and not be able to make out such an account.'[39] Nevertheless, it is possible to indicate the main categories of infantry formations serving in the British service. First there were the 'subject troops' – in other words the regiments recruited in the British Isles and also a number of independent companies serving in such out-of-the-way places as New York, Newfoundland and the West Indies. Next there were large numbers of formations, their size varying greatly at different times, of foreign troops 'in pay', that is to say hired as mercenaries from various European princelings in time of war (frequently including Danes, Prussians, Hessians and Hanoverians) on negotiated terms, usually on an annual basis, and organized and paid along lines formally approved by Parliament. Thirdly there were other formations of foreign troops drawn from Allied powers and partly paid for from British resources in the form of subsidies; these troops, of course, retained their native organization and pay. Fourthly there were a group of heterogeneous units made up of refugees and enemy deserters. Perhaps the most notable example of this type of formation were the Huguenot Regiment of Colonel Jean Cavalier (raised in 1706, the cost being divided between England and the United Provinces in two-thirds and one-third proportions), and the foot regiments wholly in English pay, made up of French exiled refugees from Piedmont, namely those of Melonière, Rochefoucauld and Belcastel (all raised in 1696), which saw service in the War of the League of Augsburg. Such units, however, were the first to disappear at the rumour of reduction or economy, and some were short-lived. Thus Major-General de Seissan's regiment of French deserters, raised in June 1711, only survived until the same October when lack of funds compelled its complete disbandment. Lastly, there were the county militia regiments, under the lords-lieutenant, which do not really count as formal infantry formations as they never saw service outside the British Isles, although they played a part in suppressing the Jacobite rebellions of the '15 and the '45.

Questions of regimental seniority were bitterly contested in the British army; not only was prestige at stake, but even more pressing was the question of continuing in employment in times of peace. The more junior regiments always went to the wall, being the first disbanded. The regiments of Guards, 1st Foot, Coldstream and Scots constituted the senior formations, and after them came the Royal Scots (or 1st of Foot); but it was not until 1712 that the foot regiments received numbers confirming their places in the line. Before that overdue reform, regimental seniority depended largely upon the standing of the current colonel. Inevitably some formations felt hardly done by when the Duke of Ormonde's decisions were published. The Royal Regiment of Foot of Ireland, for example, had hoped to emerge as the 6th of Foot, but in the event they had to be satisfied with being the 18th.[40]

It would be tedious to recount the details of how other countries made up their infantry establishment as custom invariably differed. The Habsburgs had three main categories – native Austro-Hungarian regiments, formations supplied by the states of the Holy Roman Empire, and those raised along the *militargrenze* or military frontiers – and so on. Although details varied enormously, the main categories of subject-troops, foreign mercenaries on hire, and local militias organized on provincial or cantonal bases, were reproduced in one form or another in most countries.

One further aspect of the French overall organization of their infantry arm merits a brief mention, namely the position of Colonel-General of the Infantry. This post – the most senior one in the French foot – had originally been founded by Francis I in 1544, but by the Edict of 25 July 1661 it was placed in abeyance, Louis XIV abrogating the powers to himself. So matters remained until 1721 when the post was recreated and given first to the Duc de Chartres, and later the Duc d'Orléans. The Colonel-General enjoyed truly vast influence over appointments, promotions and leaves. There does not seem to have been a true equivalent in the English or most other European armies, the 'Generals of Foot' that are met with in orders of battle only existing for the duration of a campaign.

Regimental and battalion organization

The regiment remained the basic infantry administrative unit throughout Europe. Tactically, the formation was the battalion; in many cases this was synonymous with the regiment in the British Army list, for comparatively few units sported more than a single battalion, but on the Continent many countries raised multi-battalion formations. Most of these comprised two, a few four or even more battalions. On active service it was generally the custom to group two or three regiments or battalions into brigades, but, as with the cavalry, these were essentially *ad hoc* and temporary formations.

Before describing examples of these units and a few of their national specialities it is necessary to outline the basic organization that was common to all regiments. A Regiment of Foot, whether *élite*, line or foreigners in pay, comprised two basic elements – namely a regimental headquarters or staff and a varying number of grenadier and fusilier companies which formed the regimental line. All headquarters included three officers of field rank. First the colonel, who was usually the raiser and proprietor of the regiment and frequently held a higher army rank, and was consequently as often as not absent from his regiment on campaign. His authority was exercised in his absence by the second-in-command, a lieutenant-colonel. Thirdly there was the major, responsible for the training and organization of the day-to-day life of the regiment. If there were two or more battalions there were often additional numbers of majors or *aide-majors,* and it was quite common for these officers to command the battalions in action. Thus at Malplaquet (1709), the Royal

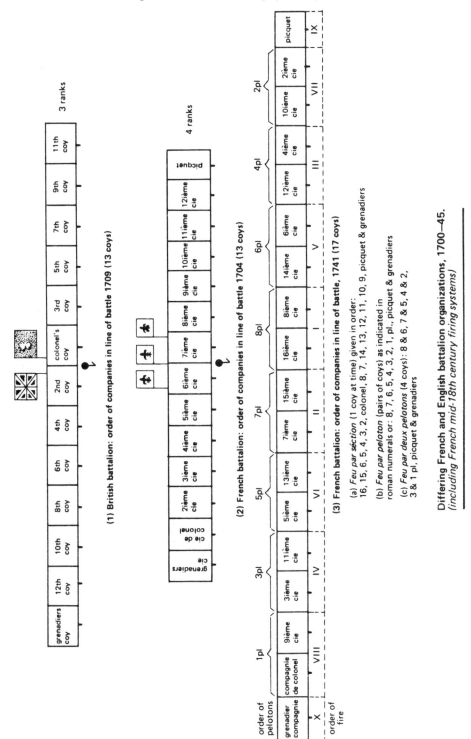

(1) British battalion: order of companies in line of battle 1709 (13 coys)

(2) French battalion: order of companies in line of battle 1704 (13 coys)

(3) French battalion: order of companies in line of battle, 1741 (17 coys)

(a) *Feu par séction* (1 coy at time) given in order:
16, 15, 6, 5, 4, 3, 2, colonel, 8, 7, 14, 13, 12, 11, 10, 9, picquet & grenadiers

(b) *Feu par peloton* (pairs of coys) as indicated in
roman numerals or: 8, 7, 6, 5, 4, 3, 2, 1, pl., picquet & grenadiers

(c) *Feu par deux pelotons* (4 coys): 8 & 6, 7 & 5, 4 & 2,
3 & 1 pl, picquet & grenadiers

Differing French and English battalion organizations, 1700—45.
(including French mid-18th century firing systems)

Regiment of Foot of Ireland was commanded by its major, Brevet-Lieutenant-Colonel Richard Kane* even though it was a one-battalion formation. The Colonel, Lt.-General Ingoldsby, was holding a command in Ireland at the time, and the second in command, Lt.-Colonel Sterne, was sick.[41] The remaining officers and men always to be found on the strength of regimental headquarters, at least from the 1700s, included an adjutant (more than one in large regiments), a chaplain, a surgeon and his mate, a quartermaster and in many cases a drum-major. *Élite* Guards formations often had additional personnel including Deputy-Marshals, solicitors and bandsmen, English fusilier regiments boasted a gun-smith, whilst some continental units and all Turkish ones included an executioner on their strengths.

The bulk of a regiment was formed by its companies. The number of these varied considerably between peace and war, but the standard number in the majority of English regiments in time of hostilities throughout the whole of our period was 13, namely one of grenadiers, which on parade took the place of honour on the right of the line (and in action often took post by platoons at the two extremities), and a dozen line companies, which drew up in a predetermined order based upon the regimental seniority of the company commanders. Each company was subdivided into a number of sections or ranks (three in the British army), the members of which often shared a tent.

The number of men in a company fluctuated enormously, but the official list for pay purposes in time of war was 60 (exclusive of officers), although in time of peace this was reduced to 40 – and in many cases even less. Thus an average one-battalion regiment on full establishment in the war-time armies of William III, Marlborough, Cumberland and George II numbered between 780 and 930 rank and file, although a number of these places would be occupied by 'widow's men' or 'dead-men's pays' and sometimes a number of officers' servants and it was rare for any unit to be up to strength even at the beginning of a campaign.

Each company was commanded by a captain, but as it was almost the invariable practice for the colonel, lieutenant-colonel and major (and sometimes the adjutant as well) to hold command of a company apiece within their regiment (and draw additional pay accordingly), actual command in such cases devolved upon the lieutenant, who was further assisted by an ensign. The average line company, therefore, had three officers – captain, lieutenant and ensign – but grenadier companies had a second full lieutenant instead of the ensign. There were also usually two sergeants (sometimes three in larger guards' companies), as many corporals and 'senior men' (or *anspessades*), and a kettle-drummer.

Such then was the basic organization of a typical regiment of foot between 1688 and 1745. It must be stressed, however, that this description constitutes only a very generalized guide, for there were a number of exceptions and special cases within every army.

*'Brevet' rank was a nominal army rank, conferred on an individual as an honour or to enable him to fill a certain post. He continued, however, to draw only the pay of his substantative or regimental rank.

It was comparatively rare for English regiments to have more than one battalion. The First Foot Guards always had two in time of war, and so at times did the Coldstream and the Scots Guards* – but these were all *corps d'élites*. The only *line* regiment which consistently sported two battalions was the Royal Scots whose regimental headquarters included two Adjutants, two Quartermasters and as many assistants, and, uniquely, a 'piper for the Colonel's company' on its strength. Outside the Guards (which at full strength had three official hautbois players in each company), the line regiments were usually expected to provide musicians (drummers apart) from their own resources until at least as late as 1725.

Other continental powers, however, made great use of the battalion system. In 1716 the 98 regiments of the French army between them provided 154 battalions,[42] whilst at the climax of his reign Louis XIV could list at least 246 infantry regiments comprising almost twice as many battalions. The crack *Régiment des Gardes Françaises* fielded no less than six in 1691, but this was an exceptional formation. But whereas the basic composition of the British regiment remained fairly consistent, that of the average French battalion fluctuated enormously. We are indebted to the *Maréchal* de Puységur's treatise on the *Art of War* for details of these variations down to 1713. They can be conveniently tabulated as follows:

Date	Bn. Strength	Officers	NCOs & Men	Gren.Coys	Ord.Coys	Formation (ranks)
1678	902	52	850	1	16	six deep
1690	745	40	715	1	13	five deep
1701	690	40	650	1	12	four deep

These figures are extended to 1741 by Guillaume Le Bond in *'Les Elémens de Tactique'*.

1733	737	52	685	1	16	four deep
1741	719	34	685	1	16	four or three deep[43]

All these figures relate to times of war. Peacetime reductions can be illustrated by what happened in 1748, when the 1741 establishment for a battalion was cut to 13 companies, twelve of 40 men and one of 45 – or 525 men in all. These statistics of course reflect full, official establishments, rather than the actual numbers in the field and make no allowance for sick, wounded, deserters, detachments and the like. A document in the British Museum dated 1706, reveals that for ordinary purposes of calculation a French 13-company battalion in the field could be considered to comprise a maximum of 624 officers and men, though many numbered barely 550.[44] These figures contrast markedly with the 'offical' strength of 690 quoted by Puységur.

Other types of French infantry operated on different establishments. Thus the Swiss contingents in *l'infanterie étrangère* were organized into battalions of four large companies of 200 officers and men each down to 1690, but thereafter they

---

*Until the Act of Union in 1707 the Scots Guards were paid for out of the Scottish establishment, and were consequently only referred to as the '3rd Regiment of Guards' from 1713.

lost a company and were reduced to a total strength of 600. This type of organization was reflected in the Habsburg service. From 1695 the nominal strength of an Imperial regiment was 1,087, distributed amongst 12 companies which for tactical purposes were divided into three battalions. In 1700, however, the total strength was raised to 2,300, made up of one grenadier company (about 100 strong) and 16 fusilier companies (some 150 men apiece) divided between four battalions. Eleven years later Prince Eugene implemented further reforms, turning one fusilier company into an additional grenadier unit, but limiting the strength of the ordinary companies to 140 men. The smallest military unit of the Habsburg forces was the *kameradschaft* of four or five men sharing a tent and a common kettle. To cite one final example of infantry organization, the Prussian army of about 1740 fielded regiments numbering between 1,550 and 1,650 men. A typical regimental establishment would be 50 officers, 118 NCOs, 196 grenadiers and 1,220 musketeers. Such a regiment was invariably divided into two battalions, each comprising one grenadier and five musketeer companies of between 114 and 126 men apiece.[45] As in most armies, however, these distinctions by companies disappeared on days of battle, when each battalion fought in two 'wings', each subdivided into a number of divisions of two or more platoons apiece. This organization will be described in the chapter devoted to infantry tactics.

The organization of Corps d'Élites, and their privileges

The household regiments were the pride of their respective monarchs and governments. It is impracticable to describe a 'typical' Guards' formation, so varied were their organizations and composition, but they all shared certain attributes in common besides a considerably larger establishment than the regiments of the line. For example, they invariably formed part of the bodyguard of their various sovereigns, and consequently had many ceremonial and escort duties to perform in addition to normal military duties. In return they received preferential treatment of many kinds, including the holding of posts of honour in camp, on the march or in the battle-line, whilst the officers invariably, and the rank and file in certain instances, also received considerable numbers of privileges including higher rates of pay which emphasized their exclusive positions in the armies.

The comparative organization of a selected number of these *élite* formations can be shown in a simplified tabulated form. This will illustrate the diversity of organization and size of this kind of formation.

Many pages could be devoted to a description of the various privileges enjoyed by these favoured formations, but there is only space here for a few specific examples.

It is significant that the contemporary or near-contemporary works which detail these matters only rarely mention the highest ranking officers in the Guards hierarchy – namely the Colonels-Proprietor. The reason is probably that these posts were almost always bestowed by the sovereign on the highest in the

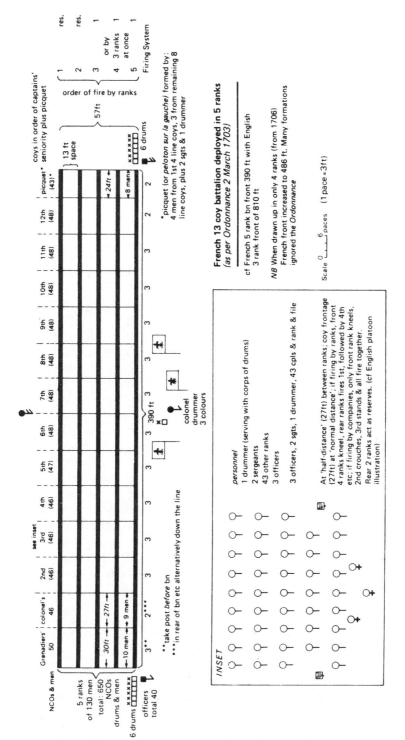

French 13 coy battalion deployed in 5 ranks
(as per Ordonnance 2 March 1703)

cf French 5 rank bn front 390 ft with English 3 rank front of 810 ft

NB When drawn up in only 4 ranks (from 1706) French front increased to 486 ft. Many formations ignored the *Ordonnance*

Scale 0 ___6___ paces   (1 pace = 3 ft)

*picquet (or peloton sur la gauche) formed by: 4 men from 1st 4 line coys, 3 from remaining 8 line coys, plus 2 sgts & 1 drummer

coys in order of captains' seniority plus picquet

order of fire by ranks

		Firing System
1		res.
2		res.
3	1	
4	or by	
5	3 ranks at once	

**take post *before* bn
***in rear of bn etc alternatively down the line

colonel
drummer
3 colours

390 ft

INSET

personnel
1 drummer (serving with corps of drums)
2 sergeants
43 other ranks
3 officers

3 officers, 2 sgts, 1 drummer, 43 cpls & rank & file

At 'half-distance' (27ft) between ranks; coy frontage (27ft) at 'normal distance'; if firing by ranks, front 4 ranks kneel, rear ranks fires 1st, followed by 4th etc; if firing by companies, only front rank kneels, 2nd crouches, 3rd stands & all fire together. Rear 2 ranks act as reserves. (cf English platoon illustration)

NCOs & men

Grenadiers 50 | colonel's 46 | 2nd (46) | 3rd (46) | 4th (46) | 5th (47) | 6th (48) | 7th (48) | 8th (48) | 9th (48) | 10th (48) | 11th (48) | 12th (48) | picquet* (43)*

see inset

5 ranks of 130 men
total: 650 NCOs drums & men

30ft   27ft
10 men   9 men

3**   2***   3   3   3   3   3   3   3   3   3   3   2   2

6 drums
officers total 40

13 ft space

57ft

24ft
8 men

Nationality	Date	Title	No. of Bns.	Nos of Coys. (a) Gren.	(b) Ord.	Regtl. Staff	Coy.estabs. (a) Offr.	(b) NCO*	(c) Men	Total
1. French	1691	*Régiment des Gardes Françaises*	6	2	30	55	5 (7)**	20	90	3,684
2. French	1720	*Régiment des Gardes Suisses*	1	–	12	28	5	36	164 (***)	2,468
3. British	1702	*1st Regiment of Foot Guards*	2	1	27	16	3	6	75	2,352
4. United Provinces	1701	*Gardes van der Köning or te Voet* plus the *Gardes Friesland and Groningen* (120 202 and 152 gren. respectively)	2	2	24	25	3	15	82	3,001
5. Turkish	1720	*Corigys* of the Janissary Corps.	1	10 *ortas*		21	3	7	100	1,031
6. Prussian	1739	The Potsdam Grenadiers plus 4 'unranked' coys.	3 4	3 –	18 –	27 –	3 3	12 12	110) 127)	65 3,067

NOTES: * – Including musicians on the company strength.

** – Figures in brackets denote strengths of grenadier company establishments when different from those of ordinary line companies.

*** – Including 16 grenadiers per company, serving with their companies.

land, in the case of France including Princes of the Blood and high ranking officers including the marshals. For example the *Régiment des gardes françaises* was successively commanded by the Duc de la Feuillade, Marshal Boufflers, the Duc de Guiche and his son the Duc de Louvigny between 1672 and 1745, whilst from 1674–1710 the Swiss Colonel-General was the Duc de Maine, succeeded by the Prince de Dombes. The prices for such exalted appointments were high: in 1672 the Duc de la Feuillade paid 500,000 *livres* for the *Gardes françaises* (although Louis xiv made him a gift of 490,000 *livres* for the purpose), and in 1693 Boufflers sold the same colonelcy to de Guiche for 500,000 francs. In the English service, Marlborough himself was Colonel of the 1st Foot Guards from 1701–12 and from 1714–22, being succeeded by his old friend, commander-in-chief the Earl of Cadogan. These dignitaries were so important and privileged already that their colonelcies of Guards formations only represented one of many similar lucrative posts. Nevertheless these appointments carried great prestige and no small financial profit – as the exalted commanding officers, like their humbler regimental equivalents, were often permitted to sell vacancies within their corps and thus earn a tidy penny. The price of a company in the English Foot Guards, for instance, was as much as £1,600 in 1706. [46] A similar position in the French Guards rarely changed hands for less than 40,000 francs* – although there were in both cases occasional appointments made purely on the grounds of merit. Nor were the other financial perquisites of these posts negligible. A colonel of the French Guards drew basic pay of 833 *livres* 8 *sols*, 8 *deniers* a month (about £38) including such additional revenue as a company commander's pay (255 *livres* – about £11.5.0 a month) but not the vast

*This post, however, carried the army rank of Colonel.

quantities of ration and forage allowances (or cash in lieu) worth a further considerable sum.* By way of comparison, a colonel of a French line regiment received 33 *sols* 4 *deniers* a day as colonel, and 50 *sols* plus 16 *sols* 8 *deniers* a day as a company commander, in all about 4/7 a day – or barely £7 a month basic pay but sundry allowances raised this sum considerably.[47] This was considerably less than their English equivalents in terms of hard cash. From 1691 an English Colonel of the Guards received £1 a day (compared to his line equivalent's 12s), together with a further 14s as captain of a company (an ordinary captain received 8s) – a total of about £51 a month,[48] whilst the colonel of a line regiment could hope to pocket about £30 (to include his company pay). Both also received a joint allowance of a further 6s a day for servants. It should be noted, however, that as a general rule English infantry officers received no rations or forage allowances in addition to their consolidated pay, whilst their French contemporaries most certainly did, a French Guards Captain, for example, being entitled to 12 rations and eight forage allowances a day,[†] whilst his regimental equivalent drew exactly half as many (or 1 *livre* a day in lieu).

In the French *corps d'élite* officers also enjoyed considerable privileges of seniority in the army list. Thus a captain of Guards Grenadiers was deemed to be the equivalent of a full colonel in the line regiments, a grenadier lieutenant rated the rank of a line lieutenant-colonel, and a *sous lieutenant* that of a captain. This privilege did not extend, however, to the rank and file. The NCOs and private Guardsmen received their recompense in terms of monetary advantage only. Sergeants of the French Guards received between 34 and 36 *livres* a month (about 31–35s) besides two rations a day, their line equivalents drawing only 12 *sols* a day – or 18 *livres* (about 16s 6d) a month in hard cash. The French Guardsman drew a little under 10 *sols* a day to the line infantryman's humble pay which ranged between 5 *sols* (before 1718) and 6 *sols* 4 *deniers* (c.1740), and the former also drew a single ration (or 2 *sols* a day in lieu) though not the ordinary *fantassin*.

The English Guards officer received no comparable advantages of 'army seniority' by virtue of his belonging to the *élite* formations, but he did receive more pay. The perquisites of colonels have already been mentioned; by way of comparison a lieutenant of the 1st Guards was entitled to 11s a day rank pay plus about 8d remuneration for a servant, whereas a line lieutenant received a total of 4/8d. The private Guardsman, on the other hand drew a total of 10d a day (off-reckonings and subsistence). The English line solider, of course, received only 8d a day.

Similarly differentials of pay and privilege equally distinguished the Guards formations of the other powers from the run of the ordinary regiments. Perhaps the most extreme case was that of Prussia, where, in 1740, a Potsdam Grenadier drew the equivalent of 1s 6d a day and a full ration besides and was entitled to

---

* For the French 'ration', see p. 44 (note). From 1702, a 'forage ration' comprised 20lbs of hay and a bushel of oats on active service; when in winter quarters, the allowance was 12lbs hay, 8lbs straw and 16lbs oats.

[†]the *livre* (20 *sols* or *sous*) was worth about 5p in the eighteenth century. All pay cited here for French officers is based on war-time rates.

free uniform, rudimentary education and medical attention at no charge, whilst his line colleague was entitled to only 1½d a day and basic rations.[49] But enough has now been said to establish that Guards formations were a privileged caste set apart from the remaining infantry of their respective armies. It should be noted, however, that all examples of pay cited are gross totals; the other ranks of almost all regiments were liable to considerable deductions from their off-reckonings for a whole series of items, which considerably reduced the amount of cash they received into their pockets, even when the paymasters were adequately supplied with specie for the purpose by their niggardly governments, which was all too often not the case.

Infantry training

The processes of turning an infantry recruit into a useful solider and an infantry company into a valuable unit were often rather haphazardly organized until well into the eighteenth century. In time of war it was common practice to send raw recruits straight to their regiments where they were expected to pick up the rudiments of their trade as best they might, and an enormous amount depended upon the conscientiousness of the regimental officers and NCOs. Some commanders such as Marlborough, Villars, de Saxe and Frederick laid down schedules of training which were supposed to be carried out during the winter or any convenient period of inactivity during the campaigning season, but the extent to which their behests were observed varied considerably, many regimental commanders preferring to practice their own forms of drill and training.

From their writings, most contemporaries seem to have favoured a four-part system of training. First, after basic foot-drill, there were 'the postures', which were wholly concerned with rudimentary handling of arms. Certain aspects of these drills have already been described in the chapter devoted to infantry weapons, and it is not intended to describe them in detail here. Suffice it to say that the pikeman (in the days before his supersession) had to learn 36 separate evolutions; the musketeer armed with the matchlock was expected to master 35 (some manuals give as many as 44); whilst the soldier armed with the flintlock had to perform only 26 (although when bayonet drill became standard practice, this added a further seven motions). A grenadier had to master a dozen movements in connection with his specialized role, ranging from slinging his firelock to 'opening' his fuse (as a precaution against damp grenade fuses were often protected with a layer of wax), to lighting it, and throwing 'with a powerful swing'. It is clear that the 'postures' altered but little over the years, or between armies except in matters of detail, once the changeover to the improved weapons was completed, although there was a tendency towards simplifying the words of command and attempts were made to reduce the number of movements. Thus a French ordinance of 2 March 1703 relating to the handling of arms specified some 67 movements; some 27 years later, by comparison, in his *Militarischen Exercitii ... mit der Flinte, Bajonet und Grenade,* Johan Jacob

Walrab describes 19 basic postures, and adds 7 more for bayonet drill, before describing the positions for presenting and sloping arms, laying them down and reversing arms (for military funerals). He concludes with a section of eight basic movements for the grenadier, and a few hints for the NCO armed with the halbert.[50] Many drill-books on these lines were published between 1688 and 1710.

From the 'postures' the recruit passed on to the manual and platoon 'Exercises' which incorporated up to 121 'motions' besides 16 warning words of command, but which were eventually reduced in the former case to some 55. The main evolutions practised were concerned with 'reducing' a unit from six ranks (the usual number employed on the march) to the three or four adopted for action by means of the 'doublings'. Other drills accustomed the soldiers to countermarching and to forming up in their ranks at close, half or full distance, these spaces relating to the varying intervals between the files needed for different evolutions and manoeuvres. The men were also often trained to obey signals given 'at tap of drum' as an alternative to the verbal word of command. When he was reasonably proficient in these attainments the soldier was regarded as trained in the rudiments of his profession. Company drill and field exercises followed – considered to be the higher branches of military training – but many of these aspects of a soldier's training are closely associated with tactics, and will be described on a later page.

The sequence of battalion training given by de Guignard in his *'École de Mars'* (1725) will serve to illustrate early eighteenth century practice. At the beating of *'Au Champ'* each company began to gather near their captain. Then, on the *'Générale'*, all the companies stood to. *'Drapeau'* was the signal for the men to take up their arms and form in close order; when this was done, the colour party marched on parade and took up its position. The battalion then marched off by companies, by either sixes or fours, the major in front acting as guide, followed by the grenadiers, then the colonel's company and the rest in order of seniority. Once arrived at the review ground or 'parade', the sergeants re-formed their men into five ranks, using supernumaries to fill gaps in other companies, the Grenadier Company taking the right of the line, the picket (drawn from all other companies) the left. Next, after opening the files, the troops prepared for arms drill, and when the major gave the signal with his cane, the drums rolled, and the officers took up their positions, half in front, and half to the rear of the battalion to supervise their men's performance. The 'Handling of Arms' was for long governed by the *Ordonnance* of 2 March 1703, which enjoined 67 movements. Arms drill was followed by *'Evolutions at the Halt'*, mostly concerned with the opening and closing of the files, reductions of the ranks, counter-marching by ranks and files. Next came practice-firing – usually divided into fire by ranks (each rank filing to the rear after discharge to reload), fire by ranks to the rear, fire to the flanks and rear, and the 'General Discharge' by the first three or even four ranks of the whole battalion. Other exercises practised included forming square by divisions (based upon the second division from the right which stood firm) and forming hollow squares or sometimes 'circular battalions', the men sometimes facing inwards to witness the punishment of offenders at the halberds. Finally came 'Evolutions on the March', and the practice of 'Salutes and Honours'. Such was the standard training programme of the French infantry in the first quarter of the eighteenth century, and it can be regarded as fairly typical of the drills practised in most other armies of the day, although, as we shall see, firing techniques were very different in some armies. However, it must be stressed once more that uniformity of training was very rare, regimental commanders continuing to please themselves for a considerable period.

The overall aim of this training was to produce a military automaton. There was no requirement for individual initiative; simply conformity and proficiency in the required movements was all that was demanded. Clearly, the training system as understood by such French Inspectors-General of Infantry as Martinet was geared to dealing with the least intelligent members of society with the intention of making passable soliders out of them, but this notwithstanding the lack of imagination it represents is somewhat horrifying.

However, as the eighteenth century entered its second quarter, there was a certain revival of interest in training aims and methods, and several notable soldiers and writers began to bend their attentions to the subject – including Santa-Cruz, Folard and de Saxe. How far their suggestions were ever implemented is open to debate, but it is interesting to study their ideas for improving the basic efficiency of the infantry.

The Marquis of Santa-Cruz, writing in 1730, made a strong plea for basing peacetime training on the realities of war. 'The troops must be accustomed to digging earth, to making fascines and positioning them, and planting barricades; they must learn to use gabions, and the methods of entrenching them, how to make ditches, parapets and fire-steps at the places the engineers have chosen . . .' The same authority called for arduous route-marches, short rations and exposure of the men to cold, heat, hunger and general discomfort in order to harden them. Santa-Cruz was also insistent on the need to train infantry to face cavalry:

> Infantry officers should mount a strong and sturdy horse . . . in the presence of their men, and then try to ride down a foot-soldier, who will stand firm armed only with a pole; they will then see that by pointing the stick at the horse's eyes or tapping its head with it, the horse will shy and refuse to advance . . . The officer should then sieze the opportunity to point out to the soldiers that if a horse will not ride down a man armed only with a pole how much less will cavalry prosper against formed battalions, whose bayonets, bullets and din of arms . . . are even more capable of scaring the horses. [51]

This was more imaginative than the requirements of the 'conventional' Puységur, who reflected the authors of earlier drill-books in his repeated insistence on the almost exclusive importance of training for fire production.

> The principal object . . . should be to teach the soldier how to load his musket properly, whether with cartridge or loose-powder, with or without the bayonet fixed; how he should give fire under the different circumstances he will

encounter; to teach him never to fire without an order, and never to do so without aiming, thus avoiding the waste of fire to no purpose.[52]

Both the Chevalier de Folard and Maurice de Saxe represented a distinct challenge to this point of view. They declared themselves unconvinced on the all-importance of the fire-fight, and preached a return to the concept of shock-action for the infantry. The methods of achieving this they suggested varied considerably, and will be discussed again in the next chapter, but both had many hard things to say about the conditions and methods of training they saw in the French armies of their day. Reflecting Santa-Cruz, Folard wrote that

> In peacetime, idleness, negligence and laxity of military law, can have dire results for a state; for, on the outbreak of war, the deficiencies are suddenly revealed, but the evil is without remedy. The officers and men are no longer the same soldiers. Work and discomfort are unbearable to them . . .[53]

Saxe commented in 1750 that 'our infantry, though the bravest in Europe, is not fit to stand a charge in a position, where infantry less brave, but better drilled and in a better formation, can close with it.'[54] The marshal's Quartermaster-General possibly hit upon the main source of the *malaise* afflicting the French forces of Louis xv when he wrote that 'the officers do not know how to command or how to secure obedience . . . Their colonels . . . are not aware of the importance of discipline and have usually no idea of it.'

Discipline 'is the soul of armies' wrote Saxe in his *Rêveries*. After the proper organization of troops he considered it the 'first matter that presents itself'. He was insistent on severe punishment without partiality or distinction of rank and birth for all cases of negligence, advocating flogging. In these views he was a typical soldier of his day. However he had many constructive suggestions to offer as well. He pointed out the value of having a nucleus of veteran soldiers in every company and, when possible, in every file to encourage and steady the raw recruits. Stressing the need to engender friendly rivalry between different formations as a means to increase *esprit de corps* and overall efficiency, he recommended kindness and rewards as well as severity. He also saw the importance of drill, but qualified its significance: 'Drill is necessary to make the soldier steady and skilful, although it does not warrant exclusive attention.'[54] Saxe strongly recommended arduous marching to strengthen the troops' endurance, for 'all the mystery of manoeuvres and combats is in the legs, and it is to the legs that we should apply ourselves,' and as a means to this end he advised the reintroduction of the cadenced step and military music, following the Prussian lead in this respect.

In Prussia, great emphasis was placed on draconian discipline and unquestioning obedience. Officers and ncos were encouraged to belabour the rank and file with staves and sticks for the slightest slip or misdemeanour, heedless of the brutalizing effect this must inevitably have on the men. The aims of military training, as expressed by the 'Old Dessauer', were 'good shooting, quick loading, intrepidity and vigorous attack', and the reputed result was an ability to fire between four and five rounds a minute (other armies could let off between two and three). Leopold of Anhalt-Dessau was also the first commander – outside Sweden – to introduce the cadenced step. But the price of such discipline and proficiency was fear and hatred. 'All that can be done with the soldier is to give him *esprit de corps* . . .' wrote Frederick the Great, 'and since officers have sometimes to lead him into the greatest dangers (and he cannot be influenced by a sense of honour) he must be more afraid of his officers than of the dangers to which he is exposed.'[55] Such was the basis of Prussian military training, which in due course was copied by many other powers.

In England, the utmost stress was also laid on the perfection of firing techniques, although the methods of inculcating the necessary discipline were somewhat less deliberately ferocious than those in vogue in the Prussian states. Writing in the early 1740s, Brigadier-General Richard Kane stressed the need for the officers to say 'something to encourage and excite the men to the performance of their duty', claiming that 'love for their officers' was a much more desirable emotion than fear or hate. Practical considerations underlay this approach as well as humanitarian feelings. 'I cannot but take notice of some gentlemen,' he continues, 'who instead of treating their men with GOOD NATURE, use them with CONTEMPT and CRUELTY; by which those gentlemen often meet their FATE in the day of battle from their own men.'* Those who treat their men well, on the other hand, 'will be sure, on all occasions, to have them stand fast by them, and even interpose between them and death.'[56]

Kane was only too well aware of the shortcomings of contemporary practice as laid down in many of the manuals of arms. 'How preposterous is it to see some of our English Jack-Boot-Men, with all their accoutrements, perform an exercise on foot!' He readily saw that one contributory cause to the confusion that often fell upon formations striving to carry out the exercise was the profusion of regimental drills used within the army.

> Everyone will allow, that 'tis absolutely necessary that the troops should be brought under one method of discipline; that when His Majesty shall please to order them together, or a General Officer is to receive them, they may perform a graceful exercise.

He also placed the blame for disgraceful performances squarely on the heads of the officers: he clearly subscribed to the belief 'there are no good or bad regiments – only good or bad officers.'

> I was once at a review, when the commanding general of the troops was reviewing a regiment of foot, where was present the Colonel, Lieutenant-Colonel, Major and most of all the captains, and yet not one of

---

*One celebrated case of an unjust major receiving his deserts at the hands of his own men reputedly took place at Blenheim. Aware that his men had it in for him, and that his exposed position in front of the battalion line might well invite a bullet in the back, he addressed his men before action was joined, promising to mend his ways if he survived the battle. 'Have no fear, we know our duty' an unidentified voice called back, somewhat ambiguously as it proved. The regiment performed its duty well, and the major came through unscathed by friendly or hostile bullet. Vastly relieved, he turned round to congratulate the men. He had just time to take off his hat and say 'Gentlemen' when several shots rang out from his battalion, and he fell, riddled, to the ground.

them capable of going thro' the discipline of the regiment, of which the general very justly took public notice.[57]

Kane particularly stressed the need for officers to become proficient in giving orders by beat of drum, and for the men to readily recognize them, against the day of action when the din of battle might make verbal orders unrecognizable. In the interests of keeping their men ready for active service, many governments attempted to impose a degree of standardization of training — but with very limited success. Ever since 1661, for example, the French authorities had ordained that battalions should exercise at least twice a week, and garrisons no less than once a month, and in due course Louvois built up a system of inspectors to ensure that these practices took place (1668). A further step was the institution of annual camps of instruction for inter-arm training in times of peace. Once again the French led the way, and some of the resultant gatherings were lavish in the extreme. In 1698, to cite one example, Marshal Boufflers was appointed to command the Camp of Coudun, ostensibly ordered for the furtherance of the military education of the Duke of Burgundy. No less than 60,000 troops were collected and besides several reviews and exercises conducted in the presence of the King there was a mock-battle, a complete mock-siege of Compiègne, and a practice grand forage. Before the camp was dispersed, 80,000lbs of gunpowder had been expended. It would seem that the attractions of the table were not exactly neglected either, for Boufflers certainly did things in style.

> He had more than 72 cooks and at least 340 domestics, of whom 120 wore livery. There were 400 dozen napkins, 80 dozen plates of silver and six dozen of enamel besides plates and silver bowls for fruit, and everything else in proportion. On an ordinary day they consumed 50 dozen bottles and when the King and Princes came to eat, 80. In one day 2,000 pounds of coffee were consumed and 268 litres of liqueurs.[58]

English governments attemped to follow the French lead — though they never attained its magnificence. A formal inspectorate charged with the duties of 'exercising ye forces and visiting ye garrisons' has been established in 1687 (its members being paid 16s 5¼d a day), and associated with this step was James II's decision to hold annual camps at Blackheath and Hounslow. The largest numbered 4,000 cavalry and 9,000 infantry, and lasted for two weeks. But both the military value and the political motivation behind these camps came in for adverse criticism. An inspector noted of the Hounslow Heath encampment of 1688 that there was

> A lack of soldier-like simplicity among the officers; regiments vied with each other in the magnificence of their mess-tents and accommodation, and in the expense of the officers' entertainments to their London friends, both male and female.[59]

Parliament liked them even less. They suspected, with some justification, that one idea in James' mind was a desire to overawe the 'loyal' Commons and

Protestant citizens of the capital with a show of military force. As a result, after the Glorious Revolution, such encampments were not held for a considerable period, although they eventually reappeared under the Hanoverians.

8

The tactical handling
of the foot

It is difficult to be dogmatic on the subject of infantry tactics, for, as with questions of regimental organization, practices tended to differ from army to army and sometimes from unit to unit within them. Until the second quarter of the eighteenth century, few countries laid down standardized drills in any detail, and much was accordingly left to the judgement and whims of the individual colonels within certain broad limits. In the search for accurate information it is also misleading to place too much reliance on the authority of the many drill-books published between 1688 and 1714. In the first place there is often scant indication of which ones received wide-spread acceptance; secondly it is impossible to claim that they even reflect the practice current on their dates of publication, as many were written many years before they were published, or merely repeat practically verbatim far earlier treatises. This difficulty is illustrated by Folard's claim to have discovered an early seventeenth century German drill-book in the Royal Libraries which was subsequently copied word for word (in translation) by the supposed French authority Lostelneau, whose *Le Maréchal de Bataille*, first published in 1647, was long regarded as the standard source of guidance, the very epitome of 'modern' practice.

Nevertheless it can be claimed that certain basic methods found wide-spread acceptance in the armies of the age, and that in certain cases special national tactical characteristics emerged which played no small part in determining the outcome of infantry engagements. A discussion of the evolution and practice of these various methods forms the subject of this chapter. At the outset it will be helpful to list the five main tactical manoeuvres that all infantry battalions had to perform at one time or another in the heat of battle. First there was the advance into close contact, giving fire periodically as the range shortened from 250 to about 60 yards. Second, the static fire-fight, in which rival battalions faced each other at 60 yards distance or even less, and blazed away at the halt until the nerve of one or other began to crack. Thirdly there were the means of conducting a further advance – or alternatively a retreat – after the static fire-fight had run its course. Fourthly there were the defensive methods adopted against hostile cavalry attack; and lastly, the means employed in defence of a breastwork or other field fortification. Each of these activities had specific drills and manoeuvres which gradually evolved as the period progressed, all of them reflecting in no small degree the development of infantry weapons.

Infantry tactics at the close of the seventeenth century

During all the seventeenth and much of the eighteenth centuries armies rigidly distinguished between marching and fighting, adopting different formations for each activity. At the start of the period, most battalions marched in column of the route on a front of between eight and twenty files; this made marching along the roads virtually impossible, and forced the massive columns into the adjoining fields, where their cross-country performance was usually painfully slow. The reason for the adoption of these unwieldy columns was closely associated with the theoretical requirements of forming the line of battle, always a complex and time-consuming process. It proved almost impossible to maintain the requisite intervals between files, ranks and formations, but without these a series of battalions attempting to form for battle from a column of march by converting to left or right were often plunged into the direst confusion which took a great deal of time to sort out. The fact that few armies (apart from the Swedes and some Germans) used the cadenced step during the 1690s still further complicated the situation. Under these conditions it is small wonder that it proved virtually impossible to surprise an opponent and force him to fight if he was unwilling to accept the challenge.

Each company took its place in the battalion column in accordance with the seniority of its commander, the grenadiers and picket usually leading the way. Most battalions still armed about one-fifth of their men with the pike, each company having its own detachment which accompanied it on the march. Thus a French company on the official 1690 establishment included ten pikemen amongst its 50 rank and file.

Once the field of battle was reached, however, the troops adopted an entirely different formation. Each infantry battalion reorganized itself into three groups, inevitably disrupting the company pattern. The pikemen left their respective companies and formed up in a solid phalanx in the centre of the battalion line, five or six ranks deep. Meantime the musketeers drew themselves up in two 'sleeves' to the right and left of the pikemen, with the exception of the grenadier company, which in some armies took post a little way apart on the extreme right, or alternatively drew up in two detachments, one on each flank. Each battalion in battle order occupied a considerable area of ground, for owing to the cumbersome reloading processes the musketeer needed a considerable amount of space. To cite one example, a French battalion, drawn up in the five ranks that were authorized from 1693, with four paces between ranks, and at least one between each man, covered an area measuring some 190 yards by 14 yards. Although details differed, this type of formation was adopted by almost all armies. Most of them were based upon the advice provided by Montecuculi in the previous generation:

The secret of success is to have a solid body so firm and impenetrable that wherever it is or wherever it may go, it shall bring the enemy to a stand like a mobile bastion, and shall be capable of defending itself.[61]

Concerning the tactical handling of these formations, it is again possible to paint a broadly standardized picture. Throughout the 1690s, despite the poor quality of most of the firearms available, the major consideration was already the production of as high a rate of fire as possible. All other considerations were deemed secondary. The ideal of incessant fire-production was the chief reason behind the five or six deep formations adopted, for in theory such a depth ensured that a fifth of the musketeers was always reloaded. Fire was delivered in one of three ways: by ranks, files or divisions. In the first case the front rank marched three paces forward, halted, fired, turned about and made its way to the rear through the files to reload. Firing 'by files', a group of two files (i.e. 10 men) would move out six paces, fan out into line, fire, and return whence they had come to be replaced by a further two. Fire 'by Divisions' – as understood in the 1690s – was an adaptation of file firing but on a larger scale; in this case the group was made up of either four or six files, half of which came forward together, deployed into two or three ranks, and then fired by ranks in turn or sometimes all at once. This type of firing was usually reserved for those occasions when a battalion was holding an entrenchment or hedge-line. The main disadvantage shared by all these methods was the disorder often caused by the continual marching and counter-marching through the files, whilst the weight of fire delivered at any one discharge was not particularly heavy. All these evolutions were normally carried through at well under 100 yards range, the maximum effective range of the matchlock being a mere 300 paces.

The nucleus of pikemen existed to defend the musketeers from the attentions of hostile cavalry. Under cavalry attack they were trained to form a hollow square within which the bulk of the musketeers sought shelter whilst a minority took post amongst the advanced pike shafts and continued to fire at the enemy horsemen. The old concept of using the pikes for shock action had almost disappeared (there were hardly enough of them in the battalion to justify their use in this way), but some armies – including the Swedes – occasionally reverted to 'push of pike' at close quarters. In many cases, however, pikemen were observed to throw away their weapons on the first opportunity to snatch up firearms from the ground.

In the 1690s it became rare for infantry to fight hand-to-hand with their opponents, although there were of course notable exceptions such as Steenkirk (1692) where the English and Dutch battalions were divided from the French only by hedgerows. Generally speaking, however, commanders deemed their foot to be a source of more or less static fire-power once they had moved ponderously up into musket range, relying on the wheeling horsemen to decide the ultimate issue.

Although it is dangerous to generalize, it can be asserted that certain nations were considered to be better than others in infantry fighting during these last days of the pike and matchlock combination. The Dutch infantry were widely

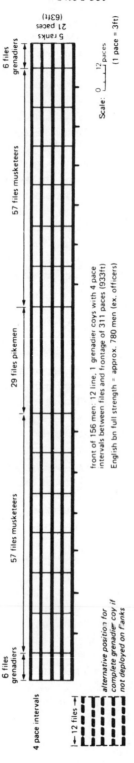

5 ranks
21 paces
(63ft)

6 files
grenadiers

57 files musketeers

29 files pikemen

57 files musketeers

6 files
grenadiers

4 pace intervals

|← 12 files →|

*alternative position for
complete grenadier coy if
not deployed on flanks*

front of 156 men: 12 line, 1 grenadier coys with 4 pace
intervals between files and frontage of 311 paces (933ft)

English bn full strength = approx. 780 men (ex. officers)

Scale: 0   12 paces

(1 pace = 3ft)

Infantry formation deployed for action in late 17th century

considered to be amongst the best serving the Allied cause. Their showing in the War of 1672 had been far from impressive, but William III had subsequently overhauled their training and organization, and by 1688 they had few peers for stalwart bravery and coolness – qualities deemed the most important in the infantryman of that day. Their conduct at Fleurus (1690) drew a warm tribute from their opponent, Marshal Luxembourg, who wrote soon after his victory that 'Prince Waldeck has very reason to be proud of his infantry.'[62] An Allied observer of the same battle, William Sawle, wrote that:

> The French infantry could not so much as dare look them in the face; could the Dutch be left alone to them, they would esteem them as nothing.[63]

Even the highly critical William III expressed himself as well satisfied with his Dutch foot's performance on a number of occasions. Their calm rallying after the defeat at Landen (1693) evoked widespread admiration.

After the steady Dutch, the comparatively amateur and immature English infantry soon earned a redoubtable reputation for valiant behaviour in action. Notwithstanding their sub-standard equipment and bad reputation for indiscipline at the outset of the Nine Years' War, they soon earned Prince Waldeck's commendation for their bravery at the action of Walcourt (1689): 'I would never have believed so many of the English would show such a *joie de combattre*.'[64] Their later conduct against overwhelming odds of five to one amongst the hedgerows of Steenkirk and their showing at the battle of Landen added further lustre to their reputation despite the unfortunate outcome on both occasions. Their years of fullest achievement, however, still lay ahead.

The French, on the other hand, were generally rated to be somewhat indifferent infantrymen in the early years of the Nine Years' War. At Fleurus, for example, French victory though it ultimately turned out to be, 'the French horse were several times forced to rally their foot and bring them up under their cover.' So disillusioned with their performance did Louis XIV become that in 1691 he ordered Luxembourg to avoid infantry action in future, for he believed that such an engagement 'involves heavy losses and is never decisive'. Nevertheless, the French foot substantially redeemed their reputation at Steenkirk and Landen, though in the former instance they required a massive superiority of numbers to convert their intial rout into a narrow success. On other fronts, however, the French infantry enjoyed a reputation worthy of their greatest days. Marshal Catinat reported in glowing terms their conduct at Marsaglia in North Italy (1693), where with great intrepidity they stormed the key to the Austrian position with the bayonet. 'I believe there never was an action', wrote their proud commander, 'which showed better what your Majesty's infantry is capable of.'[65] Such successes, however, encouraged French generals of several generations in the belief that the true *métier* of the French foot was cold steel – and this assumption led them to disregard the refinements of infantry fire tactics, with what proved to be near-fatal results in the following war.

In the almost continuous struggles in south-east Europe between Moslem and Christian, the Habsburg forces generally proved superior to the Ottoman masses.

The Turks often tried to lure their opponents from their positions into the plain, using their Arnaut snipers to sting the Austrian troops into premature counter-attack. However, the Imperial commanders soon learnt to disregard such incitements, and it became appreciated that if the basic Turkish tactic of massed, furious, all-out attack could be withstood, the enemy would soon reach a point of exhaustion which could be exploited. To this end, the Imperialist infantry often surrounded their positions with barricades of *chevaux de frise*, and remained within them until the combination of battalion fire and protective obstacles wore down the morale of their numerically massive but virtually untrained opponent. The result was a series of great battle successes for the Austrians led by such leaders as the Margrave of Baden and Prince Eugen of Savoy – including Mohacs and Szlankamen (1687 and 1691).

Such, then was the broad outline of infantry tactics commonly employed down to the turn of the century. Other methods were also in experimental use in some armies, but their description is best reserved for the following section of this chapter which covers the period when they become widely employed.

Infantry tactics during the War of the Spanish Succession

All tactical developments are inevitably closely linked with questions of weapon changes. It is unusual for the two to coincide; in most cases, there is a period during which the new weapons are available but no corresponding advance in tactical doctrine takes place, but eventually new methods emerge to make the most of the new conditions of warfare and to evade the less pleasant consequences to some degree. It is also demonstrable that the speed with which the necessary mental and administrative adjustments are made as regards tactical development varies considerably amongst different armies at different periods of their history. Somewhat ironically, it is often those countries with the most successful overall recent martial records which tend to be the most averse to accepting the need for change, whilst the governments and armed forces of unsuccessful nations have the strongest motivation to reform their methods. As a result, considerable reversals in military fortunes from war to war or even within wars are not uncommon, and in the realm of infantry tactics there are few better examples of this than in the contrast between the Nine Years' War and the succeeding War of the Spanish Succession.

In a sense the French case does not at first sight wholly support this argument. As we have seen above, the reputation of their infantry serving in Flanders under Luxembourg was not particularly notable, though on other fronts it remained high. Nevertheless, the main point holds good, for the overall success of French armies in the field remained greatly superior to that of the Allies – and as will be seen practically no steps were taken between 1697 and 1701 to modernize French infantry training, although by 1703 a large number of their troops had received the improved flintlock musket and socket bayonet. In terms of tactical effectiveness, therefore, it was to be the Allied foot that greatly improved their standard, following the adoption of more advanced methods. Nevertheless, many contemporaries spoke with awe of the fury of the initial French fire in action, although its continuity and effectiveness tended to fall off rapidly after the initial discharge.

It is true to say that the importance of infantry fire-power became even further established during the Spanish Succession struggle. One reason for this was the continuing expansion in the size of many armies which in effect implied the growth of their infantry components as cavalry were both more expensive to maintain and harder to train. Despite this increasing emphasis on fire-power, however, it is important to note that most of the great engagements of the war were won, in the last analysis, by the cavalry, closely supported by the foot. To quote Commandant Colin: 'The cavalry was the offensive element in the army; the infantry acted with its fire to destroy the cavalry's power.'[66] Nevertheless, the infantry occupied a more important place in the line of battle than had ever before been the case since the widespread adoption of firearms.

Although some French authorities continued to pay lip-service to the all-importance of infantry fire, in many ways their army remained the most conservative and backward in Western Europe. In an earlier chapter we have noted the unwillingness with which the authorities accepted the need to adopt the flintlock and bayonet; in matters of unit organization and fire-drill they remained even more unimaginative. Although the new weapons with their superior reliability and speed of reloading were potent reasons for reducing the number of ranks in a battalion formed for battle in the interests of producing greater frontal fire output, no official attempt to implement such reforms was attempted for a considerable time. Thus the *Ordonnance* of 1703 still laid down that the standard formation was to be *five* ranks deep as in the last great days of pike and matchlock, although in practice many French battalions formed only four deep – and in some cases even three – owing to the exigencies of manpower shortages as the war continued it lengthy course. It is important to note how practical considerations of this type often caused the officers and men on the spot to disregard the orders of higher authority.

The retention of five- or four-deep formations by many of Louis xiv's battalions was, to say the least, a wasteful anachronism. In the French forces they also often retained the old four-pace intervals between ranks, although this was not strictly necessary owing to the improved loading drills coming into vogue. Thus the depth of a French battalion remained about 20 paces and its frontage about 300. It is true that each battalion contained considerably more musketeers than formerly through the progressing replacement of the old pike contingents, but little effort was made to secure truly maximum fire output, although the initial discharge of French infantry remained redoubtable. Each file dressed strictly from the front, which made it impossible for more than the first three ranks to close up and fire in a concentrated volley. Thus the front rank would kneel, the second crouch, and the third stand upright, whilst the fourth and fifth stood idly by.

The French still made use of the old systems of file and divisional firings, but the method most commonly employed was the rank-by-rank discharge. There were variations within this method. Sometimes the older form (already described) was followed, but on other occasions the first rank would fire and fall on their faces to allow the second rank to discharge, who in turn would take to the ground to make way for the third, and so on. After five line volleys of this type, the whole formation would rise up – all being well – and set about reloading (the ram-rod could not be wielded properly in the prone position). A more sensible variant of the foregoing method (which did not delay the reloading process) was that described by Demorinet in *Le Major Parfait* (first published in 1686):

> The best way of firing is by ranks when it is desired to fire in line, parallel to the foe. To do this, and to fire without embarrasment, it is best to fire at the halt without making any move except that needed to make the first five ranks kneel on the ground; and the sixth is that which makes first its fire, the fifth then doing the same and the rest consecutively.[67]

All these firing methods, however, were strictly speaking out of date by 1704. Most had the inherent defects of inadequate continuity and poor fire control. Fire by ranks, whole companies and even battalions was not unknown – but the troops generally fired on the order of the major or lieutenant-colonel and were hardly amenable to close supervision by their officers and sergeants. The great majority of shots, therefore, could be expected to go wide of the mark. Fire-control was better when the file or division systems were employed, but then the output of fire was smaller, and it proved almost impossible to maintain a non-stop fire.

Similar forms of fire-drill were employed by the Austrians and Russians besides many of the smaller states of Germany, but certain countries – most particularly England, the United Provinces and Sweden – were training their infantry along very different lines. It is almost impossible to trace the real origins of the platoon firing system with any certainty. Le Blond considered that 'Fire by platoon . . . has long been in use amongst the Dutch; there is some evidence that its invention is due to them, and that they furnished the model for the other nations of Europe which have copied it.'[68] This conjecture is supported to some extent by the enquiry made of William Blathwayt, Secretary at War, by the Earl of Marlborough (newly appointed to command the English troops sent over into Flanders in 1689):

> I desire that you will know the King's pleasure whether he will have the Regiments of Foot to learn the Duch [*sic*] exercise, or else to continue the English, for if he will I must have itt translated into English.[69]

This at least shows that the English forces up to that date were not following the Dutch form; it is far more probable that they had hitherto copied French concepts in view of the close associations with France during the reigns of Charles II and James II. The copy of the French drill-book *Le Major Parfait*, it is interesting to note, is inscribed inside the cover 'this did belong to King James . . .' and dated 1686, and provides another sign of French military influence before the Glorious Revolution. However the Dutch claim is not unchallenged, and there is a school that believes that firing by platoons dates back to the

Swedish armies of Gustavus Adolphus. It would certainly appear that a form of this tactic was employed at Breitenfeld (1631) where Hepburn's Scottish Brigade served with distinction, 'the first time that platoon firing had been done . . . it utterly confounded Tilly's army.'[70], but it would seem that Charles xii's Swedish veterans had changed to a different form of fire-drill by 1708.

There were many variations of platoon firing, and it is clear that the system developed over a considerable number of years rather than appeared all at once. Marlborough and his generals thought particularly highly of it, and actively encouraged its widespread adoption throughout their infantry in place of all other firing methods, and accordingly the description that follows, based upon Brigadier-General Kane's celebrated *Exercise for the Foot* can be said to represent the English usage.[71]

In the first place the battalion or regiment took the field and drew up into line in a predetermined order of companies. The Colonel's company and that of the second-in-command invariably formed the centre of the line (in contrast to the French – see diagram p. 101), whilst the remaining ten line companies deployed to the left and right of the central nucleus in strict order of seniority of their captains. The grenadier company (which habitually marched at the head of the formation when in column of the route) meantime divided into two equal bodies, one, under the captain, remaining on the extreme right of the line, the second, commanded by the senior lieutenant of grenadiers, taking post on the extreme left. The whole battalion then reduced itself from six to three ranks, closing up to half distance ($1\frac{1}{2}$ pace intervals) in the process.

The major or adjutant next proceeded to ride down the front, dividing the 12 line companies (though not the grenadiers) into four 'Grand Divisions', and each of these groups in turn into four equal platoons* Thus a 13 company battalion was reorganized into a total of 18 platoons – 16 of them in the four 'Divisions', and two more of Grenadiers on the extreme flanks. This division into *ad hoc* platoons was only employed for fire-drill and actual fighting. On all other occasions the company was the administrative unit.

Next, the senior officers re-divided the platoons into at least three 'firings' – or groups of six platoons apiece. The Grand Divisions were of no significance in this respect, for the platoons told off for each separate 'firing' were interspersed down the whole line in a carefully pre-arranged order so as to achieve continuity of fire from very part of the battalion line. (See diagram p. 122). Each platoon would then load or check their priming before moving into close order (1-foot intervals) whilst the sergeants took up their supervisory positions in the intervals between them. The company officers took post either in front of the sergeants or four paces to the rear of the line; the colonel stationed himself and his drummer some seven paces in front of the colour party (placed exactly in the centre); the lieutenant-colonel positioned himself some ten paces *behind* the line (so as to be in a position to see everything and be ready to take over command in the event of the commander being killed or wounded), and the major and adjutant moved out

---

*At the lower establishment (as in peacetime), each 'division' would be divided into only three platoons.

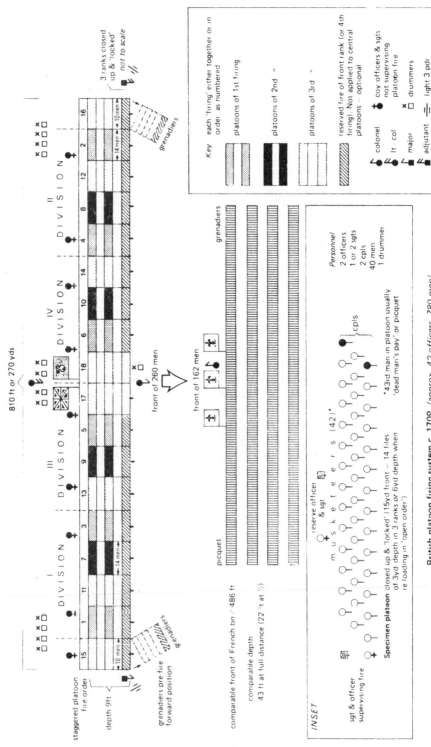

British platoon firing system c. 1709 *(approx. 42 officers, 780 men)*

onto the extremities of the regiment. The remaining drummers meantime drew up behind the centre, the right and the left wings in three groups.

The battalion was now ready to advance against the enemy. All knapsacks, tent-poles and other impedimenta would have been sent to the rear. 'If we win the Day, they will be safe; if not, 'tis no matter what becomes of them,' comments Brigadier-General William Kane. On the colonel's order, the line then marched steadily forward until it came to about 60 paces from the enemy, whereupon it halted.

On the order 'First Firing, Take Care!' (or a ruffle on the drums) the six platoons of the first firing and the *whole* of the front rank made ready to fire. The first rank all knelt, whilst the remaining two ranks of the dispersed platoons of the first firing marched into close order and 'locked'. To do this, each man placed himself with his left shoulder towards the enemy, and placed his extended left foot close behind the rearward-pointing right foot of the soldier to his front. The effect of this was to ensure that every man's presented musket-barrel was clear of the soldier in front. This sensible precaution was not practised in the French army, where the men in the files drew up immediately behind one another. This meant that at most only three ranks could fire – the first kneeling, the second crouching, the third standing upright, when a battalion volley was ordered – whilst the damage to French heads and collar-bones caused by the fierce kick of their discharged pieces caused considerable comment in contemporary medical circles. But this is to digress slightly.

On a further order – or a flan by the drums – the troops of the first firing would come to the present, and, on the given signal, open fire. Some regiments in the early eighteenth century were habitually trained to discharge their pieces one platoon at a time in a pre-set order (see diagram), thus producing a rippling fire effect down the line. Many officers, however, including both Kane and Captain Robert Parker, came to regard this as a procedure more suited for Hyde Park or the review-ground than the battlefield, and insisted that all the six platoons of the first firing should discharge their pieces together on the colonel's single order. As they were not responsible for timing the exact moment of their platoon's discharge, this enabled the platoon officers to devote all their attention to supervising their men, ensuring with the aid of their spontoons and the sergeant's halberts or half-pikes that all the musket barrels were properly aligned, pointing at the enemies' stomachs.

Immediately after the first 'firing' the platoons concerned would open-order-march and start to reload, whilst the second and third firings took up the shooting in turn if the commanding officer so ordained. If the enemy still held his ground, the process could be repeated indefinitely, and a well-trained battalion could get off two sets of three firings in a minute. It should be noted that the 'Third Firing' was slightly different from the earlier ones in that the grenadier platoons on the flanks wheeled slightly inwards to pour their fire into the mass of the enemy battalion, whilst the two central platoons aimed exclusively at the centre of the enemy's line in the hope of disabling their commanders.

Captain Robert Parker has left a description of a fire-fight between the Royal

Regiment of Foot of Ireland and an equivalent unit in the French service at the battle of Malplaquet (1709), which clearly shows the advantages conferred by the English firing system over that preferred by their opponents. It also reveals the inaccuracy of the muskets of those days if we consider the number of casualties suffered by each side in this representative action.

> We continued marching slowly on, till we came to an opening in the wood. It was a small plain, on the opposite side of which we perceived a battalion of the enemy drawn up, a skirt of the wood being in the rear of them. Upon this Colonel Kane, who was then at the head of the Regiment, having drawn us up, and formed our platoons, advanced gently toward them, with the six platoons of our first fire made ready. When we had advanced within a hundred paces of them, they gave us a fire of one of their ranks: whereupon we halted, and returned them the fire of our six platoons at once; and immediately made ready the six platoons of our second fire, and advanced upon them again. They then gave us the fire of another rank, and we returned them a second fire, which made them shrink; however they gave us the fire of a third rank after a scattering manner, and then retired into the wood in great disorder: on which we sent our third fire after them, and saw them no more. We advanced cautiously up to the ground which they had quitted, and found several of them killed and wounded . . . We had but four men killed, and six wounded: and found near forty of them on the spot killed and wounded. [72]

Here, if ever, was a test-case of the platoon firing system. Parker goes on to attribute the success to the heavier musket balls favoured by the English at this period and to the fact that 'the French at that time fired all by ranks, which can never do equal execution with our platoon-firing, especially when six platoons are fired together. This is undoubtedly the best method that has yet been discovered for fighting a battalion; especially when two battalions only engage each other.' Nevertheless, some 600 British bullets only accounted for 40 opponents – although presumably many French wounded capable of walking evacuated into the woodland and were not included in Parker's estimate.

As had already been remarked, there were considerable numbers of variations of this method in use at different times and places. Besides the 'rippling' fire within the firings, many commanding officers chose to extemporize a 'Fourth Firing'. This was done by reserving the fire of the entire first rank, the kneeling men being ordered to 'drop their Muzzles to the Ground' whilst the second and third ranks fired over their heads at their appointed moment. The front rank's fire could then be given when the colonel considered it best. This never applied to the two centre platoons, however; they invariably fired all three ranks together, the reason being the security of the colonel who had to move smartly to and fro to avoid being killed by these two platoons' volleys.

Clearly all the methods outlined above called for exhaustive practice and took no little time to organize on the battlefield itself. There were accordingly a number of emergency drills for use when a formation was attacked before it was ready. In one of these, the two complete rear ranks (less the grenadiers) were to make the first fire whilst the front rank knelt; thereafter, the front rank and the grenadier platoons took up the firing, whilst the remainder reloaded 'with expedition' to give a third volley.[73] On occasions, too, the men would be permitted to fire as individuals, but this called for a higher degree of training than most regiments could boast, at least at the start of a war.

To summarize the advantages conferred by the platoon firing system described above, it should be pointed out that these were principally threefold. First, the sub-division of formations into platoons greatly facilitated the degree of fire control that could be maintained by the officers and NCOs; this in turn, led to more accurate shooting and better discipline than was possible when a complete rank – or even three ranks – fired off all at once, as was the favourite practice in the French forces. Secondly, the three or more firings ensured that the enemy was under concentrated and almost continuous fire once the action opened; there was no let up, and the psychological effects of this on the recipients at under 100 yards range should not be under-rated; furthermore the 'fire by line' school were only too well aware that fire by ranks was extremely difficult to make continuous, but their retention (in some cases at least) of five-deep formations undoubtedly wasted a great deal of fire potential. Thirdly, one-third of a British battalion would always be loaded, and thus ready to deal with any sudden emergency; at no time would the formation – or any single sector of it – be wholly unprepared – for at least one platoon in every three all down the line would be reloaded at any given moment.

One further practice shared by England and many other continental powers (though not France until the 1740s) linked with fighting their infantry battalions deserves notice at this point – namely the attachment of two light field pieces (usually one-and-a-half or three pounders) to each battalion for the provision of close fire support. This was *not* an innovation on the part of Marlborough personally, although he probably improved its implementation. Once again it was almost certainly a Swedish development of the 1630s, for Gustavus Adolphus had attached 'leather-guns' to his brigades for this kind of purpose. In the English armies similar measures were adopted from c.1650, and James II certainly attached two 3-pounders to each of the seven battalions camped in Hyde Park in August 1686, entrusting them to the grenadier companies. Furthermore, there is clear evidence that William III took similar measures in support of his infantry in 1693 if not earlier. In his Journal entry for 16 June that year, Lieutenant-Colonel Jacob Richards of the Train in Flanders noted that 'this evening our small pieces of cannon were sent to their respective brigades with all their appurtenances as also all ammunition for each brigade, not to be touched but in time of service.'[74] This is not, however, to deny the sterling services these light cannon performed during Marlborough's great battles; light enough to be drawn by a single horse or manhandled in action by half a dozen men and capable of keeping pace with an advancing battalion, these guns – usually loaded with canister (or 'partridge-shot' in the parlance of the times) – came into action on the flanks of each battalion and cut wide swathes of destruction through their opponents. The help such guns afforded the Dutch Guards storming Taviers and Franquenay on Villeroi's right flank at Ramillies (1706), or the devotion of the gunners in dragging their pieces (both regimental

and field) through Taisnières Forest at Malplaquet to engage the French reserve
cavalry on the further side, are just two notable examples of this assistance. It
was not until the 1740s and 1750s that the French saw the need to take similar
steps by attaching a single 'Swedish cannon' to each infantry battalion.[75] Other
nations – including the Empire and Prussia – were considerably quicker in
adopting this Anglo-Dutch practice. Prince Eugene placed special emphasis on
its importance, but the Austrian army had attached 40 $2\frac{1}{2}$-pdr 'Falcons' to their
terçios as early as 1636 – doubtless learning their value in this role from the
Swedes the hard way at Breitenfeld and Lützen.

Of course there were several other basic fighting drills for battalions which we
have not yet mentioned. It is not feasible here to examine each in detail, but their
broad outline may be mentioned. All infantry regiments were trained to perform
two or three basically defensive tactical evolutions. When in retreat, the
individual battalion faced to the rear and began to march off under the
immediate command of the lieutenant-colonel, leaving the colonel free to keep a
watchful eye on the corresponding enemy movements. If the foe's pursuing
infantry threatened to come rather too close, the Colonel would order the six
platoons whose turn it was to give the next fire to halt and turn right about to
face the enemy. Whilst the remainder of the battalion continued its retreat, these
platoons would fire at their pursuers before marching 'briskly back' to reoccupy
their old positions in the line (which had been left vacant for them) and then
reload. The process could then be performed by a second group of platoons – and
as many more times as necessary. It is interesting to note that this type of
'fire-and-retire' drill was also practised by the French during the Spanish
Succession War, although they never favoured the platoon firing system as such
for the attack or for static fire-fights at this period.

The second 'defensive' tactic devised for the protection of infantry – this time
against cavalry attack – was the forming of squares. This was a complex
evolution based upon the four 'Grand Divisions' of the battalion, each of which
eventually formed one face of the square, by wheeling back and round until one
extremity of the battalion line made contact with the other (see diagram p. 118).
Fire could then be given by ranks, one face of the square at a time, as necessary.
It was customary to keep the grenadiers separate from the remainder of the
battalion under these circumstances. If the square was static, they either divided
into four detachments to protect the vulnerable angles, or alternatively they were
withdrawn within the square to shelter with the officers and colours. Under
normal conditions, however, the Colonel and the grenadiers remained outside
the square taking measures to aid the defence of whichever face seemed in
danger of attack. When pressure was not extreme, the battalion could continue
its retreat without breaking up the square, simply ordering the flank divisions to
turn in the requisite direction and the rearward face to right-about-turn. In this
instance the grenadiers normally brought up the extreme rear. It should be noted
that fire was no longer given by platoons, but by entire faces of the square firing
at once.

Very often a number of battalions would join in taking these precautions. At
Fleurus in 1690, for example, the Dutch foot formed a vast square of 16

battalions after the flight of their cavalry, and proceeded to execute a model withdrawal to Charleroi which Luxembourg was in no way able to prevent. A second outstanding example was in July 1705, when 10 Bavarian battalions under the Comte de Caraman formed up into one square at Elixhem – again after the rout of their supporting horsemen – and successfully held off Marlborough's cavalry attacks and outdistanced his foot and guns until they found safety under the guns of Louvain. 'Which plainly shews,' comments General Kane, 'that if a body of Foot have but Resolution to keep their Order, there is no Body of Horse dare venture within their Fire.' [76]

Some experts, indeed, believed that a properly conducted infantry force could repulse cavalry attacks by fire-power alone, without abandoning the linear formation, but this was extremely risky for if the enemy cavalry penetrated behind the line the infantry were doomed to almost certain destruction.

A third type of defensive manoeuvre (also applicable to the advance under certain conditions) was that of 'breaking' the battalion. In the simplest terms this meant telling the men to leave their ranks and run for it – to re-form around the colours when the colonel's drum gave the necessary signal. Many authorities regarded this manoeuvre with great and probably justifiable suspicion, and clearly its use was fraught with perils. Unless the troops were very well disciplined, for instance, there was no telling whether they would rally at the signal or just keep running. Moreover, the disorder this manoeuvre – and the subsequent attempt to re-form the line – could lead to was another potent argument against its over-frequent employment. Nevertheless, it appears to have been a favourite manoeuvre of the Dutch Duke of Schomberg. [77] However the method clearly had much to recommend it when a house or a wall was encountered during an advance in line, providing every officer and man knew exactly where to re-form on the further side of the obstacle. Once again, a very high degree of discipline and training was called upon to make such movements viable.

Finally, a few other forms of tactics need a word of elucidation. When called upon to defend an entrenchment or a breastwork, the infantry were trained to carry out 'the parapet firing'. In this case a battalion was drawn up six deep in open order with at least two paces between ranks, and each rank in turn would advance to the parapet, fire, and then retire through the intervals to the rear to reload, and in due turn move up to fire again. This method was common to all armies with minor variations, and was closely similar to one of the favourite French types of fire in the open field during the late seventeenth century. Lastly, troops were trained in drills for street-fighting in hostile towns; basically they adopted a rectangular formation, such as would fit the width of the street, certain files being charged with the duty of observing the windows on either hand ready to fire into them if a hostile head or musket barrel made an appearance. This drill was very cumbersome, and was only relevant in the conditions of a storming, which was comparatively rare at our period. Last of all, there were tactical drills devised for troops performing escort duties for convoys, in which stress was laid on the need for outlying patrols to give early warning of an enemy's approach, and for intermediate parties of troops to be available to pass the alarm back to the main body. Probably the most celebrated action fought in the defence of a convoy was that of General Webb at Wynendael in 1708, when with merely 6,000 foot he soundly defeated 24,000 French and their Allies under Count de la Motte who were attempting to destroy a vital convoy of supplies and ammunition en route from Ostend to the siege lines before Lille. 'Webb very deservedly acquired great honour and reputation by this gallant action,' noted Captain Parker, 'but then he spoiled all by making it the subject of his conversation on all occasions.'[78]

In many ways, the battle of Malplaquet (1709) marked the end of one era in tactical thought and inaugurated another. The horrific casualties inflicted on the occasion – fully one-quarter of the Allied army were killed or wounded, and the French lost about 12,000, most of them on their left or amongst the cavalry in the centre – shocked the whole of Europe and caused many men to question the validity of the methods that led to such slaughter. Another feature that attracted French expert criticism was the way that Villars had insisted on wholly defensive fighting from behind prepared entrenchments and redoubts for his infantry arm and yet was induced to weaken his centre to strengthen his flank with disastrous results. The belief grew that the French might have achieved a telling victory had the infantry of the right wing (holding the edge of the Wood of Lanières under command of Marshal Boufflers) only counter-attacked the disordered remnants of the Allied left following the massacre of the Dutch Guards under the Prince of Orange. However, at that time all contemporaries – even the great Marlborough himself – regarded cavalry as the proper instrument for the *coup de grâce*, and the idea of a massed infantry attack leading to a great victory had not yet been properly envisaged. As the discerning noted, however, at Marsala (1693), Spire (or Speyerback) 10 years later and at Denain (1712), it was heavy French infantry attacks that led to success.* Thus Malplaquet became a point of departure for French military reform. These ideas were to prove slow to germinate, but in due course they would lead to important re-evaluations of the comparative places of fire and shock in infantry tactics, although in practical terms as will be seen in the next pages, the immediate effects of these new assessments were to be distinctly limited in the 30 years – and longer – that followed the signatures of the Peaces of Utrecht and Rastadt.

Further developments in linear infantry tactics, 1713–45

For over 30 years from the Peace of Utrecht the basic infantry tactics of almost every European army bore a close resemblance to those employed with so much success by the forces of Great Britain and the United Provinces during the War of the Spanish Succession. The only exceptions were the armies of Austria and Turkey, which changed nothing – and accordingly need no special attention in this section. It is therefore generally a period of stagnation.

For once we find the French following, rather than setting, the trend. The

---

* See p. 302 below for more information on these engagements. Also p. 305.

Marquis de Puységur, for example (whose classic work on the *Art of War* was published in 1745), was convinced that the side capable of producing the heavier weight of infantry fire-power would emerge victorious, and this sentiment was continually being repeated. By the close of our period the French were training their foot to produce seven types of fire – by *séction, peleton,** by *groups of two* platoons (or 'sleeves'), by half ranks (six to eight companies at a time), by full battalions ('whole ranks'), and lastly, *'feu de billebaude',* or individuals firing at will. One further type – 'rolling fire' or *feu de joie* – was reserved for reviews or celebrations to mark great occasions.[79] Similarly, there was a move towards the official adoption of three-deep formations for battle, but this only became *de rigueur* from 1755, whilst the British practice of spreading the placing of the line companies was also copied, as was their discarded practice of firing one *séction* at a time in staggered order.

For some little time, indeed, the French forces proved extremely dilatory in producing new ideas. Although the period saw the great burgeoning of the Age of Reason and the *Philosophes*, 'only the (French) army had no sect, no philosophers, no academy, and none were seriously concerned with its regeneration.'[80] Such men who did put their minds to military affairs generally tended to multiply 'baroque' evolutions – training the troops to form circular, triangular and other complex geometrical formations which were to all practical intents completely useless on the field of battle. This French trend reached its *apogée* (or possibly, its nadir) in one M. de Chevert, who as *aide-major* of the *Régiment de Beauce*, was highly commended by Louis xv for devising a drill whereby the troops of his regiment formed the words 'Vive le Roi' before firing a *feu de joie!*[81] Such irrelevancies earned the scorn of such thinkers as Folard and de Saxe and, as we shall have cause to describe a little later, produced a reaction towards more meaningful military manoeuvres, although in some ways the reformers' 'columns' and 'legions' were equally impractical.

Despite occasional pronouncements in favour of massed fire-power, there was scant attempt made to apply one system of drill or tactics to the French foot as a whole until 1754. Regimental commanders continued to suit themselves, concentrating on smart marching and arms drill rather than firing practice. As one percipient contemporary wrote, 'our insufficiency was remarkable, above all over firing.'[82] Every soldier was supposed to fire 40 shots a year in practice, but few ever did, the excuse being that 'cold steel' was the proper French *métier*. Very gradually, however, a measure of order and reform was imposed from above. The *Ordonnance* issued for the campaign of 1733, for example, clearly defined the organization of battalions into companies, *peletons*, sleeves and *démi-rangs*, and a measure of standardization of weapons also appeared. On the whole, however, the French infantry remained unregenerate, and it took a commander with all the practical genius of a de Saxe to allow for their deficiencies and lead them to victory at such battles as Fontenoy (1745).

* It is important to note that the French term *peleton* described a group of *two companies;* thus a French battalion only comprised a total of six platoons to the British 16 (plus two of grenadiers). The French Grenadier Company (on the right), and the 'Picquet' (on the left) fired together after the 'platoons' had discharged.

The British, on the other had, continued to evolve or copy improved forms of infantry tactics – albeit founded on the platoon firing system. But once again there was no real uniformity of method between regiments. The main development was an insistence on the regiments, while mounting an attack, *continuing to advance* (instead of halting as previously) to give fire. To achieve this form of relentless pressure, the platoons due to fire were trained to step out *ahead* of the rest of their marching battalion, which at the same time stepped short; the advanced platoons then halted to fire and by the time this was completed the remaining companies would have caught up, whereupon the platoons of the next 'firing' would draw ahead ready to give their fire in turn. Of course this type of fire tended to be somewhat less accurate, but this was more than made up for by the moral effect on the foe of the continuous advance with the implicit threat of hand-to-hand contact. It is probable that this form of infantry tactics was copied from the Prussian army, but it is impossible to be certain. Similar insistence was also laid upon the desirability of inducing the foe to fire first. (See p. 139 below).

This type of attack almost brought victory to the Allies at Fontenoy (1745). Lord Ligonier's 20 battalions (totalling 13,000 British and Hanoverian troops) advanced to contact on a three-battalion front (a more extended frontage being ruled out by the restricted space), the remainder forming three sides of a vast square or rectangular formation. Facing it stood 20 battalions of French infantry. But, as Voltaire described it, 'the square continually moves on at a slow pace, never getting into confusion, and repulsing the regiments that confront it one after another.'[83] The French line gave way, and the Allied foot penetrated their lines for a distance of 300 yards and even reached the enemy encampment. There, however, their impetus exhausted itself. The Allied cavalry failed to support the infantry and exploit this great opportunity, whilst the Dutch foot failed to capture Fontenoy itself, so the remorseless advance halted. Then, as Ligonier recorded, 'we found ourselves under a cross-fire of artillery and musketry, as well as fire from their front, and it was necessary to retire as far as the line between Fontenoy and the fort near the wood . . . Having had orders to make a second attempt, our troops . . . a second time made the enemy give way; and they were once more pushed as far as their camp with great loss of men, which we too felt upon our side.'[84] Then Saxe counter-attacked with both horse and foot and light guns, and after three more hours of staunch resistance the square again retreated in good order – but leaving one man in three as a casualty. Saxe's opinion of this encounter (as written down in 1750) had already been quoted in another context* in which he stressed admiringly the superior discipline and formations of his opponents. Even more to the point was the letter he wrote to Frederick the Great in September 1746:

The French are what they were in Caesar's time, and as he has described them, brave to excess but unstable . . . As it is impossible for me to make them what they ought to be, I get what I can out of them and try to leave nothing of importance to chance.[85]

*See p. 105 above and f.n. 54.

As a result, Saxe thenceforward won his campaigns more by manoeuvre and marching than by undertaking large battles. Both Rocoux (1746) and Laffeldt (1747) became little more than *affaires de poste*, and in both cases Saxe took care, after opening the attack, to de-escalate the battle.

The British regiments remained equally staunch in defence as they were imposing in attack. At Dettingen (1743) for example, they halted the rash French attacks with the greatest coolness.* A French officer likened them to 'a wall of brass . . . from which there issued forth so brisk and well-sustained a fire that the oldest officer owned that they had never seen anything like it, incomparably superior to ours.'[86] On this occasion, the British and their Allies do not appear to have employed the usual platoon-firing system:

'They were under no command by way of Hyde Park firing, but the whole three ranks made a running fire of their own accord, and at the same time with great judgement and skill stooping all as low as they could, making almost every ball take place.'[87]

'What preserved us,' recalled an Officer of the Welch Fusiliers, 'was our keeping close order and advancing near the enemy 'ere we fired. Several that popped at 100 paces lost more of their men and did less execution; for the French will stand fire at a distance, though 'tis plain they cannot look men in the face.'[88] Colin partly accounts for the French failure at Dettingen from the fact that they fixed bayonets too soon, thus impeding reloading with the ramrod.

The British defeats at such battles as Fontenoy and Laffeldt were not to be justly laid at the door of the infantry. As had happened two generations earlier at Steenkirk and Landen, the English army had been defeated both in attack and defence. But, as Colonel Lloyd has well described it, the infantry 'showed their old hard-fighting qualities; but they were led by men who, though able and soldierly, were no match in military talent for Luxembourg or Saxe.'[89] If Saxe won victories despite the questionable talent of much of his army, 'it was because he knew the strong and weak points of his troops and had the dexterity to secure favourable conditions for them.'

However, even the redoubtable British infantry had its bad moments during this period, as at Prestonpans, where the regiments fled before the fury of the Highlanders' attack – but these were largely untried troops led by a very mediocre commander, 'Wee Johnnie Cope'. The following year at Culloden they more than made amends for their rough handlings at Prestonpans and Falkirk: 'Sure never were soldiers in such a temper', wrote Cumberland to Ligonier, 'Silence and obedience the whole time and all our manoeuvres were performed without the least confusion . . . It was pretty enough to see our little army form from the long march into three lines twice on our march, and each time in ten minutes.'[90] The time taken to form line of battle is of particular interest.

Of course the British were not alone in producing well-trained and, in the lights of the time, effective infantry tactics for their armies. The concept of always advancing to the attack without halting was probably first used by the

*For a good modern account of Dettingen, see Peter Young, *The British Army* (London: 1967) pp. 56–65.

Swedish troops of Charles XII, who throughout the Great Northern War (1700–21) attacked their opponents in four rank formations. At Narva (1700), 9,000 Swedes charged through a snow-blizzard to rout 39,000 Russian regulars and 30,000 militia. At 40 paces from the foe the Swedes were trained to let off a volley from their two rear ranks, the front two bending down to avoid the shot; then, advancing through the smoke of their own discharge, the battalion would close to 20 paces, where the front two ranks fired at point-blank range, holding fire 'until one could reach the enemy with the bayonet'. Then the troops would close with swords and bayonets.[91] Both the Swedish regulations issued at Smorgen (1708) and Wäxjö (1710) stressed the offensive role for infantry, and the *Royal Drill-Book*, first issued by Charles XI (1680) and reissued by his son in 1701 listed fifty tactical variations,. Their Russian opponents could only withstand such ferocious attacks from within entrenchments – as at Poltava (1709) – but even there the massively out-numbered Swedes – supported by only four cannon – successfully broke through eight redoubts on the Russian right and centre before nemesis overtook them with the collapse of their less successful right wing, exploited by the counter-attack of 40,000 fresh Russians issuing from Peter the Great's strong encampment, supported by no less than 100 guns.

By 1740, however, a new major military power was on the point of moving into the forefront of European history – namely Prussia. This country's military reputation had been growing since Fehrbellin (1675). In due course its dynamic ruler, Frederick the Great, would emerge as one of the greatest leaders of History, but in the early years of his reign, as he was the first to admit, the initial victories were due far more to his men than to his personal contribution; and it was the Prussian infantry above all that was to become the widely-admired cynosure of European military attention.

The Prussian infantry was groomed for greatness by two men: Frederick William II who near-beggared his small country to build an imposing army, and his cousin, Prince Leopold, 'the Old Dessauer', who trained and equipped the foot very effectively. Leopold, it is also relevant to note, was a descendant of the Dutch genius, Maurice of Nassau, whose ideas in the early seventeenth century did so much to condition and inspire the leaders of succeeding generations. He had also fought under both Marlborough and Eugene.

Leopold's reforms of the Prussian infantry covered almost every aspect. His declared over-riding aim was to produce 'good shooting, quick loading, intrepidity and vigorous attack'.[91] To achieve this he abolished the fourth rank, improved the design of uniforms (reducing the coat length), introduced the iron ram-rod for infantry (c.1720) – it had long been used for pistols – and trained up the men to a pitch at which they could fire off three to five rounds a minute. This fire was delivered – like the British – on the move, the front-rank having fixed bayonets (from 1742 all three ranks habitually did this too). To make the greatest use of this formation, he reintroduced the cadenced step. Great pains were taken to make marching formations more closely similar to fighting ones in order to speed up the formation of the battle-line, and by marching 'in columns of sections' (some 10 files or 30 men) or in 'column of sub-sections' (when a narrow way had to be negotiated) the Prussians came near to achieving their goal. It was often possible for them to form line of battle to the flank by a simple wheel of sections – and the speed with which they proved capable of deploying at Mollwitz (1741) truly astounded their less nimble Austrian opponents.

Prussian organization for administrative purposes was the two-battalion regiment, each battalion containing five companies of musketeers and one of grenadiers. For action, somewhat resembling the British practice, each battalion was divided into two *flügel* or wings, each of which were subdivided into two divisions of two platoons apiece.[92] The grenadier companies were almost always drawn off to form special grenadier battalions of four companies each. The infantry habitually fought in brigades of two or more battalions, each under the command of a major-general.

With their phlegmatic attitude and unquestioning discipline, the Prussian foot made a doughty opponent. However much their critics might sneer at the 'walking muskets' with their unquestioning obedience, ferocious discipline, parade-like movements, and frequent blasts of ill-aimed shots, they became the best infantry in mid-eighteenth century Europe. In the presence of the foe they were capable of forming column (for movement) or line (for fire-action) by executing a simple wheel of divisions (to form a line to a flank) or by halting the leading section and marching the succeeding ones half-left and half-right into the alignment (if forming line to the front).

In action, the Prussians adopted only two firings – given alternately by the odd and the even platoons; fire by individual platoons, from right to left in turn, was also still widely employed, but under certain circumstances (such as a full brigade attack) the fire of a whole battalion would be given at once. Two light field pieces were attached to each battalion, being sited in the intervals between the flanks of neighbouring battalions. The infantry were trained to fire as they advanced at the rate of 75 paces to the minute.

The rate of fire of the Prussians – even if much of it was more noisy than effective – aroused the wonder of contemporaries. It is claimed that on occasion 2,000 men were capable of letting off 10,000 shots in 60 seconds.[93] Casualties inflicted were, however, lower than might be expected. Of one battle in 1742, it was noticed that 'the Prussian infantry position was marked by a prodigious number of cartridges, which led one to presuppose the total destruction of the Austrian infantry, of which, in fact, there were barely 2,000 killed and wounded.'[94] Nevertheless, the apparently remorseless advance of the Prussian infantry was a stirring sight. At Mollwitz, for instance, after Frederick's cavalry had been totally routed and most of his guns lost, and while the monarch himself was riding fast away from an apparently hopeless field, the Prussian commander, General Schwerin, was asked to give the line of retreat for what remained of the army. 'Over the bodies of the enemy' was his reply. Then, according to an Austrian source,

> The whole front seemed to be moved by a single impulse; it came on step by step with astonishing uniformity. At the same time their artillery was served without intermission with shot and case,* and as soon as they were within

*Probably double-shotted – i.e. a round of hard shot superimposed on one of canister.

good range their musketry fire was not silent for a moment, but was like a continuous roll of thunder.[95]

Faced by such a spectacle, the Austrian infantry refused to attack, and in the end Neipperg had to concede the day and order a retreat. Clearly, the Prussian infantry was not be be scorned; but its greatest days still lay ahead.

The champions of columnar formation and light infantry tactics

All the tactical concepts described so far in this chapter were basically designed to achieve maximum fire-power at short range, utilizing linear formations of battle to this end, the aim being to blast the enemy off the field by a series of devastating volleys. Despite the aggressive 'advancing fire' of the English and Prussians, there was still little idea of forcing a way through the opponent's line by true shock action. Such an idea, it seemed, had disappeared with the pikes. However, in the second quarter of the eighteenth century a number of influential military figures began to question the validity of the almost total dependence on fire-power, advocating instead a return to tactics based on physical shock and cold steel. The resultant great contention between *l'ordre profonde* (column) and *l'ordre mince* (line) was to continue for the rest of the eighteenth century.

The Spanish Marquis de Santa-Cruz, writing in the 1730s, called for the adoption of combined linear and columnar formations. He envisaged the continued use of the two conventional lines, each four ranks deep (with some infantry in deep columns), but wished to place columns of horse and foot between the lines, the infantry ones being 30 men wide and fifteen deep. He also wished to see the cavalry interspersed with the infantry at regular intervals down the front of both lines, rather than their being kept on the wings or in massed reserve in the rear. In other words, he advocated a great increase in the strength and roles of mutually supporting formations, and the combination of fire and shock, of horse and foot, in near-equal proportions. His centrally-placed formations of the 'middle line' thus in fact became a balanced all-arm reserve, capable of redeployment as need arose.

A second writer of greater influence was the French Chevalier de Folard (1669–1752). Like Santa-Cruz, he deplored the amount of attention devoted to the production of pure fire-power, and was highly critical of linear formations as a whole on the grounds that they were very hard to manoeuvre effectively. 'The way we fight is full of vital errors,' he wrote. 'Our battalions can neither attack nor defend themselves adequately because they fight with so little depth that it is easy to break them.' He believed that by adopting deep formations and re-arming a proportion of troops with the pike, together with the deployment of large numbers of light infantry, decisive advantages would result. To support his case, he referred to two actions during the Spanish Succession struggle – namely Spire (1703) and Denain (1712) – both of which were basically won by French infantry charging with the bayonet. On the first occasion the foot had charged straight through the Imperialist forces without deploying from column of march;

on the second, victory was assured by the action of numbers of columns of varying size, headed by grenadier detachments and pickets. Although neither occasion had been a proper ranged battle, Folard believed that these examples demonstrated that the French *métier* was the infantry charge using basically cold steel; he might also have referred to Catinat's success at Marsala (4 October 1693) where victory was won by a gallant bayonet-attack by the French infantry drawn up in line; on this occasion only the grenadier companies and pickets had leave to fire at all throughout the action. On the other hand, he was particularly critical of Villars' showing at Malplaquet, where the French foot had been handled wholly defensively. This, be believed, was a betrayal of the French character, 'which is infinitely better suited for shock and for *coups de main* than for standing still and firing'.

Folard's thinking went through several stages, but in essence he desired a series of columns, between one and six battalions strong, drawn up one behind the other and screened by light infantry. The larger columns would have a frontage of between 24 and 30 files, and a depth of some 40 to 50 ranks. One man in five was to be equipped with a partizan, these troops being placed on the front and flanks. A smaller two battalion version was designed comprising 16 files and 30–36 ranks (see illustration), the main body being divided into three sections, and the grenadiers drawn up apart either in front or to the rear. He also devised theories whereby this formation could deploy into line (see diagram) for fire action when this was imperative, but basically it was a *force de frappe*. Advancing as a mighty phalanx, the column would split the enemy's lines asunder before subdividing into two halves; one would turn right, the second left, and then both would proceed (in theory) to roll up the foe's lines towards his flanks. 'The column exists for use in action; it is not required to fire, but will close with the enemy to exchange blows with cold steel.'[96]

Such ideas were bold if somewhat far-fetched. As Folard's most distinguished critic, Maurice de Saxe, observed, 'Chevalier Folard has been the only one who has dared to pass the bounds of these prejudices [i.e. those favouring linear formations]. But Chevalier Folard goes goo far. He does not realize that courage must be reborn daily.'[97] Saxe was particularly dubious about the ability of these columns to manoeuvre sufficiently adroitly to exploit the break-through, once achieved; and he also pointed out that Folard was decidedly vague about the drill movements required to carry out his column's evolutions. Nevertheless, Folard's ideas were widely borrowed by military theorists and tried out in several forms – and some of them were later enshrined in the Regulations of 1753 and 1754, and the *Ordonnance* of 1755, and survived for a considerable time. It is doubtful whether this would have happened had Saxe lived, for the greatest soldier and thinker of his time was convinced that such measures could only lead to great confusion and crowding-up under the stresses and strains of the battlefield.

The tactical ideas of Maurice de Saxe (1696–1750) were considerably more practicable than those of Folard, although their immediate impact on military thought proved mainly transitory. His military thought, as revealed in his letters to Frederick the Great and above all in his famous *Rêveries* (published seven years after his death but written in 1732), was mature and sensible if in some

Chevalier Folard's order of battle with infantry and cavalry in alternative brigades

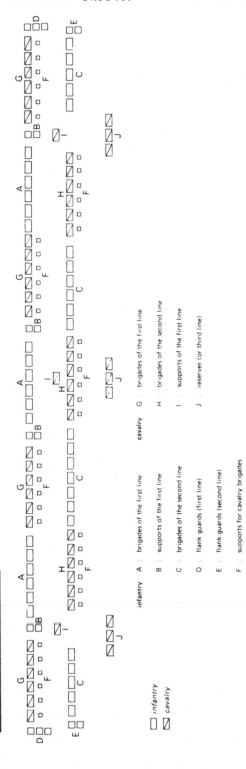

☐ *infantry*

▨ *cavalry*

infantry   A :   brigades of the first line

          B :   supports of the first line

          C :   brigades of the second line

          D :   flank guards (first line)

          E :   flank guards (second line)

          F :   supports for cavalry brigades

cavalry   G :   brigades of the first line

          H :   brigades of the second line

          I :   supports of the first line

          J :   reserves (or third line)

small respects reactionary. The *Rêveries* were composed during a period of illness. In a 'Note to the Reader' he explained the circumstances: 'I wrote this book in thirteen nights: I was sick; thus it very probably shows the effects of the fever I had. This should supply my excuses for the irregularity of the arrangement, as well as for the inelegance of the style. I wrote militarily and to dissipate my boredom. Done in the month of December, 1732.'[98] These circumstances led Thomas Carlyle to describe the book as 'a strange Military Farrago, dictated, I should think, under opium'.[99] Certainly the book roves backwards and forwards over the whole field of the military art, but most of the contents are admirably clear, concise and to the point, full of shrewd observations based on first-hand military experience.

We are only directly concerned here with Saxe's concern for the reform of infantry tactics.* Like both Santa-Cruz and Folard, he was very dubious about the great importance accorded to fire-power by most contemporaries. 'Powder is not as terrible as is believed. Few men in these affairs are killed from in front or while fighting. I have seen whole salvoes fail to kill four men . . .'[100] In so far as he supported fire tactics, in the attack, he was firmly convinced about the wisdom of the delayed volley, reinforcing the school that believed it was a vital tactical consideration to induce the enemy to fire first. Hence the famous incident at Fontenoy when the French officers invited their opponents to open fire: 'Messieurs les Anglais, tirez les premiers.' As Daniel wrote, recalling Louis XIV's precept, 'We must teach the soldier to hold his fire and to withstand that of the enemy, for an enemy who has fired is assuredly beaten when we still retain our full fire.'[101] The point was that the practical and psychological advantage rested with the troops who still had their fire to give after surviving the enemy's discharge – for they could continue to advance whilst the enemy were reloading. However, even this belief was considerably qualified by de Saxe. Admitting its general validity for combats against European opponents, he rejected it as a means for fighting the Turk. He had been present at the battle of Belgrade (1717), and had seen two Imperial battalions massacred largely *because* they held their fire until the Turks were at only 30 paces.

> The fire and the *mêlée* were simultaneous and the two battalions did not have time to flee for every man was cut to pieces on the spot. The only person who escaped were M. de Neuperg, who, fortunately for him, was on a horse, and an ensign with his colour, who clung to my horse's main and bothered me not a little, and two or three soldiers . . . (later) I had curiosity enough to count the dead: I found only 32 Turks killed by the general discharge of the two battalions – which has not increased my regard for infantry fire.[102]

Saxe, like Folard, was convinced that the combination of shock action and cold steel – *supported* by properly conducted fire-action – was the ideal form of infantry tactics. To achieve this, he advocated the reorganization of the infantry into what he termed 'legions' (3,600 men in all). Each of these was to comprise

*Saxe's proposed use of cavalry and of light infantry have been described above; see p. 58 and p. 72 respectively.

four regiments, with four 'centuries' apiece, together with a 'half-century' of light infantry and another of light cavalry. Each 'century' was to contain 150 private soldiers besides some 34 officers, NCOs and drummers at full war establishment – in a total of 10 small companies. For the legion's support he attached two 12-pounders per legion and invented an imaginary light cannon – to be called an *amusette* – firing a half-pound ball to a range of 4,000 yards and light enough to be carried by two soliders. There were to be 16 *amusettes* per legion. Instead of grenadiers, whom he believed to be killed off too quickly to make their retention economical, he suggested a grade of 'veterans' who would always form the nucleus of the centuries in times of both peace and war. As for infantry weapons, he desired a 5-foot breach-loading musket firing a one-ounce ball, with a maximum range of 1,200 paces, and a $2\frac{1}{2}$-foot bayonet (dual-purpose), of the *plug* variety, to ensure that troops attacking with cold steel were incapable of giving fire without specific direction. Instead of tentpoles, fully half the men would carry light hollow-shafted, 13-foot *démi-piques* (weighing about 4lbs) and every man was to carry a light shield into action, two of which, superimposed, were to be ball-proof.

Preparing to attack, the individual regiment would adopt a four-deep line, musketeers occupying the front two ranks, pikemen (with slung muskets) the third and fourth. Advancing against infantry in a series of small, hardy company columns, the pikes were to be lowered so as to project ahead of the musketeers, whilst the light infantry formed a screen to the front and (as the range shortened) on the flanks, firing their (imaginary) breach-loaders to harass the enemy. The cavalry sections meanwhile were to take post in the rear, ready to exploit the foe's flight.

By Saxe's system, two battalions would often fight in a single formation thus producing a total depth of eight ranks – his ideal.

> I am formed eight ranks deep and have no fear of confusion; my charge is violent and my march rapid; I do not fear confusion and I shall always outflank the enemy although equal in numbers.

And in another place, stressing the superior mobility of his two-battalion column, he writes

> I am eight ranks deep against men who are only four deep; I have nothing to check me, no loss of dressing or crowding up; I shall cover 200 paces sooner than they will cover 100; I shall be through the enemy in a moment if it comes to cold steel; and if he fires he is done for.[103]

When it came to a firefight (for example when intervening obstacles made it impossible to come to close grips), Saxe had decided views on how it should be conducted. He had no time for platoon-fire which he regarded as wasteful, inaccurate and ineffective. Instead he advocated an adaptation of carefully controlled fire-at-will by carefully selected leaders which was in some way, a reversion to a mid-seventeenth century practice.

> I should designate an officer or non-commissioned officer to every two files.

He should advance the [file-] leader of the first a pace forward and show him where he is to direct his fire, allowing him to fire at will; that is when he has found a target.

The soldier behind him will then pass his gun forward and the others in the same manner. The file leader will thus execute four shots in succession. It would be unusual if the second or third shot does not reach its mark. The commanding officer is close by him, watches his aim, directs him where to fire, and exhorts him not to hurry ...

This file having fired [i.e. four times], the officer withdraws it and advances the second which performs in the same fashion. Then he returns the first which has had ample time to load. This can be repeated for several hours.

This fire is the most deadly of all, and I do not think any other can resist it. It would silence that by platoons or ranks, and even if they were all Caesars I would defy them to hold for a quarter of an hour. [104]

Notice Saxe's conviction that carefully aimed rounds cause the most casualties – and also that it took at least two or three aimed shots to secure a hit. Saxe calculated that a man could fire off at least four aimed rounds in sixty seconds by this system – or a possible 60 in 15 minutes – so that in that period a battalion of 500 men 'will have fired 30,000 [shots], not considering the light-armed forces.' In an hour – including the contribution of the light infantry, a theoretical 140,000 shots could thus be delivered, 'all better aimed than ordinary fire'. Of course no musket of the day could have produced such a sustained rate of fire, given the fouling of the barrels by the coarse powder and the need to change the flints at regular intervals.

Concerning the employment of light infantry – a type of foot-soldier he joined with Folard in advocating – Saxe called for 70 disciplined sharpshooters for each legion. During the legion's advance, they would operate in a skirmishing line ahead of the columns, opening fire at about 300 yards. Continuing to close with the enemy, at 50 paces they would draw aside and fall back as the main body charged through, ready to deal with any parts of the enemy who might attempt to infiltrate into the twenty-yard intervals between company columns. In other words, Saxe's basic principle was that 'shock must be preceded by fire.'

His conviction that 'the attack is best suited to the French temperament' received a rude check at Dettingen (1743), where the most ferocious French efforts failed to make any impression on the British and Allied infantry. Nevertheless, some of the French infantry at Fontenoy two years later adopted his formations. Thus in their attack against the massive British column, the four battalions of the *Régiment de Normandie* advanced in two lines, and the two battalions of the *Gardes* in as many columns, and between them six battalions of Irish *'étranger'* troops, sustained by the five battalions of the Regiments of *Eu* and *Vaisseaux*. However, as we have already seen Saxe was a realist, and soon appreciated that the quality of the available French troops was insufficient to permit the implementation of his ideas without a long period of preparation, whilst the forces of military conservatism were also not to be taken lightly. Accordingly he considerably modified his infantry methods to suit the revealed foibles of the instrument, and adopted a form of fighting based on redoubts and *points d'appui* not wholly dissimilar to those employed by the much maligned Villars in the centre at Malplaquet. Their effectiveness was demonstrated at Fontenoy, together with Saxe's major conviction that 'the principles which M. de Montecuculi has given us in his Memoirs are correct. He says that infantry should always be supported by cavalry, and cavalry by infantry. Nevertheless, we do not practise it.'[105] Saxe at least tried to practise this inter-arm co-operation, and his string of victories in the War of the Austrian Succession were due to this tenet of his military doctrine to no small extent.

After his death, however, many of Saxe's ideas were forgotten or disregarded for two generations. Some officers tried to keep his principles before the military authorities – including his chief of staff, d'Herouville, who wrote his *'Traité des légions'* in the 1750s. In very many ways, however, Saxe was too far ahead of his day to gain recognition. Some credit him with devising the first all-arm divisional organization, a formation which became the norm in the 1790s. He had a far deeper insight into tactics than any other contemporary. He saw the need for a breech-loading musket, and truly light supporting weapons. He planned to break open the enemy attacks with skirmisher fire before counter-attacking in force. In the attack, he saw the need to combine fire with shock, the skirmishers again preparing the way for the columns. He reintroduced into the French army marching in step and to music. He rejected the 'sacred cow' of massed volley-firing, substituting the concept of individual marksmanship. Aware of the disadvantages of Folard's massed columns, he preached the need for smaller, more mobile formations that would yet be heavy enough to crush a way through the enemy opposition. He also believed in the ruthless pursuit, stern but humane discipline, the need to toughen the troops by hard marching, and the need for a comprehensive military organization that approximated to a divisional system. Above all, he was fully aware of the importance of moral factors in war. 'With a knowledge of the human heart,' he wrote, 'one is dependent upon the favour of fortune, which is sometimes very inconsistent.'[106] He saw straight through Folard's conviction that the bravery of French troops could be taken for granted, just as clearly as he saw the defects in his tactical schemes. But it would not be until the coming of the French Revolution that the greater number of his ideas – or adaptations of them – would receive the credit and attention they deserved. On the other hand, a few of his ideas – such as the reintroduction of pikes, and the use of shields – were hopelessly outdated and would never be adopted.

*   *   *

At this point we must leave our study of the infantry arm and its tactics and turn to consider other parts of the armed forces of the period. In conclusion, however, we can make the following summary of main points. First, that infantry was becoming more important than previously owing to its improved fire potential. Second, that the improvement of tactical techniques based upon fire-power gave the British and Dutch a great advantage on many a battlefield − whilst their main opponent (and also their Austrian ally) proved slow in the extreme to abandon out-dated and less-effective methods. Third, that this change in tactics was closely associated with improvements in infantry weapons, and led to the adoption of thinner linear formations for battle, which were, however, distinctly immobile. Fourth, that as a result the all-importance of fire received an undue amount of unquestioning acceptance, and that therefore it can be claimed that infantry tactics, taken as a whole, were stagnant for the half century from 1700, although a few enlightened military thinkers − mainly Frenchmen or soldiers serving the French cause − were beginning to prepare the way for a new approach, in which fire and shock would be given carefully balanced representation, and above all a higher degree of importance would be accorded to infantry mobility on the battlefield. Fifth, that only Saxe's suggestions for columns of attack were really valid and practicable propositions. And lastly, that the long eclipse of light infantry was drawing to a close, and with their return a further impetus would eventually be given to the adoption of extended, highly mobile formations, and a more enlightened attitude towards the individual infantry soldier, too long regarded as a form of cannon-fodder incapable of independent thought or action. It would be another half-century, however, before this became widely accepted in France, and even longer before the armies of most other European powers adopted such enlightened attitudes.

APPENDIX TO PART TWO: THE FOOT

TABLE OF REPRESENTATIVE INFANTRY WEAPONS

Type	Approx date	Calibre	Barrel length	Weapon length	Bayonet blade	Weight with bayonet
Mousquet à l'ordinaire (French matchlock)	1690	20–22 balls to lb.	3ft 8ins	5ft	2ft 8ins (plug)	6 kilograms
English matchlock	1690	.80in	3ft 10in	5ft 2in	1ft 9in (plug)	12lbs 8ozs
'William III' flintlock	1696	.85in	3ft 6½in	5ft	1ft 9in (plug)	11lbs 8ozs
Swedish flintlock	1696	.676in	3ft 8in	5ft	1ft 6in (plug)	5 kilograms
French *fusil ordinaire*	1703	.68in	3ft 8in	5ft	1ft 10in (ring)	5 kilograms
English 'Brown Bess'	1720	.75in	3ft 10in	5ft 2in	1ft 5in (socket)	11lbs 13ozs
French *fusil*	1740	18 balls to lb.	3ft 10in	4ft 10in	49cms (socket)	9lbs 12ozs
English 'long land musket'	1740	.75in	3ft 10in	5ft 2in	1ft 6in (socket)	11lbs 13ozs
English 'short land musket'	1740	.75in	3ft 6in	4ft 10in	1ft 6in (socket)	11lbs 9ozs
English 'sea-service musket'	1740	.75in	3ft 1in	4ft 5in	1ft 6in (socket)	10lbs 10ozs

NOTE: These are dimensions of specific weapons: there were, however, considerable variations within classes; the ones given, however, can be regarded as about average.

Part III

The Artillery Trains

9

Roles, representation and basic organization

The place of the artillery services in the late seventeenth and eighteenth centuries

After the Horse and Foot, the third major component of all field armies was formed by their artillery services. Throughout the seventeenth and eighteenth centuries these remained huge and complex organizations of vast authority and influence for both good and ill, and in the case of England at least the Board of Ordnance approximated in status to a Department of State. The situation was not very different in France and the Habsburg Empire, where the authority of the *Grand Maître de l'Artillerie* and his appointed officers, or of the Austrian *Feldseckhmeister* and his *Büchsenmeister* was almost as paramount as that of the English Master-General of the Ordnance over all matters pertaining to the artillery and associated services. The scope of this authority embraced every aspect of the art and science of gunnery, from the manufacture, testing and servicing of the cannon to the provision and training of artillery officers and gun crews; it also included a whole host of ancillary duties relating to the supply of weapons, munitions and other martial stores for use by the armed forces as a whole (and in the case of England this incuded responsibility for much naval equipment as well as military), whilst other tasks included the provision of bridging trains, transportation, field engineering and pioneer services, and the maintenance of fortresses and barracks. Thus the Ordnance departments wielded enormous influence over almost every field of military activity in times of both peace and war, but of all their responsibilities the provision of the guns remained the most significant.

The desirable properties of an artillery arm in any generation can be categorized as follows. High on the list comes a satisfactory degree of mobility, both along roads and cross-country, for both the guns and their ancillary services; if the pieces are too cumbersome and therefore tend to be late into action, their usefulness to a general is minimal. Secondly, a high rate of fire is clearly desirable; it must be at least as rapid as the enemy's, and ideally somewhat faster. In the third place, however, the effect of a high rate of fire is largely vitiated unless shot and shell are accurately aimed and capable of achieving a good range; here questions of weapon technology and instrumentation come into prominence. Fourthly, the ability to achieve quick repairs, and if necessary to interchange parts, is of obvious importance, whilst the provisions of adequate supplies of ammunition, readily available for both immediate use and for sustained bombardment, is another *sine qua non* of successful operation. The high degree of professional competence required to integrate these multifarious and complementary aspects of handling artillery effectively leads to probably the most vital consideration of all: the provision of well-trained and highly disciplined personnel, officers, gunners, specialist craftsmen and drivers, all working as a closely integrated team. For without a high degree of co-operation between all elements the artillery can become more of a burden than an asset in operations of war. This part of the book is concerned with showing how far these *desiderata* were achieved during the late seventeenth and the first half of the eighteenth centuries.

As will be seen, the artillery systems of this period are relatively clumsy and frequently defective in important respects. The combination of such obstacles as weighty pieces, the harnessing of draught-horses in tandem, the need to operate over execrable roads, the dependence on contractors for both horses and team-drivers, the relative under-development of practicable waterways and river-transport, and above all the financial stringency imposed by cheese-paring if not near-bankrupt governments, made the operation of effective artillery services difficult in the extreme during our period, and it would not be until the second half of the eighteenth century that such re-forming experts as Gribeauval would revolutionize the employment and organization of the artillery.

Yet no army — nor navy for that matter — could operate successfully without its proper complement of guns. In battle they were called upon to defend the lines of battalions and squadrons by silencing the opposing batteries and by unsettling (with roundshot at long range) or decimating (with caseshot at closer distance) the formations of enemy troops. High-angle howitzers were required to lob shells so as to destroy buildings or render frontal cover ineffective; airbursts were on occasions found useful for terrifying cavalry horses. The comfortingly loud discharges of friendly artillery in the close vicinity of one's own formations, moreover, served the useful psychological purpose of sustaining the morale of the rank and file during the long, anxious minutes before close action was engaged, or during equally trying lulls in the battle. In attack, the guns would help to shoot the horse and foot onto their objectives by engaging enemy strong points and hindering the deployment of hostile reserves. In the event of defeat, the guns could on some occasions cover 'the bringing-off' or withdrawal of the discomfited troops, and form a convenient rallying-place.

When sieges were undertaken, the artillery had equally vital roles to perform. Whilst the heavy guns steadily pounded breaches through the enemy defences and fortifications, thus opening a way into the heart of the fortress for the infantry assault columns, the howitzers and mortars would strive to sweep the enemy ramparts, hindering the enemy's gun-crews and garrison at their duties, thus covering the work of the pioneers and soldiers in the approach-trenches. Sometimes they would turn their destructive attentions against the houses beyond the bastions with the intention of lowering the morale of the civilian population by wreaking havoc in the town. Meanwhile, some lighter field pieces of the besieging army would be carefully sited in outward-looking positions, ready to repulse any attempt by an enemy force to interfere with the siege from without, whilst others would be ready to destroy any attempt by the beleagured garrison to make a sortie.

Artillery had as important a place at sea as on land. The gun-decks of the ships of war would roar with repeated massive broadsides, often killing the wind in the process, in attempts to bring down the enemy vessels' masts and rigging and thus render them helpless, to dismount his guns and decimate his crews with shot and deadly wooden splinters, and ultimately to pound his battered hulks to such an effect that they caught fire, blew-up, sank or struck their colours. Smaller pieces on the upper decks would be kept loaded with charges of grape and canister shot, ready to meet enemy boarders with a hurricane of fire as they attempted to clamour aboard or, conversely, ready to sweep clear an opponent's decks immediately prior to the order 'boarders away'. On other occasions ships' guns would be employed to engage enemy fortresses guarding ports and dockyards, and even to break up marching columns of enemy armies were they so rash as to use coastal roads in the proximity of deep water close inshore and thus come within range of the beautiful but deadly wooden-walls with their massed broadsides. Well might Napoleon declaim in a later generation that 'it is with artillery that war is made.'[1]

To revert from the general to the particular, by the late seventeenth century, contemporaries were becoming increasingly aware of the importance of artillery – but at the same time many experts were often highly critical of its organization and conduct. Louis xiv inscribed his guns with the motto: *Ultima Ratio Regis* – 'the last argument of the king', and writing in 1721, Père Daniel declared 'without it [artillery], nothing can be done.'[2] No general would risk the chances of a field engagement without the presence of at least a proportion of his guns; nor could a full-scale siege be undertaken without the assistance of the heavy cannon. In a letter to Cadogan (charged with escorting the 'Great Convoy' to Lille in August 1708), Marlborough urgently wrote: 'For God's sake be sure you do not risk the cannon.'[3] Some soldiers, indeed, already regarded the movements of the artillery trains as the most significant feature of military operations. Thus Sergeant Millner of the Royal Regiment of Foot of Ireland, noted in his 'Compendious Journal' that he calculated the true start and end of each campaign from the dates the train set out from, or returned to, winter quarters, 'it is being the metropolitan ensign of any army in time of war.'[4] In the English armies in Flanders it was also the frequent practice for army headquarters to move and encamp with the artillery, the convoy's standard being displayed from a special socket on a gun-carriage. There was thus a wide consensus that the trains had a large – even a determinant – part to play in the conduct of campaigns. A few generations later the greatest artilleryist of history, Napoleon Bonaparte, would declare that artillery formed the most important part of his armies, and although no early eighteenth century commander would have wholly subscribed to his view that 'great battles are won by artillery' (save, possibly the

great Luxembourg who was one of the first soldiers to advocate massed batteries)
few would have demurred from the Emperor's dictum that 'it is necessary to
have as much artillery as the enemy.'[5] Nor would the French artillery expert,
Suriry de Saint-Rémy, or Albert Borgard, first Colonel of the British Regiment
of Royal Artillery, or for that matter 'Bombardier' Ahmed Pasha de Bonneval
(the French ex-Colonel of the *Gardes Françaises* who refashioned the Turkish
artillery in the 1730s), have wholly disagreed with the conviction of Napoleon's
nephew that, 'l'histoire de l'artillerie est l'histoire du progrès des sciences, et
partant de la civilization.'[6]

Conversely, the artillery trains of our period also came in for a great deal of
adverse criticism. The most commonly voiced objection was connected with their
bulk and the slow rate of progress over the generally execrable roads of Europe
which their presence imposed on armies in the field. The majority of guns
weighed three tons apiece (trails and carriages included), and most needed six or
eight horses harnessed in tandem to draw them, whilst the trains also included
many hundreds of munition and store waggons. Clearly this volume of traffic
had to be accorded first priority on whatever roads were available, forcing both
infantry and cavalry into marching through the muddy fields in parallel
columns; this fact alone was hardly calculated to increase the love of the
fantassin or trooper for his colleagues in the artillery while on campaign. An
army's trains could cover many miles of road. Marlborough's 'Great Convoy' of
1708, to cite one notable example, required no less than 16,000 horses to drag its
80 heavy guns, 20 siege mortars and 3,000 assorted waggons, and its two
sections covered a total of 30 miles of highway. Such vast convoys were special
cases, and in most instances the heavy siege trains moved separately from their
parent armies, being called up from the rear — whenever possible by river or
canal barges — once a particular siege had been decided upon. Nevertheless,
many trains of field artillery were sufficiently large to form a considerable
hindrance to the movement of the armies, often ruling out schemes of
imaginative or bold manoeuvre. William III's relatively small Train of 1692, for
example, comprised 38 brass cannon and some 240 four-horse waggons of
munitions and ordnance stores (besides further large numbers of baggage and
supply waggons). Fifty-six years later, the French artillery train intended for
Flanders (1748) totalled 150 cannon, 397 waggons and 2,965 horses.[7] The
transportation of such formations and the provision of adequate forage for their
draught-horses often presented almost insoluble problems for every commanding
general, however brilliant, and in the event of unseasonable weather the
aggravated problems could bring major operations to a halt until conditions
improved. As Captain Robert Parker noted, wet weather halted operations in
Flanders for three weeks in 1707, and 'it was late July before the artillery could
be raised from the ground',[8] and many similar instances could be cited. Only a
very few generals were prepared to circumvent this problem by leaving their
heavier pieces behind in order to achieve superior mobility (as Marlborough did
in May 1704 for his rule-defying march from the Netherlands to the Danube,
and it would be still some considerable time before the experts designed lighter
cannon, improved gun-carriages and limbers, or better ways of harnessing the

horses in order to tackle the problem from its foundations.

A second perennial complaint was that the guns were often late into action. Responsibility for this was often laid wholly at the door of the train conductors – somewhat unfairly, for until about 1713 it was common practice for commanders-in-chief to relegate their artillery to the rear of the army with the baggage trains; thereafter, as will be seen, it became increasingly the practice to give the guns higher movement priority and even to divide them into brigades accompanying the various columns near their head so as to facilitate their entry into battle. Similarly, difficult conditions of ground often accounted for the late arrival of guns into battle. As Colonel Jacob Richards recalled of the artillery's march down to the Scheldt on 25 August 1692, shortly after Steenkirk, 'the soile [*sic*] is richest in these parts so that the roads were not able to beare the great weight of our artillerie, which made our march very tedious and was the reason that the army was engaged before we could come up with them.'[9]

Another frequent complaint was that the artillery tended to be unreliable in action. This was not so much a criticism of the competence or courage of the actual gunners, or of the quality of their pieces, as of the civilian drivers and boys who were in charge of the horse teams for both guns and waggons. It would still be many a long year before these personnel became truly militarized in any European army, the main reason being that the bulk of every army's transport and horses was still acquired one campaign at a time, by arrangement with civilian contractors, who insisted on supplying their own drivers (doubtless in the hope of keeping an eye on their property). Such civilian-drivers had obviously even less desire to find a 'glorious death' on a hard-fought field than the average soldier, and tended to flee in droves when danger threatened. Thus, when the Duke of Monmouth's West Country rebels attacked Feversham's camp at Western Zoyland on the misty night of 5-6 July 1685, it needed the services of Dr Peter Mews, Bishop of Winchester and former Cavalier in the Great Civil War, a chance visitor to the Royal camp, to bring up the guns from their park by harnessing his coach horses to each of them in turn. We can also hazard a guess that the professional gunners (or a proportion of them) had shared in the drivers' flight at this same battle of Sedgemoor, for Sergeant Weems of Dumbarton's Regiment was later awarded a special grant of £40 for the part he and other infantrymen had played in manning the guns.[10] Nor were the drivers of the ammunition waggons any more trustworthy, if we may judge from the 'Wynendael' tapestry at Blenheim Palace, which clearly shows a sergeant 'encouraging' a faint-heart with the point of his halberd (see illustration 13). Such difficulties were not, of course, special to the English army. Writing of Blenheim, the Comte de Mérode-Westerloo recalled a similar instance affecting the French guns: 'I then re-formed some sort of a line,' he wrote, 'and placed four pieces of artillery in front of my position – I had noticed them trying to sneak off and promptly commandeered them.'[11]

Underlying many complaints against the artillery – and consequently vitiating much of their validity – was the rankling knowledge that many of its personnel received higher rates of pay than the ordinary rank and file, and that their uniforms and equipment were generally of better quality. Some officers of cavalry and infantry also professed to scorn their artillery colleagues on account of the training they were expected to undergo and the examinations they were usually called upon to pass before promotion. The gentlemen 'amateur' tended to distrust the more truly 'professional' engineers or gunners. But probably the greatest source of contention that existed until at least the 1720s was the awareness that most gunners, pioneers, 'tin-boatmen' and 'matrosses'* were not really to be deemed proper soliders at all, recruited and paid as they were by a semi-autonomous and civilian organization existing outside the regular army which could often ignore or evade the directions of even senior generals with complete impunity. Here lay the source of much friction, and it would remain to bedevil military relations to a greater or lesser extent until the creation of regular Regiments of Artillery within the main army frameworks led to a closer *rapprochement* between the two rival military authorities. Nevertheless, throughout the period the artillery organizations and their trains gave generally sterling service to their respective armies, as even their most grudging critics usually had to admit in the last analysis. We shall have occasion on a later page to describe some of the gunners' most outstanding feats, which helped found the great traditions and *esprits de corps* of the various national regiments of artillery. In sum we can avow that all military commanders and the bulk of their armies regarded their gunners with considerable (if concealed) respect; the artillery trains might often constitute a grievous burden on the prosecution of effective military operations, but it was widely recognized by the 1700s that their services were indispensable.

The representation of the artillery within armies

'A numerous artillery is necessary for forming great enterprises, for attacking a foe with advantage, and for facilitating the defence of an army.'[2] So wrote Le Blond in the latter half of the eighteenth century. Balancing the advantages and disadvantages his conclusion was that the ideal size for an army was 50,000 men equipped with 50 cannon (mostly 8- and 4-pdrs with a few pieces of 12 and 16), with an additional artillery reserve of 20 spare guns 'especially if the defence or reduction of entrenchments is contemplated'. What Le Blond termed 'the ancient idea' of providing a proportion of one gun for every 1,000 men, certainly dates back to the reign of Louis xiv if not earlier. Surirey de St Rémy, whose great work, *Mémoires d'Artillerie*, first appeared in 1697, also advised a force of 50 cannon for an army of 50,000 men (viz. four 24-pdrs, six of 12, and 20 each of pieces of four and eight), claiming that such an artillery force operating in Flanders would require 1,225 horses and 183 waggons.[13] Such standards, however, were not always obtainable during the long Spanish Succession War. Writing in 1733, de Saxe reached considerably different conclusions, postulating an army of 46,000 men supported by 50 16-pdrs, 12 mortars, and 160 of his

---

*A 'matrosse' was an assistant gunner, who often wielded the rammer and sponge and was armed with a musket to help defend the pieces in hand-to-hand fighting. See p. 206 below.

imaginary $\frac{1}{2}$-pdr *amusettes*. Thus as the eighteenth century wore on there was a gradual trend towards increasing the proportionate representation of the artillery arm in terms of cannon both in theory and in fact (see p. 150 for the comparative table of guns used in a selection of battles over the period). This growth was due on the practical side to the increasing number of improvements being slowly incorporated in the equipment of the trains as regards weight and mobility, together with a growing awareness of the theoretical tactical value of the arm as a potential battle-winning weapon, although it would not be until the Napoleonic wars that a proportion of up to four cannon per 1,000 men would be deemed either advisable or feasible.

A number of considerations had to be taken into account before the generals could settle the ideal number of guns for their armies. Besides the obvious question of availability (not often a problem in our period as almost all the governments of the *ancien régime* proved quite capable of meeting all requirements for artillery *matériel*), matters concerning the type of terrain over which the campaign would be fought were often of tantamount importance. Thus an army about to conduct a mountain campaign in the Alps or Pyrenees would reduce its guns to a minimum, leaving behind all the larger and most of the medium pieces in the interests of retaining some degree of mobility. Similarly, it was widely held that armies serving in 'the cockpit of Europe' and, as a general rule in North Italy, would require considerably less in the way of field guns and munitions accompanying them into the field than those serving in Germany or Eastern Europe. The main reason underlying this calculation was that in both the Netherlands and the Po valley – both of which regions were amply provided with fortress-towns and cities – it would be possible for commanders to draw a considerable part of their requirements from local sources; for campaigns in sparsely populated Germany on the other hand, or for operations associated with frontier wars, particularly in South-East Europe, where towns were often few and far between and distances for magazines would be inevitably greater, a more elaborate and comprehensive provision of guns and munitions had to accompany the armies from the outset.

A further major consideration was the type of rôle envisaged by contemporaries for the artillery on active operations and the consequent number of guns they deemed necessary for its implementation. This subject will be treated at greater length in the chapter devoted to gunnery tactics (below) but it is relevant here to note some salient points. Until the 1730s the main concepts remained defensive so far as battle was concerned, and only partly offensive in the even more circumscribed field of siege warfare. In battle, the artillery was expected to perform a double rôle – namely to sustain the over-extended and potentially fragile lines of battle, and, secondly, to form batteries to support key points in both attack and defence.

There were, however, somewhat more aggressive ideas prevalent in those armies that had extemporized a form of regimental artillery, more particularly the English, Austrian, Swedish and Dutch, where the infantry battalions' 3-pdrs accompanied their parent formations in attack as well as defence. Even larger guns were occasionally re-deployed to meet mobile tactical requirements, as was the case with the battery led up by Colonel Blood at Blenheim over the Nebel stream during the critical fighting around Oberglau, or with the guns brought into action against Taviers village by the Dutch Guards at Ramillies. Nevertheless, until the greater number of artillery pieces became lighter and handier, their rôle remained fundamentally defensive and static, and these considerations did much to determine the number of guns needed by an army in the field. Even in the 1750s Le Blond could assert that the basic criterion was that sufficient guns should be provided to ensure adequate *protection* for every sector of the battle-lines which might become exposed to enemy attack. [14] Sixty years earlier, St Rémy had written that 'what is really of importance in the final analysis, as experience has taught me, is that you should be able to place one brigade of cannon on the right of your army's line and another on the left . . . to prevent the enemy from taking the army in flank.' This he firmly regarded as far more important than numerical parity or superiority in cannon, believing that batteries placed in this way would keep the enemy 'respectfully' at a distance – again basically a defensive concept. So far as siege warfare was concerned, the requirement was again two-fold: firstly the ability to mount sufficiently strong heavy batteries to create one or more breaches, associated with enough howitzers and mortars to sweep the enemy's defences; and secondly, to retain sufficient field pieces to ensure the adequate defence of the lines of circumvallation protecting the besiegers' positions from any danger of attack by a relieving army. These matters will be treated at greater length in the next section of the volume.

It is extremely difficult to reach even an approximate idea of how many guns of all kinds were held by the various powers at different periods. All that is possible here is to give a few examples of suggested national statistics, before considering a selection of particular armies serving in the field about which more is known. It is estimated that Louis XIV could call on some 13,000 cannon (fortress, siege and field) between 1689 and 1697, and perhaps as many as 14,000 during the Spanish Succession War. [15] In 1727 a British report placed the peace-time artillery resources of the six frontier provinces of Alsace, the Moselle, Roussillon, Guienne, Dauphiné and Flanders (about half of the Provinces of France) at 332 fortress and siege guns and 260 field guns – perhaps about a third of Louis XV's total resources. In 1748, on the other hand, at the end of a major war, the total French artillery would seem to have comprised 12,377 *canon de foule*, 2,354 iron guns, and 2,778 mortars and pierriers, or almost 18,000 pieces in all, but in this case naval artillery was included in the figures to the tune of almost 5,000 guns. [16]

Such numbers of guns seem enormous until we learn that Russia, which only founded its first proper artillery service in 1700, owned 13,000 brass and iron cannon by 1713, during the Grand Mastership of Count Bruce, whilst Great Britain, one of the smaller powers in terms of ostensible military power, had stored in her 54 'forts, castles, fortifications etc' in 1716 no less than 3,219 guns of iron and brass, mortars and howitzers included, besides a further 196 pieces of all kinds at Gibraltar, 199 at Port Mahon and 22 at Placentia – or a grand total, presumably excluding naval armament, of 3,636 pieces, at a time when the army numbered only 26,000 men and the fleet but 100 ships. Small wonder that

Marlborough, as re-appointed Master-General of the Ordnance, was desirous of implementing a reduced home establishment that would hold the more realistic number of 1,254 guns, although it is more difficult to appreciate the reason for his further suggested economy, namely the reduction of the 51 'flaggs at present' to merely 26.[17]

For other European powers it is more practical to consider the numbers of field guns they proved capable of putting into the field at different periods with specific armies, although at best it can only represent a very generalized guide on account of the special circumstances that often affected gun allocation. Turkish armies, however, would seem to have been consistently well provided for. The army that defeated Peter the Great at the River Pruth (1711) is reputed to have possessed all of 444 cannon. This, however, was exceptional even for Turkey, her armies beaten by the Imperialists at Szlankamen and Zenta having 154 and 200 guns respectively. Russian armies, as might be expected from the previous paragraph, were also well off for guns, having 179 at Narva and 122 at the Pruth, though precious little good they did them on either occasion. The most generously gunned army that fought in battle in Western Europe between 1688 and 1713 would seem to have been the Allied forces at Ramillies, which disposed of 120 guns (see table), but the Confederate Army that took the field in Flanders on 15 April 1709 reputedly numbered 262 pieces of cannon (siege and field) besides 20 mortars and howitzers.[18] Turning to later in the century, it would appear that the 27,000 strong Prussian army that invaded Silesia (1740) was provided with 42 guns, and four years later the 71,843 Prussian troops serving in the three main Prussian armies shared 182 field guns and 56 siege pieces, the total artillery in the field in 1744 (not including fortress guns) numbering 298. The Austrian forces (108,563 strong) serving in Sudetenland and Bohemia that same year were served by 197 guns, whilst the 75,300 strong Austro-Saxon army of late April 1745 (prior to the battle of Hohenfriedberg) sported 121 pieces of all calibres. By way of comparison the largest recorded number of siege guns in action at any one time were those deployed by Marshal Luxembourg against Mons (351 pieces in all) in 1691. For the siege of Lille, 17 years later, the Allies amassed some 180 siege guns and mortars and Eugene commanded over 200 before Belgrade in 1717.

The table that follows shows the artillery believed to have been present at a selection of major engagements between 1688 and 1745. Of course it only represents guns actually on the battlefield, and takes no account of breakdowns or other batteries performing secondary roles, but it does provide some indication of comparative representation, revealing a slight overall growth in proportionate representation by 1740, if due allowance is made for the earlier disproportionate numbers of Turkish and Russian guns.

Artillery authorities in France and England compared

The origins of the various artillery authorities go back to at least the fifteenth century. Père Daniel claimed that the French *Grand Maître d'Artillerie* developed from the officer commanding the *Arbalastiers* in the Early Middle

TABLE OF ARTILLERY PRESENT AT SELECTED ENGAGEMENTS*

Date	Battle	Victor's strength (approx.)	Guns[1]	Prop. per 1,000 men (to 2 places of decimal)	Loser's strength (approx.)	Guns[1]		Prop. per 1,000 men
1690	Fleurus	50,000	70	1.40	38,000	50	(49)[2]	1.32
1691	Szlankamen	50,000	n.d.	n.d.	100,000	154	(154)	1.54
1692	Steenkirk	57,000	60 (8)[2]	1.05	70,000	70	(10)	1.00
1693	Landen	80,000	71	0.88	50,000	91	(84)	1.82
1693	Marsaglia	40,000	30	0.75	36,000	31	(24)	0.86
1697	Zenta	50,000	60	1.20	100,000	200	(45)	2.00
1700	Narva	10,000	37	3.70	60,000	179	(179)	2.98
1704	Blenheim	52,000	60	1.15	56,000	90	(72)	1.61
1706	Ramillies	62,000	120	1.93	60,000	70	(54)	1.16
1707	Almanza	36,000	40	1.11	15,000	30	(24)	2.00
1708	Oudenarde	80,000	110	1.37	80,000		(25)	
1709	Malplaquet	110,000	100	0.91	80,000	60	(16)	0.75
1709	Poltava	80,000	100	1.25	21,500	4	(4)	0.18
1711	Faltschi-on-the-Pruth	260,000	444	1.71	40,000	122	(n.d.)	3.05
1716	Peterwardein	63,000	80	1.27	60,000	135	(130)	
1741	Mollwitz	21,600	53	2.45	15,800	19	(7)	1.20
1742	Chotusitz	28,000	80	2.85	28,000	40	(16)	1.43
1743	Dettingen	35,000	98 (1)	2.80	26,000	56	(nil)	2.15
1744	Velletri	24,000	30	1.25	16,000	40	(n.d.)	2.50
1745	Fontenoy	60,000	70	1.16	50,000	101	(5)	2.02
1745	Kesselsdorf	35,000	68	1.94	35,000	72	(40)	2.06

NOTES: 1. Gun totals reflect *all* guns present, whether siege, field or regimental.
2. Losses (given in brackets) are the usually accepted ones.

Ages, but dates the real emergence of the post from 1546 in the reign of Francis I. In the first years of gunpowder, all monarchs kept a tight control on such perilous resources; in England King Edward III retained the cannon that appeared at Crécy in the Royal Wardrobe.† The first emergence of the Master-General of the Ordnance's title would seem to be in 1414, when Henry v appointed a 'Master of our Works, Engines, Cannon, and other kinds of Ordnance for War'.[20] This special relationship with the throne partly accounts for the separation of almost all European artillery organizations from their native army authorities. The division was further reinforced by strong ties with certain trade guilds which provided the original Fire-Masters and Fire-Workers who made up the personnel of the artillery, and as late as the early eighteenth century the Austrian *Buchsenmeister* continued to regard themselves as guildsmen rather than soldiers, whilst in Turkey the *Topeys,* or cannoneers of the Sultan, retained similar professional barriers between themselves and the military. Nor were relics of such attitudes hard to find in the western armies.

To all intents and purposes, however, we can assert that the first truly comprehensive organization of these institutions in France and England took place in the second half of the seventeenth century. Although it would be many

*This table should be used in conjunction with Appendix pp. 302–309.
†The Wardrobe was the most important part of the personal governmental machinery employed by the later Angevin and Plantagenet kings. Its officials were all royal servants under the monarch's personal direction.

more years before a truly united regimental organization would emerge in France, it was in 1668 that Louvois, working on the foundations laid by his father's creation of the specialist gunner cadres, instituted an Inspectorate of Artillery under Claude du Metz and brought a measure of order and classification into the *Grand Maître's* powerful but diffuse organization. Although the Cavalier and the 'New Model' armies had employed reasonably well-organized field trains during the Great Civil War, in England the moment of true departure was probably 25 July 1683, when Charles II issued the first 'Instructions for the Government of our Office of Ordnance'. This document, originally drawn up under the supervision of James, Duke of York, and subsequently repromulgated with considerable additions by James as king on 4 February 1686, forms the basis of the artillery organization, and subsequent monarchs re-issued the document at the commencement of their respective reigns.[21] In certain respects the English Masters-General enjoyed wider powers than their French counterparts, in others they were rather more circumscribed; but both their respective authorities and privileges were truly immense, ensuring that both posts remained high in the lists of Officers of State.

Only an outline of these great institutions can be given here. In the first part of his *Mémoires d'Artillerie*, St Rémy lists a total of 40 different French functionaries besides 32 kinds of specialists, ranging from the *Grand Maître* at the summit of the hierarchy, his deputy the *Lieutenant-Général* and varying numbers and grades of *Trésoriers-Généraux de l'Artillerie*, all members of the *'Conseil de Guerre'* (or governing body) to the gardener at the Arsenal de Paris (kept at the Bastille), giving exhaustive details of their duties, privileges and status. What was to become known as the *Corps Royal d'Artillerie** comprised some 1,000 officers and civil functionaries in the 1690s (but subsequently shrank to about 500), most of them distributed among the 240 garrisons and fortresses of France, many being required to serve with the trains in time of war. These officers were divided into five 'Estates', each with a set of regulations governing terms of employment, many deriving all their authority and emoluments from the King, others from the *Grand Maître*, but a number holding joint-commissions. From 1679 a school was set up at Douai regulated by St Rémy,[22] followed by new establishments at Metz and in Italy. Those at Douai and Strasbourg survived to 1720 when they became absorbed into the new Artillery School organization. There were four classes of student – namely *Commissaires-Ordinaire*, *Extraordinaire*, *Officiers Pointeur* and *Aides du Parc*.

A clear distinction must be drawn between the officers of the *Corps Royal* on the one hand, and the officers and men of the *Régiment Royal d'Artillerie* (known as the *Fusiliers du Roi* until 1693) with its 12 companies of incorporated *canoniers*, the formations of miners, and the *Régiment des Bombardiers* (raised in 1676), on the other. The former was an all-officer institution, forming the basis of the provincial organization of the artillery, some of whose officials, however, would also be called to serve and often command in the trains; the

---

*The *Corps* bears certain resemblances to the active personnel of the English Board of Ordnance, but generalizations are dangerous.

latter were mostly recruited (until 1697 at least) from serving infantry, initially to guard the guns and later to serve them in action and to carry out various other specialist functions in battle or siege, and thus retained close links with the army proper as well as with the *Grand Maître,* who was ex-officio Colonel-General of the *Régiment-Royal* and Colonel-Lieutenant, under the king, .of the *Bombardiers.* From 1693 the *Grand Maître* only retained the sole right to issue commissions in the *Corps d'Artillerie;* all other officers of the Regiments received normal royal commissions, but these were always addressed to the *Grand Maître* as Colonel-General, and were of course often made out in favour of his nominees. This type of double-commission continued until 1720.

The differing organizations of the *Régiments Royal d'Artillerie* and *des Bombardiers* (destined to be merged in 1721 into a single comprehensive Artillery formation) will be described in more detail in the next chapter, but something must be said here about the provincial gunnery authorities operating directly under the *Grand Maître* and manned by the *Corps.* Until 1703, all posts in the Corps had been non-venal, but in that year Louis XIV made all commissions and promotions purchasable, and in certain cases hereditable as well, in return for payment of the *Droit de reversibilité* and the *paulette* (or office tax). This was probably a dire moment for the future governance and overall quality of the French artillery, and it was not until 1716 that the Regent, le Duc d'Orléans, began to dismantle the pernicious system, a process completed in the great reforms of 1720.

Under the same reorganization of 1703 the old provincial Lieutenants of Artillery were replaced by seven lieutenant-generals (for Alsace, Flanders, the Moselle, Roussillon, Île de France, Dauphiné, the Western Frontiers and the Western Coasts). Over the next ten years a further nine lieutenant-generals were appointed, making a grand total of 16 by 1715, between them covering the whole of France. Besides undertaking the training of local personnel, each was responsible for manufacturing and storing cannon, firearms and munitions in their respective provinces, and forming them into field or siege trains on the *Grand Maître's* order; they could not, however, be employed on active service without his special warrant.

Each lieutenant-general had a staff of Provincial Commissaries (the most senior of whom usually commanded the trains in the field), *Commissaires Ordinaires* and *Commissaires Extraordinaires,* whose equivalent army rank had been fixed since 1693 as First Captains, Second Captains and Lieutenants respectively in a somewhat vain attempt to end the ceaseless friction and bickering about relative status. Each province also held four *maréchaux des logis,* a Captain General of Waggons (with subordinate Captains of Waggons), and a staff of Conductors, *officiers pointeurs* (gun-aimers) *officiers déchargeurs* (gun-firers) and a *Major d'Artillerie,* charged with day-to-day administration. [23] There was also an officer grade called *'les Gardes-Magazines',* often old officers and quartermasters permanently attached to the various garrisons and arsenals*

---

*Arsenals, other than the main one in the Bastille, were situated at Metz, Chalôns, Lyons, Amiens, Narbonne, and Calais.

with *Gardes Provinciaux* and *Gardes Particuliers* to assist them.

Before giving a brief summary of the *Grand-Maître's* powers, it is interesting to note that no equivalent provincial organization existed in England at this time (probably the country was too small to require one),* but a similar system existed in the Habsburg Empire. In Austria, there were under the *Feldseckhmeister* four Generals of Artillery, each with his own region from 1636; they were each expected to able to provide on very short notice 1,000 men, 500 horses and 7 guns with all equipment ready for service, and further large numbers of cannon and mortars after a further period of time. To assist them, the Austrian generals had a staff including a colonel, lieutenant-colonel, 'major-general' (or staff officer) and an establishment of junior officers closely analogous to that of an infantry regiment.[24] This organization was retained with only slight changes well into the eighteenth century.

To revert to the French artillery, we have seen how it possessed a provincial as well as a central organization. Over all sectors presided the powerful figure of the *Grand Maître*[†], invariably a Prince of the Blood or very senior officer. His authority extended over every corner of the realm, and he was empowered to exercise criminal and civil justice throughout the artillery – exercising it through the court at the Arsenal. He had the lucrative right to nominate officers to almost 1,000 posts (and receive fees accordingly), and he alone could authorize the movement of artillery and munitions within the kingdom. He issued orders in the king's name, and was accountable only to him on all matters of expenditure. He was entitled to 100 rations a day (or the monetary equivalent), a salute of five salvoes 'of the great guns', and had the right to dispose of the church-bells and cannon of every captured town (or a cash sum in lieu). He was responsible, like the English Master-General, for the upkeep of fortresses as well as for the provision of munitions, and the supervision of their manufacture. In terms of financial independence, he was considerably better off than the English Master-General, who was ultimately responsible to Parliament for all heads of expenditure. On the other hand the French *Grande-Maître's* powers were somewhat diminished when the pernicious venal and hereditary system (operated

* However, the British Isles were divided into eight 'divisions' for artillery purposes before 1716, see p. 155.
† Lists of the French *Maîtres-General* and English Masters-General, 1688–1745.

(a) French: (1685) – 1694 : Louis de Crevant, Duc d'Humières, Marshal of France
　　　　　 1694 – 1710 : Louis-Auguste de Bourbon, Duc de Maine
　　　　　 1710 – (1755) : Louis-Charles, Comte d'Eu (2nd son of the Duc de Maine and heir to the title)

(b) English: (1682) – 1688 : George, Lord Dartmouth
　　　　　 1689 – 1693 : Frederick, Duke of Schomberg
　　　　　 1693 – 1702 : Henry, Viscount Sydney (later Earl of Romney)
　　　　　 1702 – 1712 : John Churchill, First Duke of Marlborough
　　　　　 1712 – 　　　 : Richard, Earl Rivers (died August *idem*)
　　　　　 1712 – 1714 : James, Duke of Hamilton and Brandon
　　　　　 1714 – 1722 : John Churchill, First Duke of Marlborough
　　　　　 1722 – 1723 : William, Earl of Cadogan
　　　　　 1725 – 1740 : John, Duke of Argyle and Greenwich
　　　　　 1740 – (1749) : John, Duke of Montague

wholly to the Crown's advantage by royal servants) became fully operative, and further he wielded no authority whatsoever over the navy – that was the special province of the *Commissaire-Général de l'Artillerie de la Marine*. His English equivalent had by comparison, almost as much naval as military authority over all matters pertaining to gunnery. [25]

Passing on to consider the English Board of Ordnance, we find an august institution of great standing in the realm. The Board was headed, of course, by the Master-General of the Ordnance, always an important personage assisted by 'Five Principal Officers' – namely the Lieutenant-General, the Surveyor-General, the Clerk of the Ordnance, the Keeper of Stores and the Clerk of the Deliveries. Most of these officials, like the Master-General himself, were appointed under the Great Seal, their commissions bearing the signature of the Secretary of State. [26] Beneath these powerful officials clustered a number of lesser luminaries of 'Under-Ministers' and 'Attendants', perhaps 160 in all divided into 14 categories, of whom the most important were the 'Treasurer of our Ordnance' and the 'Secretary to the Master of our Ordnance', both of whom are frequently found listed amongst the 'Principal Officers' in later lists. The junior members of what may be deemed subaltern status were often called 'Gentlemen of the Ordnance'; these officials were the main component of the 'active' element; some were attached to every operational train, being in charge of the guns at all times except in action.

The scope of the Board's authority was truly vast, and it may be said to have had a finger in every military pie, only the all-pervading power of the Treasury being more influential. Its primary task was the supply of cannon to both the army and the fleet (an early Master-Gunner of England on the 1683 establishment was a sailor, Captain Richard Leake R.N.), together with the myriad accessories and stores – including firearms and other hand weapons – required to make their employment effective. Further clearly defined duties included the provision of all engineering services for the construction, maintenance and repair of fortresses and barracks (the particular responsibility of the Surveyor-General), the finding of horses and transport for the movement of the trains (supervised by the Waggon-Master-General), the training and certificating of gunners for both army and navy (the charge of the Master-Gunner of England) besides the manufacture, supervision and testing of a large range of weapons for all arms of the services. The Master-General was also responsible for many minor duties ranging from providing candles for Chelsea Hospital to arranging salutes of cannon and other celebrations for august occasions. On one occasion, for instance, we find Colonel Richards, as Second Engineer, being repayed £30 on 2 November 1695 'on account of fireworks for His Majesty's Birthday in St James's Square òr otherwise'. [27] Even such minor prerogatives were jealously guarded against interlopers.

The powers vested in the Master-General and his officers were impressive, though not quite so totalitarian as in France. The Board was in no way subject to the normal military or naval authorities (except insofar as trains in the field were under the *de facto* control of the commander-in-chief), and indeed were only subordinate to the Monarch, the Treasury, the Auditors of Imprest for

Accounting, and the Secretary of State for the issue of military equipment. [28] They were ceaselessly exposed, however, to the purse-conscious supply committees of the House of Commons, but at least the Board was distinguished by being permitted to present its private financial estimate every year. Absolutely uniquely, too, the Master-General could authorize expenditure in emergencies for which a Parliamentary vote had not been sought in advance. The Master-General directly commissioned most of the Board's subordinate officers, who were strictly forbidden to buy or sell their commissions throughout the period (in contrast to the rest of the forces of the Crown).*

The Board maintained small groups of officials and assistants in all the forts and garrisons of the islands – often only a gunner, an assistant and a store-keeper – and sometimes an armourer in addition. These 'out-stations' were divided between eight 'divisions' in the British Isles besides a varying number of truly distant posts in the Mediterranean, West Indies and North America. Many personnel were paid only months in arrears – the fact that many of them also drew pay from *army* sources complicating the issue – and sometimes groups of minor officials were forgotten for years: and in such a vast organization cases of long undetected dereliction of duty were not unknown, particularly in time of peace. Thus in 1702 Marlborough found it necessary to re-impose several of James II's orders which had fallen into desuetude since 1697 – largely for want of men to command, so savagely had the Ordnance been cut back after the Peace of Ryswick.

The full effects of peace-time laxity were again experienced in 1715, when the Jacobite emergency found the Board totally unprepared. 'Things are in such confusion as cannot be described,' wrote Albert Borgard from the North; [21] a request for 10,000 firearms could only be met with 4,000, and the field train's departure from the Tower of London for the campaign was delayed week after week. Nor were the fortresses found to be in good order; General Maitland, for example, found Fort William indefensible, with no sign of gunners or stores, whilst the accommodation for the garrison could not be occupied 'without being exposed to the inconveniences of all weathers'. At Chester, guns were found but no carriages; the Governor of Carlisle reported that there were exactly four barrels of powder in the arsenal there. The reaction to this confusion and incompetence led directly to the reform of the organization and above all to the creation of the 'Royal Regiment'.

On the whole, however, the Board of Ordnance, at least in time of war, proved capable of meeting the greater part of the demands made upon it, and somehow or other the campaigns went on. If Flanders received greater priority than other, more distant theatres, it was because it was the principal area in all major wars England engaged in between 1688 and 1748 – but there is evidence that the

---

*The status of the Master-General *vis à vis* the military hierarchy had originally been settled by a Royal Warrant of 13 May 1686. By this, the Master-General should 'have the rank, as well as the respect, due to the youngest Lieutenant-General'. He was entitled to gun salutes and an escort of an officer and 21 other ranks when on duty, but was never given a field command by virtue of his Ordnance rank only. By 1745, he was entitled to the same honours as a full General of Foot or General of Horse, and was 'to be saluted by all officers, colonels excepted'.

Spanish front received less than its share of support between 1705 and 1712. And if, as we have had occasion to note in several earlier chapters, the relationships between the Board and individual regiments and ships tended to be somewhat contentious and distrustful on both sides, then the reverse of the medal must also be mentioned. Given the right conditions, the Board fulfilled its many duties well; even under unfavourable circumstances it generally got by somehow.

There were few major structural changes affecting the Board up to the foundation of the Royal Regiment of Artillery in 1716, although many minor administrative adjustments were made, and its senior officers proved very prone to political pressures – far more so than was the case in the French service (as is reflected by the length of the list on p. 153). After the raising of the first Regiment of Artillery the organization eventually settled down into its adjusted role with relatively little difficulty, and the service as a whole benefited from the consequent changes.

It would be tedious to detail the artillery organizations of other countries – but in many ways they generally reproduced the main aspects of those already described. The Dutch under their *Meesters-generaal* possessed a somewhat closer *rapport* with their armies and navies from the outset of our period, but in general terms the efficiency of their organization was in decline by 1700. The Austrians, as we have had occasion to mention, were in a generally out-dated condition so far as the higher control of their ordnance was concerned, and would remain so until the mid-eighteenth century when their gunners would emerge as amongst the best in Europe. The Prussian senior gunners, under the eagle eye of first Leopold of Anhalt-Dessau and later Frederick the Great, would eventually produce an artillery service more than capable of outstripping their rivals. To summarize, then, we may assert that the machinery for the administration of the guns and ordnance was generally cumbersome and somewhat hidebound, in the late seventeenth and early eighteenth centuries, considerations of caste dividing soldiers and civilians, between 'amateur gentlemen' and 'expert artisans', not doing anything to facilitate close co-operation; but as the eighteenth century progressed, and the artillery became more closely associated with their armies – finishing by becoming integral parts of a single whole – the situation would steadily improve, and greater military proficiency both at the front and in the rear areas would be the eventual outcome.

10

Personnel and field organization

In the previous chapter we have described the organization of the headquarters artillery institutions in France and England, giving some indication of their personnel and functions, noting that their antecedents and development was mainly outside the framework of the standing armies. In this chapter we shall examine the emergence of the second major component of the artillery (which grew for the most part *within* the army establishment), namely the respective Royal Regiments of Artillery, and then outline the way these troops joined up with their *Corps Royal* or Ordnance colleagues in time of war to form the field trains which accompanied the armies into the field. Personnel drawn from both sources also manned the siege trains, but their description will be reserved to the section of the volume devoted to Siege Warfare and Military Engineering, where we shall also deal with engineers and miners, although the arbitrary division is only for purposes of convenience.

The development of the royal regiments of artillery in England and France

The processes which eventually gave birth to regularly-constituted regiments of professional gunners were both complex and lengthy, for many strands eventually merged to create the end-product. The first attempts to organize specialist troops within the French army framework can probably be traced with reasonable accuracy to the regiments of fusiliers raised in the 1670s and 1680s, and to these must be added the creation of a number of independent *Compagnies des Canoniers* for service with the French army at various dates.

The French fusilier's original *raison d'être* was the protection and handling of the guns (assisting the Corps personnel in the latter function). The original *Régiment des Fusiliers du Roi* was wholly a specialist formation, comprising (1671) one company of '*Canoniers du Grand Maître*', another of '*sapeurs*', and two of workers in wood and iron, but in the second year of its existence 22 more companies of ordinary troops were added, including two of grenadiers, making a regiment of two battalions. This number rose to six battalions in 1677 (but subsequently dropped to five), and in due course a further twelve companies of *canoniers* were added to serve as holding units for professional gunners. In 1693 this large formation was renamed the *Régiment Royal d'Artillerie*. Most of its men had been drawn from line infantry regiments up to this time, and all the officers bore commissions from the King, and although these were addressed to the *Grand Maître* as Colonel-General as already related, the artillery connection remained unpopular. It was recorded, indeed, that some 'fusilier' officers regarded it as a point of honour *not* to stay by their guns in action, but insisted on drawing their men away to serve as infantry. By 1695, however, the Regiment was becoming increasingly distinct from its infantry antecedents and very shortly afterwards was recruiting itself separately.[30] Thus assimilation into an artillery service was proceeding apace, although there were the usual immense fluctuations in composition over the years and by 1721 the Regiment had been reduced to four battalions.

Besides further companies of *Mineurs* and *Canoniers* (including the Free Company of Coastal Gunners – raised in 1702) another regiment closely associated with the *Grand Maître* and the workings of his Department, was the *Régiment Royal des Bombardiers*. First raised in 1676, this formation grew from a couple of companies to a total of 18 (in 2 battalions) by 1707. Most companies numbered an average of 50 men apiece, except between 1697 and 1701 and after 1714 when they sank to some 30. The Lieutenant-Colonel's Company and the Second Company were on slightly larger establishments – fluctuating in strength between 105 and 90 men in the first case (including 40 cadet-bombardiers and 10 workmen), and between 70 and 60 (including ten cadets) in the second. The Regiment's specific duties were manning the mortars and providing garrisons for frontier fortresses (in time of peace). All commissions were granted by the *Grand Maître* who also controlled the appointment of the Captain-General of Bombardiers. Both the Bombardiers and the Royal Artillery Regiments served during campaigns in detachments with the various trains and armies as required. On the march, troops drawn from these regiments generally headed the train column, whilst another detachment brought up the rear.

Vauban suggested the creation of an amalgamated Artillery Corps of three regiments, each of 18 companies, as early as 1691, which would have brought the fusiliers, bombardiers, free companies of cannoniers and miners into a single organization, under the king as Colonel-General, but Louis XIV ignored his advice. So matters rested until 1720, when on 5 February, a Royal *ordonnance* empowered Lieutenant-General de Broglie to merge the two formations into a single *Régiment Royal d'Artillerie* organized on a five battalion basis.* Every battalion received a staff of a colonel, a major, an aide-major, a chaplain and a surgeon-major, and included eight companies of 100 men apiece, each divided into three 'squadrons'. The first 'squadron' contained mainly gunners and bombardiers; the second miners and sappers;† the third craftsmen; all three held

*The First Lt.-Cols were Pijart, de Certemont, de Thorigny, de Prosi and de Romillié. All other officers were redeployed accordingly, while the troops were divided into 50 equal groups, ten being assigned to each battalion.
† But see also p. 223 below for the eventual separation of the miner and sapper squadrons from the artillery in 1729.

a proportion of apprentices. It was also decreed that the new amalgamated regiment should doff the white Bourbon uniform, and adopt a blue coat and red trousers.[31] All officers were chosen by the king (Colonel of the Regiment) but commissioned by the Grand-Master.

Each battalion of the Royal Regiment was allocated a garrison town where an Artillery School was to be established, under the overall supervision of M. des Touches, Director of Schools, and M. de Vallière, Inspector of Schools. These depots were established at Metz, Strasbourg, Grenoble, Perpignan and La Fère. The syllabus was carefully designed, and newly commissioned officers were trained as ordinary gunners, then as commanders of a single gun-crew, before having their appointments confirmed. Sixty years later the young Napoleon would go through the same mill. At any one time in days of peace a quarter of each battalion would be under instruction, working a six-day week divided equally between practical and theoretical work. The latter side was directed by a Professor of Mathematics (appointed by the king at a salary of 1,000 crowns a year), aided by the regimental officers and a few selected NCOs. The battalions were also expected to perform routine garrison duties although some officers and skilled tradesmen were exempted.

On campaign, the new regulations continued, the Regiment was invariably to camp with the Train. When involved in a siege, it was never to serve in the trenches in a holding rôle, but only in the main batteries or saps under construction. Writing in 1721, Père Daniel avowed that 'this Regiment is the principal nerve of any war.'[32] Such, then were the main features of the reconstructed French Royal Regiment of Artillery. Before we pass on to consider the situation in the English army, the following table will give an indication of the relative strengths of the various components of the French artillery service at different epochs within our period.

FRENCH ARTILLERY ESTABLISHMENTS, 1689–1748 [33]

	1691		1710		1729		1748	
	Offrs.	*Men*	*Offrs.*	*Men*	*Offrs.*	*Men*	*Offrs.*	*Men*
Régiment des Fusiliers du Roi			270	3,790	–	–	–	–
(subsequently *d'Artillerie*)*				(1720)	225	2,800	275	5,000
*Régiment Royal des Bombardiers**			80	1,300	–	–	–	–
*Compagnie des Mineurs***			20	340	25	250	30	435
Coastal Artillerymen***			6	200	–	–	–	–
Craftsmen**			nd	nd	10	200	10	320
Corps Royal d'Artillerie			321	nil	321	nil	321	nil
TOTALS	6,480		697	5,630	581	3,250	636	5,755

NOTES: * – Subsequently merged into the *Régiment Royal d'Artillerie* (from 1720).

** – These were independent companies; the *R. R. d'Artillerie* of course also included both miners and craftsmen in its 2nd and 3rd 'squadron' establishments until 1729.

*** – This represented the Free Company of Coastal Gunners, raised by Sieur Ferrard de Cossay in 1706 (some sources claim 1702); it was specifically organised to accompany expeditions overseas, but was eventually disbanded. Ordinary coastal gunnery duties were under the charge of the Provincial Lt-Generals and the personnel of the *Corps Royal d'Artillerie* (an all-officer organization).

As usual, strengths varied considerably between the dates specified.

In the case of England, the growth of a regular artillery service within the framework of the standing army followed a somewhat different and more haphazard course. In the first instance, the regiments of fusiliers – instead of becoming assimilated into and eventually indistinguishable from the artillery as in France – increasingly reverted to an infantry role, a process that was virtually completed by the early 1700s. As a result, the distinction between the artillery and the rest of the army remained clear-cut throughout Marlborough's campaigns, although this did not of course prevent considerable numbers of infantry officers and men being temporarily drafted into the trains in time of war to assist in the handling of the guns. Indeed, some of these temporary gunners proved extremely versatile in the functions they performed. The celebrated case of Captain Richard King's service at the siege of Menin (1706) will adequately illustrate this point. Originally commissioned into the Royal Scots Fusiliers, he successively served in the following capacities in the short space of four and a half weeks: controller of the train, conductor of artillery, supervisor of rations and munitions, engineer in charge of entrenchments, commander of the breaching battery, before finally reverting to his original duty as an infantry commander in the last days of the siege! Small wonder such a versatile and busy officer wrote to an acquaintance: 'I have very little time to myself.'[34]

Although the fact that officers were sometimes called upon to perform such multifarious duties might seem to indicate a somewhat haphazard atmosphere within the Ordnance as well as a high degree of individual talent, there were certain tentative experiments leading towards the adoption of a regimental organization for the trains serving in the field long before the formal raising of the Royal Regiment of Artillery in 1716. The need for such an organization was firstly tacitly recognized in the Royal Warrant of 22 August 1682, which reorganized the 100 extraordinarily incompetent 'feed gunners' at the Tower, reducing their number to 60 and bringing them under a form of discipline, with the strict proviso that they were to be exercised once a week in winter and twice a week in summer by the Master-Gunner of England. Such was the first, small beginning. The next real step was taken 11 years later, when the Flanders Train of 1693 was reorganized into something approaching a regimental organization – probably on the lines of the Dutch model. It was provided with a staff of 27 officers and civilians including the 'Kettle-drummer, John Burnett, and his coachman, John Humphreys', whilst the main body of the personnel of the train proper were divided into four companies, each comprising a captain, two lieutenants, two Gentlemen of the Ordnance, 4 sergeants, 36 gunners, 4 corporals of matrosses and 56 matrosses – a total of five officers and 100 other ranks apiece. These companies divided the cannon between them, but it is significant to note that the howitzers were left in charge of the firemaster, 10 fireworkers and 12 bombardiers, who were not organized into a company structure, although the 'tin-men' (in charge of the pontoons) had an equivalent organization with three officers, four NCOs and 50 private men.[35] Excluding waggoners and other ancillary personnel, this train numbered 675 officers and

1   Three prominent Allied commanders of the War of the Spanish Succession:
top Prince Eugene of Savoy; *centre* John Churchill, First Duke of Marlborough;
bottom John William Friso, Prince of Orange

2   The Battle of Blenheim, by Louis Laguerre. In the left-hand panel, English grenadiers wade the River Nebel to attack the village; in the centre, French cavalry flee into the Danube, deserting their infantry; to the right, Prince Eugene amidst his staff and escort of Austrian cuirassiers

3 Light cavalry of the mid-18th century. Drawing by Marcellus Laroon

4 Charles XII, King of Sweden—a skilled, if rash, exponent of 18th century warfare

5 & 6 Illustrations from 'The Grenadier's Exercise' for the First Regiment of Foot Guards, by Bernard Lens, c. 1735. *Above* 'Guard your Fuze'; *right* 'Throw your Granade' (*sic.*)

7 Detail from the Blenheim Tapestry. An English grenadier with captured trophies. Note the artillery and the medical team depicted in the background

8 Detail from the Oudenarde Tapestry: Infantry marching into battle and deploying for action

9   Battle of Oudenarde, 1708. A line engraving by J. Huchtenburg showing the climax of the fighting

10 Hermann Maurice, Comte de Saxe, the celebrated commander and military theorist

11 The artillery park at the Arsenal of Toulon, by Claude-Joseph Vernet

12 The Battle of Peterwardein, 1716. Prince Eugene's success paved the way for
his even greater success before Belgrade the following year. Note the Turkish
Janissaries depicted in the right foreground

13 Detail from the Wynendael Tapestry, showing the two-wheeled supply waggon favoured by Marlborough and certain details of infantry clothing and equipment, *c.* 1708

14 Sebastien Le Prestre, Seigneur de Vauban and Marshal of France—the doyen of scientific siege warfare

15 The Bouchain Tapestry, Blenheim Palace, depicting Marlborough's celebrated penetration of the Lines of the Ne Plus Ultra in 1711

16 The Siege of Ostend, 1706. Note the artillery batteries, bomb vessels and details of ancillary equipment behind the Allied siege lines

17 The Crossing of the Scheldt, 1708. Marlborough's brilliant manoeuvre forestalled French attempts to raise the Allied siege of Lille. Note the pontoon bridges

men, with 66 cannon, four howitzers and a total of 292 waggons.

Henceforward this company organization of the artillery component was regularly adopted for field trains (though not for siege trains). Following the Peace of Ryswick, a 'Peace Train' of four companies was mooted in May 1698, but Parliamentary economies all but killed this off within six months. With the outbreak of the Spanish Succession War, the work of organization had accordingly to be begun again, and Queen Anne's first 'Holland Train' comprised a staff, two artillery companies (each consisting of three officers, six NCOs and 50 other ranks), and two innovations – a 'Company of Pioneers' (two sergeants and 20 pioneers) and a 'Company of Pontoon Men' (a Bridgemaster, two corporals and 20 pontoon men),[36] dragging behind them 34 guns and howitzers.

One major administrative drawback of all these trains was their impermanence: at the end of a war they tended to be immediately disbanded; the greater number of the rank and file re-entered civilian life; those officers fortunate enough to be retained were either distributed around the garrisons or 'attended the service (at the Tower), as formerly', like Albert Borgard between 1720 and 1722. In the event of a sudden emergency – like the rising of the Scottish clans in 1715 – the Ordnance was almost certain to be caught at a disadvantage. There was also a growing requirement for a permanent regimental organization in England which could support and sustain the long-term overseas garrisons which required artillery detachments. Chief amongst these were Gibraltar (from 1704), Minorca (from 1708), and the even more distant posts over the Atlantic – Annapolis (1710) and Placentia (1713).

But it was the lack of preparedness revealed in the Autumn and Winter of 1715 that persuaded the last doubters on the Board of Ordnance that their house needed to be put in order. As a practical commander and great administrator, the Duke of Marlborough, the restored Master-Gunner* was more than happy to approve the suggested improvements put up to him on 10 January 1716. These called for the establishment of a permanent regiment of four companies and a staff, responsible for home and overseas artillery commitments. It was pointed out that the implementation of certain economies – mostly notably the running down of the Train of North Britain, and the gradual abolition of sundry posts, including that of Master-Gunner of England – would reduce the annual charge of the service's pay from £16,829 to £15,539. As we have already noted earlier, economies in material were effected in September the same year (see p. 149 above), but for our present purposes the most important date was 26 May 1716, for it was on that date the British Royal Regiment of Artillery formally came into existence.

The full recommendations of the Ordnance Board were not immediately implemented. In its initial form the Regiment possessed no formal staff

---

*Following his disgrace in late 1711, Marlborough had been deprived of all his posts and dignities. These were restored by George I on his accession. Marlborough's Board in 1715 included Thomas Earle (Lt. General), Col. Michael Richards (Surveyor-General), Col. John Armstrong (Chief Engineer), Edward Ashe (Clerk of Ordnance), James Craggs (Clerk of Deliveries) and Harry Mordent (Treasurer).

(although an irregular one existed from 1718) and comprised only two companies in England (costing a mere £4,891 p.a.) which had no responsibility for the two weak detachments overseas at Port Mahon and Gibraltar. Over the following 20 years of the Regiment's infancy, however, these deficiencies were slowly made good as officers on the 'old establishment' (i.e. Ordnance) wasted out. In 1722 the Regiment received its first colonel – the veteran Albert Borgard.

The career of Albert Borgard (1659–1751) is worth summarizing. During it he participated in 23 sieges and 19 battles and expeditions. In 1675–89 he served in the Danish service; from 1689 to 92 he served the King of Prussia (also serving in Hungary at the Battle of Salankamen) before transferring to the service of William III. He was subsequently present at both Steenkirk and Landen, and at the siege of Namur (1695). After the Peace he was one of only two foreign soldiers invited to remain in the English artillery service. In 1702 he commanded five bomb-vessels at Cadiz, and, later, at Vigo Bay; 1703 saw him briefly in Flanders before being sent to Spain. After losing his left arm at Valenzia (1705), he saw further service at Alcantara (1706) and Almanza (1707), before commanding the artillery in the successful attack on Minorca (1708). In 1710 he received four wounds at Almenara, and was taken prisoner for a spell after Villa Viciosa. He was repatriated to England in time to arrange the fireworks for the Peace of Utrecht (1713). Two years later he served in Scotland. In 1716 he was wounded in an explosion at Moorfields gun foundry, and spent the next two years conducting further experimental work. In 1719 he served at Vigo, and in 1722 became the first Colonel of the Royal Artillery (being promoted Lt.-General in 1739). He died in 1751 aged 92 years.

In 1727 a Lieutenant-Colonel and a Major were added (in the persons of Jonas Watson and James Petit respectively), whilst Borgard became Colonel-Commandant, and a full establishment of four companies (commanded by Captains J. Richard, Thomas Hughes, J. Deal and Thomas Pattison) was attained for the first time – largely due to the requirements of the siege of Gibraltar. The years passed relatively quietly, the only dramatic events being the unsuccessful Spanish siege of Gibraltar (1727) – during which Colonel Jonas Watson commanded 200 Royal Artillerymen in the Regiment's first sustained defensive action (it had been its first offensive operation under Borgard's personal command at the bombardment of Vigo (1719) during Lord Cobham's brief expedition to Spain – when an artillery force of 12 officers and 79 regular rank and file (besides conductors, drivers and clerks) had manned 14 cannon, eight mortars, two bomb-vessels and some 42 smaller 'coehorn' and 'royal' mortars with great success), and the preparation (also in 1727) of a field train for Flanders of 24 cannon and six 'royal' mortars, manned by one company supplemented by attached personnel – but the expedition never sailed. These excitements excepted, the Regiment carried out a routine existence for almost 20 years, one or two companies finding the artillery garrisons for the overseas posts, and the home-based echelons providing contingents for such events as 'the Campaign [sic] in Hyde Park' of 1716 (10 guns in all), the Hyde Park Camp of 1723, where 20 guns supported the manoeuvres of six regiments of dragoons and twice as many of foot for the delectations of the citizens of London.

For most of this period the total strength of the English army rarely rose far above 26,000 men, so naturally the size of the Regiment of Artillery remained small. The original suggested establishment for an artillery company (1716) had been one captain (at 10s a day pay), two lieutenants, as many Lieutenant-Fireworkers, three sergeants, three corporals, three bombardiers, 30 gunners (1/4d a day) and 50 matrosses (1s a day), and this had been implemented (but only for two companies) on 26 May the same year.* In 1720, the establishment of both companies was considerably adjusted, a Captain-Lieutenant being added together with four fireworkers, eight more bombardiers and five cadets for both the gunners and the matrosses, besides two drummers; at the same time, however, the two Lieutenant-Fireworkers were suppressed, the gunners were reduced to 25 and the matrosses to 43 per company. The following years saw small fluctuations in detail (thus in 1727 an additional officer and 8 pioneers were added for the proposed Flanders Train Artillery Company, besides a regimental staff of 13, a group of 12 artificers, nine 'Civil Officers', and a Bridgemaster with 22 pontoon men), whilst other changes saw the re-establishment of Lieutenant-Fireworkers (from 1734 to 1745). The status of the artillery officers was still occasionally the subject of acrimonious dispute, and it was only (apparently) in December, 1735, for instance, that a gunner colonel was first appointed as President of a Court Martial (with six or more artillery officers and six from the Guards, as members).

The next major adjustment took place between 1739 and 1741. A new company was added to the home establishment (to make a total of three), the strength of each being made up to 150, whilst the two weaker companies serving at Gibraltar and Minorca were augmented to 100 men apiece. These changes became operative from the Royal Warrant of 21 April 1740. A year later it was decided to reorganize the three companies of the home establishment into four, largely for reasons of administrative convenience, and by March 1742 two further companies had been extemporized, making seven in all.[37] Nor was this the end of the expansion, for as the War of the Austrian Succession gathered momentum, the regiment grew to eight companies in June 1743, thence to 10 in March 1744, whilst the addition of a cadet-company in 1745 brought the total to 11 – seven serving in Great Britain, and one apiece in Gibraltar, Minorca, Newfoundland and Louisburg. After the ending of the scare occasioned by the Rebellion of the '45 in Scotland, two of the home companies were redeployed in Brabant. Further proof of the increasing prestige of the Regiment is provided by the addition of yet another three companies in 1747 (making a total of 14 companies including cadets) – and within the space of six short years the company strength more than doubled.[38] Even after the Peace of Aix-la-Chapelle only three companies were reduced or disbanded, and the personnel of the individual companies underwent very slight diminution, as the following table indicates:

---

*It is interesting to compare these rates of pay with those received by equivalent ranks in the Trains in 1693. See p. 160 above.

APPROX. PERSONNEL OF THE REGIMENT OF ROYAL ARTILLERY, 1716–1748 [39]

Dates of specimen years (total companies in parenthesis on top line)

Ranks	1716(2)*	1727(4)	1741(6)	1743(8)**	1744(11)	1747(14)***	1748(11)
A. STAFF	26 May	1 Nov.	30 Apr.	June	8 Dec.	n.d.	n.d.
Colonel	–	1(25s)a	1	1	2	2	3
Lt.-Colonel	–	1(20s)	1	1)	3 'field	) 3	1
Major	–	1(15s)	1	1	officers'		1
Adjutant	–	1(6s)	1	1	1	1	1
Bridgemaster	–	1(5s)		1	1	1	1
Chaplain	–	–	1(6s 8d)	1	1	1	1
Surgeon	–	–	1(7s 6d)	1	2	2	2
Surgeon's Mate	–	–	1(3s)	1	–	–	–
Quartermaster	–	1(6s)	n.d. b	1	1	1	1

B. TOTAL REGIMENTAL STRENGTH
Officers:

Ranks	1716(2)*	1727(4)	1741(6)	1743(8)**	1744(11)	1747(14)***	1748(11)
Captain	2 (10s)	4	6	8)	21'captains')	27)	21
Capt.-Lieutenant	–	4(7s)	4	8			
1st Lieutenant	2 (6s)	4	8	8)	53 'subal-)	68)	53
2nd Lieutenant	2 (5s)	4	6	8	terns'		
Lt.-Fireworker	4 (3–4s)	12	19	24			

NCOS *and Other Ranks:*

Ranks	1716(2)*	1727(4)	1741(6)	1743(8)**	1744(11)	1747(14)***	1748(11)
Sergeants	6(2s)	12	17	24)	140 (est.))	182'NCOS')	140
Corporals	6(1s 8d)	12	17	24			
Bombardiers	6(1s 8d)	32	80	64			
Gunners	60(1s 4d)	80	141	160	200	260	200
Cadet-Gunners	–	–c	16	–	–	–	–
Matrosses	100(1s)	256	294	512	640	832	616
Cadet-Matrosses	–	–c	16	–	–	–	–
Drummers	–	8(1s)	12	16	20	26	21
Gentlemen-Cadets	–	–	–	–	48	48	48

TOTALS:

Ranks	1716(2)*	1727(4)	1741(6)	1743(8)**	1744(11)	1747(14)***	1748(11)
Officers	10	34	50	65	85	106	85
Men	198	400	593	800	1,048	1,248	1,025

NOTES:　Engineers, tinmen, pontoonmen, etc., although often serving with the 'marching companies' on active service, are not normally included in the Regimental establishments.

Distribution of Companies in specimen years
* : both in British Isles; Gibraltar and Port Mahon garrisons still Ordnance 'Old establishment'.
** : 2 in British Isles (4 in 1741); 1 each in Gibraltar & Port Mahon.
*** : 2 at Woolwich; 3 in Flanders; 1 each at Gibraltar, Port Mahon and Newfoundland.
**** : 7 in British Isles; 1 each at Gib., Port Mahon, Newfoundland and Louisburg.
***** : 3 at Woolwich; 1 Scotland; 5 in Brabant; 1 each at Gib., Minorca, Newfoundland, Louisburg and Pondicherry.
****** : (after peace) 7 in British Isles; 1 each at Gibraltar, Minorca, Newfoundland, and Nova Scotia.
a. Daily rate of pay for specified rank throughout period (with minor changes).
b. Q.M. not listed in 1741 return, but has reappeared by 1742. Possibly an error.
c. Although no Gunner- or Matrosse-cadets are listed for 1727 there had been a total of ten of each in June 1720, and eleven Cadet-Gunners are given in the establishment of 1725. Their omission here therefore is possibly an error.

This evidence of dramatic growth in the Royal Regiment of Artillery – although it does demonstrate the rising standing of the Regiment in the British

Army – also reflects the phasing-out of the Board of Ordnance's 'old establishment', especially in overseas posts.

As will be appreciated, the gunners and matrosses still retained slight advantages of pay over their infantry equivalents – and this remained the cause of some envy. Similarly, their uniforms tended to be of better material than many issued to the 'poor foot' or some cavalry troopers. As early as 1695 we find a Mr Gibbon being paid for 224 suits 'for the service of the matrosses of His Majesty's Train of Artillery in Flanders' at a rate of £4–5–0 a suit, the coats being of red cloth faced with blue; the same year a Mr Graham received £7–15–0 apiece for 144 suits for gunners – described as follows:

> Coats of crimson cloth lined with blue serge, with a flap on the button holeside, the sleeves lined with blue cloth with a narrow gold galloon round the sleeve cuff, a button of the same cloth, and thereon and the button holes tapt with gold.
> Waistcoast of blue cloth and small brass buttons.
> Breeches of ditto lined with linen and leather pockets.
> Strong shoes of neats's leather waxt.
> Blue worsted stockings for rowling [*sic*].
> Black hats edged with gold.
> Gloves with tops lined.[40]

As for the pioneers, at that time an integral part of the Ordnance and artillery services, they were outfitted *inter alia* with blue waistcoats, red cloth caps faced with blue bearing Lord Romney's coat of arms* and pioneer trophies, and white yarn stockings.

The distinctive blue coat of the Royal Artillery seems to have come in with the foundation of the Regiment. In 1734 'the uniform dress of the officers was a plain blue coat, lined with scarlet; a large Argyle cuff, double-breasted, and with yellow buttons to the bottom of the skirts, scarlet waistcoat and breeches, the waistcoat trimmed with broad gold lace, and a gold-laced hat.'

'The sergeants coats were trimmed – the lapels, cuffs and pockets with a broad single gold lace; the corporals and bombardiers with a narrow single gold lace; the gunners and matrosses, plain blue coats; all the non-commissioned officers and privates having scarlet half-lapels, scarlet cuffs, and slashed sleeves with five buttons, and blue waistcoats and breeches; the sergeants hats trimmed with a broad, and the other non-commissioned officers and privates with a narrow gold lace. White spatterdashes were then worn. The regimental clothing was delivered to the non-commissioned officers and privates once a year, excepting regimental coats, which they received only every second year; and the intermediate year a coarse blue surtout which served for laboratory work, cooking, fatigues etc. and was delivered with the usual small mounting.'

'The arms of the officers were fuzees without bayonets, and not uniform. The sergeants, corporals and bombardiers were armed with halberts and long

---

*The famous 'broad arrow' ⬆ which remains in use on the insignia of the Ministry of Defence to this day.

brass-hilted swords; the gunners carried field staffs about two feet longer than a halbert, with two linstock locks branching out at the head, and a spear projecting between and beyond them. Great attention was paid to keeping these very bright. A buff belt over the left shoulder, slinging a large powder horn, mounted with brass over the right pocket, and the same long brass-hilted swords ... The matrosses had only common muskets, with bayonets and cartouche-boxes.'[44]

The Regimental Drummer and his coachman wore even more splendid finery, the former's uniform costing £50, the latter's £15, and they drew 4s and 3s a day respectively.

A final word must be devoted to the methods of training employed. Until his position became redundant, this was the special charge of the Master-Gunner of England (paid £190 p.a.). He was, in time of peace,

> To profess and teach his art to our under-gunners in the exercise of shooting of great ordnance, mortar pieces etc. in such publick places as by the Master of our Ordnance shall be allotted and appointed for that purpose, and there to exercise them once a month in winter and twice every month in summer ...

He was also responsible for the testing and certification of proficient gunners (receiving a fee for each document issued) and was also expected to maintain a list of all gunners in pay as well as a register 'of all our great guns as well brass or iron belonging to any of our ships, forts, castles, blockhouses or garrisons.'[42]

The practice was widely followed of sending off promising young officers to understudy continental armies in any convenient war. In 1688, for example, Lord Dartmouth dispatched Jacob Richards to Hungary to study Habsburg techniques. He was specifically enjoined

> ... to observe and take notice of their method of marching, encamping, embattling, exercising, ordering their trains of Artillery, their manner of approaching, besieging, or attacking any town, their mines, batteries, lines of circumvallation and contravallation, their way of fortification, their founderies, instruments of war, engines, and what else may occur observable.

For this dauntingly comprehensive curriculum he was to receive the princely pay (for the time) of £1 per diem.[43] In similar fashion, nine years later, the same Jacob Richards was sent to Corfu to observe the current war against the Turk.[44]

As the eighteenth century progressed, the practice grew of attaching a number of Gunner-Cadets and Matrosse-Cadets to the various companies of the Regiment of Artillery where they learned their profession 'at the cannon's mouth'. This system was partially replaced by the foundation of the Royal Military Academy at Woolwich in 1741. The regimental cadets were to be joined by other young men desirous of acquiring a scientific education. The syllabus was broad. The 'Theoretical School' concentrated on pure and mixed mathematics with some Latin; the 'Practical' taught gun-drills, fortification, laboratory duties, and drawing. But it is open to conjecture how much of the teaching was wasted effort, for in its early years the Academy was noted for the indiscipline and uproarious behaviour of its students. Absenteeism was rife, and many a muster-entry ends laconically with 'I know not where they are' or 'A very idle fellow'. When the Regiment was inspected in June 1744 by the Duke of Cumberland, a disorderly mob without officers or even uniforms was observed milling about on the right of the line – the cadets of the Royal Artillery. Matters improved somewhat with the creation of the Cadet Company with a proper establishment of officers in 1745, but the Lieutenant-Governor still had to patrol to check the ragging inflicted on the hapless professors by their unruly charges, and a stream of edicts poured fourth forbidding such misdemeanours as 'smouching ('liberating' other people's property) and 'shutting their desks with violence', whilst two unfortunates at this time were described as 'scabby sheep, whom neither lenity will improve, nor confinement to a dark room and being fed on bread and water.'[45] Nevertheless, from such unpromising material there emerged the young officers of the trains, whose services in Flanders in 1747 and 1748 earned Colonel Belford's warmest praise. The Cadet Company varied between 20 and 48 cadets at different periods, and for all its shortcomings it would be recognized that Woolwich was the only British military Academy until the very end of the eighteenth century. The situation in France, as we have already had occasion to mention, was considerably more advanced.

The organization of the artillery trains

Until the foundation of full-time artillery regiments, artillery trains were raised when specifically needed and almost invariably disbanded after the completion of the task. Despite the dislocation, delay and confusion such an unsatisfactory arrangement inevitably caused in time of emergency (as in Britain in 1715), all early attempts to establish permanent 'Peace-Trains' (as in 1697) foundered as we have already noted on the rock of financial stringency. From 1716 onwards, however, there was always a nucleus of trained gunners and their assistants to hand, and by the 1730s these 'marching companies' were a permanent aspect of the military scene.

The means by which trains of artillery were called into existence were fairly standardized throughout Europe. The system pertaining in England in the 1690s can be taken as reasonably representative of the period as a whole until at least as late as 1714. The initial step was the issue of a warrant (in France an *ordonnance*) by the Secretary of State on behalf of the monarch, addressed to the Master-General or his Deputy, warning him of a forthcoming requirement. Thus on 27 February 1691/2, Lord Nottingham instructed the Lieutenant-General of the Ordnance, Sir Henry Goodricke (The Master-General, Schomberg, being absent on duty in Ireland) that a train was 'to be made ready' for Flanders, comprising eight brass demi-culverins, 10 brass sakers, 20 brass 3-pdrs, four 8-inch howitzers and two small petards.* The Warrant also mentioned that this field train would require the provision of 11,200 cannon-balls, 560 rounds of case-shot, '600 horses for Guns and tin

*See p. 180 below for definitions of these cannon.

boats' besides '200 waggons with 600 horses for stores', the whole to be manned by a force of some 70 officers, 53 NCOs and craftsmen, 40 gunners and 80 matrosses, 49 'private men' and 9 miners.[46] As time passed additional warrants were often issued authorizing reinforcement or augmentations of the trains in the field, often due to the need to make good losses sustained in action or by accident. Thus on 5 March 1693/4 an 'Addition to the Flanders Train' was ordered by Lord Shrewsbury (Secretary of State), calling for the finding of a further 64 cannon (30 sakers, 10 demi-culverins, 20 3-pdrs and four howitzers) 'to be forthwith provided and sent into Flanders for our future service'. The size of this demand was almost certainly due to the need to make good the losses sustained at Landen, where, according to Lieutenant-Colonel Jacob Richards, the Allies 'left the field, their artillery and what baggage they had with them'; it seems that the Allies lost 84 out of 91 cannon with William III's army that unfortunate day, and Albert Borgard, future Colonel of the Royal Regiment, noted that 'our Army was beat, and sixty-three pieces of English cannon lost.'[47] This number fits closely with Shrewsbury's subsequent replacement warrant.

Documents have survived to show how accurately, or otherwise, these Warrants were executed. In a 'certified and True copy' dated 5 April 1692, all 38 cannon called for by Nottingham are listed as being in the field, although there is no mention of the four howitzers – probably held back in the rear that year to form part of a siege train. There is also corroborative evidence for the 'Addition' of 1694. In his 'List of the English Artillery that was in the camp in the Years 1694, 5, etc.' Jacob Richards mentions for 1694 10 demi-culverins, 36 sakers, 20 3-pdrs and six howitzers – the six extra sakers and two howitzers above Shrewsbury's issue order being probably recovered cannon, survivors of the previous year's debâcles, or repaired pieces.[48] It would seem, therefore, that William's Ordnance Board was quite capable of providing all gun requirements as need arose.

It is clear that the same procedures were in vogue during the succeeding reign. Thus the 'Warrant for Holland', dated 14 March 1701/72, was the genesis of what became the 'Blenheim Train', consisting of 14 sakers, 16 three-pounders and four howitzers. This original provision was subsequently reinforced as a result of warrants dated 8 February 1702/73, 17 January 1703/74 (stores only) and 16 June 1704.[49] Six years later, on 7 May 1708, Marlborough inspected the 45 cannon of the British Artillery at Brussels – probably the entire Flanders contingent at that date. However, there is considerable evidence that Flanders received the lion's share of available Ordnance resources. As it was the major overseas theatre in all campaigns fought by the British army between 1688 and 1745 this was justifiable enough, but it must be recognized that subsidiary fronts – as, for example, Spain and Portugal – frequently fared badly in terms of administrative priority. The original artillery force sent to Portugal in 1703 boasted but five sakers and a single $5\frac{1}{4}$-pdr, served by precisely two officers, 20 gunners, six engineers, five bombardiers and 10 miners. This was slightly augmented the following year (by six 3-pdrs, three officers, 42 matrosses and one fireworker), but it was not until January 1707 that a reasonably balanced 'Combined Train' of two company strength was organized by merging the

Portuguese, Spanish and Rivers's expeditionary trains together.

In its defence, however, the Board of Ordnance could list the number of trains and other artillery services it had provided between 1701 and 1713. Besides at least 15 bomb-vessels fitted out at different dates with 13-inch brass mortars (most carried two), each provided with artillery personnel comprising one or two fireworkers, four bombardiers and one carpenter, and ignoring the all-important Flanders Train and its augmentations, the Board produced a total of 16 other trains over the period of a dozen years,* ranging in size from the tiny West Indies Train (if it merits the name) of 30 December 1702 (namely two brass $7\frac{1}{4}$-inch mortars, accompanied by a couple of engineers and three bombardiers) to the vast expeditionary train provided for the Duke of Ormonde in 1702 for the abortive Cadiz raid, which included 30 cannon, 26 mortars, and 10 petards manned by a company of gunners, another of miners, and 49 officers and staff.

After the Peace of Utrecht only five were retained – namely the train in North Britain (based on Edinburgh, Stirling and Fort William), those serving with the garrisons of Gibraltar, Port Mahon, Placentia (with Annapolis), and lastly the very reduced armament retained within England itself. But when the moment of testing came late in 1715, the hastily organized trains only reached Scotland in January 1716 although the first warrant had been issued on 4 August the previous year – hardly an impressive performance. The establishment of the Royal Regiment of Artillery thereafter ensured that there would never be a recurrence of such a humiliating episode.

Enough has been said on how trains were raised, and the size of the commitment for one power in the course of a major war and immediately

---

*These 15 trains were as follows (excluding Flanders):
6 April 1702 : Ormonde's Train (see text).
30 Dec. 1702 : West Indies Train (see text).
12 April 1703 : Portugal Train (see text).
3 Oct. 1704 : Gibraltar Train – 24 naval cannon, six 13-inch mortars; 4 officers, 6 NCOS, 55 gunners.
10 Aug. 1705 : Addition to the Portuguese Train (see text above).
12 April 1705 : Peterborough's Spanish Train – 8 cannon, 2 mortars; six officers, 11 NCOS, 10 gunners, 2 engineers, 8 craftsmen, 4 conductors.
3 July 1705 : Newfoundland Train – 14 cannon with 16 spare gun-carriages (for use with captured cannon); 1 officer, 3 craftsmen, 2 gunners.
13 May 1706 : Lord Rivers's Expedition – 40 cannon; 20 staff and officers, 18 NCOS, 32 gunners, 64 matrosses, 17 miners, 12 conductors, 10 craftsmen.
18 Jan. 1707 : Lord Galway's 'Combined Train' for Spain.
16 Dec. 1708 : North British Train – 30 cannon, 7 mortars; 4 officers, 7 NCOS, 10 gunners, 18 craftsmen.
16 Jan. 1709 : Minorca (Port Mahon) Train – no guns (much captured material *in situ*); 9 officers, 9 NCOS, 20 gunners, 10 miners, 60 matrosses, 19 craftsmen, 4 conductors.
30 July 1710 : Annapolis Royal Train – no guns; 5 officers, 7 NCOS, 11 gunners, 40 matrosses, 2 craftsmen.
1 Feb 1711 : Col. Richard King's Expeditionary Train – 30 cannon, 4 mortars, 4 petards; 13 officers, 14 NCOS, 20 gunners, 40 matrosses, 8 craftsmen, 2 conductors, 3 labourers.
May 1711 : Quebec Train (abortive raid); no guns; 15 officers, 14 NCOS, 20 gunners, 40 matrosses, 8 craftsmen.
6 May 1713 : Placentia Train – 30 cannon, 2 mortars; 2 officers, 20 gunners, 4 craftsmen.
23 June 1713 : Dunkirk Train – no guns; 5 officers, 8 NCOS, 30 gunners, 60 matrosses, 3 craftsmen, 2 conductors.

thereafter. We must next turn to describe the internal organization of these cumbersome field formations. The overall size of trains varied greatly according to local conditions, but most followed certain basic principles concerning personnel and organization. Every train in our period comprised two main sections – the active part which undertook the fighting; and the passive part, which provided support and munitions not only for the guns but also for the armies as a whole. Whilst the second category remained fairly static in organization, the first underwent considerable changes in the continuous search for increased operational efficiency.

Within these two categories there were a total of five sub-sections, namely the staff, the artillery, the engineers, and specialist workers, the Ordnance stores organization, and lastly the transportation services. The engineers and craftsmen, although an integral part of the trains well into the mid-eighteenth century, will for convenience be described in the next section of the book. The staff included the commander of the train, and the higher-paid 'comptroller', the senior Ordnance civil representative, and their deputies, aides and assistants, including as often as not a number of specialist officers and civilians; in the English armies in Flanders it also generally included from 1693 the magnificent drum-carriage which was regarded with the same pride and affection as the colours of an infantry regiment or the guidons and banners of the cavalry. Three representative artillery staffs were as follows, but it should be appreciated that the personnel remained fluid from year to year:

English Train (1691)	*French Train (1700)*	*Dutch Train (1701)*
Colonel Goor (& clerk)	*Colonel*	*Kolonel* O. van Verschner
Comptroller (& clerk)		
Lt.-Colonel Jacob Richards (& clerk)	*Lieutenant-Colonel*	*Luit. Kol.* A van Mijill
Major John Schlund	*Major*	*Majoor*
Captain-Lieutenant		
Battery-Master (& assistant)		
Adjutant	*Aide-Major*	*Officieren van het Brugwegen*
Quartermaster	*Marechal des logis*	
Chaplain	*Aumonier*	
Auditor		
Paymaster & 1 assistant		
Master-Surgeon & 1 assistant	*Chirugien*	
Waggon-Master & 2 assistants	*Vaguemestre*	*Wagenmeesters van het Lager*
Provost Marshal & 2 assistants	*Provot & 5 archers*	
Kettle-Drummer		
& Coachman	*Le Borreau* (executioners)	

Each departmental head had his special responsibilities, and by roster the officer-of-the-day, the captains and conductors would be expected to ride up and down the slow-moving columns ensuring everything was in order.

Next there were the guns with their crews and attendants. In English armies these were divided from 1693 into a number of companies according to type (although this sensible sub-division does not appear to have been applied to the siege-trains); in similar fashion the Dutch had their *compagnien,* and the French their *brigades.* Besides containing the guns, their horse-teams and an allocation of officers, gunners, matrosses and drivers, each of these sub-units included a number of waggons carrying munitions for the infantry regiments. It is hard to give a generalized but accurate impression of these 'companies' and *'brigades'* for it was in these sections of the trains that most experimentation took place.

St Rémy's suggested organization for a French train of 50 guns (divided into five brigades) accompanying an army of 50,000 men – late seventeenth century

Personnel (Staff excluded)	Equipment
Premier brigade	
1 *commissaire provincial* (equiv. 1st Captain)	Ten eight-pounder cannon.
2 *commissaires ordinaires* (equiv. 2nd Captain)	One tool-waggon (50 spades & 50 pickaxes).
2 *commissaires extraordinaires* (equiv. Lt.)	One spare gun-carriage (4 horses).
1 *officier pointeur*	Six waggons of 8-pdr ball (at 150 a gun).
1 *officier déchargeur*	Three waggons of powder (at 1,000lbs a gun).
1 *capitaine des voitures*	Six waggons of 400lbs powder, 400lbs lead and 300lbs match.
3 *ouvriers*	Three waggons of tools.
(plus indeterminate number of *canonniers*, matrosses, etc.)	One waggon for the officers' equipment.

Summary: 10 8-pdrs, one spare gun-carriage, 20 2-wheel waggons. 144 horses (at six per 8-pdrs and 4 per waggon). 12 officers and staff; perhaps 60 gunners, assistants and civilian drivers, etc.

Deuxième Brigade	As above (10 8-pdrs, etc.)
As above	Ten four-pounders; otherwise as above; 134
Troisième Brigade	horses (at five per 4-pdrs); waggons as before.
As above	Ten 4-pdrs; otherwise as above.
Quatrième Brigade	Four 24-pdrs; six 12-pdrs; 100 waggons; 3 field
As above	forges, 9 chariots, 6 caissons of surgeon's,
Cinquième Brigade or 'du Parc'	chaplain's stores, etc., 20 copper boats on flat
As above but with additional transport staff and specialist craftsmen.	trucks; 2 spare flat trucks.

Summary: four 24-pounder and six 12-pdr cannon; two spare gun-carriages (at 4 horses); 140 vehicles, (boats at 6 horses, chariots at 5, waggons at 4: spare vehicles at 4 = 669 horses); perhaps 25 officers and 800 other ranks of all types.

Thus in the late 1690s, St Rémy's suggested artillery train drew 50 cannon of assorted sizes, and needed a total of 1,225 horses (exclusive of officers' mounts) to draw the guns and the total of 220 waggons and carts that accompanied them.[51] Its total personnel (including drivers) must have approached 1,000 officers and men. This 'theoretical' train compares interestingly with William III's actual English train in Flanders (1692) already described above; this, it will be recalled, comprised 38 cannon, and required a total of 1,200 horses and 200 waggons to make it up, and some 250 officers and men, besides perhaps 400 waggoners and boys. A description of the enlarged English train of 1693 will be found on pp. 200–201 below.[52] But it is pertinent to note that it included in all 240 waggons for 70 cannon and howitzers besides 40 pontoons and the 'warning-gun on its special carriage.'* Once again, the scale is closely comparable to St Rémy's and there is no reason for believing that either Marlborough's or Prince Eugene's later trains varied significantly save in detail.

As the eighteenth century moved towards its half-way mark, many armies tended to grow in size and this process was generally shared by their artillery trains. The earlier trend in the French army towards making each *brigade* a miniature train capable of taking care of all its own requirements was partially reversed, and the tendency grew of keeping the parks highly concentrated, this often reducing their ease of movement still further, although, as we shall see later the guns themselves often moved well forward in sensible detachments. Let us examine the 'Artillery Train intended for Flanders in 1748', a document preserved in the French *Archives de l'Artillerie*. This organization was planned to include 150 cannon, 397 waggons and 2,965 draught horses, divided between 16 *brigades*, a *Grand Parc* (holding the ammunition for the infantry and cavalry together with their tools), a *Petit Parc* (comprising the field forges and artificers' vehicles), a bridging-train with 100 pontoons, and lastly an *équipage des officiers* and one *'du grand-maître'*.

FRENCH ARTILLERY TRAIN FOR FLANDERS, 1748

No. of Brigades of each category	No.	Calibre	Tool Waggon	Spare carriage	Shot waggon	Powder waggon
Two, totalling	14	16-pdrs (at 11 horses)	2 (at 4 horses)	2 (at 6 horses)	14 (at 4 horses)	4 (at 4 horses)
Two, totalling	16	12-pdrs (at 9 horses)	2	2 (at 4–5 horses)	14	6
Three, totalling	30	8-pdrs (at 6 horses)	3	3	18	9
Eight, totalling	80	4-pdr. 'Ordinaires' (at 4 horses)	8	8	2 of cartridges	3
One, totalling	10	4-pdr 'suedoises' (at 2 horses)	1	1 (at 2 horses)	2 of cartridges	3
Grand Parc –	–	–	4	–	90 of inf. cartridges	
Petit Parc	–	–	23	4 forges (at 5 horses)	–	–
Bridging Train		100 pontoons (70 'French', 30 'Swedish')	10		20 forges & waggons	
Officers' kit	332 horses					
Grand Master's kit	100 horses		NB. Where no figure is given for number of horses it			
Sutlers transport	120 horses		can be taken as four.			

Total: *16 Brigades, 150 guns, 397 waggons, 2,965 horses.* [53]

The personnel of so vast an affair cannot have been much short of 2,000 officers, men and drivers. It is revealing that although the cumbersome 24-pdrs of St Rémy's day have been discarded, and the recently introduced practice of harnessing the horses in pairs had made it possible to increase greatly the number of horses for each of the larger guns, and despite slight advances in the design of gun-carriages and trails that had been carried out under the reforming

---

*This was a signal gun, used to mark such important moments of the military day as reveille or 'setting the watch'.

La Vallière the Elder, yet there seems to have been no marked improvement in over-all mobility; doubtless the problem of massed transport counter-balanced the improvements for each individual gun.

Turning to consider the Ordnance stores carried by trains of the type we have been describing, we find an aspect of the organization that was absolutely vital to the armies but which was nevertheless all too often ignored or violently abused by contemporary chroniclers. The perennial problems that tended to bedevil the relationships between the various Commissaries of Stores, their clerks and store-keepers were such knotty questions as which stores were issuable at public charge, and conversely which were liable to repayment from unit resources (i.e. by means of stoppages of pay and deductions from the 2d a day 'off-reckonings' which constituted so considerable a part of the individual private soldier's pay). The question of replacements for weapons and equipment lost or worn out on active service was particularly the focus of contention, as many a heart-felt letter to the Board of Ordnance complaining of sharp or inconsistent practice testifies. To cite two instances; on the one hand the Board was quite prepared to accept the responsibility of replacing the pikes and muskets surrendered to the enemy at Dixmude in 1695 by the five Regiments of Foot that were subsequently repatriated. (To the not inconsiderable number of 528 of the former and 1,131 of the latter besides 935 bandolier and cartridge boxes, and 11 halberds.)[54] But when, on the other hand, it became a question of replacing pikes by socket bayonets throughout the army (as in 1700) the Board dug in its heels and steadfastly refused to countenance a free issue to Colonel Hodges' Regiment on the rather specious grounds that a socket-bayonet was a type of sword, which had always indisputably been issued on repayment.

The leading representatives of the Ordnance Stores department serving with the English trains were the Commissaries of Stores, but to these officials were added two or more Controllers of Army Accounts from 1703 onwards.[55] Their inclusion led to the avoidance of many abuses and anomalies in the field, whilst the creation of the Board of General Officers in London (1706) to investigate *inter alia* serious allegations of misdemeanours was a further positive step forward – both improvements owing much to the inspiration of the Master-General of the day, the first Duke of Marlborough.

The quantities and types of munitions and stores these officials were responsible for controlling could be vast. The primary responsibility was of course the provision of sufficient powder and shot, as well as spare instruments and replacements, for the guns. The calculation of what constituted a 'sufficiency' varied considerably from army to army and generation to generation. Thus the 38 cannon (excluding the howitzers) of William III's 1692 field train left England for Flanders provided with 11,200 cannon-balls (or an average of 295 a gun) and 560 rounds of case (about 15 a gun). The statistics given by Colonel Richards for the English Train of 1692 corroborates that this quantity of shot did in fact accompany the army to Flanders. For the 38 'brass ordnance' he listed a total of 3,200 'rownd shot' for the 8 demi-culverins, 4,000 for the 10 sakers and as many for the 20 three-pounders and the provision of case-shot for the same categories to the number of 160, 200 and 200 respectively;

this scale of ammunition required 200 barrels of 'corne-powder' and 20 more of match, whilst the four howitzers shared 200 seven-inch grenades.[56] Much of these munitions were doubtless held in arsenals in rear of the army, ready to replenish the trains as need arose. St Rémy, by contrast, held that '100 rounds per gun is ample for 50 pieces, it being almost impossible that they could shoot them off in a single day's affair',[57] and estimated that at least some 50 rounds per gun should accompany each *brigade,* together with some 1,000lbs of powder. Each cannon ball required up to two-thirds of its weight in gun-powder; thus a 24-pdr could require 1,600lbs of powder for 100 rounds. By the 1740s, the French army seems to have carried 150 rounds per gun into the field, 'sufficient for two large battles and a retreat'.[58] Additionally there were quantities of 'hair-mats' (used for greasing the balls before loading them into the barrels), a spare carriage for every five or more guns, and quantities of spare rammers and training-levers besides vast numbers of hand-tools for improving the rough roadways to aid the passage of the weighty guns and their attendant waggons, and a number of tents (some 100 in all), ridge-poles, 'tent-pinners' (2,896 'in 11 hampers') and a total of 92 mallets.

In addition to this basic duty, every train carried substantial munitions and other equipment for the use of the army as a whole. At the very outset of a campaign, each infantry soldier would usually be issued with 24 rounds of powder and shot from the train waggons, and in addition to this a further reserve of between 24 rounds (according to St Rémy) and as many as 50 rounds per soldier would accompany the army into the field, besides vast numbers of grenades and tools. Thus William III's 1692 Train dragged with it 600 barrels of corne-powder, 10 tons of match, four tons of musket shot and one of carbine shot, besides 12 barrels of hand-grenades (4,000 in all) and 6,000 fuses for them. St Rémy was insistent that the munition scales should be calculated at a pound of powder per man for each day of anticipated action (sufficient for 24 shots), a pound of ball (between 22 and 23 rounds) and as much of match. On this scale, to supply an army of 50,000 men for a major battle would require some 30,000lbs of powder and as much again of shot (it being assumed in St Rémy's day that a substantial proportion of the infantry would be pikemen). The same authority also estimated that such an army would require a total of 6,000 spades, shovels, axes, etc. borne by the train transport. Many authorities mention the need for a further 'ultimate reserve' of one day's worth of powder and shot for use only in emergencies.

The large number of munition waggons required now becomes understandable. Most of them in the late seventeenth century were four-wheel affairs drawn by four or more horses in tandem. The French habitually loaded 200 rounds of eight-pounder or 300 rounds of five-pounder ammunition into a single waggon; alternatively they placed 1,250lbs of powder, 1,143lbs of lead, 1,238lbs of match, or 1,000 charged grenades into each cart. In Richards' day the English Ordnance specified different quantities for their transport, for example 160 ball and 40 rounds of case-shot for a 6-pdr saker, or 93 rounds and 18 of case for a 24-pounder demi-culverin – substantially lighter loads than their opponents. Marlborough's famous two-horse two-wheel light carts carried a maximum of two-hundredweights. By 1748 the French were loading their four-horse waggons still more excessively: for instance the six waggons allocated to carry 154 roundshot for each gun of a *brigade* of 10 8-pdrs packed a total of 2,048 pounds apiece, and some four-horse teams were expected to drag up to 4,000lbs of powder although this was exceptional.[59] At this period the French had a reputation for overestimating what a horse could draw or carry, their load being 550lbs. This was a possible burden for good going, but under rough conditions it placed a disproportionate strain on the animals and inevitably led to exhaustion and delays.

11

Artillery pieces and equipment

In the early seventeenth century, the German gun-founders had been considered the best in Europe, but by the 1650s it was generally acknowledged that the Dutch and the Swedes excelled in the design, manufacture and handling of artillery. The former were especially renowned for reducing their calibres to four whether for sea or land service, namely 6-, 12-, 24- and 48-pdrs, and for developing a standardized gun-carriage for each. The latter had made great advances under Gustavus Adolphus in reducing the crippling weight of many of their pieces; the two-man 'leather-guns' of the Swedish armies (subsequently replaced by Tortensson's cast-iron 4-pdrs weighing 500lbs) virtually introduced the concept of practicable regimental artillery, whilst the production of mathematical artillery tables and the improved status of the Scandinavian artillerists were further advantages.

To some extent the Swedes retained their original reputation throughout our period, and in 1745 we shall find the French authorities divided into bitterly contesting factions over the desirability of introducing the 'Swedish gun'. The reputation of the Dutch, however, had declined to a considerable degree by the 1690s – largely due to their own complacency – and the lead may be said to have passed successively to France, England, and later Austria. No single power was really paramount in influence during the eighteenth century before the days of Gribeauval; rather each excelled in one particular field or aspect of gunnery. Thus the French produced the greatest theoreticians of the day in such men as Lieutenant-General Surirey de Saint-Rémy whose writings were to gunnery what the works of Vauban were to military engineering and siegecraft); Vallière the Elder who took the first hesitant steps towards major reform of the artillery as a whole; and Bernard Forest de Bélidor and Blondel who founded the school of modern ballistics – preparing the way for the truly revolutionary reforms of later years. Between them these remarkable men prepared the way for Gribeauval. The English on the other hand produced the best practical artillerymen during the long Spanish Succession War led by such famous gunners as Holcroft Blood, the Richards Brothers and Albert Borgard, although by the mid-century the Austrian artillery was in the process of earning an extremely impressive reputation, especially in regard to their horse artillery, first introduced by Prince Eugene early in the 1700s.

Types of artillery

The classification of artillery at the opening of our period is complicated by the profusion of calibres in use, many of which were constructed according to different principles. It will only be possible here to indicate the main divisions and to discuss the characteristics of a few representative pieces.

There were three main categories of weapon. First the cannon, divided into two groups: *pièces de place* or *de batterie* (fortress, siege and naval guns) and *pièces de campagne* (field pieces generally of somewhat lesser bulk and greater manoeuvrability). All cannon employed direct fire, except siege guns which often adopted ricochet fire. Secondly there were the mortars, used almost exclusively for siege warfare, which lobbed bombs of varying sizes over a high trajectory to fall behind fortifications or other forms of cover. And thirdly there were howitzers, weapons which enjoyed some of the characteristics of both cannon and mortars. These last were perhaps the most economical artillery of the day in so far as they were mobile, considerably lighter than the bulky cannon, and fired a larger projectile than field guns of a similar weight (albeit over rather a shorter range). The main characteristics of a selection of these various pieces will be listed below.

Besides being divided into the two main categories of siege and field according to role, the French artillery of the 1690s and 1700s – and those of several other powers – was further split into two types, namely *'les canons de vielle invention'* and those *'de nouvelle invention'*. The 'old' guns in the French service had been reduced to six calibres by the 1690s – namely 'Spanish' pieces of 12- and 24-pdr and 'French' of 33-, 16-, 8- and 4-pdr. This would have been a reasonable system had it not been for the regional variations permitted in the design and casting of the various calibres. There were, for example, three brands of most classes of cannon, namely 'bastards', 'legitimates' and 'doubly fortified' according to how thick the founder cast the walls of the bore. The thicker the metal, the larger the powder-charge that could safely be used. Thus a 'doubly-fortified' cannon could take the full weight of the ball's worth of powder, a *'légitime'* up to four-fifths, a *'bâtarde'* only two-thirds. Alternative terms were 'greater', 'standard' and 'lesser' guns of a particular calibre. Each artillery department jealously conserved its own points of variance, and although every gun in France bore the royal coat of arms con-joined with that of the Duc de Maine *(Maître-Général)* this was practically the only point of resemblance common to the artillery as a whole. Thus solid shot cast to fit the bore, of for example, a 33-pdr *canon de France* produced in the foundries of Saint-Gervais in Dauphiné could not be used for a similar piece cast in the forges of Charleville or Périgord. This inability to interchange ammunition presented obvious logistical and operational problems, and a similar lack of standardization affected gun-carriages and other equipment, whilst the cost of gun-founding varied considerably from region to region. Some guns were long in service. For example one of the guns taken by the Allies at Namur (1695) bore the cipher of Henry IV of France (1594–1601). Most French cannon of the 'old invention' however, shared one feature that was an advantage and a disadvantage at the same time, namely a broadly similar barrel length. This not only applied to guns of the same calibre but also to those of every calibre – although classes of 'short' 8- and 4-pdrs were developed as well. The supposed advantage gained by this was that it made possible the employment of almost any gun for the defence of fortifications. A cannon with a short barrel whose muzzle failed to protrude beyond an embrasure was liable to inflict a considerable amount of damage to the masonry through the flash and force of the exploding charge. The standardized barrel lengths, which ranged only between 11ft 1inch and 10ft 7in for the whole range of six calibres, overcame this difficulty. On the other hand, this resulted in the *weight* of many smaller pieces being out of all proportion to the size of ball they fired, gravely aggravating the eternal problem of gun mobility.

Many attempts were made to overcome this grave disadvantage, one of the most noteworthy being the founding of cannon according to the 'new invention.' This originally seems to have been the idea of one Antonio Gonzalès in about 1679. By refashioning the powder-chamber at the base of the bore into a spherical form in place of the old standard cylindrical shape, it was found possible to reduce the weight of the propellant charge from the standard two-thirds of the weight of the ball to merely one-third, and still obtain the same range and penetration power. The discovery of this interesting fact is sometimes attributed to Claude du Metz, Inspector-General of Artillery. The reason was that the spark of the linstock could be introduced into the centre of the charge (instead of at its rear extremity as formerly), thus inducing faster burning and a more devastating explosion. The reduction of the powder charge in turn made possible a considerable proportionate reduction in the cannon's mass – producing a dramatically lighter piece. The saving in weight can be seen by comparing the following specimen figures:

'Old' *démi-canon de France* (16-pdr) weighed 4,100 livres (or 256 calibres – i.e. weight of ball)
'New' *démi-canon de France* (16-pdr) weighed 2,100 livres (or 137 calibres)
'Old' *'la moyenne'* (4-pdr)   weighed 1,300 livres (or 325 calibres)
'New' *'la moyenne'* (4-pdr)   weighed 600 livres (or 150 calibres)
(N.B. – all weights refer to barrel only)

In this way almost half the weight of the 16-pdr and rather more than half that of the 4-pdr could be saved, the latter approximating to Tortensson's Swedish cast iron pieces, which required only two horses to draw them.

Unfortunately there was another side to the story. To achieve such dramatic reductions involved, *inter alia,* increasing the thickness of the breech metal and the shortening of the barrels of the pieces, which recreated the problem of embrasure damage. For example, the 'new' 24-pdr barrel measured only 6ft 3in (plus cascabel) to the 'old' 10ft 10in. Secondly the old-fashioned trails and gun-carriages tended to disintegrate under the strain of the recoil from the more violent explosion. The cause of this was misconstrued, and instead of devising truly superior carriages the experts advocated a pear-shaped chamber – the invention of the Marquis de la Frézelière, Lieutenant-General of Artillery – which lessened the discrepancy between the chamber's diameter and that of the bore – but little advantage was ultimately gained thereby. The hope that improved ranges would result proved illusory, and a further complication was the continuing difficulty of swabbing-out the chamber with the wet rammer between rounds. A sponge or rammer that would fit the bore could not reach every crevice of the new-type chambers – and if any smouldering material remained from the previous shot the results were likely to be unfortunate for the man at the end of the rammer as he attempted to drive home the next charge. De la Frézelière was an energetic man and tackled each problem in turn, devising slightly longer barrels, better trails, and gun-carriages, but these still tended to fall to pieces. Undeterred the Lieutenant-General refounded most of the culverins held in the fortresses of the eastern frontiers according to the 'revised new invention', sometimes called 'the German fashion' as they were founded in Alsace-Lorraine, but his enlightened reforms stirred up such a heated controversy that on his death the authorities insisted on recasting all his improved pieces, with the result that they became almost as cumbersome as formerly. This victory for reaction was to cost the French dear during the wars that followed.[60]

Further experiments were conducted by many powers in the early eighteenth century. Some related to materials employed for casting; alongside the old brass cannon were put pieces made of bronze, forged iron and cast-iron, although many of these inventions tended to produce heavier guns than ever and therefore were soon scrapped; thus the cast-iron 16-pounder weighed 4,200lbs to the brass culverin's 4,100lbs. Guns of bronze, however, soon became the standard type. Considerable advances were made in methods of construction, although early attempts to bore-out the barrels failed owing to inadequate machinery, and the old method of casting cannon in a mould with a central core remained the usual practice in all countries, imprecise though it tended to be. This process could be perilous; on one occasion in 1716 for example, a considerable explosion destroyed the English foundry at Moorfields – caused by molten metal being poured into damp-moulds – killing many spectators and wounding a great number more, including Colonel Armstrong, Surveyor-General of the Ordnance. Other reforms related to general design. In 1704 the French arsenals produced a secret-weapon in the triple-barrelled cannon, of which a great deal was expected, especially by Marshal Villeroi. Such hopes proved unfounded, however, and several of these pieces fell into Allied hands during Marlborough's Passage of the Lines of Brabant in 1705, and after Ramillies the following year the idea was discarded. Other experimental designs included double-cannon, firing pairs of balls joined by a metal bar, but these soon shared the fate of the triple-cannon. Of more lasting value was the development of a tiny one-pounder mountain gun, mounted on a special carriage, probably the inspiration for the imaginary *amusettes* advertised by Marshal de Saxe as an infantry-support weapon in the 1730s.

Inevitably different armies employed different cannon – but in broad terms we can assert that the greatest differences distinguishing the rival artilleries related more to methods of siting and employment than to dramatic variations in *matériel*. Commanders also tended to differ in the proportions of heavy, medium and light cannon they placed in their artillery parks. In most French armies, the proportions were 7 per cent of pieces of 36-, 24- and 16-, 33 per cent of 12- and 8-pdrs, and 60 per cent of 4-pdrs or smaller cannon. Many European armies adopted this pattern, but the English field trains of Marlborough's day rarely contained pieces larger than 16-pdrs. Tallard's artillery at Blenheim, however, included four 24-pdrs, as Mérode-Westerloo bears witness.[61]

TABLE OF FIELD ARTILLERY IN GENERAL USE, 1688–1730

Calibre	Other name	Wt. of Barrel in lbs.	Barrel length excluding cascabel[1]	'Old' Wt. in calibres	Point Blank[2] Range in paces	Max. Range at 45°
24-pdr)	Demi-canon d'Espagne	5,100 (3,000)[3]	10ft (5ft 10¼in)	212	800 paces	5,000
	English 24-pdr	5,600	c.12ft (6ft 5in)		900 paces	
16-pdr)	Demi-canon de France	4,100 (2,200)	10ft (5ft 6¼in)	256	800 paces	5,000
	English culverin	4,500	c.12ft			
12-pdr)	Quart-canon d'Espagne	3,400 (2,000)	10ft (5ft 5¾in)	283	450 paces	5,000
	English 12-pdr		(5ft 1in)			
8-pdr)	Quart-canon de France	1,950 (1,000)	10ft (4ft 5½in)	243	400 paces	4,500
	English demi-culverin	2,000			400 paces	
6-pdr)	English saker	1,500	c.9ft 6in (4ft 1in)		500 paces	4,000
4-pdr)	'La Moyenne' &	1,300 (600)	10ft (4ft 4in)	325	300 paces	3,500
	French courte-moyenne		8ft 6in			(?)
3-pdr	English minion	800	c.7ft 6in (3ft 3in)	266	450 paces	3,200
½–2½- pdrs	Falcons & Falconets[4]	150–750	c.7ft		150–260 paces	1,200– 2,500

NOTES: 1. Cascabels (the rounded knob at the rear of a barrel) varied in length between 5 and 11 inches. Most authorities exclude them when giving barrel lengths – calculated by measuring from the muzzle to the first *platte-bande* of the breach.
2. Ranges. Authorities vary enormously in this respect, and it is impossible to give more than a rough approximation. Different types of gun existed within each class (thus there were 'least', 'ordinary' and 'greatest' classifications within the English culverin category). Ranges given here refer to 'ordinary' guns. 'Point-Blank' range was defined in 1702 as 'the shot of a gun, levell'd in a direct line without mounting or sinking the barrel'.
3. Weights and lengths in parentheses relate to cannons of the 'New' invention.
4. These classes of small guns were rapidly disappearing in most armies, although the French 1-pdr mountain gun remained in use.
SOURCES: the French specifications are taken from St Rémy, Vol. II pp. 57–60; the English from the *New Military Dictionary* of 1702 (slightly suspect in some respects); and the ranges from Favé, Vol IV pp. 22–6 and 69. All specifications are to be regarded as approximate but may be said to represent rough averages.

The second major class of artillery – namely the mortars – belongs more properly to siege warfare, and accordingly will be described more fully in the next section. As the third class – howitzers were used increasingly in the field, they can be considered here for convenience, although their major employment also remained reserved for siege warfare. Contrary to popular belief, these were not fired at an extreme angle, the maximum elevation of the barrel being generally 15 degrees from the horizontal. It was widely considered that the English excelled in the design of this weapon, although the Dutch had been the first to introduce this type of ordnance in the seventeenth century. The English 'haubitzer' barrel weighed about 1,500lbs and measured about 3ft 7½in (not including a 9in cascabel), and was mounted on an exceptionally sturdy and well-constructed carriage which was the envy of many armies. By comparison the standard Dutch howitzer weighed only 900lbs and measured about 42 inches, but it was considered far inferior to the English version. The diameter of the bores were commonly 10 inches and 6 inches respectively, yet the better-designed English shell was lighter in weight than its Dutch equivalent, and accordingly could be fired further. The maximum range of the English howitzer would seem to have been about 1,300 yards. By the 1750s, the English armies had 5ft 8in, 8in and 10in versions, the last weighing 3,500lbs and measuring 4ft 2in. in barrel length

The French do not seem to have taken to howitzers on a large scale until the 1720s, although there would appear to have been at least a few in service earlier – possibly captured Allied pieces. The major disadvantage of the early howitzer – which it shared with most mortars – was that it often required two 'fires'; first the fuse of the shell had to be lit (often a hazardous procedure for the danger of the spark reaching the propellant-charge beneath was always present) and then the piece itself had to be discharged. Obviously it was very difficult to gain accurate results, for every fraction of a second the fuse of the shell burnt before the howitzer was discharged brought the explosion point nearer, and as a result ineffective air-bursts were frequently encountered. It was not until the late seventeenth century that a means was discovered for firing both charge and shell at the same instant by use of a double-linstock, and for a further period these remained somewhat unreliable.

Lastly, we must briefly consider naval cannon. As their role was generally to fire in broadsides, they were generally regarded as static pieces, and as such had more in common with fortress artillery than field guns. Indeed, both in design of cannon and type of carriage, naval and garrison guns were often inter-changeable and can be treated together.

The French navy commonly employed seven calibres of gun for the sea-service, namely pieces of 36-, 24-, 18-, 12-, 8-, 6-, and 4-pdrs. There were also a few 64-pdrs in service, but as Père Daniel noted, 'such pieces are dangerous on board',[62] and from the 1720s the use of 36-pdrs was also restricted, being reserved almost exclusively for the French first-rate three-decker vessels which mounted between 70 and 120 guns. A naval 36-pdr weighed some 6,200lbs, measured 11ft 1in (cascabel excluded), had a point-blank range of some 600 paces and a maximum range of about 6,000, although at sea it was rare for guns to be discharged at more than 300 yards range (lesser ranges were common), and it may be said that a practical maximum for accurate fire was some 800 yards (the restricted space of the gun-port making it impossible to fire lower or main deck guns at a very high elevation). The basic dimensions of the other naval pieces listed roughly correspond with those tabulated for field artillery, with the same restriction on maximum effective ranges as cited for the naval 24-pdr.

Other navies employed broadly similar guns, although as always there were regional variations. Thus the Spanish navy included a small number of 40-pdrs in the late seventeenth century, whilst the Russian fleet in 1735 placed 32-pdrs on the lower deck, 18-pdrs on the main, 9-pdrs on the upper, and 6-pdrs on the quarterdecks of their first-rate warships, which included the 100 gun *St Peter* and, interestingly enough, the 70 gun *Marlborrow* [sic] and *Prinz Eugen*. Lesser vessels mounted 24-, 18-, 12- and 6-pdrs.[65] The Dutch, we have already noted, used identical calibres whether ashore or afloat, namely 6-, 12-, 24- and-48-pdrs. The Royal Navy employed much the same types as their perennial French opponents, but tended to place lighter guns in ships of the same class. Many complaints from English captains of the period lamented the fact that French ships mounting 60 to 70 guns included a proportion of 24-pdrs in their armament, whilst such large pieces were only to be found in Royal Naval vessels of 70 guns and above. Similarly, French 50-gun ships carried 18-pdrs, a type of cannon only issued to English vessels of 60 guns or more. What the French presumably sacrificed in terms of taking on additional weight they more than made up for in being more heavily gunned, a point of no small significance in ship-to-ship duels between vessels of much the same size.[63] On the other hand at least half of Queen Anne's 200-odd warships mounted 50 or more guns.

Wherever possible, Admiralties preferred to equip their ships with guns of bronze rather than pieces of forged iron. Bronze guns were far less likely to burst their barrels and that was a peril to be rigorously avoided in the highly inflammable 'wooden-walls' of the period. The life of an iron piece was generally computed (for both land and sea) at 1,200 rounds; thereafter, cracks would rapidly appear around the vents or in the bore. But when there were not enough bronze guns to go round (which there rarely were in our period), steps had to be taken to ensure that the more important vessels received a higher proportion than their slighter sisters. Thus a French *Ordonnance* of 1669, amended by that of 1689, laid down the following standards. First rate ships (70–120 guns and 3 decks) were to have none but the best – iron-guns were banned from them. Second rates (56–70 guns and three decks, one being a 'half-deck') were to have two-thirds bronze guns and one-third iron, unless they were designated to carry an Admiral's flag in which case they enjoyed the same privilege over armament as first rates. Third rates (40–50 guns and two decks) were to carry only half guns of bronze. Fourth rates (30–40 guns) merely a third and any insignificant fifth rates (18–26 gun two-deckers) were to carry a mere quarter of their armament in bronze guns, although the presence of an admiral could revise the state of affairs in all instances.[64]

ENGLISH BRONZE NAVAL CANNON, MID-EIGHTEENTH CENTURY (all of 'New' invention)

Calibre	Barrel length	Calibre	Barrel length
42-pdr	8ft 4inch	18–pdr	6ft 4inch
36-pdr	7ft 10inch	9–pdr	5ft
24-pdr	7ft	3–pdr	3ft 6inch

(NB there were also bronze 6-, 12-, 24- and 42-pounders of the 'old' variety, and nine calibres of 'old' iron guns and as many again of 'new').

Another type of artillery used at sea was the mortar — reserved for the bomb-vessels. Those of Queen Anne's navy habitually carried two 13-inch mortars, together with a crew of 30 men, including a team of three or four 'experts' (usually a 'fireworker' and three bombardiers per vessel) provided by the Board of Ordnance, and displaced between some 150 and 300 tons. These mortars were used to good effect on such occasions as the bombardments of Le Havre (1694) and Dunkirk (1706), or during the operations against Cadiz in 1727, but the description of their characteristics can be reserved for the pages devoted later to siege-mortars from which they differed little if at all. The English and the Dutch were the first to make widespread use of such weapons at sea, but the French were following their lead on a limited scale.

Projectiles, propellants, equipment and gun-carriages

There were three main types of ammunition in common use in the late seventeenth and early eighteenth centuries. First there was solid shot, spheres of stone or cast-iron, manufactured in various sizes to fit the different bores allowing sufficient 'windage' to facilitate loading. To ensure that balls were neither too big nor too small, every one was passed through a ring gauge which the Spaniards called a *pasabala* (literally a 'ball-passer').

Round shot was the standard ammunition for all field artillery. It was used against enemy batteries, formed bodies of men or against fortifications and buildings, and at sea of course against enemy vessels or targets ashore. The use of richochet fire gradually came into widespread use (probably first advocated by Vauban for use in siege warfare), whereby the ball was fired in such a way as to strike the ground ahead of the target with a glancing blow, and then bound onwards in one or more 'hops', sending up fragments of stone or earth which could wound numbers of troops who managed to avoid the passage of the ball itself. In due course this type of 'skip-firing' was applied to war at sea as well, the ball being bounced off the surface of the water and into the victim beyond, where the worst hazard to the crew was always caused by flying splinters. This type of fire could increase the maximum range considerably, though clearly the exact effect of the shot was determined by a whole number of variable factors including the weather, the state of the ground (or sea), and the accuracy of the powder-charge. Red-hot shot was also occasionally employed particularly by shore-batteries against vulnerable ships, as well as in a few sieges, but this was tricky to handle: wet wads had to be placed between the powder charge and the missile, and it was clearly desirable to be clear of the muzzle (and the rear) before these were burnt through, or a premature explosion and recoil might have dire results.

Solid shot was generally fired directly at the target. Penetration power varied according to local conditions, but at sea it was estimated that a 24-pdr ball fired at 100 yards could penetrate up to $4\frac{1}{2}$ feet of seasoned oak. On land, St Rémy taught that a 24-pounder, firing at 150 yards from a stone-and-earth bastion could penetrate as much as 35 feet of packed earth.[65] Smaller pieces had a lesser effect. At the siege of Castillo de San Marcos (Florida) in 1740, the defenders noted that the English 18-pdrs – sited at 1,000 yards from the fort – were capable of sending their cannon balls only 18in into the main fortifications, but that the same guns were wreaking great havoc with the slenderer parapets which were only three feet thick.[66] Of course, breaching batteries were normally advanced stage by stage to the optimum range of 200 yards or even less, but we shall return to this subject in the following section. Obviously a cannon-ball could do great harm to troops drawn up in the open if they were caught in enfilade (or from a flank).

There were other variants of solid shot in use. Some of these – like bar-shot – were experimentally used on land, but most were reserved for service at sea. These included chain-shot, two balls linked with a few feet of chain, a missile particularly useful against an enemy's rigging. Reputedly an adaptation of this weapon was employed experimentally against a land enemy. On this occasion a long chain was joined to two cannon-balls, and each was loaded into a separate cannon, the idea being to cut a swathe of destruction through the enemy. Alas, the end result was the cutting in two of the gun crew, not their opponents. One of the cannon had misfired!

In the second place there were various forms of case-shot. This was known in the English army as 'partridge' – a reference to sporting practices of a more peaceful nature. The French – and most other armies – used three varieties, namely *'la cartouche'* (a wooden-box, linen bag or tin full of musket-balls or other small missiles), *'la grappe de raisin'* (a wooden base fitting the bore, with a number of grape-shot secured to it by metal straps), and a variant of the latter idea, *'les pommes de pin'*. These were used for anti-personnel work in close-quarter fighting – usually at ranges of 200 yards or less – and all worked on broadly the same principle. After the gun was fired, the case-shot would be propelled at high velocity from the gun, and as it left the muzzle the container would disintegrate causing a spray of shot to burst forth over a considerable area. A form of this projectile much used at sea for close-quarter work was grape-shot (rather larger balls collected around a wooden core, the whole enclosed in a linen bag) which had to have a measure of penetration power to pierce the wooden-walls and other cover provided around ships of war. Many types of mortar were also designed to fire this type of projectile. The French *pierrier* and Spanish *pedrero* are two examples. One version threw a whole pattern of stone balls from a series of cup-discharges as well as a shell in much the same fashion as the modern grenade-throwers used on some types of tank or as depth-charge patterns are fired against submarines. In 1740, the Spanish fort at San Marcos held 6,000 stones for use in mortars besides 2,000 sacks of grapeshot.

Thirdly there were 'hollow-shot' *boulets creux,* shells and bombs, used by howitzers and mortars. These were hollow globes filled with explosive or occasionally case-shot (but never a combination – shrapnel still lay a century ahead); the former were discharged by a lighted fuse protruding from the sphere, and the calculation of the correct length of match for a given range was clearly a very difficult matter. It also often involved a double-lighting (i.e. fuse followed by the powder charge propellant), as contemporaries found it impracticable to load the bomb or shell fuse-downwards (so that the exploding charge lit the fuse and achieved precise synchronization), but several ingenious if unreliable means were devised in the early eighteenth century for achieving simultaneous fuse-lighting and discharge. Many of the larger bombs used for the big mortars also sported a pair of carrying handles. As a 12in mortar bomb of 1740 weighed all of 145lbs these were clearly necessary adjuncts. This type of shell was mainly used to set fire to houses, to terrify cavalry with air bursts, or to reach targets behind cover, but it was often possible for cool recipients to pluck out the burning fuse as the shell or bomb lay smoking on the ground. Wet ground could also put them out of action. Thus an account of the action at Walcourt (1689) related that

> a bomb fell among the officers of Collonel [*sic*] Hayne's (Hale's) Regiment without doing any harm, the Fuzze being stifled; two more fell in a Meadow near our Guards, with the same success.[67]

It is not clear whether these were enemy shells or Allied short-falls. Most French experts stress that the French army was slow in adopting howitzers – but all armies had mortars. Many shells and bombs were designed with thicker metal near the base than in the region of the touch-hole, in the over-optimistic hope that this would induce the missile to fall base-first to the ground, reducing the likelihood of the fuse being extinguished in some inopportunely placed puddle on first impact. Different shapes of shell were also experimented with but most were basically spherical.

Passing on to describe the gunpowder in use at our period, we again find a story of regional variation in composition. All gunpowder, however, was of the black variety, which inevitably led to rapid fouling of cannon and musket barrels and caused dense clouds of gun-smoke to obscure the battlefields. According to the definitive French *Ordonnance* of 18 September 1686, the composition of gunpowder was supposed to be 75 parts saltpetre to $12\frac{1}{2}$ parts sulphur and a similar proportion of charcoal. An English formula, on the other hand, placed the proportions at 75, 10 and 15 respectively. The saltpetre was very carefully refined, being boiled three times in special containers for 24 hours, and the end-product was carefully graded according to colour. Although exactly the same powder was used for the cannons as was employed for the muskets, some armies supplied special priming powder of a 'corned' variety, which was supposed to make a brighter flash. On ignition, ordinary black powder, it may be noted, liberated gases occupying about 300 times its own space, but it was both dangerous and unstable, and in store tended to absorb dampness with remarkable alacrity. This proved a major problem in tropical climes.

Much of the powder was moved in and issued from barrels (many holding a quintal or 98lbs). Most shells and grenades were transported uncharged in bulk and were only loaded and fused immediately prior to action. However, reliance on the old wooden powder buckets for measuring correct quantities was gradually superseded (in part at least) by pre-packaged powder bags of linen 'stuff' or canvas holding a fixed quantity. This innovation dates from the armies of Gustavus Adolphus in the 1630s, but some armies including the English, long preferred to ladle out their powder from barrel to gun. Indeed, in the 1720s, La Vallière insisted that the French gunners return to the use of 'la lanterne'. Thirty years earlier, on the other hand, St Rémy had advocated cartridges of parchment (as these almost entirely disappeared in the discharge, making it necessary to swab out the touch-hole only every four or five shots. French *gargousses* (cartridges) measured three calibres in length, and held amounts of powder varying between half and two-thirds the weight of the ball. Every variety of cannon had its own recommended charge; too much led to the danger of exploded barrels and 'bushed' touch-holes; too little reduced the range and penetrating power of the ball. Contemporary artillerists spent much time and paper arguing about ideal charges, but not until the 1720s was much real scientific progress made.

To prime a cannon using a cartridge necessitated the bursting open of the bag where it lay under the touch-hole. This was often done with a small pick, but in the early 1700s a powder-filled tin tube was introduced which was driven into the bag through the touch-hole. When the top of this was touched with the smouldering end of a piece of slow-match — attached to the end of a forked linstock to enable the *déchargeur* to keep well clear of the recoil — the spark was passed directly to the charge and the piece went off.

Shell and bomb fuses were wooden tubes with tightly tamped down 'slow' powder charges placed in the quarter-inch hole running through their length. The head of the fuse was often slightly wider with a cup-like aperture to facilitate lighting. To achieve the right burning time, the bombardier either cut the fuse to the required length, or alternatively bored a small hole at the correct point to let the special powder, finely 'mealed' and moistened with alcohol, flash at the requisite moment. Some English variants used two strands of very narrow match instead of this inflammable substance. The heads of all fuses were protected by paper caps (or sometimes tin) when not in use. A fuse was driven home into the bomb-aperture until only 2/10ths of an inch was protruding. To withdraw a fuse there was a fuse extractor somewhat resembling a pair of pliers.

A considerable amount of ancillary equipment accompanied every gun into the field. In 1694, for instance, and English demi-culverin 'complete' required one ladle, one sponge, a bucket, two rammers, a wadhook, one set of 'coynes' (wedges for altering the barrel's elevation), three drag ropes (sometimes chains), one handspike, three lashing ropes, one iron chain and one pair tompions (metal caps that fitted over the cannon's muzzle).[68] Similar scales of issue existed for all sizes and types of cannon of all nationalities, and differed hardly at all in basic type from generation to generation, although details of manufacture varied enormously, and hardly any pieces of equipment were interchangeable. Furthermore relatively little care was taken to ensure good design or reliable materials went into the manufacture, resulting in many complaints.

Lastly we must devote a word to gun carriages and trails, around or upon which most of the items just listed were hoisted or slung. In this field, despite the efforts of men like de la Frézelière and St Rémy, there was little uniformity of design or quality of manufacture, although as the eighteenth century wore on simpler, stronger and less encumbered designs made their appearance. Basically the French artillery used three classes of carriage, one for each major class of cannon, namely heavy, medium and light. For many years little care was taken to ensure a truly sensible proportionate weight relationship between carriages and gun barrels. The carriages of larger guns should have been proportionately larger than those for smaller pieces, but this was not always the case. Thus a 'long' 24-pdr was placed on a carriage that weighed half the barrel weight; a 'short' 24-pdr on the other hand had a carriage one third of its weight; similarly different types of 4-pdr had carriages weighing between 65 per cent and 85 per cent of the barrel weight. Many different designs of gun-carriage were experimented with – and no less than 85 pages and almost as many plates of St Rémy's definitive work are taken up with describing and illustrating these – but most remained badly designed with little iron-work to strengthen them against the stresses of discharge and recoil, and in consequence many simply fell to bits. The 'spare carriage' that accompanied every brigade or battery into the field was certainly often employed.

English designs of gun-carriage proved remarkably superior to those of France, and this factor partially underlines the superior reputation earned by Marlborough's gunners. Particularly admired was the English howitzer carriage which was strong, elegant, and relatively light.

Almost all field and siege gun-carriages had the same basic features, namely a pair of wheels, an axle, two trail-slides or 'cheeks' (usually one calibre thick), with differing means of changing the barrel alignment (most used wedges), two trunnion-caps for holding the cannon in position, and various types of reinforcements and transoms. By the late seventeenth century, almost all guns were also provided with an *'avant-train'* or limber, a pair of wheels on an axle furnished with a pole or shafts to which the horses were harnessed. The rear of the trail of the cannon was lifted onto the *avant-train* for easier movement along such roads as there were, although some experts deplored the extra time it took to bring a piece into action on account of this. Nevertheless, gradual improvements in design of trails redistributed the gross weight between the four wheels, and this made it possible to reduce the number of draught-horses. Some small pieces – such as the English 3-pdr 'regimental' pieces – dispensed with a limber and instead had a forked-trail, which made them handy pieces to manoeuvre whether by hand or by horse.

Garrison and ship gun-carriages were very different from land carriages. Although Vauban designed an experimental all-purpose two-wheeled marine carriage for coastal and naval artillery in about 1700, almost all of these were mounted on four small, low-slung wheels (or 'trucks') of cast-iron or wood. In order to fit the restricted space on shipboard or rampart, such gun- or 'truck'-carriages were considerably lower in height than their field equivalents, and virtually dispensed with the trail altogether. Aboard ship they were tethered by a complex system of ropes and pulleys to absorb as much of the recoil as possible, to facilitate running up and back for reloading purposes, and to avert the peril of the guns running amok in bad weather. Many minor variations of design were employed in attempts to ease wear and tear. Thus English naval manufacturers put copper on the bottom of the spindle on which the wheels (or trucks) revolved; the French by contrast preferrd t put it on the top. By the 1750s, many fortress guns were being mounted on special platforms which could be traversed.

Mortars were a separate case altogether. They had wooden 'beds' and,-for use on land, 'travelling carriages' or mortar waggons of varied design. The bed consisted of a pair of wooden cheeks held together by transoms, the whole being sited upon a timber platform, and never had wheels. A mortar's trunnions were normally situated close to the breech (as compared to those of a cannon or howitzer which were sited near the point of balance), and many were designed to give a fixed elevation of 45 degrees, for long considered the optimum for range until mid-eighteenth century experiments showed this concept to be wholly fallacious. When aboard a bomb-vessel, mortar-beds were so designed as to enable them to swivel.

The design of ammunition waggons and caissons varied enormously. Most armies employed four-wheel tumbrils, but many (especially the English and British armies from 1702 onwards) also used lighter two-wheeled sprung carts. Pontoon-waggons were invariably four-wheel flat-tops, with vertical forks fore and aft to hold the 'tin-boat' in place.

Such, then, were the ammunition, propellants, equipment and transport used by the artillery between 1688 and 1745. We must next turn to consider the major improvements that were eventually adopted.

Improvements in matériel *and advances in theory to the mid-eighteenth century*

The truly revolutionary improvement in European artillery would date from Gribeauval's great range of comprehensive reforms in the last quarter of the eighteenth century, but considerable preliminary spadework was carried through during the period 1720–50 by a series of more or less enlightened artillerists and professors, many of them Frenchmen.

Perhaps the most significant (if ultimately impermanent) changes were those that went to make what is known as *la système Vallière*. Jean-Florent de Vallière (1667–1759) was Lieutenant-General of the French Artillery from 1733. On appointment he set out to bring a measure of order to the sadly confused artillery service left by Louis xiv, with its profusion of calibres, types and special versions. In this mammouth task he was assisted by the considerable period of relative peace in Europe that lasted from 1714 to 1730.

As his son, Joseph-Florent de Vallière (1717–76), destined to be the bitter opponent of Gribeauval and his ideas in the 1770s, wrote of his father's work:

It was not arbitrarily or on conjecture that M. de Vallière based the important work of reform entrusted to him. During the last 18 years of Louis xiv's reign he had noted the strengths and weaknesses of the different European artilleries, and he had meditated at leisure during the long peace enjoyed by

France at the beginning of Louis xv's reign. After long study he conceived the extraordinarily simple and fertile idea of creating *a single class of artillery of only five calibres from 4- to 24-pounders.* [this author's italics], all of them equally suited for the attack or defence of towns, and the first three of which, organised according to circumstances, particularly suited for work in the field; thus, in case of need, the towns could furnish the armies [with guns] and the armies the towns.[69]

Here lay the kernel of Vallière the Elder's work. With considerable success he undertook the gargantuan task of achieving uniformity of cannon-specification throughout France, issuing detailed tables which were rigidly enforced on the manufacturers by the Royal Inspectors. According to the *Ordonnance* of 7 October 1732, the French artillery was to comprise the following calibres:

FRENCH ARTILLERY ACCORDING TO THE 'SYSTÈME VALLIÈRE', 1732–65

Calibre	Wt. of Barrel in lbs	Wt. in 'calibres'	Measurement of bore	Wt. of carriage	No. of horses	Rounds per minute
24-pdr	5,400	225	156 mm	Information not	n.d.	1
16-pdr	4,200	262	137 mm	available	n.d.	1
12-pdr	3,200	266	124 mm	4,966	9	1–2
8-pdr	2,100	263	109 mm	3,579	7	2
4-pdr	1,150	280	86 mm	2,438	7	3

Additionally there were to be 12-inch and 8-inch mortars and a 15-inch *'pierrier'*.
SOURCES: Picard and Jouan, pp. 54–9; J. Colin, *Les Campagnes de Maréchal de Saxe*, Vol. I, p. 58

It will be appreciated by comparing this table with the one to be found on p. 180 that these changes constituted both forward and retrograde steps at the same time in different respects. Great advantages accrued from the simplification of cannon types to a single variety, although continuing defects in manufacturing processes partially thwarted the achievement of real standardization and inter-changeability and ranges remained about the same. On the other hand, the gross *weight* of both guns and their carriages took a notable step upwards, sacrificing practically all the advantages of superior mobility that the 'new' and 'revised new' systems had provided.* Furthermore it is noteworthy that the list of Vallière's guns does not include any provision for howitzers; indeed it was only to be in 1747 that the French army formally adopted this useful class of weapon.

Thus Vallière's changes looked forwards and backwards; they represented both reform and reaction. However, his basic principles of design for the barrels were advantageous, resulting in improved weight-distribution on gun-carriage and limber. Thus the trunnions were so placed as to give the barrel a slight preponderance of 1/30th of its weight towards the rear; the dolphin-handles or

*The matter of weight constituted a major difference between the rival Vallière and Gribeauval systems. For example, a Gribeauval-type 12-pdr (*c*.1800) weighed some 2,172lbs (barrel) and its carriage about 2,192lbs, representing approximately a 50% saving in weight.

anses were placed to counter-balance this displacement, and if a cannon were suspended from them it balanced exactly.

Both the 24- and 16-pdrs were provided with a powder-chamber *smaller* than the bore. A detachable ready-use chest holding a number of rounds and charges, resting between the cheeks of the trail, became a standard feature. Attempts to improve the manufacture of powder were somewhat forwarded by the contraction of the French gun-powder industry from 26 mills (in 1713) to 20 (1744), but Vallière set his face against cartridges and insisted on return to ladling loose powder, in many ways another retrograde step. Charges remained between one-third and one-half the weight of the round, but it proved hard to truly standardize the manufacture of the latter. Case shot was reduced to one variety – contained in a canvas bag.

Such were the main 'improvements' in the Vallière system. Most of them were copied – or in certain cases anticipated – by the major European powers. The British army placed great importance on its 8in and 10in howitzer contingents, and by the 1740s it had been established that a 'single-fire' could be relied upon to light the shell-fuse. Providing no wad was placed between charge and missile, the flash of the explosion passed round the windage of the shell to light the fuse in the first split-second of the explosion before the shell began to travel up the bore.

In Great Britain considerable advances were also made in methods of cannon manufacture. From 1739, the adoption of a Swiss invention made it practicable for the first time to cast barrels in one solid piece of metal, and thereafter 'bore' the chamber to the required calibre. This led to the achievement of a far 'truer' piece with improved accuracy and facilitated mass-production which in turn made possible far larger British artillery trains during the War of the Austrian Succession. Experience gained in this war, however, induced the authorities to drop the lightest calibres – particularly the out-dated $1\frac{1}{2}$-pdr – and increase the proportion of 12- and 9-pdrs in the field trains. At the same time, problems of mobility experienced during the Highland Revolt of the '45 encouraged experimentation with lighter carriages and better harnessing methods.

With the supersession of $1\frac{1}{2}$-pdrs and some 2-pdr field guns there came a complete reliance on 3- and 4-pdrs to provide the 'regimental' pieces. Although Vallière's system included a 4-pdr, this was rather too heavy for regimental use, and over the question of a satisfactory alternative there soon developed a major quarrel, especially but not exclusively in France. The *canon à la suedoise* was the focal point of this argument. This type of 4-pdr weighed only 600lbs (150 calibres) and measured only 17 calibres in length, compared to the 1,150lbs and 26 calibre length of the standard variety. The Swedish gun could take a charge of between $1\frac{1}{4}$ and 2lbs in weight, and was useful for ranges up to about 600 yards, it being theoretically possible to fire between 8–10 rounds a minute. It seemed that mobility and a high rate of fire-power had at last been achieved.

This was by no means a new weapon. The Swedish armies of Charles XII had used pieces of this nature (based upon Gustavus Adolphus's reforms), and several German countries continued to add four similar light pieces to each of their regiments without a break. Marlborough's armies, as we have seen, made good use of two 3-pdrs per battalion. However it was not until 1737 that the French became fully aware of this type of gun's value, when experiments conducted by the Chevalier de Bellac, Lieutenant-Governor of Metz, revealed its full latent possibilities.

This was the signal for the forces of reaction to unleash a virulent campaign of abuse designed to prevent the adoption of the new weapon by the French army. Nevertheless, the Minister of War of the day, M. de Breteuil, ordered the experiments to continue, and in 1740 the king in person commanded 50 Swedish pieces to be made. The weapon's opponents fought back, insisting on the introduction in lieu of a far inferior French piece with a forked trail; but following the disastrous campaign of 1741 which wiped out so much of the French field artillery, the renewed clamour for ever lighter guns could no longer be ignored, particularly as the great de Saxe lent the weight of his influence to the cause. For once he was in full agreement with the Chevalier de Folard, another champion of the weapon. As a result, by May 1744 the Flanders Artillery Park (60 guns in all) included 40 4-pdrs of French design and a further 10 'à la suedoise', and the following year Saxe's artillery (100 cannon in all) included no less than 50 Swedish pieces (with 200 rounds per gun) to only 36 French 4-pdrs (with 150 rounds apiece).

It seemed that the Swedish gun's champions had won the day, but after Fontenoy, where it failed to live up to its full expectation, the number of this type diminished again, and by 1748 there were only 10 of them in the Flanders Park as against no less than 80 French 4-pdrs out of a total of 156 cannon. The biggest disadvantage of the weapon had proved to be the large number of personnel each required – a sergeant and 14 men per piece – and as the Duc de Maine absolutely refused to countenance the employment of infantry soldiers for this purpose (cf the British Army where this practice had long been established for Regimental artillery), it was found that the heavier batteries were very short of trained artillerists. Only in 1757 was this difficulty to be overcome when each piece was given three horses, one sergeant and 16 infantry soldiers. [70]

Other experiments which proved short-lived included the Marquis de Rostaing's attempt to introduce an even lighter piece, weighing only 200lbs and firing a $2\frac{1}{2}$lb ball, and capable of being carried into action by four men or dragged by a single horse. Some authorities claimed that this was capable of firing 10 rounds in one minute, but this is highly unlikely. Sixty rounds were to be carried in the ready-use chest, whilst a further 120 were to be carried on a mule. This concept was blessed by de Saxe – who probably inspired the development by writing of his *amusettes* in his *Rêveries* – but although a few were attached to file battalions they proved very disappointing in action and had been discarded by 1748.

Great advances were made during the last two decades of our period in the science of ballistics. This aspect of the artilleryman's art had really been started by Gallileo's observations on the laws of movement, and Nicholas-Francois de Blondel (1618–86) had developed the master's work and devised rules for the effective firing of mortar bombs. This notwithstanding, most soldiers of all nations continued to employ empirical methods, calculating the distance bombs might be fired by the angle of the piece to the horizon. Even the great St Rémy reflected the prevalent ignorance about the movement of projectiles. Only two methods of aiming had widespread acceptance, namely direct aim (operable up to a maximum of some 800 yards) by squinting along the centre line of the barrel (few guns had even rudimentary foresights at this time), or alternatively fire at an elevation of 45 degrees, widely and erroneously held to achieve a maximum range. Such methods were hardly superior to the rule-of-thumb advocated by Montecuculi in 1636:

> The good master [-gunner] aims his piece by placing his feet at the rear of the trail, his elbows on his belt, his hands clasped in the centre of his body, fingers stretched; looking between them along the centre of his mortar he takes his aim without difficulty, judging the necessary elevation to reach his target as well as the range of his piece and the requisite amount of powder. [71]

Such *ad hoc* methods, however functional, hardly represented a scientific approach to gunnery – although as late as the 1720s Vallière would permit no other sighting besides direct aim. However, in Bernard Forest de Bélidor (1693–1761), France produced a mathematician of no common merit, who vastly developed the work of Blondel. We may guess that his father before him was in the same line of business, for the 1702 edition of St Rémy acknowledges a debt to 'M. Blondel's Treatise'[72] for the ranges obtainable by mortars. The son, however – if such he was – went far further, publishing in his book *Le Bombardier Français* (1731) a full set of ballistic tables giving ranges of bombs for various charges, angles and elevations. He proved that most gun charges commonly used were excessive and wasteful, leading to premature wearing-out of both barrels and carriages to no good purpose – neither the range nor the velocity of the shot being improved thereby.

As Professor at the La Fère Artillery School, he demonstrated convincingly that range was not proportionate to powder charge, exploding the ancient theory that the closer the weight came to two-thirds of the ball's weight the further the ball would travel. His findings inevitably raised a storm of protest, and he even lost his position for a time, but was reinstated in 1740 and eventually died 'in the odour of sanctity' as Royal Inspector of Artillery in 1761.

Bélidor's findings were based on the theory that the explosive power of a powder charge was greatest at the *end* of the explosion, and accordingly he advised a return to spherical chambers to achieve more powerful discharges. Despite criticism, the War Minister Belle-Isle ordered the reduction of all powder charges to one-third of the ball's weight, a step that made possible the design of shorter and lighter cannon (although pitifully little was achieved in these directions before 1765).

The following ranges were then found to be obtainable:
24-pdr at 15° elevation – 3,340 yards: at 45° elevation – 4,600 yards
12-pdr at 15° elevation – 3,100 yards: at 45° elevation – 3,600 yards
 8-pdr at 15° elevation – 2,880 yards: at 45° elevation – 3,360 yards
 4-pdr (Ord.) elevation – 2,600 yards: at 45° elevation – 2,920 yards [72]

Most contemporary 'experts' remained insistent as late as 1744 that 'effective' cannon range could not be more than 500 *toises* (1,000 yards) as the aimer could not distinguish targets clearly at greater distances, nor observe the fall of shot, and gunners were advised not to fire at over 800 yards. Such dogmas, as Saxe revealingly commented, 'did not prevent a battery situated 800–900 *toises* from Antoing [at the battle of Fontenoy 1745] from stopping the offensive movement of the Dutch.'[73]

Thus far greater ranges were in practice obtainable than the pundits believed, although in effect no elevation angle greater than 8 degrees was permitted on active service which limited firing to ranges of up to 1,000 *toises* (2,000 yards), whilst the 4-pounder at six degrees could hit targets at 1,600 yards.

It would be erroneous to suppose that all major advances in artillery theory emanated from France, but the men we have cited here were the most important influences on European gunnery in their day. This is not to deny the sterling work of Major-General John Armstrong, FRS (1674–1742) and Colonel Albert Borgard of the British army or, of Andrew Schlach (1686–1776), First Superintendent of the 'Warren' foundries (also known as 'The Gun-Yard) at Woolwich, the nucleus of what subsequently became the Royal Arsenal. Nor should the work of John Müller be neglected, though his important *Treatise of Artillery* was not to be published until 1756. Other powers – including Spain – produced notable gunners in the first half of the eighteenth century, and by the Seven Years War the Austrian gunnery services directed by Prince Lichtenstein would be of redoubtable quality. Turkey, of course, enjoyed from 1729–47 the services of Ahmed Pasha de Bonneval, the renegade colonel of the French Guards. Although his degree of influence varied enormously during his years in Turkey, he was instrumental in reforming the organization of The *Khumbaradjis* (or Bombardiers) of the Sultan's army in 1735. This corps was increased by 300 men above its normal establishment of 7,000, and became an *élite* organization. De Bonneval's other reforming activities, however, met much conservative opposition, and after his death in 1747 almost all of his work was undone.[74] Suffice it to say that there were many contemporaries of Vallière and Belidor working along broadly similar lines towards generally similar conclusions – but that the France of the last great flowering of *l'ancien régime* was the most distinguished source of artillery lore and development. This supremacy would reach its apogee in the next generation in the work of Jean Baptiste Vacquette de Gribeauval (1715–89), the creator of the weapons that underwrote most of Napoleon's great successes. As the fallen Emperor was to write with gloomy nostalgia at St Helena, 'It is with artillery that war is made.' This may not have been quite so true of the first half of the eighteenth century as of the years towards its close, but the seeds of future developments in both theory and *matériel* were already burgeoning long before 1745.

12

On campaign

The handling of the field artillery on campaign produced a myriad difficulties for the responsible officers and personnel, but it can be claimed that basically their duty to their cumbrous charges comprised three main fields of activity; namely the supervision of the trains on the march, the organization and siting of encampments, and lastly the employment of the guns in action on the field of battle.* As 1688–1745 saw few really radical changes in respect of these functions, it will be convenient to describe each activity in turn for the complete period instead of breaking it down into shorter periods of time. As in earlier chapters, the main emphasis will be placed on French and English practice, but the trains of the other European powers differed little from them in terms of handling in the field.

The trains on the march

The movement of iron and brass monsters weighing an average of three tons apiece clearly required the services of vast numbers of horses and drivers, as did the drawing of the large number of attendant waggons already listed in an earlier chapter. The first problem facing every train commander at the outset of a campaign was the finding of adequate draught-animals and transport. Officially, in most armies the Board of Ordnance or equivalent authority was expected to provide a minimum of transportation for the artillery trains. In England, the Waggon-Master-General was one of the 'Under-Ministers' of the Ordnance at a salary of £100 pa, and his official duties included the finding of transport and horses for the cannon. In the field this functionary was represented by officials called Waggon-Masters, Conductors and Commissaries of draught-horses. In practice, however, many an artillery colonel found himself left largely to his own devices, which meant in effect the wholesale requisition of local animals and waggons as 'contributions' if the army was presently operating on hostile territory, or the striking of bargains with contractors in horse-flesh if

---

*The duties of the trains in siege warfare are reserved for the next section.

the forces were due to move off from a home or allied region. At times, as might be supposed, desperate officers were prepared to resort to bare-faced seizure of local animals no matter how 'friendly' the area, and this malpractice was often tacitly approved by authority despite the strident clamour of the aggrieved peasantry for restitution or compensation. Clearly the ability of any army to take the field at the opening of the campaigning season depended to no small degree on the success of the officers at wheedling, cajoling or stealing horses and oxen, and delays were not unknown. Jacob Richards noted in his diary on 25 April 1693 that 'the Gunnes were fitted up and all the pontoons fixed for a march, wanting nothing now but Colonel Goor with the Contractors' horses and waggons, as also Mr Fletcher with our recrute [*sic*] stores from Rotterdam.' It was not until 18 May, however that the train commander made his somewhat belated appearance with 'the greatest part of our horses and waggons so that now our traine will soon be fixed for the first orders that may come.'⁷⁵ William's armies were notoriously slow off the mark compared to the French each year, and under Marlborough earlier mobilizations were achieved. However, it is revealing that so important an officer as William Cadogan, Marlborough's Quartermaster-General, no less, found it necessary to undertake such tasks in person. Writing to Lord Raby on 20 September 1703, he records:

> I have been till now on the road of all posts, being employed to find horses in the country for drawing the cannon from Liège to Limburgh; those whose business it properly was having so wholly neglected it that there wanted above 1,000 which with much ado I have got at last and sent away to Liège.⁷⁶

Clearly some of Goor's successors in the English Trains were even less successful in their performance of this primary duty than the worthy Colonel of William III's wars. However it is equally notable that these difficulties overcome 'with much ado' by Cadogan in 1703 probably bore important fruit in the comprehensive preparations implemented next year for the far longer march to the Danube. By careful planning, and above all the provision of a well-stocked military chest, Marlborough's army found nothing but co-operation from the local population. Noted our friend Captain Robert Parker,

> As we marched through the countries of our Allies, commissaries were appointed to furnish us with all manner of necessaries for man and horse; these were brought to the ground before we arrived . . . Surely never was such a march carried on with more order and regularity, and with less fatigue both to man and horse.⁷⁷

Doubtless the artillery train of Colonel Holcroft Blood shared in these excellent administrative arrangements despite the difficulties encountered near Mainz owing to wet weather. A guinea or two of English gold could produce more willing co-operation from the local populations than a thousand promissory notes issued on behalf of Louis XIV for redemption at some future (and usually unspecified) date.

Other English and Allied armies were not so fortunately endowed or administered. The campaigns in the barren vastnesses of Spain and Portugal between 1703 and 1713 often came near to foundering on questions of mule or horse availability – and enemy-inspired obstruction and intrigue had to be carefully countered. Thus we find Colonel John Richards (brother of Jacob) writing a 'Memorial' for the Duke of Marlborough, 'to be read in the Privy Council, February the 8th (indistinct in original), 1706' as follows concerning the need to purchase 500 horses through the Consul at Lisbon:

> They would come out att under 50 dollars [each] and less if we would pay them in ammunition but the secrecy in this matter is absolutely necessary, for should the French that are there get wind of it before it be concluded, it will not be difficult for them by the help of a little money to break our treaty with these mercenary people . . .[78]

Even when the horses were produced by the contractors, many often had to be rejected as unsuitable. In 1689, for example, General Schomberg felt compelled to turn down horses intended for use in Ireland on the grounds that 'they appear to me too slight . . . Besides one was lame, another an old cart-horse and most of them faulty.' Small wonder that generals were continually assessing and reassessing local resources in the areas they expected to be operating in. One such document survives from 1692 in which it is regretfully noted that the district of Liège – currently under French contribution – might prove capable of providing the foe with 2,353 waggons and as many as 14,000 local pioneers, whilst on the other hand Flanders could provide the Allies with only 'four to five hundred waggons which would serve to transport that which is coming from Brussels'.[79] William III in person was plagued with transport considerations: in his hand-written 'Memorandum on Military Matters' dated 6 December 1689 we find under the heading 'Artillerie and what depends on it' an item reading 'contracts for wagons and horses. To send for Flanders.'[80] If it is true to assert that armies could operate only over such distances they could carry their bread, it is equally clear that they could only conduct effective operations against such places as their guns could reach. In both respects, one key consideration was the availability of horses, drivers, waggons and fodder.

The problems associated with the continuing reliance in many armies on civilian drivers and boys for the trains have already been alluded to. These personnel constituted a considerable martial hazard, through their well-known proclivity for flight the moment danger threatened and through their general intransigence towards those in authority over them. Even the able and long-suffering Colonel Goor was moved to request William Blathwayt, Secretary at War, 'that a representation be made to his Lordship [the Master-General] of the want of a Comptroller upon the place to look after the civil part of the Trains in Flanders, Colonel Goor now *absolutely refusing* to concern himself therewith – that some fitting person may be sent over for want whereof His Majesty's affairs suffer daily.'[81] Again, this problem was a source of continual complaint from commanders in every corner of Christendom – and Islam too. This difficulty was not immediately solved by the formation of the regular regiments of artillery; only in 1794 was the British Royal Corps of Waggoners established on a quasi-military footing, and in the case of France it would not be until the time Napoleon was made First Consul (1800) that the driver elements of the French artillery would finally become militarized.[82] Until these dates, almost every army and artillery train relied on civilian drivers supplied on a contractual basis.

Probably the most intransigent basic problem involved in moving the trains was the poor quality of European communications in the late seventeenth and early eighteenth centuries. Although Louis XIV improved the four great 'strategic' highroads traversing France running from Picardy to Bayonne, Lower Brittany to Marseilles, Languedoc to Normandy and Santoigne to Bresse, these main arteries were of little tactical significance. Most roads in Europe were little more than earthen tracks, often deeply rutted, turning into quagmires in wet weather or miles of frozen, axle-breaking ruts in winter. Hills presented major problems – whether going up or down – and the efforts of the pioneers could do but little to ameliorate the situation. This was one major reason for the restriction of campaigning as a general rule to the period from April to September each year. Even at the height of the 'season', the movement of the trains could be hell on earth in the event of unusually wet weather. Jacob Richards describes one such day in his Journal (31 July – 1 August 1692) shortly before the battle of Steenkirk and it is worth citing the entry at length to illustrate the frustrating and herculean tasks that often faced the gunners and their burdensome charges:

> The artillery was stirring before day but it was six of the clock before they got off the grounde being a verry wet morning. We marched off first the Dutch and Spanish followed. We continued Brussels Causey way for above three miles and then struck off to the left. The Army marched to the Rt. wh. we did not see (again) until we came within sight of Otibreigue. The wether proved extreamley wett and the Way so verry that the Army had (to) cut (its) own march. We lost our Guide for some time and when he came he turned us backward [with what difficulty for all concerned we can imagine] to Otibreigue, a verry soft way. The Entrance into the village for above 200 paces was not passable. We made the artillery to halt for above fower howers being forced to cut a newe way wh. we made of straw and fascines. We (then) had a great Hill to get up and bad way so that severall guns stuck, but the night comeing on we were forced to lye by the way upon a great Hill. Most of the Dutch guns and all our waggons was left on the other syde of the Defile. The Troops of Hannover Encamped in viu (view?) of us facing ffrom us. Mr Van Hill came from the King to order uss to get up (forward) the Pontoons, but it was impossible, if not to march up verry early and joine the Army.

We can imagine the reception this helpful staff aide received from the sorely tried officers of the Train after such a day – even if most of their heartfelt comments were made *sotto voce*. The same Aide-de-Camp also ordered the waggons to take another road, '. . . wh. they did but it proved verry bad ffor the Army had marched that way before.' The guns made the best of their way towards Lemburg along the River Senne in the wake of the army. Even then the tale of tribulation was not complete. Having reached the camp site between Hal and Tubise: 'It was late before we got our baggage, the Hanoverians having cut

the way ... We were not a little glad (to reach camp) after so tedious and
ffatiaguing [*sic*] a march. The Ffrench are att Enghein two leagues from this
place.'[83] The men frequently had to lay hold of tow ropes and chains to aid the
floundering teams – and cases of death through heatstroke or exhaustion were
not unknown in the hot weather of mid-summer.

The reference to the Hanoverians 'having cut the way' illustrates possibly the
major military crime that could be committed during an army's march. For
reasons of tactical flexibility (such as it was) it was vital that the artillery trains
should proceed without let or hindrance. Formations that broke into the
slow-moving column could cause havoc with timetables, and the strict forbidding
of such intrusion was the subject of many orders-of-the-day. Stiff penalties could
be exacted on violators of this rule – however distinguished. One such case took
place on 18 August 1705, and is recorded by Parker as follows:

> We were now drawing near the enemy, and his Grace (Marlborough) had sent
> orders that the English train of artillery should make all possible haste up to
> him: but as they were just upon entering a narrow defile, Slangenberg* came
> up to the head of them, and stopped them for some hours, until his baggage
> had passed on before them, a thing never known before even for the King's
> (William III's) baggage. And this delay it was which prevented the Duke from
> attacking the enemy . . . The Duke made a proper representation of
> Slangenberg's behaviour to the States-General, who knowing the pride of the
> man, readily laid hold of this opportunity, and sent him a dismiss.[84]

The negotiation of bad roads and difficult terrain, exacerbated by poor traffic
discipline, were by no means the prerogatives of the trains of England and her
Allies. The military experts of all countries frequently referred to these
over-riding difficulties. Marshal de Saxe, for example, called for the use of oxen
to draw the artillery, 'because they damage the road less.'[85] Clearly Saxe was not
primarily concerned with achieving fast mobility when he gave his advice. In any
case, the heavy guns of the Vallière system tied any army's rate of advance to a
bare crawl, and it proved extremely difficult on several occasions to take the
heavier cannon into Germany. Thus in 1741, Marshal Belle-Isle only just
managed to drag his eight 24-pdrs through the defiles of the Black Forest, and so
disillusioned did he become with their performance on the roads that in the end
they were put into park at Ingolstadt and left there for the best part of two years.
As a result, the French found themselves attempting to undertake the siege of
Prague with no heavier metal than Swedish 4-pdrs.

The priority accorded to the artillery in the column of march varied
considerably from army to army. It is revealing to note the placing of the French
artillery in the heighday of Louis XIV. First came the Treasure, followed by the
Royal baggage (comprising the equipment of the sovereign, the Princes, the
Royal Household etc.); next came the effects of the Commander-in-Chief, those
of the Quartermaster-General, the waggons of the Provost-Marshal and the

---

*General Frederick van Baer van Slangenberg (d.1713) was General of the Dutch Foot, and a
continuous thorn in Marlborough's flesh from 1701–5.

equippages of the War Commissaries. Only then did the guns and their supporting services figure in the list, being followed by the kit of the *Maison du Roi*, that of the advance guard cavalry, the mass of the regimental baggage (in strict order of unit seniority), with the volunteers' waggons and the carts of the *vivandières* and the sutlers bringing up the rear.[86] English and Austrian armies often gave their guns somewhat greater priority (as is implied in the Parker extract cited above).

Surirey de St Rémy gives exhaustive instructions for the conduct of trains on the march in the second volume of his work. The average French train of the 1690s and 1700s would seem to have been organized into five brigades, each being more or less self contained. At the head of the column marched a sizeable detachment of fusiliers with engineers and 40 pioneers whose duty it was to improve the road, the necessary tools being carried in a waggon. Behind this advance party came four loaded 4-pdrs and their gun-crews with another waggon holding fifty rounds and all necessary powder and equipment. Then came the army's treasure and the Royal baggage, followed by the pontoons of the bridging train and the vehicles of the specialist workers associated with it, followed by the bulk of the guns, divided into some five brigades moving in carefully regulated order. In the first (10 8-pdrs) were placed ten more pioneers, a waggon of tools, the guns themselves, a spare gun-carriage, 15 waggons of ball and powder, three more of tools and lastly one with the officers' kit. The second echelon of the guns consisted of the third brigade (six 4-pdrs) with detachments of miners and their equipment as before, followed by the *brigade du parc*. This was the largest sub-unit, holding the four 24-pdrs and the six 12-pdrs, the heaviest components of the field train in fact, together with their waggons and all surplus transport of the train, including the field forges and 20 pontoons. There followed the second brigade (ten 8-pdrs), followed by the fourth (10 4-pdrs). Behind these would come:

The mortars
Caissons of the Guard
Waggons of the Paymaster and Quartermaster
The equipment of the miners and specialist craftsmen
The general of artillery's baggage
Officers' baggage (escorted)
A few highly-privileged *vivandières*
Waggons of powder, match, sandbags, rope, bomb and grenade fuses, lead, grenades, tools, spare mortar carriages, bombs, roundshot, etc., etc.
Waggons of the pioneers

and, bringing up the rear, a second force of fusiliers. Small detachments of these troops would also accompany each brigade, dropping off at all cross-roads and junctions to ensure that army baggage did not cut the column, for it was always axiomatic that the artillery train must be kept closed up.

A complex roster of duty-officers was maintained. The captains and conductors of each brigade carefully reconnoitred the way ahead, and controlled the speed of the convoy. The train commander moved at its head, with the provincial commissary of the day at his side, moving at the pace of the draught-horses and stopping from time to time to permit the rear elements to close up. The provincial commissary of each brigade appointed a junior officer to watch the brigade immediately behind, and gave instant news of any delays. Ahead of the whole column moved a camp party consisting of the Major, two other officers and one conductor seeking out a convenient site for the next night's camp in the general area designated by the General Officer of the Day at his morning orders session (which the Major or his deputy was always expected to attend).[87]

The Standing Orders for William III's English Train in Flanders of 1693 reveal Colonel Goor's similar convictions on these matters. Those relating to the Trains on the march (Nos. 8 to 13) make the following points. Captains of 'Companies' were to parade their men on march days one clear hour ahead of the specified time of departure. The Gentlemen of the Ordnance were to be particularly responsible for seeing that the guns themselves were ready to move, and that each piece had its full complement of gear; noted deficiencies were to be made good by application to the artificers and storemen well in advance of the hour of departure. On the march itself, each company was to be divided into temporary 'plotoons' [sic], and the personnel specifically told off to attend the guns or waggons under the Gentlemen of the Ordnance's instructions. All lieutenants, sergeants and corporals were also divided between the platoons, charged with their general supervision and above all with ensuring that no baggage or sutlers' waggons hindered the movement of the munitions. Lastly, any breakdowns were to be immediately manhandled off the road, and left with a detachment, whilst the Captains of the Companies were to post themselves at the head, centre and rear of the column when not patrolling their sectors; 'they shall admit of no body on the guns, nor permit any baggage to be put upon them.'[88]

During the campaigns of Louis XIV and William III, of Villars, Marlborough and Eugene the artillery remained painfully slow and difficult to move, but as the infantry proved equally slow in preparing for battle this normally provided enough time for the guns to come up. It was not, however, unknown for them to be late, until the helpful idea of dividing the train into 'active' and 'passive' elements was widely adopted. What we may term 'Echelon A' (comprising the guns and their immediate requirements) marched with the main columns of the army in the centre. 'Echelon B' (the mass of munitions and store waggons) was relegated to the head of the baggage trains well to the rear. However, although brigades or companies of artillery were occasionally detached from the main trains to serve with the advance or rear guards, and it was not unknown for brigades to move with the outlying flanking columns of an advancing army when close to the foe, as a general rule the bulk of the trains and the guns were kept together in a single closed-up column.

This remained the general picture almost until the 1760s. De Feuquières and Chevalier Folard in their respective generations made strong pleas for the attachment of brigades to individual columns as a standard practice, especially for fast marches, and the Spaniard Santa-Cruz went so far as to demand their permanent deployment in this way but military opinion only slowly moved towards these points of view. Thus in 1741 Baudet de Villeneueve in his *Cours sur la Science Militaire*, was still declaring that generals should place their 'artillery in the centre on the best road ... Marching to attack, the baggage keeps to the rear; the guns keep to the centre except for certain brigades placed at the head of each column.' [89] During the Austrian Succession War, the French and Allied trains continued to move in massive columns, divided into brigades as formerly. At the head marched a battalion of the Royal Artillery, together with the miners; behind them came the brigades or companies, an example of one of these consisting of a tool waggon, 10 4-pdr guns drawn by four horses apiece (and carrying 30 rounds in each trail chest besides a further 100 in the caissons), a spare carriage, a pair of powder waggons, three caissons holding some 100 rounds apiece, five waggons of composite munitions, and lastly two coaches for the officers – in all a total of 24 vehicles drawn by 96 horses. As earlier, the main park moved further back, accompanied by some 50 spare horses, together with the pontoons etc. [90]

It is thus clear that there were few significant changes in the problems or methods of moving the trains between the years 1688 and 1745. The artillery on the march remained large, cumbersome and delay-prone, but its services were indispensable.

The Trains in camp

Before the outset of a campaign, an assembly camp would be organized, often in close proximity to the main magazines of the army. It was important that the munitions waggons of the assembling train should be cited in a convenient location, for the first task of the organization was to issue every soldier with his initial amount of ammunition – usually two dozen rounds of powder and shot. It was equally important that the powder waggons should be dispersed to avert the danger of a mishap to one becoming a catastrophe for all – and probably for the neighbouring town as well. Fire precautions were strictly maintained, and the guards and patrols responsible for the security of the army's powder were not permitted to carry firearms – but only half-pikes or staves – lest the spark from a musket or pistol carelessly discharged should set off a chain of disastrous events.

Once the campaign had begun, the trains were invariably expected to form nightly field parks, or, if they were involved in a siege, a semi-permanent siege park (the description of which is reserved for the next section). Nightly field parks were usually roughly square or rectangular in shape, and were often sited 300 yards to the front of the centre of the main army encampment. The guns were at first placed in a line along the face nearest the enemy, largest on the right, smallest on the left, but from the early eighteenth century the far more sensible practice of deploying the pieces by brigades in order of march became increasingly adopted. The attendant waggons and specialists' vehicles were drawn up to the rear in various groups, but the powder was invariably kept apart and carefully roped off from the rest of the park, often to the central rear. The encampments of the train personnel and the fusilier detachments were sited some hundred paces to the left and right of the square, and it was not unknown for the quarters of the commander-in-chief to be sited within the area as well. This was certainly often the practice of William III, but such a prestigious presence in their midst was not always an unmitigated advantage for the officers and men of the trains. In his *Journal* for the period 29–31 June 1693, Jacob Richards noted that 'we still continue quiet on both sides.' However he also reported that the cannon were suddenly ordered to be moved – no small undertaking – 'by reason we were so nigh to the King's quarters that our Gunn wh. sett the watch was offensive.' [91]

All armies had a number of signal guns; these were either small cannon carried in waggons (St Rémy advocates the positioning of four such pieces 20 yards to the front of the main gun line, controlled by a captain's guard), or else a number of field pieces told off for this time-keeping duty. Besides setting the watch at night, gun signals were used to recall foragers, and of course to give the alarm. Thus on the morning of 13 August 1704, the Flemish cavalry general, the Comte de Mérode-Westerloo, records how he was told by Marshal Tallard to 'send an aide-de-camp to the artillery to order the two signal salvoes fired for the recall of the foragers ... My aide-de-camp with noteworthy rapidity got himself recognized and obeyed by the gunners [and interesting if unconscious revelation of the latent distrust between regular soldiers and the personnel of the French trains of the period], and we soon heard the 24-pounders fire the two salvoes. There were in all four pieces of this calibre.' [92]

When choosing the next camp site for the artillery, certain priorities had to be carefully balanced. First, and obviously, the spot chosen had to be large enough to take all the train and its appendages and at the same time be reasonably convenient for the issue of reserve ammunition to the infantry and dragoons. This was performed in a very orderly manner from waggons set well apart from the main park area. Secondly, as the guns were habitually placed ahead of the army and thus usually nearest to the enemy, the security of the encampment against surprise attack had to be carefully considered. The English army learnt this the hard way in Ireland in 1691, when the brilliant Jacobite commander, Sarsfield, surprised the Orangeite artillery in a night attack (1 August) and killed almost every man and boy, civilian drivers included, besides ham-stringing the horses, and did so much damage to the *matériel* that William was compelled to order the formation of virtually a new train to make good the damage. [93] After such a sharp lesson, security was left in the hands of a comprehensive system of picquets, main guards and grand guards, a reserve of 100 men being under arms every night ready to tackle emergencies.

A third major consideration was the reduction of the risk of fire – the ever-present peril bedevilling the trains with. their bulky and often leaking waggons of powder kegs. Doubtless this was one reason for the trains camping apart from the main army; in closer proximity to the myriad camp-fires lit every night by the rank and file the danger of a chance spark being blown into the powder laager was too grave to be risked. Conversely, the cooking-activities of the train personnel and guards had to be severely controlled, often being centrally organized in a safe area. One possible reason for the superior cloth used for gunners' and matrosses' uniforms (the cause of considerable envy from less well-clad soldiers as we have already noted) may have been that they were often forbidden to light bivouac fires to sleep by, and consequently had to be issued with warmer clothing to ward off the incidence of fevers and agues – but this is merely surmise.

Once the site was selected, the commander of the advance party would send back an officer to lead up the trains to their night's lodgement area whilst the remaining members set about subdividing and pegging out the areas for the various components. In the French army, St Rémy laid it down, the Commissary of Artillery was responsible for the overall perimeter (a frontage of 400 paces being required for a 50-gun train), whilst the Provincial Commissaries set out the fusilier camps, gunners quarters and horse and waggon lines, leaving at least 300 clear paces all round the powder dumps. The horse lines were chosen after consultation with the Waggon-Master-General. Sometimes these duties were neglected, as on the evening of 5 July 1692, when Jacob Richards grumblingly and somewhat apprehensively noted that 'we found here (Genappes) Mons. s'Gravemore with all the quartermasters, but no ground marked out. With much ado we encamped our artillery. We are howerly expecting allarms.'[94]

Ferocious orders were continuously being promulgated to reduce the fire risk. Enemy arsonists caught red-handed attempting to carry out their suicidal missions were liable to be burnt alive – a fate that certainly befell one French patriot in August 1691, when he attempted to destroy William III's park in Flanders.[95] Almost equally severe penalties were exacted from friendly soldiery who were caught within the roped-off area for no good reason – they were often shot or hung after a hasty trial. Richards recounts the case of Matrosse Berry Blackbourne, who was court martialed by Count Solmes for stealing a quantity of powder for his pistol by cutting small slits in some of the barrels – hardly a sensible action on his part. The unfortunate miscreant was lucky to escape with his life; but on the grounds that he had never had the Articles of War read to him, and was thus technically still a civilian, the court martial took a lenient view, and Blackbourne was let off with a whipping from the hangman, branding on the hand, and ignominious discharge from the army. Such misdemeanours were occasionally experienced in every army.

Genuinely accidental fires were another hazard – especially during prolonged dry spells. 'This day some forage belonging to the officers of the Train took fire wh. was seasonably put out,' wrote Richards on 26 July 1692, 'otherwayes (it) might have proved of very dangerous consequence being within 20 paces of our ammunition waggons.'[96] Life in the artillery parks clearly held moments of 'seasonable' excitement.

In attempts to avert such perils, all trains received strict standing orders regulating activities in camp. St Rémy was insistent that three officers and one conductor should be on duty each and every night, with a comprehensive series of patrols to inspect and reports to make. The senior officer on duty was to attend the commander-in-chief's orders sessions, and was to report to the Grand-Master (or his representative) every morning with an account of the night's happenings; he would then be given the pass-word for the next day. If the camp was established for a considerable period, this routine was continued *sine die*, and the duty officers would receive an additional duty – the supervision of any foraging forays authorized for the personnel of the Trains.[97]

Similar arrangements were commonplace in all armies. William III's Train of 1693, for instance, had the following standing orders for duties whilst in camp. The officers were charged with keeping the gunners and matrosses in good order, inspecting the tent-lines to ensure that the area was kept clean and neat. For the purposes of providing guards and fatigue parties, the personnel was divided into eight 'brigades' (sections), four of gunners and as many of matrosses, each under a sergeant or corporal. No officer was permitted to leave the camp area without higher authority, and no man was allowed out without his Captain's specific leave. On the firing of the warning piece to set the watch each night, the sergeants and corporals were to visit the tent lines and report any absentees. Once every 15 days the captains were to inspect the arms and clothing of their men, and ensure that any deficiencies were made good by new issues set against stoppages of pay. In cases of death or desertion, the captains were enjoined to report the circumstances immediately to the colonel, and secure the personal effects of the men concerned. Every Monday morning, the Captains were to give the Colonel a full parade state of their men, indicating the number on it, sick, deserted or detached. Needless to say, a nightly guard was to be set, and the officer in charge was personally responsible for escorting any visitor to the park area, both in and out, for supervising the issue of stores and munitions 'at the kettledrum,' and for ensuring that the Guard tent was safely stowed aboard the picquet waggon before the train set out next morning. These are mere specimens of the myriad rules and regulations deemed necessary to ensure the safety and efficiency of the artillery train organization while in camp – most of them being based on sound common sense.[98]

The Trains in battle

By the end of the long reign of Louis XIV, generals had come to regard the symmetry of their twin battle formations to be sacred, just as admirals considered the maintenance of their ships' line of battle at sea an inviolable principle. It was rare for an army to have a reserve – although sometimes a force of dragoons was retained in the rear – and as armies grew gradually larger so the extent of their lines developed. Extended lines stretching over three to four miles (as at Blenheim or Ramillies) were potentially vulnerable, and the prime duties of the artillery in battle were considered to be to sustain the individual sections of the line and to form batteries for the support of key strongpoints for use in attack or defence. The first task was particularly the responsibility of the regimental artillery – the pair of 2- or 3-pdrs which English, Dutch and Austrian battalions habitually took into battle with them – but in armies like the French which possessed no real regimental pieces until the 1740s, both tasks depended upon the resources of the field park.

Armies moved up for battle in between three and ten columns, each following its own route. As we have noted the guns often came either well to the rear, or all in the centre (as at Fleurus in 1690) when Luxembourg advanced on Waldeck's forces in five columns, the central one consisting wholly of the train). Then, whilst the horses and foot slowly took up their precisely regulated battle positions, the senior officers of the artillery would ride forward to select the best available battery positions. As a general rule they sought the highest ground available with the least impeded and longest field of fire; the size of the batteries they established varied according to circumstances between four and twenty pieces; thus at Entzheim (1674), St Hilaire drew up his 32 guns in four batteries;[99] whilst at Malplaquet the battery destined to wreak so much havoc with the Dutch Guards numbered 20 pieces. Colonel Blood's battery at Blenheim five years earlier, which did so much to save the day near Oberglau, totalled 'nine field-pieces loaded with partridge-shot' according to Captain Parker.

It was often the practice for the guns to advance some little way ahead of the main battle line to engage the enemy with fire whilst the troops behind made ready for combat. If the foe advanced to the attack, the guns, St Rémy tells us, were to retire with the screening cavalry into the intervals of the first line. Alternatively, if their own troops advanced, the heavier guns would be forced to cease fire, but guns up to 4-pdrs were expected to accompany the advance to a range of half-musket shot if this was at all possible. 'This is the way to assure victory.'[100] It was comparatively rare, however, for guns to be retained ready-limbered and prepared to accompany an advance at this time, although it seems that this was done by Catinat's artillery at Marsaglia (1693). 'Our cannon served to perfection,' reported their proud commander, 'M. de Cray making them follow our troops continually.'[101] Marlborough might have written in equally glowing terms of Blood's performance at Blenheim already cited, when the sweating and toiling gunners had to negotiate the Nebel stream and its marshes under heavy fire to bring succour to Holstein-Beck's hard-pressed battalions. At Ramillies it was the fact that the Dutch Guards managed to manhandle two field guns forward with their infantry that accounted for their rapid capture of Francquenay and Taviers villages on the French right, whilst at Malplaquet the massed battalions of Marlborough's right wing dragged their pieces through Taisnières wood at the height of the battle to engage the French cavalry beyond. In similar fashion, the Swedes moved their guns forward with the infantry on their ill-fated attack at Pultava. The fact that it proved possible to deploy the lighter guns so far forward in this way should not disguise the scale of the problems generally involved in so doing.

The guns were equally expected to cover any retreat by the main forces. On many occasions it proved impossible to bring the guns off at the end of an unfortunate engagement, but on others a great deal was in fact achieved. Colonel Jacob Richards writes as follows of the Allied defeat at Steenkirk in 1692:

In our retreat the enemy got 12 pieces of our Cannon, but we retook the four of them again (of wh. 4 was Dutch). The heat of this dispute held (lasted) about three howers, that is ffrom one to four, about wh. time all ffires ceased, and by the King's command we retreated wh. was done in great order, the Enemy never attempting to make any advantage thereby untill we were all on March, and then appeared the left of their army wh. advanced as ffar as the Grounde wh. we stood upon. *But our cannon was so advantageously posted that they thought it was not discretion to come fforward* and so wee parted ffor this cause, but through the ffear and neglect of the carters some ammunition waggons were overset wh. wee ourselves afterwards burned. [102]

All in all this represented a dignified withdrawal, despite the incident of the munition-carts. It was not repeated next year at Landen however. On this occasion the Allies 'left the field, their artillerie and what baggage they had with them' to the tune of 84 cannon. Such loss of metal was not exceptional amidst the confusion and panic of defeat. At Blenheim the French lost some 60 guns and mortars, whilst at the disaster of the Pruth (1711) Peter the Great lost all his 122 cannon.

Cannon and howitzers were served by carefully drilled gun-crews. Once again, French practice, as recorded by St Rémy, may be taken as fairly typical of the period. He advised the posting of at least twelve men with every gun to ensure a reserve for emergencies and the replacement of casualties. It would seem that the average piece needed at least two gunners and six matrosses or soldiers deputizing for them to keep it in action. The first gunner stood to the right of the gun, with a bag of loose powder and two *dégorgeurs*. His main duties were to close and open the touch-hole at the beginning and end of the loading process, and to prime the touch-hole after placing the main powder charge in the bore. After discharge, he was responsible for checking the gun at the end of its recoil with a lever to prevent it rolling forward again. The second gunner was posted to the left; he was responsible for bringing up the powder-charge from the ready-use magazine (either loose in a leather sack or powder-bucket, or else in a linen pre-packaged cartridge), and for pouring it into the measure held ready by the first gunner; he also had charge of the linstock or *porte-feu*, and had to ensure it was ready for use whenever required. The remaining assistants stood by in two groups, three on each side. The first pair wielded a sponge and rammer respectively, and according to the French drill operative in the early eighteenth century, the powder charge was supposed to be tamped home with eight blows of the rammer, and the ball with four more. Moreover, the barrel had to be thoroughly sponged out at least once every 10 to 12 shots. After seeing to this, the two matrosses were to seize handspikes and help lever the gun forward to its firing position again. The third assistant (stationed on the right) ensured that there was an adequate supply of wads for keeping powder and shot in place in the bore (earth or dung was occasionally used in lieu of the standard straw or cloth wads), whilst his opposite number was responsible for seeing that some 50 round-shot were kept within reach of the gun, and for easing each ball in turn into the muzzle ready for ramming home. Both the matrosses then also helped their colleagues run the gun up to the firing position. Finally, the two 'Number Threes' were equipped with levers with which they manhandled the gun trail to right or left as necessary to align the piece with its target; an additional duty of the left-hand gun-number was to ensure that the light used for the linstock was kept well covered during the reloading process to guard against the ever-present fire hazard, whilst his mate controlled the coigns or wedges which were employed to alter the elevation of the cannon. This last was no easy task in the days before the introduction of screw elevating gear, and accordingly both 'Number Twos' were also expected to assist if required. The aiming of the gun was usually the responsibility of the battery commander or *officier pointeur*, who passed from gun to gun once reloading was completed. Hardly any pieces had even the most rudimentary of sights until the mid-eighteenth century so it required the combination of experience and rule-of-thumb to procure an accurate fall of shot, especially as many guns developed their own special characteristics which had to be carefully allowed for. The firing of each gun was similarly an officer's responsibility in several armies.[102]

Similar drills were used for fortress and naval guns. One speciality for the former – especially for coastal batteries engaging shipping – was the employment of red-hot shot. The cannon-balls were heated on special grids well to the rear of the firing platform, and were adjudged ready for use when a well-aimed shot of saliva refused to stay in contact with the darkly-glowing metal but danced on the surface. The shot was then carried up on special bearers and gingerly eased into the cannon's mouth. Before this stage was reached several wet wads would have been carefully placed atop the powder to keep the red-hot metal from causing a premature discharge. Nevertheless it was still a ticklish process running up the gun with a wisp of smoke winding up from the muzzle as the red-hot shot slowly burned its way through the successive wads, and it was clearly in everybody's interest to fire the piece before this inevitable process was completed. It was hardly advisable to be standing behind a cannon of any calibre squinting along the barrel when it went off on account of the ferocious recoil – as an incautious or unfortunate matrosse would learn precisely once.

Red-hot shot was never used at sea for obvious reasons (although in the late 1790s the out-classed French Revolutionary navy was to experiment disastrously with the idea in an attempt to regain something approaching parity with their British foes in ship-to-ship duels). At sea it was also clearly impracticable to allow a discharged gun its natural recoil distance, and much use was made of 'restraining tackles' – strong ropes working on a pulley-system and attached to rings on the inside of the bulwarks. These ropes facilitated running out the guns, and of course were used to secure them when not in action. Terrible havoc could be caused by a naval gun which broke loose in a storm, as readers of Victor Hugo or C. S. Forester will recall.[103]

Howitzer drill was somewhat different, a crew of five men (two 'fire-workers' with three assistants) normally being required. After a shell had been fired, the first task was to close the touch-hole. Next the the charge was placed in the bore, and rammed home with a wad; three sharp blows were specified for the powder, followed by nine more *sur la terre* (or wad) to ensure that the powder beneath filled the chamber. The time had now come to ease the shell into the bore, fuse outermost and pointing along the centre line. To ensure that the missile did not move out of alignment it was next wedged with earth. The howitzer was now ready for pointing and elevating, the most popular elevation at our period being 45 degrees until Belidor and others proved conclusively that this was not always necessary. Before firing, the touch-hole was unstopped and the protective covering (often made of tin) removed from the shell-fuse. It now only remained for two of the crew to light the fuse and charge as nearly simultaneously as possible (sometimes a special wide-branched linstock was used which made it possible for the fire-worker to perform the double-function). Despite all precautions, however, malfunction of the fuse was frequently met with as has already been mentioned on an earlier page.

In battle, round-shot was used in attemps to silence the enemy's batteries or to wreak havoc amongst his densely aligned formations of troops. Canister or 'partridge' was used against troops at close ranges. Conversely, solid-shot could be employed to destroy earthworks, buildings or fortifications. Ricochet fire, strongly advocated by the great Vauban, could greatly increase the effect and range of a single shot as the ball bounded on through the enemy forces, sending up showers of wounding stones and earth at each 'hop'. Howitzer shells, on the other hand, were mostly suitable for setting fire to buildings or for unsettling the hostile cavalry with well-placed air-bursts. It seems that it was possible to see a round-shot coming for most of its flight so low was the muzzle velocity of the day, and sometimes evasive action could be taken. A graphic, if somewhat illiterate description of what it was like to be under fire in the mid-eighteenth century comes from the pen of Sam Davies, footboy to a Major Honeywood, who wrote as follows to his friend Abraham Debart, a drawer at the 'White Hart' at Colchester, describing his part in the battle of Dettingen in 1743:

> . . . our battel lasted 5 ours, the first they played upon our baggage for about 2 ours with there cannon . . . the balls was from 3lbs to 12lbs each . . . We stayed there till the balls came flying all round us. We see first a horse with baggage fall close to us, then seven horses fell apeace then I began to star about me, the balls came whistling about my ears. Then I say the Oysterenns (Austrians) dip there heads and look about them *for they doge* (dodge) *the balls as a cock does a stick, they are so used to them* . . . A 12 pounder came within a few yards of me. Then I began to stear indeed, it was about the size of your light puddings but a great deal hevyer. [104]

Being under close enemy fire of this type was obviously most unsettling for all concerned whether officer or man. As our prickly friend, the Comte de Mérode-Westerloo, recalled of the lengthy artillery prelude to Blenheim, which lasted from about 10 o'clock until midday: 'I was riding past Forsac's regiment when a shot carried away the head of my horse and killed two troopers; another of my Spanish mounts was killed behind one of the Orléans squadrons, whilst yet a third received a hit which carried away the butts of my pistols, the pommel of the saddle and a piece of flesh as large as the crown of a hat . . .' [105] In an attempt to minimize the number of casualties, Dr Hare, Marlborough's chaplain, recalls that at the same battle the Duke ordered the rank and file to lie down in formation until the time was ripe for them to attack.

Of course cannon-balls were no respecters of persons, however exalted. In the course of the war Marlborough himself had several narrow escapes from enemy fire – he was showered with earth at Blenheim, but no enemy shot came closer than in the celebrated incident recalled by Lord Orkney of the battle of Ramillies (1706):

> Milord Marlborough was rid over, but got other sqadrons which he led up. Major Bingfield holding his stirrup to give him another horse was shot with a cannon ball which went through Marlborough's legs; in truth there was no scarcity of 'em – indeed I think I never had more shot about my ears – both musketry and cannon.[106]

Other senior commanders were less fortunate; Marshal Villars was seriously wounded in the knee at the climax of Malplaquet (1709), and of course King Charles XII of Sweden was killed outright at the siege of Fredriksten in 1718 by a small round-shot through the head. But inevitably it was the regimental officers and men who bore the brunt of the casualties. Charles James Hamilton (then aged about 16) recalled of the battle of Fontenoy that:

> . . . we have had a most bloody battle with ye french; yesterday we began at 5 in ye morning & left off at 2 in ye afternoon, all wch time ye french kept canonading us; I was forced to be very civil & make a great many bows to ye balls for they were very near me . . . the foote were very sadly cut to pieces, for ye french put grape shot into their cannon & cut them down as just if they were sheering corn.[107]

Of course the maintenance of such sustained bombardments called for careful placing of artillery ammunition reserves, and we must next examine the way the supporting elements of the artillery were drawn up on days of battle. St Rémy, it will be recalled, was convinced that '100 rounds per gun is ample . . . it being almost impossible that they could shoot them off in a single day's affair.'[108] He was equally insistent that all ammunition issues prior to the opening of the battle should be made from the Train Park – leaving the spare ammunition waggons attached to each brigade for emergency issues only; these munitions normally accompanied the brigades to their selected action stations in the front line. This practice was also prevalent in William III's (and presumably Marlborough's) armies. Colonel Richards noted in his Journal for 16 June 1693 that 'this evening our small pieces of cannon were sent to their respective brigades with all their appurtenances as also all ammunition for each brigade, *not to be touched but in time of service.*'[109]

Arrived at the selected point (indicated by officers of the train who had attended the battlefield reconnaissance), the guns often drew up some 100 yards ahead of the infantry line, leaving the waggons *between* the two main lines of battle. Initially each gun would often be provided with some 30 rounds, and then the horse-teams and the *avant-trains* would move back to rejoin the waggons in the brigade park, whose immediate security would be in the hands of a detachment of fusiliers or other infantry told off for the purpose. Not a few contemporaries disliked the presence of so much gunpowder in such close proximity to the main positions, particularly as it was bound to be vulnerable to enemy fire, and the danger of a general explosion and conflagration could never be wholly ruled out. Meanwhile, behind the army and at a safer distance, the 'Main' or 'Grand Park' would be established, holding some 150 rounds for each gun besides the reserve infantry and dragoon ammunition, which would be issued as need arose, either before or during action.

Such was the standard procedure well into the eighteenth century. In the 1730s the experienced Spaniard, Santa-Cruz advocated a more elaborate ammunition-holding system. He wished to place his guns 200 yards ahead of the line, leaving only three rounds with each piece; a further 57 rounds per gun were to be kept some 200 paces back, together with the gun-limbers and horse-teams. A third supply would be placed 500 paces back, including a number of waggons and handlers; 1,000 yards from the guns was the site of the reserve park, with another 60 rounds for every gun, and finally, at 1,500 yards distance, the officers were to establish the Grand Park, where the bulk of the transport would be held. A series of carrying-parties would move to and fro from dump to dump, maintaining the specified ammunition level. This system was designed to reduce the danger of accidents and also to minimize the devastation caused by unfortunate enemy hits, but however sensible this might seem in theory, in practice the excessive decentralization of the munitions tended to lead to confusion and break-downs in forward supply, and it seems never to have been seriously adopted. Nevertheless all armies made attempts to reduce the incidence of 'friction' brought on by the confusion and uncertainties of battle. The English trains for example, numbered and labelled every waggon of their trains from the time of William III onwards to facilitate the identification of its contents in the heat of action.

It only remains to describe such advances in the employment of the guns in action as took place between 1688 and 1745. In fact there were remarkably few changes in either tactical doctrine or practice, except in so far as it became more usual for a number of guns to accompany advancing infantry as the period wore on. However, the siting of the individual batteries remained very much the affair of each *chef de brigade*, a possible exception being Marlborough's armies where Duke John earned considerable contemporary comment for the care he took in placing his guns. But then we should remember that by a happy coincidence for British martial fortunes the Duke combined in his person the posts of Master-General of the Ordnance and Captain-General of the Horse and Foot, and consequently was more likely to take a personal interest in his artillery. Such a degree of personal application *vis à vis* the guns was unusual at so exalted a level; all such tedious gunnery matters were usually delegated to the senior Ordnance representatives accompanying an army.

In the earlier years it appears that brigade commanders tried to site their guns in such a way as to secure their safety and at the same time make it unnecessary to redeploy them when the line moved forward. Rising ground on the flanks were therefore particularly favoured. However, Catinat at Marsaglia (1693) and Marlborough at Blenheim, Ramillies and Malplaquet, provided convincing examples of the way in which guns could be handled more imaginatively and effectively, even over difficult ground, and it became increasingly the rule for armies to concentrate on taking a larger number of lighter pieces into the field with them, relegating such immobile monsters as 24-pdrs to the park of the siege trains. Between 1715 and 1740 this tendency continued to develop. The defensive role remained probably the dominant consideration, but at both the battles of Parma and Guastalla (1734) the French artillery proved capable of a fair measure of manoeuvrability on the battlefield. On the first occasion the French guns arrived on the field 'towards the fore', were quickly deployed, and opened a destructive fire at the enemy at 200 yards range. An Austrian attempt to site a battery so as to enfilade the French line was countered by a forward movement on the part of four French pieces, and after ten hours of fighting the foe relinquished the field. It was noted that the French had handled 'the greater part of their battalion artillery like a troop of infantry'.[110] Guastalla was more of an encounter battle, and 'during the battle's course,' Brunet writes, 'the French batteries several times changed their position to take the enemy attacks in flank; at the end, two batteries pursued and cannonaded the Austrian retreat.'

There were still few signs of the development of truly massed batteries; the heavier guns tended to be placed towards the centre of the battle-line, the lighter on the flanks, but almost all guns were still drawn up along or to the fore of the front line in small detachments. Santa-Cruz, for example, divided his 18 guns into six three-piece batteries, 12-pdrs on the flanks of the infantry and 8-pounders between the infantry brigades, and ordered all battery positions to be enclosed within *chevaux de frise* – a practice that would hardly have served to encourage much further movement. Most generals paid lip-service to Montecucculi's earlier precept that 'once deployed, the artillery should fire as soon as the foe appears,' but in practice it was rare for guns to engage at ranges of over 600 paces, whilst case-shot was of little use at more than 300. Both Santa-Cruz and and the French expert de Quincy advised the gunners to concentrate on the enemy infantry and horsemen rather than his guns, but it is not clear how far this advice was adopted. Anyone desirous of studying a typical set of standing instructions for this period is directed to the 'General Order for the Artillery on Day of Battle' issued by Major-General Camus-Destouches, Inspector-General of the Artillery, on 12 September 1720,[111] from which much of this account has been drawn.

From 1741 to 1771 the influence of Vallière the Elder remained dominant in French artillery circles and in many another army as well. Siege operations tended to predominate, although the increasing allocation of 4-pdrs encouraged the ever-wider employment of regimental artillery. In battle, however, there was little change of role or emphasis, although Saxe's handling of his guns at Fontenoy was unusually successful, if in certain ways reactionary. On this occasion the French light guns were almost wholly restricted to defensive fire tasks, which they conducted very effectively. Saxe had at his disposal, after detaching guns for the siege of Tournai, some 100 pieces, including 50 'Swedish'. After leaving further detachments to cover the bridgehead over the Scheldt and the trenches at Rumignies, the French were left with some 60 guns for the battlefield itself. It is interesting to note how these were deployed. Six were placed near Antoing village, with a further four a little way to the East; six more were deployed in groups of two on three sides of Fontenoy village, and two larger batteries of six guns apiece were established on the flanks of the village. Six heavy guns were sited near Calonne Mill so as to enfilade the approaches to Antoing. The remainder were distributed along the French front, with the exception of 12 held in reserve between the two lines of infantry. This creation of an artillery reserve was practically unique at the period and really foreshadows Napoleonic practice – and equally notable was the degree of care Saxe took in selecting his battery positions. Not since the days of Marlborough had a commander-in-chief taken such pains based on careful thought and study of the ground.

The results proved the value of attention to topographical detail. The Fontenoy batteries engaged a British column and 'killed many of the foe, taking them in flank; it also attracted a hot fire from the (Allied) battery facing the redoubt, which the enemy redeployed.'[112] At 10 am four 'Swedish' guns pulverized the right-hand corner of the massive Allied square, pouring in seven salvoes and reducing the target area to a shambles. This also attracted the counter-fire of every Allied gun within range, but this in turn enabled the other French guns to concentrate on the Allied square, which constituted the main attack of the day, and in the end it was compelled to withdraw after terrible loss. This decided the battle, and the part played by the French artillery in securing the favourable outcome was very important, although the rather disappointing performance of the light Swedish pieces led to their number being considerably reduced for future French campaigns. This is not wholly to decry the efforts of the Allied gunners. The 3-pdr battalion guns attached to each British battalion were dragged to within 30 yards of the enemy line, whilst the 6-pdrs engaged the enemy artillery, but the flight of the Allied artillery drivers and their horses early in the day limited the support these guns could offer.

But if the French had on this occasion substantially reverted to defensive artillery tactics of the sort that had taken such a heavy toll of the Dutch Guards at Malplaquet a generation or so earlier, the British guns retained their reputation for operational mobility. If they had tended to allow their attention to be distracted at Fontenoy, the following year at Culloden they made a substantial contribution to victory – albeit against an opponent inferior in guns. The Duke of Cumberland sited his 10 6-pdrs in pairs between the battalions of his front line, and placed six howitzers in two batteries to the left of his Foot. Prince Charles Edward, conversely, placed his 12 guns more conventionally in three four-gun batteries, one on either flank and one slightly ahead of his centre. Colonel Christopher Teesdale of the 3rd Buffs recorded that:

> ... The Royal army marched in three columns and formed battle (in view of the enemy) in two lines and a corps de reserve, with the dragoons on the flanks, and these moved forward with ten field pieces (short 6-pdrs) in the front, and when we came within reach of cannon-shot our field pieces got into a bog, so that the horses were obliged to be taken off and the soldiers to losing their arms in order to drag the guns across the bog, which required some time. If the enemy thought our artillery could not be drawn across the bogs their ground was certainly well chosen.[113]

However, the guns were in due course brought into action and opened a far more effective fire against their opponents than the Young Pretender's gunners could return. The Highlanders on the right and in the centre became restive under the sustained bombardment, and were ultimately provoked into a premature massed-charge, which, although briefly successful against the 4th and 27th Foot, which had to give ground, proved of no avail whatever elsewhere, and the day ended in the rout of the Highland army and the virtual collapse of the Jacobite Rebellion.

British skill in handling their guns in a mobile fashion was to increase still further as the years passed. By the time of the Seven Years' War it had become necessary to arm the gunners and matrosses with carbines and bayonets, so exposed did they at times become through bold forward deployment. One climax was reached at Minden (1759), when 10 12-pdrs were rushed unseen by the foe to a critical point:

> We accordingly drew up our ten guns close to the six Regiments on the right and there waited undiscovered till the Enemy came almost within pistol shot, like a cloud, with numbers, and when they were just going to gallop down sword in hand amongst our poor mangled Regiments, we clapt our matches to the ten guns and gave them such a salute as they little expected, as they have since told us.[114]

One feels that the spirits of Jacob and Michael Richards, of Holcroft Blood and Albert Borgard, had they been present, would have joined in a rousing if ghostly cheer.

Part IV

The Engineering Services

13

The place and organization of military engineers

Although it was only gradually that military engineers received full recognition or a regular establishment within the structure of the armies of the day, there is no denying that they made vital contributions to the conduct of military operations between 1688 and 1745. On the one hand they facilitated the movement of the cumbersome armies, building or improving roads and tracks, bridging rivers, marshes and streams. On the other, they were responsible for the design and building of defences and lines, and above all for the technical aspects of siege warfare – both in attack and defence – in other words for the whole science of fortification in all its complexity.

The great commanders of the age varied in their opinions of the engineers' services. Of course the famous Vauban's position and reputation was unassailable, and in 1693 he even received a letter from Louis xiv which declared that 'nobody can have more consideration, esteem or friendship than I have for you'[1] – no mean mark of royal favour. His only serious rival, the Dutchman Menno van Coehoorn, earned the golden opinions of William iii and even of Vauban himself for his skill and spirit at Namur (1692 and 1695), and when he learnt of his death in 1704 Marlborough described himself as 'strongly affected' by the news.[2] The Duke was not always so impressed by his lesser engineers. During September 1708 he was continually denouncing the 'very ill conduct of our engineers and others' before Lille, going so far on the 27th as to describe himself as 'so vexed at the misbehaviour of our engineers that I have no patience' – a rare sign of temperament in the usually urbane and unruffled Marlborough. On the other hand, such outstanding engineers as Colonel John Richards, 'having on all occasions distinguished himself during the war in this country, but particularly at the siege of Bouchin,'[3] earned the Duke's full confidence and patronage – and even the ultimate accolade of being represented three times in the series of tapestries embellishing Blenheim Palace. A generation later, Maurice de Saxe in his *Rêveries* (1732) declared, somewhat tendentiously,

I am not particularly wise, but the great reputations of Vauban and Coehoorn do not overwhelm me. They have fortified places at enormous expense and have not made them stronger. The speed with which they have been captured proves it. We have modern engineers, hardly known, who have profited from their faults and surpass them infinitely . . .[4]

True or false, such views serve to illustrate the considerable importance accorded the engineering services, such as they were; in an age when whole campaigns and even wars often revolved around certain key fortresses and fixed lines, military engineers occupied a central position, and their importance could not be ignored.

Considering the part they were expected to play in the prosecution of warfare, it is strange how slowly regular engineering services emerged. Of course one indubitable reason was their long-standing association with the Boards of Ordnance or equivalent quasi-military bodies, whose special status *vis à vis* the military has already been described on an earlier page. In consequence engineer officers, like their artillery colleagues, often faced strong prejudices and sometimes actual hostility and obstruction, particularly when equivalent ranks, privileges or shares of prize-money were in question. In 1703, even the famed Coehoorn left the army in a huff after a great dispute with Deputy Hop and General Slangenberg over his army rank as Master-General of the Ordnance and Director of Fortifications of the United Provinces.[5] In England and France, it will be seen, it took all the prestige and position of Marlborough and Vauban respectively to lay even the first foundations of properly constituted organizations, but it would not be until many years after their deaths that the work came to full fruition, and many setbacks were encountered on the way.

In England, the Surveyor-General was, under the Master-General of the Ordnance and his deputy, particularly responsible for all matters pertaining to military engineers and their calling, receiving £500 for his pains. He was seconded* by a Principal Engineer (paid £300 per annum), charged with being skilled 'in all the parts of the mathematicks', the keeping of models and plans of all fortresses and the inspection of works as directed, and with the finding 'for our service good and able engineers, conductors and work bases' together with the necessary examination of all aspiring applicants; he was also responsible for the planning and conduct of sieges.[6] To aid him he was permitted two 'Inferior Engineers' (with salaries of £250 and £150 respectively), often called the Second and Third Engineers of England. Any, or even all, of these officials could be civilians, but in time of war the practice was to appoint soldiers to vacancies. Thus Holcroft Blood was appointed Second Engineer in February 1696, illustrating the way in which ordnance officers were often expected to be jacks-of-all-trades, for on 20 February 1702 he was promoted colonel of what eventually became 'the Blenheim Train', basically a gunnery post.[7] Such inter-departmental fluidity was frequently encountered, especially in the English forces. Lastly, there were varying numbers of engineers and sub-engineers including a few 'young men to be bredd up in the Art and Knowledge of Fortification etc.', often by being sent abroad for a period to study. These officers, then, together with a number of minor functionaries, clerks and artisans, formed the 'headquarters' organization that would one day form part

---

*Under William III there was also an Assistant-Surveyor, but this post disappeared in 1702.

of the Corps of Royal Engineers. The posts were permanent, a situation that did not pertain in the siege trains (to be considered later) where the engineers were essentially temporary appointments (until 1716), most of them being officers drafted in from the line regiments as required. A possible exception to this was the obscure body known as 'the King's Company of Engineers', approximately 27 strong, which apparently came directly under the Crown and not the Board, being paid by special Treasury warrants at rates varying from 10s to 5s a day. It disappears from sight, however, about 1700.

In France, as might be expected, a more complex system pertained. Louvois, Secretary of State and Minister of War, had suppressed the senior engineer post, namely that of *surintendant des fortifications,* but on his death in 1691 Louis xiv recreated it for Le Pelletier. The second senior post, namely *commissaire contrôleur général des fortifications,* fell early to the lot of Vauban (1678), and some time later the highest appointment was merged with this office under the title of *directeur général des fortifications du royaume.* By 1690 Vauban had created the first clear headquarters hierarchy. Beneath the *directeur général* came *directeurs des fortifications,* (controlling 'Maritime' or 'Frontier' provinces) a considerable number of *ingénieurs-en-chef* (commanding major fortresses etc), and lastly the junior officer grade, *ingénieurs-ordinaire.* How the French engineers organized themselves for field service will be described later, but all Vauban's efforts to create a firm rank structure came to naught. A later Director, the Marquis d'Asefeld (1667–1743), made minor improvements, but it was not until 1744 that Comte d'Argenson secured an *ordonnance* really defining the rank and status of engineer officers.[8]

Approximately similar central organizations existed in the United Provinces, Austria, Sweden and (after 1700) in Russia. As in both the cases cited above, the engineers remained for many years in most respects integral parts of their national Ordnance organizations. Within these, in many cases, they also remained subordinate to and dependent upon the artillery arm. The gunnery organizations for instance usually proved the tools used by the sappers as well as their powder and arms, whilst financially they were included in the overall Ordnance votes and estimates. Thus the engineers on campaign had scant administrative and even less financial responsibility for their work, whilst the artillery authorities were expected to administer services they did not direct. This contradictory situation survived well into the eighteenth century; but it seems to have worked fairly well in practice despite frequent disputes over priorities and allocations and slow improvements were made. Thus in Russia, the German engineer, Burchard Christophe Münnich (1683–1767) greatly improved the status of both engineers and gunners, securing the transfer of the Department of Artillery and Fortification from Moscow to St Peterburg in 1730.

For many years the position of the engineer serving with the field armies remained anomalous. Although it became generally recognized that engineers enjoyed officer status (indeed, they for long remained an exclusively officer organization in many countries), there was little agreement about equivalent army ranks or their privileges. Endless disputes about precedence and prize-money led to some slow amelioration of the situation. In 1692, for instance,

William III ruled that an engineer should receive 15 shares of prize-money, heedless of his seniority within the profession.[9] But so long as a proportion of engineers remained civilians rather than soldiers it proved harder to create a proper rank table. Of course many field sappers were recruited from the officers of the line regiments, and in these cases they retained their infantry ranks. Gradually the practice grew of either appointing engineers to companies of infantry as such, or, particularly in the French and Spanish services, of giving them brevets as *reformado* officers. Senior engineers often commanded regiments of infantry in the earlier years of our period: for instance Coehoorn was given the colonelcy of a regiment of Dutch infantry as one of many rewards for his services at Namur (1695), and Holcroft Blood commanded the 17th Foot between the years 1705 and 1707.[10] Such double-positions sometimes led to divided loyalties, and attempts were made in at least the French service to compel officers to choose one career or the other, although engineers deprived of actual infantry commands were permitted to retain brevet-ranks.[11] But Vauban and Marlborough were continually pressing for a regularized promotion table, but it was not until after their deaths that this was fully achieved. On the other hand, patronage could sometimes be employed to reward deserving sappers deprived of the opportunity of promotion within their profession, and in England there was always the possibility of appointment to an established post within the Surveyor-General's branch of the Ordnance to serve as an incentive for loyal and valorous conduct. Similar opportunities existed in all services. In Russia, for example, Münnich rose to the rank of Field Marshal in 1732 and firmly established the Russian sappers, many of them foreigners like himself, as integral parts of the Russian army.

Engineers serving in the field operated at one of two levels. The senior experts invariably gravitated towards the staff of the Commander-in-Chief or Captain-General; their more junior brethreen served as members of the trains in a number of capacities.

The roles of the senior engineers on the staff need not detain us long at this stage. In the academic sense they formed probably the most skilled section of the staff – numbering anything from three to a dozen or more – but they received their appointments by personal invitation of monarchs or generals rather than through intervention by the Ordnance authorities, although consulation was not unknown. Besides overseeing their junior colleagues, these staff engineers really came into their own when sieges were undertaken. A Director of the Trenches and other specialist posts would be appointed from their number. However from beginning to end they remained strictly subordinated to the Captain-General or Commander-in-Chief; they rarely were given a free hand for the conduct of sieges although their advice would be sought about the technical aspects. Nevertheless their counsel would not necessarily be followed. No doubt the suggestions of a Vauban would not be lightly disregarded, but it is perhaps significant that he wrote his treatises on fortification and siege warfare primarily for princes and generals rather than for fellow-engineers. Coehoorn's plan for the siege of Kaiserwerth (1702) was disregarded by the Prince of Nassau-Saarbrücken who imposed his own until the rising waters of the Rhine foretold by the Director-General compelled him to abandon his attack from the riverward in favour of one from the heights.[12] By way of contrast, however, Marlborough adopted the advice 'that it might be done', of Colonel Armstrong at the opening of the siege of Bouchain (1711) in spite of the otherwise unanimous opinion of the council of war that it was impossible, because he 'well knew the capacity of the man in that respect'[13] – displaying a confidence that was amply justified by subsequent events.

Passing on to consider the inferior engineers, their organization within the trains remained haphazard for much of our period. In the French service they were often grouped into temporary *brigades* of six or seven men apiece, including a *brigadier* and a *sous-brigadier,* but these were appointments rather than ranks. Vauban advised that an army should hold at least six such brigades to allow for a shift system of sieges by two groups at a time – 'this means that the trenches are never without engineers.'[14]

Vauban was always dissatisfied with the conditions of service of his juniors, '*avec qui Je vis comme des frères.*'[15] He did what he could to safeguard both their lives and career interests. Together with Le Pelletier, he strongly opposed Louvois' sweeping reduction of the serving engineers from 600 to 300 after the Peace of Ryswick, particularly as no pension or compensation was offered. The result of this impolitic act carried out in the name of economy was ultimately to send several hundred talented engineers into the English and Austrian services, where they joined their Huguenot colleagues (already driven overseas by the Revocation of the Edict of Nantes in 1685) in fashioning excellent engineering services as France was to learn to her cost in the next war.[16]

Defeated on this issue, Vauban turned to attempts to secure army rank for the survivors of the purge, and in due course obtained *reformé* commissions for those not already holding infantry appointments. At the same time, Vauban laid down rigid standards for his assistants. They were to be proficient in mathematics, geometry, trigonometry, surveying, geography, military architecture and drawing, and were to be regularly examined by M. Sauveur of the *Academie des Sciences.* He also set his face against promotion by favour. 'Merit and capacity alone should earn people positions'[17] he wrote, foreshadowing Napoleon, but in this respect he was hopelessly ahead of his time. Nevertheless, many of his lieutenants and protegés proved extremely capable engineers.

Vauban always deplored the deaths or maiming of his juniors on active service. When nine were killed and 15 wounded at the siege of Phillipsburg (1688) he described them as 'the martyrs of the infantry'. By way of comparison, the Allies lost all of 70 during the long siege of Lille 20 years later.[18] From first to last the Frenchman was convinced that one way to reduce such losses was by the creation of a regular corps of engineers which would exist and train in peacetime and contain other ranks as well as officers. 'If the war continues it will be necessary for you to procure from the King the Company of Sappers which I have so often demanded . . .' he informed the Minister of War; 'I am tired of leaving everything to chance, and having to train new sappers for each siege.'[19] But although Louvois was personally well-disposed towards the forthright engineer-general, he would not support these repeated requests, and his successors remained equally obdurate. Near the end of his life, Vauban made yet another appeal in 1705 for a company of specialists, nine officers and 212 sappers strong* pleading that it would cost only 50,000 livres a year, but again his plea fell on deaf ears. Only after 1715 – the year when the term *genie* was first employed – did any of his suggestions bear fruit – but it would not be until the 1760s that the engineers became finally separated from the artillery.

English trains had a smaller proportion of engineer officers than the French, but then both William III and Marlborough could call on numerous Allies, particularly the Dutch, to make good the deficiencies. William's trains habitually contained five or six engineers (paid 10s or 5s a day), but the one proposed for the 'Summer Expedition' of 1693 listed all of fourteen. Marlborough's trains were furnished on much the same scale, although there are indications that the prestige of the profession was rising during his campaigns. From 1716–17, moreover, dates the first emergence of an all-officer corps of engineers, largely independent of the artillery, although the Ordnance train formed to accompany Lord Cathcart's expedition in 1740 included a Chief Engineer and 12 engineers, still listed as of old under 'the officers and ministers and other attendants'. [20]

The British changes of 1716–17 need further mention as they were of the greatest significance in the formation of a permanent engineer organization. In May 1697 an attempt had been made to include six engineers (designated 'Captains' for possibly the first time), four sub-engineers and six Gentlemen of the Ordnance in the 'Regimental Train of Artillery to be kept in pay in time of peace', but less than a year later Parliament forced the King to disband the whole formation. However he managed to retain the officers' paid services, although this did not amount to creating a permanent organization. So matters rested until, on 19 June 1716, the Board of Ordnance submitted new proposals to the Duke of Marlborough (recently restored to all his offices by George I) for a major recasting of both the artillery and engineers. For the latter they proposed to allow 19 engineer posts (mainly well-paid sinecures) on the old establishment to waste out, replacing them with 28 engineers on a new organization in the interest of both economy and efficiency. A graded rank structure was also put forward, ranging from a Chief Engineer, through three Directors, six Engineers-in-Ordinary, as many Engineers-Extraordinary to six Sub-Engineers and a similar number of Practitioners. These proposals were not accepted without query or adjustment, but on 22 August 1717 King George I in Council approved a revised 'New Establishment' for 29 engineers in England† and a number more serving in two overseas garrisons – Gibraltar and Port Mahon. However for many years a dual system was destined to operate, for the changes were only 'to take place as vacancies shall happen on the three old establishments.'[21] Nevertheless, this document represents the first cautious emergence of a permanent and more independent corps of British engineers,

---

*Namely a Captain (paid 10 livres a day), four *Lieutenants* (at 5 livres), four *sous-lieutenants*, 12 sergeants, as many corporals, and 188 sappers.

† A Chief Director (paid 27s 6d *per diem*); two Directors (at 20s); 2 Sub-Directors; otherwise as suggested in 1716, with pay ranging between 10s and 3s a day.

albeit still an all-officer organization, and still (until the end of the century) subject to the Board of Ordnance.

What assistance could engineers call upon to carry out their projects? In terms of regular toops it was very limited in both extent and value – but most armies included companies of miners, pioneers and bridging personnel. Of course these formations – save the miners – were primarily concerned with aiding the artillery, but the engineers had residual claims on their services.

As early as 1671 a company of the French Regiment of Fusiliers was instructed to perform a double-function, adding sapper tasks to the duties of artillery protection, but this did not work well in practice and soon became a dead-letter. Miners were more successful. The French army contained three, and later four companies, each holding about 80 men, but following their full integration into the Grand-Master's organization and the practice of appointing artillery officers to command them in place of engineers (1705), they rapidly lost their traditions and subterranean expertise under the double-yoke of artillery administration and engineer direction.[22] Miners appear in the English army in weak company strength in the train created in April 1702 (consisting of a lieutenant and 20 miners), and in that of 1740 they were still present in identical numbers.

Pioneers are mentioned by St Rémy as performing road-improvement duties at the head of the French train columns on the march, and William III's 1693 Regimental Train included a detachment of a lieutenant, four sergeants and 54 pioneers. Thenceforward these units are almost always present with the army, and all nations developed the same practice. As an arm of the service, however, their prestige was low, and it had long been a punishment in many armies to degrade an offender to the rank of 'abject pioneer'.

Additionally, every army included a bridging detachment equipped with pontoons of copper or wood. The Spaniards held a high reputation as bridge-builders,[23] second only to the Dutch, whose canal- and dyke-crossed provinces afforded them with plenty of practice for native skill. Their *Compagnie Pontonniers* in 1701 comprised three officers, six *korporals*, two *blikslagers*, ('quartermasters'), six *timmerleiden* ('tinboat-men') and 60 *pontgasten*.[24] The English train of 1693 held a bridging company of three officers, four NCOs and '50 private men, 10 to be English watermen, at 2s each'. Like the pioneers and miners, it would seem that in most armies these formations were disbanded at each peace.

As a general rule these different specialist companies had individual existence, but d'Asefeld, who succeeded Le Pelletier on his retirement (1727), experimented with joint-companies holding gunners, sappers and miners altogether. This fusion did not succeed, however, and in 1729 the French sappers were again re-formed into five distinct units, one being loosely attached to each battalion of artillery, and the miners similarly reverted into autonomous sub-units.

All trains also included numbers of craftsmen – smiths, carpenters, harness-makers, wheel-wrights, coopers, tent-makers and 'tin-men' (fuse experts), on whom engineers could call for a measure of skilled assistance. These specialist companies and craftsmen described above could hardly be expected to afford the engineers with the amount of assistance they would require in a major siege, especially as their first duty lay with aiding the artillery. So engineers had often to be content with working parties detailed from the line regiments, and large numbers of local peasantry rounded up by entrepreneurs. Major operations required large numbers of *boors* serving as a labour force. Vauban suggests that at least 15,000 to 18,000 workers and perhaps 4,000 local carts with their horses were required for constructing a line of circumvallation between four and five leagues in length[25] around an invested town. For the siege of Mons (1691) he collected no less than 21,000. The necessary numbers could not always be collected before the opening of a siege. Thus on 12 August 1711, three days after the Allies invested Bouchain, Marlborough wrote to the Dutch Council of State requesting the use of 700 waggons drawn from Flanders and Hainault; 'I find myself obliged,' he urbanely continued,

> to make at this time a similar demand for 6,000 pioneers with their work tools, from the Provinces of Flanders, Brabant and Hainault . . . It is with regret that I find myself forced to make this request, and nothing but the necessities of the service would induce me to do so.[26]

Turkish armies, on the other hand, never seemed short of all the labour they required. It is estimated that no less than 100,000 slaves and pressed peasantry were with their army that challenged Eugene before Belgrade in 1717.

Christian forces were rarely so well provided for in this respect, and there were inevitably squabbles between the artillery and the engineers over the allocation of the amount of workmen available. At the same siege of Belgrade we find Brigadier-General de la Colonie, serving a spell in charge of a section of the Imperial trenches, recording that:

> I was not unaware of the fact that the gentlemen of the artillery are not always in agreement with their brethren in the engineers as to the employment of work parties, and that they get hold of them on their respective accounts whenever they can if they have any works in hand.[27]

Labouring under such competitive stresses in addition to the normal perils of siege life, it is small wonder that engineers were sometimes men of nerves as well as men of nerve. A few were downright disgraces to their profession in the tradition of one famous firemaster in the Tangier garrison (1668) of whom it was reported that he was 'certainly a most ignorant person as to the knowledge of any ingredient except brandy'. Others shared in the vice of officer-absenteeism. In October 1708, Marlborough was forced to take action against one such malingerer. 'Mr Chater not having attended his duty as an engineer this whole campaign, as he was directed, I desire his pay upon the establishment of the Ordnance may be respited till further orders.'[28] Most, however, were conscientious enough if prone to fits of temperament when frustrated in the conduct of their duties. In any case their services were indispensable. As Lord Galway wrote from Spain in 1704:

It is no easy thing to find good engineers, and a Commission from the Board of Ordnance is not sufficient to make one ... good engineers are so scarce, that one must bear with their humours and forgive them because we cannot be without them.[29]

14

Engineering tasks in
peace and war

In times of peace or winter quarters the engineer spent much of his time inspecting fortifications and undertaking their repair or improvement. For this purpose officers were often sent off to join garrison staffs at home and abroad. The more distant overseas posts were not particularly popular with some of the British Ordnance's personnel, and considerable pressure had sometimes to be exerted to fill vacancies – caused as often as not by disease. Detachments – often two or three strong – were habitually present at Gibraltar (from 1704), Port Mahon and Minorca (from 1708), and at different times at Placentia, Annapolis (Nova Scotia) and New York. At home, numbers would be retained at the Tower of London (where instructional courses were held) and Edinburgh Castle, whilst others conducted tours of inspection. During wartime winters, a majority would stay in Flanders, preparing fortresses against the possibility of future siege, or repairing the ravages of last year's campaigning on the latest conquests. On 4 September 1692, for example, William III ordered all the English engineers to foregather at Ostend to assist in the fortification and repair of Furnes and Dixmude. At the former, the Dutch engineer M. Tobias was already at work aided by 5,000 peasants, making it 'fit for winter habitation'.[30]

Such engineers as were retained 'in pay' after the cessation of hostilities would frequently be called upon to assist with civil engineering projects, though many of these of course had military implications. One of the most celebrated engineers of the period, the Comte de Münnich (who wandered from employ to employ until he entered Russian service in 1721 at Peter the Great's invitation), was famous as a canal builder. He had already built a 30 kilometre canal linking the Rivers Diemel and Fulda for a previous employer, the Margrave of Hesse-Cassel, and built the port of Carlshaven (1715) before moving on to drain marshes at Ujardowsk for Augustus II of Poland, but his greatest work was performed in Russia. First he improved the navigation of the River Neva by means of a series of weirs (1722); he next undertook the completion of Peter's favourite project – the linking of Moscow and St Petersburg by waterway. From 1706 some 20,000 serfs had laboured to link the River Tvertsa (a tributary of the Volga) with the River Tsna, and to create Lake Metus, but 12 years later the work was still incomplete. The main problem was hazardous Lake Ladoga, hard-by the new capital. In 1718 the Tsar ordered a canal to be dug around the lake, and entrusted the task to an engineer named Pisarev, a protégé of the favourite Prince Menchikoff. Four years of work, however, saw only 13 kilometres completed at a cost of over a million roubles. A furious tsar after consulting his Grand Master of Artillery thereupon appointed Münnich. Not only did he immediately make more progress than his predecessor, but he used only 2,900 troops and some 5,000 serfs, reducing the cost per *verste* by a third. Peter was delighted: 'The works of my Münnich have astounded me,' he declared after one of his many visits to the site; 'One day I count on embarking with him at Petersburg and next setting foot in the Gollowin Gardens in Moscow.'[31] In fact the work was not finished until seven years after the Tsar's death. At completion in May 1732, Münnich had constructed 111 kilometres of canal, which was 10–11 feet deep and 70 feet wide, and overcome the most daunting difficulties of natural and human obstruction in the process. His reward from the Empress Anna was appointment as Field-Marshal and President of the War College – virtually Minister of War.

In France, military engineers were often involved one way or another with the palace and gardens of Versailles, and after the Peace of Utrecht they supervised the construction of the Picardy canal. They also were responsible for supervising the work of the local *corvées* in maintaining the four major strategic highways and building new roads.

Indeed, road improvement figured high in the list of engineer tasks of all nations. In Russia, Münnich constructed the strategic road from St Petersburg to Schlüsselbourg (1733). On campaign, officers would scout ahead of the marching columns assessing the state of the roads and undertaking repairs with pioneers and local peasants as necessary. St Rémy advised French generals to place a waggon of spades and pickaxes at the head of the artillery trains for the use of *la chèvre* – a Captain of Workmen and his labourers.[32]

Amongst the most famous road-builders of our period was General George Wade (1673–1748), who built 250 miles of strategic highways through the Highlands between 1726 and 1738. Writing to King George I on 31 June 1726 Wade stated:

> I presume also to acquaint your Majesty that parties of regular troops have been constantly employed in making the roads of communication between Killymuire and Fort William.[33]

These were primarily intended as military roads to facilitate the disarming and control of the clans, but of course they also served to open up the country for trade and some measure of development.

About 500 regular soldiers, 'Wade's Highwaymen' as he jocularly termed them, were employed on this duty at any one time (with local labour) and although the task was not wholly completed by the time of the Revolt of the '45, they left their mark on the land, justifying the traditional doggerel:

> 'If you had seen these roads before they were made,
> 'You would have held up your hands and blessed General Wade.'

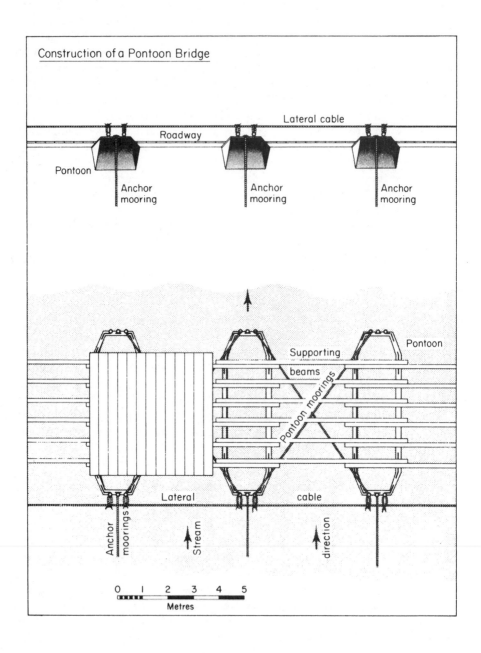

Construction of a Pontoon Bridge

Lateral cable

Roadway

Pontoon

Anchor mooring

Anchor mooring

Anchor mooring

Supporting beams

Pontoon

Pontoon moorings

Anchor moorings

Lateral

cable

Stream

direction

0 1 2 3 4 5

Metres

The engineers and soldiers also built 40 bridges over the same period, their masterpiece being the bridge over the River Tay at Wearn, described as having:

> Five arches, nearly 400 feet in length, the middle arch 60 feet wide, the starlings of oak, and the piers and land-breasts founded on piles shod with iron.[34]

Bridging assignments were also of great importance when armies were in the field, though few army-built crossings were so elaborate as the one just described. Most were either rough causeways over marsh and stream constructed by covering the obstacle with a thick layer of fascines with planks laid over the top (five such were laid over the Nebel stream under enemy fire during the morning of 13 August 1704), or pontoon-bridges over larger waterways, put down and taken up again as required. Engineers were required to select the best sites for the work, and thereafter left the work to the tin-boatmen.

Every army included at least one pontoon train; many had several. The Allied army took the field in Flanders in 1710 equipped with 40 pontoons; 30 years later a French army prepared to enter a campaign in the same region with all of 100.[35] Most pontoons were approximately 17 feet long, and were carried upside down on special waggons. Constructed of wood, many were sheathed with copper plates (hence 'tin-boats') nailed onto the timbers.

For obvious reasons, the pontoons were often among the first units to move off from the army's camps. 'The pontoons are sent away,' recorded Jacob Richards on 30 July 1692, 'and we have orders to march at the break of day.'[36] Marlborough's dash from Lessines to Oudenarde in the early hours of 11 July 1708 was headed by Cadogan and the pontoons. On reaching the proposed bridge-site, the pontoons would be launched into the water and anchored at set intervals from one another, fore and aft (see illustration). Beams were next secured to link the pontoons, and over these a plank roadway would be laid. The approaches and exits required careful preparation, and great care had to be taken at the bridgeheads; the mooring arrangements had to be capable of adjustment to meet sudden spates or drops in the water level, and it was even more important to impose strict traffic control to ensure that the pontoon bridges were not overloaded. What might happen if this was not done was drastically illustrated on 2 July 1704, when a large part of Count D'Arco's routed Bavarian garrison headed for the Danube, 'where they had a bridge of boats, but this breaking under them great numbers were drowned.'[37] The scale of Marlborough's victory at Oudenarde was also compromised by the collapse of a bridge.

Bridging operations tended to be taken for granted by many contemporaries, but a few feats deserved citation. At Blenheim, some gallant Allied engineers repaired the main stone bridge over the Nebel under heavy French fire besides laying the causeways already referred to. A year later, no less than 24 bridges were laid over the River Mehaigne in a single day as part of Marlborough's plan to fool Villeroi as to his intended crossing-place through the Lines of Brabant. This penetration was effected for minimal loss near Wanghé, the crossings over the Little Geet being equally promptly constructed.

Colonel Michael Richards, one of the Duke's adjutants, and who had the
direction of making the bridges, and who had behaved himself very well in
this action, was sent to the Emperor at Vienna with the welcome news. [38]

Equally celebrated were the laying of seven temporary bridges over the Scheldt
near Oudenarde the morning before the battle in July 1708 already referred to,
or the bringing of the River Scarpe near Bouchain in 1711 – both feats carried
out under the very noses of superior enemy forces. Bridges and their
maintenance also figured largely in the reduction of fortresses situated near
rivers – as the sieges of Namur and Belgrade well illustrate.

In an age when great importance was laid on the physical occupation of
territory for reasons of prestige and the subsisting of armies, engineers were
frequently called upon to construct fixed defensive lines to protect important
areas in the seats of war. The function of such lines was to provide an
early-warning of enemy attack and to delay his invasion until the main defence
forces could be marched up to contest the passage. Their function was therefore
temporary rather than permanent, so it would be erroneous to compare them to
the trench-systems of the First World War or the Maginot Line of 1940 which
were intended to be impregnable to attack.

The nature of these lines varied according to local topographical conditions.
Wherever possible use was made of high ground, scarped when necessary to
increase the gradient, and local waterways – rivers and streams – which were
often dammed to create areas of morasses. Causeways traversing the inundations
and watersheds were often breached and commanded by redoubts;
double-ditches and earthern ramparts, small forts and abattis of fallen trees,
were employed to cover open stretches, where the advantages of nature could not
be put to sufficiently good defensive use.

Some of these lines were very extensive. Amongst the longest were the
earthworks of the Ukraine, started by Tsar Peter I and completed by Münnich in
1730, designed to halt the incursions of Turkish and Tartar marauders, later
known as the *Tsaritzine* (or Tsarina) Line; these ran for all of 250 kilometres. [39]
In Flanders, the Lines of Brabant (1702–5) linked Antwerp and Namur – a
distance of 60 miles, whilst the Lines of *Ne Plus Ultra* constructed by Villars
in 1710–11 ran for almost 90 miles from the River Canche on the Channel Coast
to, once again, Namur. Similar extensive areas of fortification existed along
parts of the Habsburg-Turkish borders, including the Iron Gate region. Others
were shorter, for example the 12 mile Lines of Stolhoffen, built in 1703 to
dominate the ground between the east bank of the Rhine and the Black Forest
mountains, or the Lines of Corinth, designed to withstand the advance of the
Turks into the southernmost area of the Balkan peninsula.

The use these lines were put to in actual war has been described in earlier
chapters devoted to the consideration of cavalry and infantry. A few
contemporaries scorned reliance upon them; most made the fullest use possible of
them. Controversy invariably centred around their physical siting. The Comte
de Mérode-Westerloo was scathing about the location of the lines constructed in
1702 by the Flemish engineer, Verboom at the behest of Marshal Boufflers and

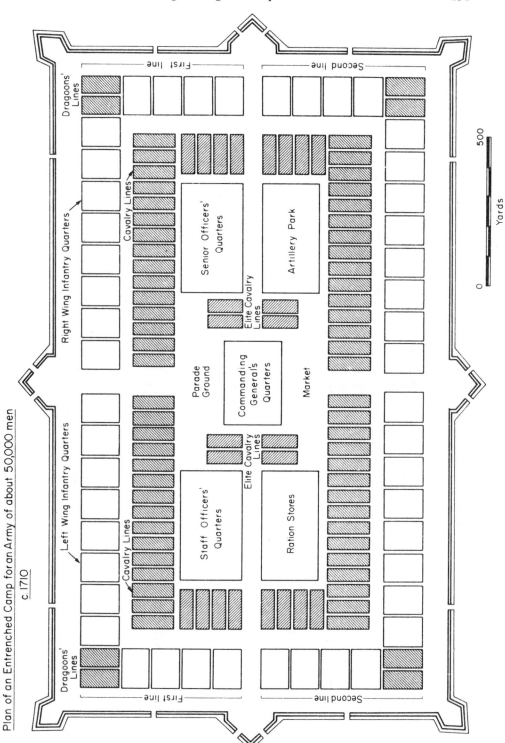

Plan of an Entrenched Camp for an Army of about 50,000 men
c. 1710

the Marquis de Bedmar, describing them as 'more profitable to the purses of the engineers who built them than for the country they were supposed to protect,' but his evidence is rendered somewhat suspect by the fact that they ran through his estates, destroying 'incalculable amounts of my trees and land . . .'[40]

Field defences were also often constructed to sustain the arrayed hosts in full panoply of battle. Redoubts, trenches and barricades were used to shield batteries, form *points d'appui,* and obstruct the advance of the enemy. At Landen (1693), the French were forced to storm William III's entrenched position – with success. In 1709, the Swedish infantry of Charles XII proved less fortunate at the battle of Pultava, where the Russians had built a dozen redoubts which absorbed most of the impetus of the Nordic attack whilst Peter the Great's main forces bided their time within a strongly entrenched camp. The same year Marshal Villars similarly entrenched the gap between the forest of Taisnières and Lanières Wood at Malplaquet, only to be manoeuvred out of them by Marlborough's consummate skill which enabled the English foot to occupy the redoubts for negligible loss. Imperial armies made considerable use of entrenched positions to compensate for their numerical disadvantage in battles against the Turk such as Zenta and Peterwardein, practices also adopted by the Russian armies until Münnich in the 1730s abolished both the pike and reliance on trenches, substituting the use of *chevaux de frise in lieu*[41] – a device widely used by Swedish, Austrian and other German forces. Finally, at Fontenoy in 1745, de Saxe made excellent use of earthern redoubts and battery positions to hold, and ultimately defeat, the Allied army of the Duke of Cumberland. The design and supervision of the building of these positions were often a task shared between the Gunners and Sappers.

One other duty was the laying-out of defences to shield permanent encampments. If an army halted for more than a week in one place it was customary to add perimeter ditches and parapets, with outworks to protect the gates (see illustration). The Austrians and Russians particularly favoured this type of position, and so did the Dutch. Vauban had much to say in support of the idea of constructing permanent encampments as integral parts of major fortresses – and built an experimental one at Toulon – but the consideration of his concepts is best reserved for the last chapter as in cases such as these they approximated to regular fortifications, a subject yet to be treated.

Other examples of entrenched camps include William III's position at Landen in 1693, the contemporaneous encampment outside Bruges in the Netherlands – Camp St Michel (see illustration) – Overkirk's position (1705) hard by Maastricht on Mont St Pierre – and of course we should not forget Marlborough's fortified encampment between the Rivers Deule and Marque in September 1708, the only time Marlborough adopted a wholly defensive position – from which he defied the daunting combination of Vendôme, Berwick and Burgundy, during a critical period of the siege of Lille; four miles of circumvallation were eventually dug around Ennetières – and so strong did the position become that even Minister of War Chamillart, sent from Versailles with direct royal orders for an immediate assault, went against the letter of his instructions and supported the generals' caution.[42] Marshal Villars also made full use of a camp of the sort commended by Vauban in his (abortive) attempt to sustain Bouchain during Marlborough's final great siege.

15

The art and science of
fortification and siegecraft

Few periods of military history can have been more dominated by siege warfare than the 60-odd years between 1680 and 1748. The following table gives some indication of the relative frequency of sieges *vis à vis* field actions:

Period	Major Sieges	Land Engagements
1618–1679	22	77
1680–1748	167	144
1749–1815	289	568 [43]

No doubt the Earl of Orrery was exaggerating when he wrote in 1677: 'We make warre more like Foxes than Lyons; and you have twenty sieges for one battel.' [44] – but the trend definitely existed in his day and became ever more pronounced as the eighteenth century progressed into its second quarter. Indeed, it is claimed that the French army conducted no less than 84 sieges in Flanders alone during the War of the Austrian Succession [45] – but this staggering total must include many minor blockades not included in Bodart's estimates listed above.

Without exception, all the great commanders found themselves frequently involved in siege warfare. Some commanders deliberately set out to avoid battle under any but the most favourable circumstances. Their number included such notable soldiers as Marshal Luxembourg during the Nine Years' War and the great Maurice de Saxe a half-century later, although each also had a record of notable field successes to his credit. The latter went so far in his *Rêveries* as to assert:

> I do not favour pitched battles, especially at the beginning of a war, and I am convinced that a skilful general could make war all his life without being forced into one. [46]

Other leaders might deplore the need to spend so much time and *matériel* in the tedious toils of siege warfare, but even such stormy petrels as Prince Eugene and Charles XII of Sweden were frequently compelled to indulge in the practice, whilst Marlborough, for all his well-deserved reputation as a battle-seeker, conducted only four major engagements and two actions and over 30 sieges in ten campaigns. For the rest, many lesser commanders welcomed the opportunity of disguising their lack of initiative or military ability behind the convenient cloak offered by the need to indulge so frequently in such static and relatively predictable operations. As Daniel Defoe sarcastically remarked in 1697:

> Now it is frequent to have armies of 50,000 men of a side standing at bay within sight of one another, and spend the whole campaign in dodging – or, as it is genteely called – observing one another, and then march off into winter quarters.[47]

The basic design of permanent fortifications

The art and science of defensive engineering made considerable progress under the inspiration of such influential figures as Vauban, Coehoorn and Rimpler. Each expert founded a 'school' of followers and imitators, and developed his own specialities of design, but in almost every case these improvements were merely variations on a theme. Although details might differ considerably, the broad aspects of design remained common to all; they shared, for instance, the concept of a polygonal trace or ground-plan; similarly, most of the component parts of a defensive scheme were used by every nation, although regional variations certainly existed. As Coehoorn himself wrote, 'It is not a wonderful thing that in a whole Age (1588–1700) there should be such small improvement made in the Art of Fortification?'[48]

Throughout history, fortifications have been designed to perform certain functions, although the order of priority and emphasis amongst them has frequently shifted, reflecting changes in weapon capabilites and the methods of construction.

Perhaps the most important concept since the onset of the age of gunpowder has been that of producing a maximum of effective firepower; certainly in the late seventeenth and early eighteenth centuries it was axiomatic that the approaches to all sectors of a fortress should be swept by converging fields of fire, both cannon and musketry. Most experts put emphasis on the former, but the followers of Fournier laid special emphasis on the musket as the most important defensive weapon, pointing out that gun-crews needed considerable experience to be effective, and the heavy man-power commitment their use involved, the general vulnerability of the pieces themselves, and the expense in terms of casting the weapons and providing them with powder and shot which the large cannon invariably incurred. On the whole, however, the gunnery school triumphed, for it was deemed advisable to destroy an attacker before he could get within close range of the defences – and the effective range of cannon was over 600 yards whilst the maximum carry of a musket-ball was little more than 250 yards. Of course the requirements of immediate defence were not disregarded, and all fortresses were supposedly capable of producing effective curtains of fire of both the close and distant varieties. Acting upon this assumption, every position and outwork had to be carefully designed to permit the freest use of all the defenders' weapons and the maximum degree of mutual support.

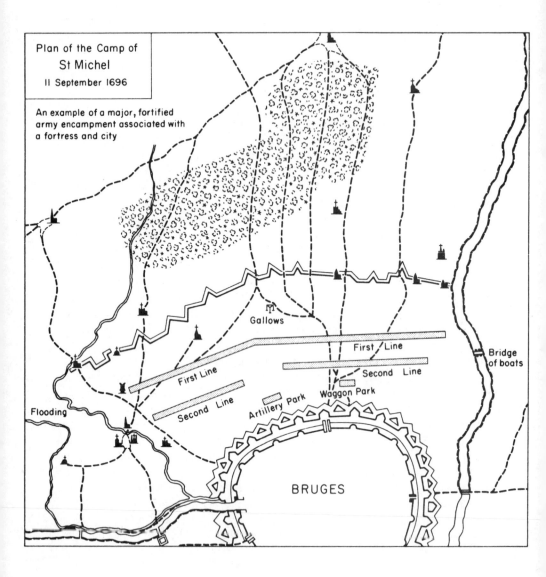

Plan of the Camp of
St Michel
11 September 1696

An example of a major, fortified
army encampment associated with
a fortress and city

Gallows

First Line

First Line

Second Line

Second Line

Bridge
of boats

Artillery Park

Waggon Park

Flooding

BRUGES

A second principle was the function of protection – for garrison, citizenry and real estate within the perimeter. This was partly a question of designing defences strong enough to withstand the effects of shot, bomb and shell, and partly a question of compelling the hostile batteries to operate from as long a range as possible. The former consideration was very much a question of design. The towering walls of mediaeval castles had given place to squat, immensely thick bastions and curtain walls, let down into the ground, as engineers strove to reduce the destructive power of the increasing numbers of cannon becoming available by opposing to them stone-reinforced positions of rammed earth and deep ditches. The second *desideratum* was obtained by adding ever more outworks in closely related series in order to push the enemy's batteries further and further away from their ultimate target. As cannon became more numerous and (marginally) more powerful and effective, so defensive systems became increasingly complex, as one ring of outworks was superimposed upon another until the point was reached in the eighteenth century when fortresses were ringed with several successive layers of defences.

A third object in the design of fortifications was the obstruction of the enemy foot-soldier's approach by means of both fire and physical obstacles; his arrival at hand-to-hand grips with the garrison was to be delayed for as long as possible. For if the production of maximum fire-power was one cardinal principle of defence, the winning of time was another. Every day that passed increased the possibility of relief by a friendly field army – or the exhaustion of the attacker's patience and resources – although as we shall note on a later page, the desirable length of a sustained resistance was clearly defined and in many ways curtailed by contemporary customs and regard for the 'laws of war',

In modern times a further principle had been added to these three – namely camouflage or concealment. This concept did not really arise in our period although the innermost details of defences were kept as secret as possible. But it was an age notorious for its lack of security. More or less accurate engravings of most towns were on sale in profusion all over Europe. 'There are presently few places in Europe,' observed Vauban, 'of which there are not plans; most are even engraved; and although these plans are often inexact one should not refuse to use them . . .'[49]

Passing on from the general to the particular, we must next examine how these concepts of fire output, protection and obstruction were applied in the type and design of fortifications commonly encountered throughout Europe.

The outermost part of the vast majority of fortresses was the glacis, an area of ground between 200 and 400 yards wide entirely encircling a town or fortress. The glacis was often carefully sloped gently upwards towards the main defences, and was completely devoid of all forms of cover and inequalities of ground so as to provide the garrison's sentries with a clear view, and the guns with an ideal killing ground. In some instances the outer edge of the glacis was protected by a ditch, but many engineers, including Vauban, discouraged this practice as likely to interfere with the effectiveness of sorties as well as providing the enemy with a ready-made source of cover for use as a *place d'armes*. Sometimes the glacis was dispensed with – as when a fortress was placed on top of a hill.

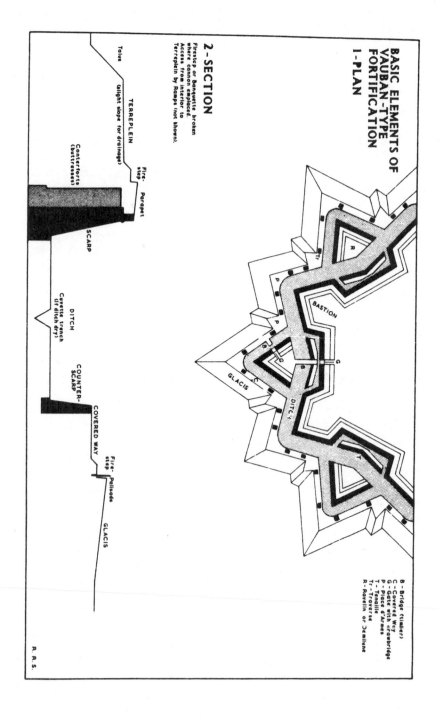

BASIC ELEMENTS OF
VAUBAN-TYPE
FORTIFICATION

1 – PLAN

2 – SECTION

Firestep or Banquette broken
where cannon emplaced.
Access from interior to
Terreplein by Ramps (not shown).

Talus

(slight slope for drainage)

TERREPLEIN

Fire-
step   Parapet

Counterforts
(buttresses)

SCARP

DITCH
Cuvette trench
(if ditch dry)

COUNTER-
SCARP

COVERED WAY

Fire-   Palisade
step

GLACIS

BASTION

GLACIS

DITCH

B – Bridge (timber)
C – Covered Way
G – Gate with drawbridge
P – Place d'Armes
T – Tenaille
Tr – Traverse
R – Ravelin or Demilune

A. R. S.

The inner edge of the glacis merged into the covered way – the first regular outwork. This also ran all the way around the fortress on the outer side of the main ditch. The covered way usually comprised a circular access road and a parapet provided with a firestep, from which musketeers could engage an advancing opponent. This was generally an earthern construction strengthened by palisading. The average depth of this area was some 20 feet, but at certain intervals larger *places d'armes* or redoubts were let into the glacis.

From the rear of the covered way dropped the counterscarp wall, the outer face of the ditch – a steep bank occasionally revetted with bricks or stone. Sometimes let into its face were counterscarp galleries, fire positions commanding the bottom of the ditch and the foot of the facing scarp walls. Ditches varied in width and depth according to the size of the positions beyond or within their area which would usually have been constructed with the earth dug out from them. Vauban advocated a width of 95 feet and a depth of between 18 and 20 feet (below the ground level of the fortress interior).

There were three varieties of ditch: dry ones – which would be provided with a deep trench running down its centre to obstruct assaulting troops and intercept enemy mining attempts – and wet ditches of two kinds, namely those filled with still water (which represented a health hazard in those days of primitive sanitation and disease prevention), and those holding moving water as at Namur and Lille (which presented the difficulty of erosion and the danger of flooding at intemperate seasons of the year). Nevertheless this last kind was regarded as the best form of obstacle as it was very difficult for an attacker to bridge it under fire. Both types also hindered sorties to some extent, although sally-bridges were provided.

Many dry ditches contained a *fausse-braye* or earthern rampart running round the foot of the rampart, but these were becoming obsolescent by the late 1690s. Within the ditch area were also situated numbers of further outworks of growing complexity, all designed to protect this or that part of the main position. These included *ravelins, démi-lunes* and *tenailles*; sometimes there would also be *caponnières* let into the angles of the ditches to command the foot of the ditch; to protect major gateways into the town or fortress vast crown-works and horn-works were often constructed abutting the glacis (as at Lille and Bouchain).

The scarp (or inner-wall) of the ditch was almost invariably faced with stone, and adjoined the main curtain wall with its projecting bastions. Both the *courtine* (or curtain) and the bastions were relatively low structures – projecting about 12 to 15 feet over the edge of the glacis, but this height associated with the depth of the ditch made them into considerable obstacles. Their real strength lay in their thickness, many measuring perhaps as much as 66 feet at the foot, tapering to some 30 feet at the level of the gun-platform. Curtain walls were somewhat less strong, but nevertheless still redoubtable enough, many parapets being up to 24 feet thick. They were constructed of rammed earth, and were usually provided with sloping outer faces in an attempt to minimize the damage done by the impact of cannon balls. These faces were habitually sown with wiry turf (Vauban particularly recommended *four de Bourgogne*), or osier saplings, in order to bind the earth together with the roots. Of course these were not permitted to obstruct lines of fire, but were burnt or cut down periodically. Neglect of this precaution could cost a Governor dear, as the commander of Fort St Michael learnt in 1702. Captain Parker was one of a group of hardy souls led by Lord Cutts who stormed into the position hard on the heels of part of the garrison.

> They that fled before us climbed up by the long grass that grew out of the fort, so we climbed after them . . . Had the Governor kept the grass, by the help of which we climbed, close mown, as he ought to have done, what must have been our fate?[50]

Bastions projected forward from the main trace in order to achieve patterns of flanking fire with neighbouring positions for the guns placed upon their respective platforms. They presented a number of faces towards the glacis – normally two but the angle at the apex and the precise shape of the flanks linking them to the rampart of the *courtine* led to much contention between the rival schools of engineering (see next chapter). The distance separating bastions was often calculated on the musket-range of the day, but this was not invariably the practice. At Maubeuge, for example, they were no less than 600 yards apart. In such cases the use of *tenailles* to protect the exposed length of curtain wall was very important.

Within the bastion was situated the gun-platform, protected by a strong parapet provided with a firestep and pierced with wide gun embrasures. A popular practice was to add 'guérites' or small watch towers at the apex of the bastions or at intervals along the curtain walls to serve as observation posts, but these were later superseded, especially in France, by *tours bastionnées* of two or more stories (a speciality of Vauban's later years), which were designed to hold the guns as well. Along the summit of the rampart ran a *chemin de rondes* paced by the sentinels. Finally, behind the bastions would run a military road to enable the garrison reserves to reinforce a threatened sector, with staircases running up to the ramparts or earthen slopes up to the gun platforms.

Siegecraft: the attack and defence of fortresses

The mechanics of siege warfare in our period are nowhere better described than in Vauban's *l'Attaque des Places*, whilst further illuminating detail is provided in Surirey de St Rémy *Mémoire d'Artillerie*. The intention of both authors was to instruct their contemporaries rather than to describe historical events, so here it will be desirable to illustrate their ideas by reference to actual sieges, thus adding example to precept. For this purpose the sieges of Namur (1 July – 5 September 1695), and Lille (12 August – 10 December 1708) will be referred to in particular, supplemented by further examples drawn from other campaigns when it is necessary to illustrate specialized aspects.

As Vauban wrote, 'the choice of sieges is a cabinet matter.' Whenever possible, the decision was taken well in advance as there were usually vast preparations to be undertaken, at least for a major siege. Thus the French prepared for the unseasonably early siege of Mons (15 March – 10 April 1692) throughout the preceding winter, illustrating Vauban's dictum that 'It is a very favourable circumstance to be able to attack before the enemy takes the field in strength . . . to achieve . . . (this) . . . it is necessary to have large magazines of forage within range of the target.'[67] William III went to great pains to complete his plans for the recapture of Namur three years later by late February.[52] Similarly, Eugene's preparation for the siege of Belgrade (1717) went back to the period immediately following his victory at Peterwardein in August 1716.

Such foresight was not always possible. The siege of Lille, for example, was only seriously considered after the Allied victory at Oudenarde that same July (the first definite steps being taken on the 22nd of the month); similarly, the Austrian siege of Prague in 1742 was hurriedly exemporized without benefit of lengthy preparation.

Preparations for a siege
Any important siege involved the collection of large numbers of men and animals and huge quantities of munitions, rations, forage, stores and waggons, together with all possible information about the town to be attacked, the size of its garrison and the morale of its citizens. These preparations were hard to conceal from enemy agents, and Vauban deplored the common lack of security surrounding such projects. He advised that a besieging force needed to be at least 10 times the estimated size of the garrison, and in any case no less than 20,000 strong if the construction of lines of contra- and circumvallation was envisaged. He also called for the employment of 15,000 peasantry and several thousand local waggons and horse-teams. St Rémy believed that 32,000 foot and 18,000 horse, supplemented by 10,000 peasants, was sufficient for most operations. Perhaps the largest besieging force of our period was that used by the French at Philipsburg in 1734, where some 117,000 men were deployed; the sieges of Lille (1708), Landau (1713) and Belgrade (1717) were conducted by armies orginally totalling between 80,000 and 110,000 men apiece, but the average for a major fortress would seem to have been in the region of 50,000 to 60,000 which accords closely with St Rémy's estimate.

St Rémy is equally exact concerning the quantities of munitions and rations required for an army of 60,000 men. Calculating on the basis of a forty days period, such an army and its labour force would need 3,300,000 rations and 730,000 issues of forage. As for munitions, he calculated that at least 40,000 rounds of 24-pdr shot, 16,000 more for guns of lighter calibre, and some 9,000 bombs for the mortars should be available, besides 40,000 grenades and 30,000 rounds of musket ammunition. Such a fire programme called for 793,750lbs of powder and an additional reserve of 150,000lbs. Additionally he lists every store the besiegers might need, from 550,000 cubic feet of timber for gun-platforms and trench-shoring to 18,000 picks and mattocks, 4,000 baskets and huge quantities of ropes and nails.[53] The gathering and transportation of so much varied material clearly called for administrative ability of no mean order, and the more time available the better for those responsible. The financial backing

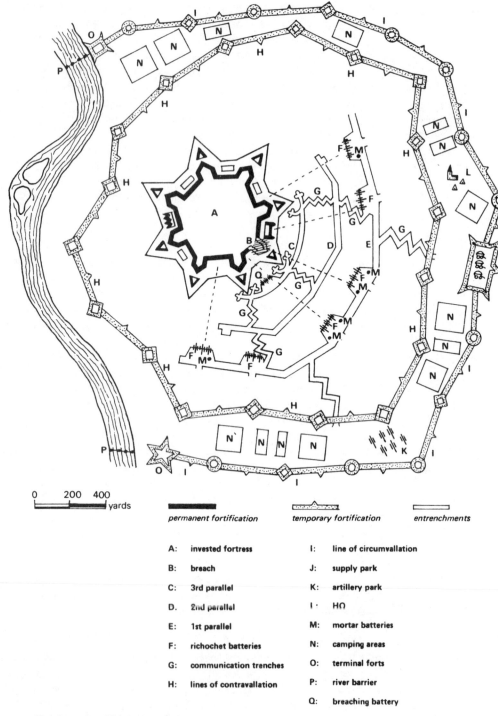

0   200 400
yards

permanent fortification   temporary fortification   entrenchments

A: invested fortress   I: line of circumvallation

B: breach   J: supply park

C: 3rd parallel   K: artillery park

D: 2nd parallel   I·   HΩ

E: 1st parallel   M: mortar batteries

F: richochet batteries   N: camping areas

G: communication trenches   O: terminal forts

H: lines of contravallation   P: river barrier

                                Q: breaching battery

The siege of an 18th century fortress

required for such enterprises also took considerable contrivance to arrange. A sufficiency of heavy guns was the *sine qua non* of proceeding with a regular siege. St Rémy advised his army to provide itself with a siege train of 110 cannon (including 50 33- or 24-pdrs) and 40 mortars. In practice this standard was often surpassed. To besiege Mons in 1692, Vauban amassed 130 cannon, 44 mortars and 8 *pierriers*.[54] To recapture Namur, Coehoorn deployed 147 cannon and 60 mortars. At Lille, the Allies sited 120 'battering cannon' besides mortars and lighter pieces, whilst nine years later Eugene deployed over 200 guns of all sizes before the defences of Belgrade.

Siege trains usually did not accompany the armies in the field, but remained in rear ready to move ponderously forward when required. As might be expected these were vast organizations. In 1693, William III ordered a 78-gun heavy train to be prepared against 'this summer expedition', comprising 20 24-pdrs, as many coehoorns, 18 sakers, and 10 13in, and as many 10in mortars. Commanded by Colonel Sir Martin Beckman, this train had an establishment of 87 assistants of officer status (including 14 engineers – Holcroft Blood being of their number), 30 bombardiers, 26 conductors, 22 bridgemen, 100 gunners and as many matrosses, 61 craftsmen and 96 drivers – almost 550 officers and men in all if we include boys.[55] This will serve as a representative example of a siege train, although larger ones certainly existed. It was unusual to find an English siege-train's components sub-divided into companies until the eighteenth century, but this then became increasingly the practice. By the time of George II this was firmly established; in March 1740 a Royal Warrant ordered the formation of a heavy train of 30 cannon, four mortars and 50 coehoorns for Lord Cathcart's army in Flanders, and this document clearly enumerates companies of gunners and miners.[56]

Most siege trains were very slow-moving and, with their myriad attendant waggons, filled many miles of road. The 'Great Convoy' of July 1708 covered (in two sections) some 15 miles of roadway, consisting of 80 siege guns (drawn by 20 horses apiece), 20 mortars (requiring 16 horses each) and 3,000 four-horse waggons. Under Cadogan's watchful eye it moved exceptionally swiftly, taking only seven days to cover the 75 miles from Brussels to Menin *en route* for Lille, and directly or indirectly some 90,000 men were engaged in ensuring its security from French raiding parties. 'For God's sake, be sure you do not risk the cannon,' wrote Marlborough to his Quartermaster-General.

Whenever possible, siege trains were conveyed by water. Thus Jacob Richards travelling to Ostend in September 1692 'met a great number of well-boats in which was [*sic*] all our Sea Trains and all the Stores of Warr belonging thereunto which were going to Nieupoort.'[57] It was military considerations of this type that partly underlay the construction of so many canals in France, Russia and above all in the Netherlands.

If commanders of field armies contemplating making a siege had to make elaborate preparations, so of course did commanders of frontier garrisons as a routine precautionary duty. Although Vauban was explicit in his opinion that no fortress, however well defended, could hope to hold out for an indefinite period, he was equally insistent that no fortress should be lost prematurely by default. In

La défense des places he gives explicit instructions on the proper composition of staffs and garrisons, and the exact weapons and stores the governors should lay in against the evil day. Basing his calculations on the number of bastions a fortress possessed, he provided exhaustive lists for 15 different sizes of towns, (but excluded the needs of the civil population as irrelevant to his particular survey)* A six-bastion fortress, for example, needed to be garrisoned, armed and stocked on the following scale to stand a 48 day siege:

(Garrison, peace): 1,200 infantry, 100 cavalry and a skeleton staff
(Garrison, war): 3,600 infantry, 360 cavalry and 200 staff; 120 gunners, 80 bombardiers, and 40 miners.
Weapons: 60 cannon, 30 mortars, 60 wall-muskets; 3,000 spare muskets.
Shot: 24,000 cannon-balls, 15,600 bombs and grenades.
Powder: 340,000lbs, besides 419,240lbs of lead and 300,000 lengths of match.
Rations: *inter alia* 3,495 *septiers*† of grain and rice, 5,051 boxes of onions, 1,424 quintals of beef, 480 quintals of mutton 'for sick or wounded officers', as much of veal for wounded rank and file, 385 quintals of cheese; 8 quintals of plums 'for the sick', 275 *muides* of wine, 825 *muides* of beer and 108 more of *eau de vie,* 'for distribution at a rate of two small tots a day'.

This list represents only a representative selection of his very full recommendations, but one further item deserves mention as it illustrates both Vauban's thoroughness and his concern for the state of morale of the ordinary soldier. 'Tobacco', he writes, 'is necessary to keep the soldier happy', and he conscientiously advised the provision of 12,900lbs for 4,000 men as 'one pound tobacco contains 112 pipefulls, let us say 100 to allow for waste.'[58] He also stressed the importance of governors keeping their water cisterns clean and full, of frequent inspections and testing of arms, and of constant maintenance of their defences in a proper state of repair. He also advised regular observance of strict fast days, to help innure the troops to possible future hardships.

How far this represents an 'ideal' rather than a practical state of affairs it is difficult to assess. In 1691, it would seem that the Dutch garrison of Namur (8,800 strong) was equipped with 62 24-pdrs and 28 lighter guns and mortars, besides 442,736lbs of *luspolver* (loose powder) and 46,000 made-up charges; 41,137 shot were available for the 24-pdrs.[59] Other representative garrisons were as follows: Marshal Boufflers had 16,000 men with which to defend Lille in 1708, and some 80 cannon. The Austrians tried to hold Belgrade against the Turks in 1690 with only 5,000 men – far too few, as the immediate storming indicated. Twenty-seven years later, the Turks tried to defend the same place with no less than 30,000 – the largest garrison recorded for the period – and held out rather better. The French placed 26,000 men in Prague in 1742, and the Turks defended Oczakov with 22,000 against Münnich's Russian army in 1737.

---

*In another paper, devoted to a scheme for the defence of Paris, Vauban calculated that 25,200,000 bushels of wheat would be needed to feed a total population of between 700,000 and 800,000 people for twelve months.

†A *septier* = 235lbs; a *quintal* = 112lbs; a *muide* = 280 pints.

Of course the size of garrisons varied enormously according to a large number of circumstances, but Turkish ones generally tended to be larger than Christian owing to their large numbers of slaves and supernumaries.

The progress of a siege – as conducted by both the besiegers and the garrison
With certain exceptions, the prosecution of sieges had become a highly ritualized affair by the late seventeenth century. Although there were unique features in each operation, there were also certain fixed conventions which both besieger and besieged generally observed. Unless treachery could be counted on to open the gates (as at Bruges and Ghent to the French in July 1708) or to permit an unopposed crossing of a vital waterway to surprise the enemy camp (as at Limerick in 1691 where a Colonel Lutterell 'to preserve his estate', allowed Orange forces over the Shannon), or the known-weakness of a garrison and the defences encouraged an immediate storming (what Vauban refers to as 'an accelerated attack', as at Belgrade in 1690 and Oczakov in 1737), a commander usually had to undertake the performance of a regular siege in all its stages.

The lengths of sieges varied enormously. The longest in our period was that of Milazzo (1718–19), where an Austrian garrison defied their opponents for 219 days (see Appendix Two), but the Swedish defence of Riga in 1700 was only one day shorter. In 1742 the French held Prague for 152 days before capitulating. Marlborough's longest siege was that of Luttich (131 days). At the other end of the scale, if we exclude immediate stormings, came the six-day sieges of Huy (1705) and Marchiennes (1712).

Of course many factors might account for the duration of a siege besides the size of its garrison, the state of the town's defences, or the presence of disaffected elements. The morale of the defenders could be a decisive factor: thus after Marlborough's great victory at Ramillies in 1706, a dozen major fortresses fell into Allied hands in the space of three weeks, only the garrison of Ostend offering even a token resistance. Similarly, Allied towns fell with depressing speed to Marshal Villars when his band-wagon began to roll after his success at Denain in 1712. It was not unknown for the attitude of the civil population to overwhelm a weak governor. At Mons, in 1691, Louis xiv hastened the conclusion of the siege by threatening to levy a fine of 100,000 crowns from the prosperous citizenry for each further day the city's resistance continued; the result was a capitulation after only 26 days.[60]

Nevertheless, a great many sieges fit into the 40 to 60 day range, which partly supports Vauban's dictum that a defence of 48 days' duration was respectable. His master, however, came to deplore the frequency with which French commanders beat the *chamade* after the expiry of this period heedless of the state of their defences, and on 6 April 1705, Louis xiv addressed the following circular letter to all governors:

Despite the satisfaction I have derived from the fine and vigorous defence of some of my fortresses besieged during this war, as well as from those of my governors who have held their outworks for more than two months – which is more than the commanders of enemy fortresses have managed when besieged by my arms; nevertheless, as I consider that the main defences of my towns can be held equally as long as the outworks ... I write you this letter to inform you that in the circumstances of your being besieged by the enemy it is my intention that you should not surrender until there is a breach in the body of the *enceinte*, and until you have withstood at least one assault ...[61]

This homily does not appear to have unduly impressed the commandants of the Netherlands fortresses in 1706 if we can judge by their actions. Nevertheless, Vauban's timetable for the capture of a well-appointed and resolutely held six-bastion fortress provides an interesting commentary on the 'standard' proceedings of a normal siege, however much practice might vary from precept in matters of detail.

To invest a place, collect material, and build lines	– 9 days
From the opening of the trenches to reaching the covered way	– 9 days
The storm and capture of the covered way and its defences	– 4 days
Descent into and crossing of the ditch of the *démi-lune*	– 3 days
Mining operations, siting of batteries, creation of a fair breach	– 4 days
Capture and exploitation of the *démi-lune* and its defences	– 3 days
Crossing of the main ditch to two bastions	– 4 days
Mining operations and siting of guns on the covered way to making a practicable breach	– 4 days
The capture of the breach and its supporting positions	– 2 days
Surrender of the town after the capitulation	– 2 days
Allowance for errors, damage caused by sorties, a valorous defence	– 4 days
	Total: 48 days[62]

This was only intended to be a rough guide to assist commanders estimate what they were up against, and if complications could be expected further days were to be added to allow for the capture of outlying hornworks, redoubts etc. Against these Vauban balanced the effects of mounting casualties and worsening conditions in the town.

To form a clear impression of the conduct of a siege it is necessary to trace the various stages in rather more detail, giving specific examples.

The Investment
Once the many preparations were completed or at least far advanced, the attacking army would advance on its objective, leaving the siege train and heavier convoys (suitably escorted) to follow at a slower pace. In attempts to retain the advantage of surprise, feints were often mounted to distract the enemy's attention; in 1691 this did not prove necessary before the French attacked Mons, for the early date of their arrival there (second week in March) caught the Allies hopelessly unawares, but in more conventional campaigns a measure of deception was habitually attempted. Thus in 1694 the Allies feinted towards Dixmude before besieging Huy. In the case of Lille (1708), the Allies after Oudenarde were equally well-placed to besiege Tournai, Ypres or Mons, and kept the French guessing until 10 August – only two days before the

investment actually began. Indeed, 'he (Vendôme) did not think so wise a commander as Prince Eugene would venture upon so rash an enterprise'[63] given the proximity of so many French troops to the Scheldt area – a factor that further reinforced the degree of surprise obtained. By the time the French at last fully awoke to the Allied intention it was too late to intervene, and on 12 August, while Marlborough and the main army covered the last stages of the Great Convoy's journey to Menin, the Prince of Orange descended with 31 battalions on the Lower Deule near Marquette Abbey (barely two miles from Lille) whilst General Wood closed in on the city with 34 squadrons from the direction of Potteghem. Thanks to the gallantry of Grenadier Sergeant Littler of the 16th Foot, who swam the river and single-handed let down a draw-bridge by cutting through the securing ropes with his axe, the Prince was able to complete the investment from the north-western side. Next day Prince Eugene arrived on the scene via Pont-à-Tressin to complete the investment by the evening of the 13th.

At this juncture it was often the practice to beat a parley and invite the Governor to surrender with no more ado, but except in cases where treachery or defeatism had prepared the way, neither side regarded this too seriously. At times considerable badinage would be exchanged during lulls in the early parts of the siege. Captain George Carleton, present at the siege of Maastricht in 1676, recorded some witty exchanges with the Spanish Governor, Count Calvo.

> That Governor, by a messenger, intimating his sorrow to find we had pawned our cannon for ammunition bread (the guns were late arriving), answer was made that in a few days we hoped to give him a taste of the loaves which he should find would be sent him into the town in extraordinary plenty ... I remembered another piece of raillery which passed some days after between the Rhinegrave and the same Calvo. The former sending him word that he hoped within three weeks to salute the Governor's mistress within the place, Calvo replied that he would give him leave to kiss her all over if he kissed her anywhere in three months.[64]

Such pleasantries were not always exchanged in such comradely and chivalrous taste. The Turks, for instance, had a habit of firing severed heads of captives into their objectives to lower morale.

With the establishment of cavalry posts on all roads leading into the town, the state of investment was complete. The garrison and townsfolk could still make contact with the outside world cross-country, and it was not unknown for reinforcements to force their way through into the fortress at this stage. The Allies invested Namur on 1 July 1695, but two days later William III reported to the Prince de Vaudemont that 'M. de Boufflers entered yesterday evening with two regiments of dragoons, whose horses he had since sent away which is most annoying for the presence of M. Boufflers there will change the aspect of affairs.'[65] No such incident occurred at Lille; Marshal Boufflers was present in the city from 28 July, and its garrison of 20 battalions, 7 squadrons of dragoons and 200 spare horses[66] was complete from the 10 August when reinforcements from Berwick's army were incorporated. On this occasion Boufflers was seconded by two lieutenant-generals, namely de Surville and de Lée, aided by the

Engineer-in-Chief, M. de Puy-Vauban, nephew of the recently-deceased Marshal.

At any siege where there was the least chance of enemy intervention from outside, the besieging forces would divide into two parts. One wing would take charge of the siege works whilst the other took post some distance from the town as a covering force, ready to head off and intercept any attempt at a relief. Thus at Namur in 1692, Luxembourg's army covered the siege conducted by Louis xiv and Vauban; three years later, William iii and Coehoorn supervised the trenches whilst the Prince de Vaudemont kept watch and ward; in 1708, Prince Eugene undertook the siege of Lille with 50 battalions* whilst Marlborough performed the covering role with 137 squadrons and 83 battalions from the vicinity of Helchin.

The first task of the troops near the invested town was the construction of lines to complete the isolation of the target. Whilst the cavalry busied themselves making six-foot fascines of branches and some of the sappers constructed hollow gabbions, eight feet tall, the infantry and workmen would set themselves building lines of contravallation – positions facing towards the town beyond cannon-range, usually consisting of a ditch and a parapet, which were occasionally strengthened by projecting redans or redoubts – along sites carefully surveyed by the engineers. Once these were complete, it was theoretically impossible for the beleaguered to make contact with the outside world or to send out or receive news, though stalwart messengers were on occasion known to make their way through, the lines and sentries notwithstanding. The line of contravallation would be supplemented, if there was a possibility of a hostile field force appearing on the scene, by a line of circumvallation, facing *outwards*. In the intervening area of ground the camps, train-areas and magazines would be carefully sited, together with headquarters, whilst the pontoon men busied themselves building crossings over any intervening rivers and streams running through the attackers' lines so as to link up all sectors. Although Vauban allowed nine days for the completion of these works, at Namur in 1692 he only needed three owing to special circumstances; in 1695, Coehoorn took 10 days to achieve as much, and at Lille the lines were completed by 21 August (or in seven days) despite a minor French sortie by 1,000 men which only inflicted minimal damage.

Meanwhile the commander-in-chief and the Directors of the Trenches would have been conducting careful reconnaissances of the defences seeking out the best sector to attack. Vauban advised that these activities should be completed by the seventh day, but was full of warnings about generals or senior engineers going too close for fear of capture – a fate he himself narrowly avoided on a number of occasions. However, ruses could be employed to get a close look at the enemy's defences. Very often a governor would seek the permission of his opponent for the evacuation of non-combatants. In 1692, for example, Louis xiv

*Eugene was well provided with high-ranking officers: there were seven full Generals, nine Lt.-Generals, 12 Major-Generals and 13 Brigadier-Generals. The chief engineers were Des Roques and Du Mey. Five British battalions were included in the 50 – namely the 16th, 18th, 21st, 23rd and 24th Foot.

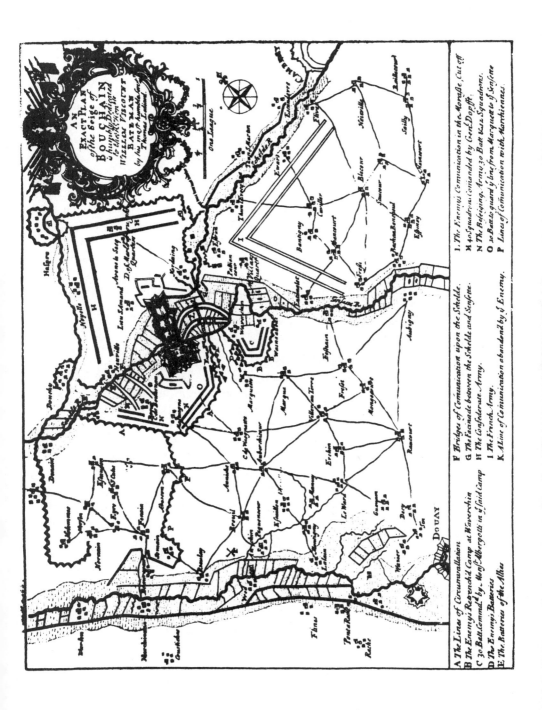

allowed the Comte de Barbançon to send out a large party of women and children from Namur, but Vauban immediately profited from this humane gesture to obtain a close look at the enemy defences, disguising himself as a common soldier in the escort sent down under flag of truce to receive and escort the party.

Such permission was not always forthcoming, however. Prince Eugene refused to receive a delegation of citizenry from Lille, despite the 'compliments and refreshments' they wished to offer him, for he believed that 'a besieged town ought to be kept very close' and had no wish to strengthen Marshal Bouffler's capacity for resistance by easing his ration problem. From time to time horrible incidents occurred when a Governor and his adversary remained equally obdurate over the issue. Robert Parker recorded, of the siege of Ballymore in Ireland (1690) that

> ... here the miserable effects of war appeared in a very melancholy manner; for the enemy, to prevent a famine among themselves, had drove all useless mouths from among them the last winter, to our side of the Shannon; and we, for the same reason, would not suffer them to come within our frontiers, so between both they lay in a miserable starving condition. These wretched came flocking in great numbers about our camp, devouring all the filth they could meet with. Our dead horses crawling with vermin, as the sun had parched them, were delicious food to them; while their infants sucked their carcasses with as much eagerness as if they were at their mothers' breasts. [67]

Such scenes are worthy of Goya's 'Horrors of War', and contrast most markedly with the chivalrous badinage exchanged at Maastricht already mentioned. Marshal Villars, too, had an unsavoury reputation in regard to enemy civilians. In September 1713, after receiving the surrender of the city of Freiburg, he flatly refused to allow the non-combatants or wounded to be evacuated, and threatened to destroy the town and massacre the wounded, both civil and military, if the citadel continued to hold out. Clearly, even in the supposedly 'humane' eighteenth century there were commanders prepared to demonstrate General Sherman's later dictum, 'war is hell'.

When the reconnaissances were complete, a detailed map would be drawn up showing both the defences and the proposed lines of attack. At Lille, for example, it was decided to attack the city from the northward, the gates of St Mark and St Magdalen with their protective horn- and crown-works being selected as the main targets. At the same time, a full duty roster would be drawn up listing every general's and every formation's roles and responsibilities. The exact location of camps and trains would be indicated (St Rémy gives very full instructions concerning the siting of the siege trains and the exact duties of their personnel[68]) and careful security measures to guard against surprise sorties would be implemented, ranging from cavalry patrols and 'grand guards' in no-man's-land to the maintenance of a sizeable 'trench guard' ready to reinforce any threatened sector; in 1708, Eugene kept 10 battalions in the trenches before Lille day and night for this purpose.

Once the encircling lines were completed, it often proved possible to send off sizeable detachments to join the covering army. Thus on 20 August 1708 Marlborough wrote: 'we are at liberty to draw off a considerable strength from the siege to reinforce the army.'[69] As will be described a little later, further large reinforcements would similarly be sent from the siege lines when danger threatened the covering force.

Siege guns and mortars

By this juncture the heavy guns would have made their appearance in the lines; thus the Allied 'Great Convoy' reached Eugene on 17 August, and 10 days later no less than 88 heavy pieces were in action. However on this occasion they proved to be sited too far back to have the desired effect, and the confident predictions of the engineers that 10 days' bombardment would suffice to bring Boufflers to terms proved over-optimistic – the first of many miscalculations and disappointments that would earn an unusual degree of ireful comment from Marlborough. The main purposes of these first batteries were to dismount the enemy cannon, harass the defenders and make it hard for them to man their outworks, rather than to create a breach. Consequently much use was made of mortars at this stage of a siege.

This is a convenient place to insert a description of siege-guns in general and mortars in particular. The former came in a large variety of calibres, ranging from huge 42- or 36-pdrs to 24- and 18-pdrs, the majority of pieces being of the latter two types. Occasionally even larger guns were used, especially in Turkish armies. Jacob Richards recalls inspecting some tremendous pieces captured in 1697 after the siege of Megara near the Isthsmus of Corinth:

> We visited some Turkish cannon which was designed to be embarked but fownd them of such an unmeasurable greatness that we were forced to give over that designe for want of machines to move them. They carry about 400 £ [*sic* i.e. pound weight] ball and are computed to weigh about 18, or 20,000 pounds.[70]

Siege guns were principally intended to destroy fortifications and enemy batteries and to create breaches. Their powder charges tended to be greater than normal (except for ricochet fire) and in order to absorb the greater force of the explosion their gun carriages had therefore to be more massive than those for their field equivalents. Thus a British 24-pdr, mounted on a siege carriage, had cheeks (or sides) 13 feet long by 5 feet 8in thick, and was provided with wheels of 58 inches diameter, whereas a field gun of the same calibre employed a carriage whose equivalent dimensions were nine feet, $4\frac{1}{2}$in and 50in respectively.[71] These greater proportions inevitably increased the weight ratio, and made movement dependent on large teams of horses. On other counts, however, the main characteristics of siege artillery were very similar to those of the field cannon described in the previous section.

Siege artillery was usually placed in five, eight or 10 gun batteries, the construction of which will be touched on later. They employed either direct or ricochet fire. The latter was one of Vauban's specialities which became widely copied. The object of this type of fire was either to brush the top of the enemy's parapet with the shot which would then bounce into the interior to cause maximum mayhem, or to ricochet off the rear wall of enemy outworks so as to damage the main defences beyond. Smaller charges than usual were required which reduced both recoil and wear and tear on the cannon, and once a gun was correctly aligned and the powder-quality checked, it was feasible to fire-day and night provided great care was taken in measuring out the correct powder-charge. 'One soon gets accustomed to richochet fire,' counselled the master, 'and it is the best and most excellent method of usefully employing cannon in a siege.'[72] Guns were normally fired one at a time rather than in salvoes in order to maintain a ceaseless and harrowing rate of fire.

Of course such a sustained bombardment called for vast quantities of ammunition. St Rémy estimated that each 24-pdr could fire between 90 and 100 shots a day, whilst 16- and 13-pdrs could get off as many as 200 rounds each in nine hours of daylight. Small wonder, therefore, that major sieges often became battles of munitions in which the critical factor was the ability or otherwise of the besieger to restock his magazines from his rear arsenals. This was certainly the cause of the crisis at Lille between September and October 1708.

Mortars, too, came in a profusion of sizes and types. The French army habitually employed eight varieties for siege-work, but St Rémy lists four main types as being in widespread service in the 1690s.

Caliber	Diameter of Shell (note windage)	Explosive charge
18 in	$17\frac{5}{6}$ in	48 lbs
$12\frac{1}{2}$ in	$11\frac{2}{3}$ in	15 lbs
$8\frac{1}{3}$ in	8 in	4 lbs
$6\frac{1}{4}$ in	6 in	$3\frac{1}{2}$ lbs[73]

The bore length of many French mortars was one and a half times the calibre; British versions tended to be larger, two or three times the calibre. This made British mortars considerably heavier than the French: thus a 13in mortar weighed just over two tons in London and only about half as much in Paris. As the eighteenth century passed its half-way mark improvements of design and casting would reduce the bulk of these pieces. Müller in particular achieving considerable advances. By 1748, British armies were equipped with 4.6in, 5.8in, 8in, 10in, and 13in land mortars, whilst special versions of the last two calibres were adapted for use in bomb vessels at sea. An Austrian mortar, cast in 1714, had a 17cm calibre, a 26cm barrel length, and weighed 156 kilograms (without bed).

Mortars shared a number of common characteristics. Most were embellished with a pair of dolphins to assist mounting, and like the Spanish *mortero de plancha*, were mounted on a bed (or sturdy timber base); as they were not wheeled, they had to be transported in special waggons. In action, mortars were habitually mounted on wooden platforms, often nine feet by six feet for a 12in mortar. Many had a fixed elevation of 45 degrees, adjustments of range being achieved by varying the propellant charge. Blondel's table, for instance, claimed that a $12\frac{1}{2}$in mortar, charged with a standard 2lbs of fine powder, and fired at an angle of 45 degrees, would carry 720 yards. A $2\frac{1}{2}$lbs charge could send a shell

940 yards, and one of 3lbs (the maximum), could attain a range of 1,035 yards. [74]

Other mortars had trunnions at the base of the barrel and consequently could be adjusted by means of wedges for elevation. Elaborate mortar tables were worked out, the basic calculation for a 12in mortar using a 2lb charge being that one degree more or less of elevation would cause a rise or drop of 60 feet in range – to a maximum elevation of 48 degrees. An 8½in mortar on the other hand (using a 1lb charge) would vary in range by 82 feet per degree. Special instruments were developed to aid the calculation of correct angles for given ranges and powder charges.

A third type of mortar-weapon was the *pierrier*, an anti-personnel weapon of more limited range which fired stone missiles. These were collected into baskets (measuring in some cases 15in in diameter by 20in long) and were capable of achieving a scatter effect; some versions had a ring of smaller cup-dischargers gathered around the main barrel, and were thus capable of firing a pattern of missiles. In later years this variety was adapted to fire off hand-grenades, as a sort of multiple coehoorn. *Pierriers* required crews of three men. A mortar needed a team of five bombardiers. The first man (on the right of the piece) charged the chamber and rammed the powder down (with three blows) before adding two wads (rammed home with nine blows). The second (from the left) handed up the wads and cleared the touch-hole. The third and fourth bombardiers brought up the ready-charged bomb from the magazine, and the whole team then lent a hand in manhandling it into the bore, making sure it rested squarely atop the wads. Thereupon 'Number One' tamped earth or dung around the shell to block up the windage and ensure the shell remained correctly placed. The mortar was next levered forward to the firing position (marked in chalk on the platform), and the *officier pointeur* or battery commander advanced to aim the mortar whilst the first bombardier primed the touch-hole. Meanwhile the 'Number Five' would have been guarding the smouldering linstock at a safe distance, waiting to hand it to the senior bombardier whose duty it was to fire the mortar.

As with howitzers, it was for long the practice to light the fuse of the shell before lighting the charge beneath it, but a method was eventually worked out for simultaneous firing, and in due course it became possible to use the flash of the exploding charge to ignite the bomb-fuse.

Once it had fired, the crew manhandled the mortar back ready for reloading, whilst the fifth detail thoroughly swabbed the barrel out with the wet rammer. The charging powder was generally kept some 20 paces to the rear of the platform in a small magazine, the loaded bombs being laid out in a specially protected bay a further five paces away. Although basically an anti-personnel weapon, mortars could bring off notable coups upon occasion. A famous 7in mortar is kept at the Heeresgeschichtliche Museum in Vienna, which bears the following inscription: '14 August 1717: I was placed before the fortress of Belgrade to the great terror of the enemy. My little bomb awakened many to their death; it struck a magazine and left nothing except a pitiful sight – death, horror and the most dreadful ruin.' [75]

The opening of the trenches

It is now necessary to revert to the progress of a siege. Once the lines were finished, and the first batteries about ready to open fire, an important moment arrived – the 'opening of the trenches'. This was the beginning of the formal attack against the sector of defences settled upon after the reconnaissances already described. When man-power, material and other conditions allowed, it was sometimes the practice to open trenches at several places simultaneously to confuse the defence. Vauban made a major contribution to siegecraft in respect of this stage of the operation. Formerly the approach trenches had been dug towards the objective more or less directly, with occasional zig-zags to avoid the penalties of enfilade fire. By the Vauban method, the attackers began by digging a large trench *parallel* to the defences at a distance of some 600 yards (maximum cannon range). The ground-plan for this first *place d'armes* was pegged-out in advance by responsible engineers, and work was started overnight by carefully organized parties. Ahead of them would move a guard of grenadiers and cavalry, carrying fascines. Then parties of 50 workmen, supervised by captains, would advance to dig at their allotted sectors, the aim being to get below ground level before daybreak. Two or three days would be spent perfecting the trench, which would be made both wide and deep and furnished with a fire-step and terminal redoubts if these were deemed necessary.

Meanwhile, further parties of workmen, supervised by engineers, would be busy digging a number of narrow approach trenches forward from the First Parallel towards the town; these would usually be undertaken at two or three places or even six at once, further confusing the foe as to which 'attack' to take seriously. At a distance of about 400 yards from the enemy defences the sappers and workmen, protected as before, would construct the Second Parallel along much the same lines as the first, which would now be occupied by the battalions of the main trench guard and be used as a supply point for tools, fascines, gabbions, and other material. This second *place d'armes* was to be started on the third day and completed by the fifth.

Forward of the Second Parallel, which by day would inevitably be exposed to the attentions of enemy cannon, it was necessary to proceed methodically by means of saps, dug by four-men teams, regularly relieved, according to a strict work-pattern. Protecting themselves with mobile screens (or, more often, embedded gabbions filled with earth and interlaced with fascines), the sap-parties would creep forward over No-Man's-Land. The first man dug an area 1 foot 6in square, leaving a 12in step at the foot of the gabbion. The second sapper then took over, and enlarged the area by six inches each way, followed by the third and fourth men in turn until a three foot cubic area had been excavated. Whereupon, a second team would take over, and the first fall back to rest for an hour. As the sap-party made progress, further groups of workmen would set to behind them to develop the approach trench to a width of some 10 feet and a depth of three (the line of earth-filled gabbions and supporting slopes and sandbags projecting some three more feet out of the ground), also constructing *démi-places* or re-entrants at the angles in the trenches where garrisons could be stationed.

Everything depended on good organization, close supervision, and willing toil on the part of the workmen. To ensure the first, two teams of engineers would work by rota, responsible to the Directors of Trenches, whilst large parties of troops or conscripted peasantry served as carrying parties or made fascines in rear. To secure full co-operation from the sappers and workmen, Vauban indicated a system of cash rewards for progress and degree of danger, ranging from 2 *livres* 10 *sous* for each fathom of the Third Parallel completed, to 10 *livres* per *toise* of work successfully carried through in the enemy's water-filled main ditch. By providing incentives of this kind, Vauban was confident that 480 feet of trenches could be completed in a 24 hour period. He sounded one note of warning to engineers:

> ... Sappers often intoxicate themselves at the sap-head, and are then slaughtered like beasts as they take no care what they do; this must be prevented by allowing them only well-watered wine.[76]

Similar (though smaller) cash incentives were paid to encourage the fascine-makers. The process of sapping forward would be carried on with extreme caution towards the proposed site of the Third (usually the final) Parallel, situated on the glacis itself. This position would be constructed with the greatest care, being very exposed to enemy fire; by this stage, however, it was to be hoped that the siege batteries would have silenced the greater number of the hostile cannon.

Vauban was much opposed to kings, statesmen or other notables visiting the works. Everyone forward of the First Parallel, he considered, was potentially very dangerous as enemy shot and shell could not be relied upon to distinguish between common peasants and men of quality. Any senior officer whose duty took him further forward was to avoid being attended by an entourage which might attract the attention of the enemy. Such strictures were well-advised. Both King Charles XII of Sweden and Marshal D'Artagnan were killed in the process of supervising sieges (at Altranstadt, 1722 and Maastricht, 1673, respectively), whilst Eugene was incapacitatingly wounded in the head before Lille on 21 September 1708 (leading a storming-party it is true) – an eventuality which placed a double-burden on Marlborough's shoulders for the succeeding five weeks. Civilians visiting the front were equally vulnerable. William Blathwayt, William III's Secretary-at-War, had a Deputy-Governor of the Bank of England, Michael Godfrey, killed at his side during a sight-seeing tour of the siege of Namur in 1695.[77] Such perils were aggravated still further by the likelihood of contracting disease in the insanitary and stinking entrenchments. Well might Vauban conclude, 'there is no safe place in a trench.'

Counter-measures: sorties, mining and external relief attempts
Up to the present it may have seemed that a siege unrolled with remorseless precision whilst the governor and garrison of the place under attack helplessly watched their fate creeping towards them. If the governor was a man of spirit, however, nothing was likely to be further from the truth, for the prosecution of an 'active' defence could cause a besieger, however strong numerically, much

anxiety and no inconsiderable delays. Vauban describes a number of counter-activities open to the defence – together with the necessary security measures to thwart them. First amongst them came sorties, sub-divided into 'external' and 'internal'.

The first category was designed to cause damage to a besieger's works and ideally to lure his troops within range of the fortress cannon as they followed up the retiring sortie parties. These sallies were often timed for dark, moonless nights when the chances of surprise were greater. After over-running the drowsy sentries and picquets, one part of the garrison would push ahead down the trenches to meet and delay for as long as possible the forces of retribution which would inevitably appear on the scene as the alarm was given, whilst the rest laid aside their weapons and set to with spades, picks, torches and powder charges to inflict as much damage as possible on the overrun trenches, filling them in wherever possible. When the pace became too hot, the sortie would retire back whence they had come, carrying as much portable equipment from the trenches as the circumstances permitted. Lastly, if the enraged besiegers followed them up too far, the great guns would speak and sweep a swathe of destruction through the troops on the glacis, the scene being illuminated by blazing barrels of pitch.

Operations of this type were often employed during the earlier stages of a siege before the attacker had really completed his security arrangements. Thus on 21 August 1708, Boufflers led a sortie by 800 infantry and six squadrons of dragoons, but only caused superficial damage – 200 trees cut down and a couple of houses burnt – to Eugene's siege lines. Mustapha Pasha was notably more successful in this respect against the same opponent at Belgrade nine years later; the repeated Turkish sorties seriously impeded the development of the siege and afforded ample time for the huge relief army to make its appearance; in one such encounter, on 17 July, the Turks surprised General de Marcilly in an isolated position near Sembin on the left bank of the River Save, and butchered him and several hundred Imperialists. Another notable sortie took place on 27 November 1781, when part of the garrison of Gibraltar attacked *Las Lineas* and caused great havoc and dislocation to their Spanish beleaguerers.

Alternatively, a major sortie might be timed to coincide with the appearance of a relieving force, when the attention of the besieger could be expected to be very distracted. Such was the case on 5 September 1708, when the energetic Boufflers sallied forth on a wide front to make the most of the absence from the lines of Prince Eugene and 72 squadrons and 26 battalions, summoned away from the siege to aid the outnumbered Marlborough repulse the anticipated (though ultimately abortive) challenge by Marshals Berwick, Vendôme and the Duke of Burgundy near Ennetières.

The second type of sorties – 'internal' – were smaller, more localized operations designed to regain part of the covered way, reoccupy a breach, destroy enemy mine galleries, or challenge the besieger's attempts to pass the ditch. Such desperate fights would see much use of grenades, small mines and carcasses (barrels filled with combustibles), besides other 'infernal engines of warre'. Obviously affairs of this kind would most probably occur towards the conclusion of a siege as the defender desperately made bids to stave off surrender for a little longer. They frequently proved very costly to both sides.

Naturally, a besieger who knew his business could take steps to reduce or nullify the effects of these sorties by the garrison. Comprehensive security precautions – cavalry picquets, outpost lines, strong main guards – could do much to reduce the chance of surprise; furthermore, if the main *places d'armes* and the intervening *démi-places* were well constructed and supplied with adequate garrisons 24 hours a day, Vauban concluded there was no good reason why a sortie should penetrate further than the Second Parallel. Vauban advocated, indeed, the deliberate abandonment of incomplete forward positions to give the besiegers' cannon the chance to wreak havoc upon the garrison before the infantry were unleashed from the trenches to deal with the survivors. Similarly, he strongly advised against over-energetic pursuits of discomfited sorties.

> It is not worth an affair to prevent the foe overturning a dozen or so gabbions or setting fire to unfinished works, for if your fire is well directed he will pay dearly for his gains.[78]

On occasion, however, a very bold party might enter part of the enemy defences hot on the heels of the defenders, but sally-ports and draw-bridges were carefully provided with supporting defences to make this extremely hazardous.

Second in the defender's repertoire came the construction of counter-approaches. As the besiegers' trenches crept closer over no-man's-land, so the garrison's engineers and sappers would dig outwards from neighbouring sectors of the covered way and attempt to drive a trench across the exposed flanks of the enemy parallels, to rake them with enfilading musketry fire. The Allies encountered considerable difficulties owing to this type of operation at the siege of Namur (1695): the capture of French outworks protecting the Porte St Roche sector was particularly protracted for this reason.

In the third place, a defender would make great use of mines and counter-mines. Before abandoning an outwork, whenever possible the garrison would construct mines and lead back powder trails and fuses to within their new positions ready to inflict grievous losses on the advancing attacker. Similarly, the garrison would sometimes drive subterranean galleries under the glacis and dig out chambers beneath the besieger's positions in the hope of causing heavy damage to his major installations – especially powder-magazines and battery positions – the destruction of which could considerably put back the progress of a siege and even render its continuation pointless.

For mining the basic calculation was that 'two ounces of powder will raise two cubic feet of earth';[79] $12\frac{1}{2}$lbs would lift 200 cubic feet (each cubic foot of packed earth weighing 124lbs). According to St Rémy, an 'average chamber' was designed to hold between 400 and 500lbs; the larger variety held 1,000lbs.

Of course what was good for the goose was equally good for the gander, and mines often played a prominent place in the besieger's operations; it was particularly used for breaching a fortification. Certain sieges, indeed, were dominated by these fearsome methods; Tournai (1709), for instance, was notorious for both mining and counter-mining. Recorded Thomas Lediard, quoting *The Tatler,*

> The manner of fighting in this siege discovered a gallantry in our men, unknown to former ages; their meeting with adverse parties under ground, where every step was taken with apprehensions of being blown up with mines below them, or crushed by the fall of earth above them, and all this acted in darkness, has something in it more terrible than was ever met with in any other part of a soldier's duty. However this was performed with great chearfulness. [80]

It seems that several dozen mines and counter-mines were sprung during this 10 week siege; one destroyed almost a complete Hanoverian battalion; another entombed 300 men alive. Mrs Christian Davies (*alias* Mother Ross) recalled the gruesome atmosphere prevailing at this time:

> Wherever my husband was ordered I always followed him, and he was sometimes of the party that went to search for and draw (neutralize) the enemy's mines; I was often engaged with their party underground, where our engagements were more terrible than in the field, being sometimes near-suffocated with the smoke of straw which the French fired to drive us out; and the fighting with pickaxes and spades, in my opinion, was more dangerous than with swords. [81]

The Turks also used mine warfare extensively; at Belgrade (1717), when the huge Turkish relief army had completely invested Eugene's besieging army in its turn, the Turks proceeded energetically to mine the Imperial positions at many points – a circumstance that partly persuaded the Prince to risk a major battle in order to win or lose all – a gamble that in the event paid off handsomely.

Perhaps the most dramatic siege dominated by mining was that of Alicante on the eastern seaboard of Spain (1708–9). Situated upon a huge rock, the citadel to which Major-General John Richards withdrew his garrison after surrendering the town (2 December) was not vulnerable to routine siege methods. So the French commander, Comte d'Asefeld, spent three months driving a gallery deep into the rock in order to place a huge charge of powder beneath the internal water cistern situated under the main parade of the fortress.

General Richards was well aware of this development and the peril it represented to his slender garrison, but he was determined to hold out until relief arrived, and dared d'Asefeld to do his worst. Not strong enough to make a sortie, Richards tried to smoke out the enemy miners and also to flood the galleries, but without success. In a letter smuggled out to General Stanhope, dated 25 February 1709, he described his situation most graphically:

> The confidence which you have in the natural strength of this Rock is undoubtedly the reason why we have not bin succour'd all this whyle, but the enemy having actually Mined the noblest part of this Castle where we had allmost all our provisions of War and mouth, and especially our water, there is now an absolute necessity of speed relieve for wee juge the enemy to be now

verry neare if not under our Greate Cysterne where they are actually making there chamber which they pretend to charge with 1,200 barrels of powder. The consequence of which noe mortal can judge it being the first attempt of this kind that ever was heard of for I believe that we are above their mine 200 feet. But be it what it will you may be assur'd that we shall stand it, tho' there may be some who are not alltogether of this minde. And indeed it is very uncomfortable to heare our Enemy night and day working under ffeet . . . [82]

Day by day the tension grew, but his resolution did not waver. It was not an act of unthinking bravery on Richard's part, but a carefully calculated risk. He believed that internal fissures within the rock would divert much of the force of the explosion when it came, and that accordingly the castle and garrison might survive unscathed. So at least he wrote in another letter dated 25 Feburary, written to his brother Michael Richards, serving as commander of the main Allied trains in Spain. This missive touchingly ends on a personal note: 'Good night, Micky. Pray God send us a merry meeting.'

Another surviving document is a reasoned assessment of the dangers faced in which the *pros* and *cons* of continuing resistance are carefully balanced.

For the Surrender. 1. That we have a terrible mine under us, the effect of which cannot be certainly known but it is possible that it may blow into pieces the upper part of the Rock, att least it will open it and destroy our water and it may be the Hospital . . .
Answers. 1. That we have a terrible mine beneath us is certain, but the effects of it are nott. It is therefore unjustifiable in the highest degree for men of our profession to do a certain Evil out of fear of an uncertain one, for all that we shall probably lose by the mine is our great cysterne . . . [83]

So, despite the understandable anxieties of many of his men, the Governor soldiered doggedly on. On his orders a shaft was sunk through the parade ground in the hope of dissipating part of the coming blast. By late February d'Asefeld had massed 1,200 barrels of powder, each holding a hundredweight, in his mine chamber. In a humane gesture (and possibly in the hope of saving all of 60 tons of gunpowder), d'Asefeld had invited two Allied officers from the garrison to inspect the mine on 20 February, but nothing could shake Richard's resolution. Two further offers of terms were rejected on 1 and 2 March.

The anticipated climax came on the morning of Monday 3 March. As the apprehensive townsfolk vacated the town below, General Richards, in order to set an example for his men – deliberately placed himself on the parade immediately above the smoking mine. Behind him there drew up all senior officers off-duty. Prior to this demonstration of sublime courage, Richards had reduced the guards to the minimum compatible with security, and sent all the rest of his men into the castle.

Shortly after six am a tremendous explosion convulsed the region. When the dust cleared it was seen that several huge fissures had sundered the parade. Of Richards and his party no sign remained: they had been swallowed into the earth. In all 12 officers and 42 soldiers had shared his fate. But Richard's faith in the strength of his position was justified – if only posthumously – for the castle, defences and hospital of Alicante had successfully withstood the shock and stood unscathed. Moreover the survivors, led by a Lieutenant-Colonel d'Albon, conducted as resolute a defence as ever. But in the end a disgruntled d'Asefeld gained possession of the castle when, on 15 April, the long-overdue sails of Admiral Byng's fleet, from Minorca, appeared over the eastern horizon; the Admiral decided not to attack but to negotiate for the free evacuation of the garrison in exchange for the castle. D'Asefeld agreed. The Allies could ill afford to lose such officers as John Richards. [84]

Enough has been written on mining and garrison activities; but a few paragraphs must be devoted to the types of operations a relieving army might mount in attempts to compel the besieger to abandon his enterprise. The great siege of Lille includes examples of almost every available move and counter-move.

The over-riding aim of the relieving field armies was to compel the besieger to abandon his operations. In the first place this might be achieved by marching up with a superior army and forcing a direct confrontation. Burgundy and Berwick collected some 110,000 troops in late August 1708 and advanced from their rendezvous at Grammont to attempt a circuitous march on Lille. As the French moved round the eastern and southern approaches to the siege lines, Marlborough took care to keep his 50,000 men between the foe and their objective, moving on a shorter arc, until he came to the Ennetières–Seclin sector where he halted and began to prepare a strong position, summoning Eugene and part of the besieging force as already related to bring his strength to about 75,000 men (209 squadrons and 109 battalions) for a limited period while the crisis was at its height. However, despite their continuing superiority of force, the French commanders based on Mons-en-Pévêlle were sufficiently in awe of Marlborough's hard-earned reputation to hesitate to attack him, and despite direct orders from Versailles to engage, and Bouffler's sortie on 5 September, they ultimately gave up the project after facing up to the increasingly strong Allied position from 4 to 14 September. Even Louis xiv's messenger, the Minister of War Chamlay, came to endorse the views of the doubters, and so, after a heavy bombardment on the 10/11 September, the French began to march away. Eugene, incidentally, had taken his men back to the siege as early as the 7th after the 'Twin-Generals' had accurately devined the lack of determination in the enemy camp; for his part, on the 14th, Marlborough unwillingly forebore to attack the retiring French. So ended the first French attempt to force a relief by direct means. A renewed effort on 6 October from the North also failed when Vendôme again had second thoughts and fell back to Roulers.

Similar direct confrontations occurred during many other important sieges. Suffice it here to mention Villars' abortive attempts to drive Marlborough from before Bouchain in 1711, and the Turkish army's massive advance to trap Eugene before Belgrade six years later. Both interventions failed with varying degrees of disaster for the would-be relievers. Indeed, with certain notable exceptions such as Vienna (1683), the naval breaking of the boom outside Londonderry (1689), or the relief of Barcelona (1706), such attempts seem to have achieved their purpose comparatively rarely. William III, for instance, proved completely incapable of saving Namur in June 1692 thanks to Luxembourg's shadowing and Eugene did little positive to save Landau or Freiburg in 1713.

If direct confrontations were not possible, a foe might resort to logistical interdiction – a war of supply. Such operations were aimed to intercept and destroy the besieger's support convoys of munitions and rations without which his position would become untenable. Thus in September and October 1708, the French armies drew off from Mons-en-Pévêlle to sieze the Scheldt crossings, and thus interrupt the Allied line of communications running back to Brussels. With his usual strategic flexibility, however, Marlborough was equal to the new challenge. Switching his communications to the port of Ostend, he conveyed his stores by barge from the Brussels area to Antwerp, and thence by ship along the Scheldt to the Channel and Ostend where General Erle had established a strong position, having convoys waiting to carry the stores to Lille via Menin.

The local French forces did all in their power to cut the new supply route. First General La Motte collected 22,000 men and set out from Bruges to intercept General Webb's crucial convoy of munitions. The outcome was the action of Wynendael (28 September), where Webb with only 7,000 men inflicted a sharp defeat on his opponent. As a result 250,000lbs of powder and two weeks' supply of shot and shell reached the Lille lines, and the siege, which was badly behind schedule at this stage, could be continued with greater efficacy.

One example of a successful – if minor – raid on a besieger's convoys took place in 1692, when the Allied garrison of Charleroi sallied forth to trap and destroy a French grain convoy in the Pass of Slenrieu. Twenty waggons of flour were burnt (Louis XIV's huge army needed 30,000 bushels of wheat and oats a day) but this minor success did not in fact seriously impede the French siege of Namur.

Conversely, a relief force might resort to extreme measures to force a way through a besieger's lines in order to deliver urgently-needed material to the garrison or reinforce it. Once again Lille furnishes a famous example. On 28 September, the Chevalier de Luxembourg boldly tried to bluff his way through the Allied lines at the head of 2,000 horsemen each of whom was carrying a sack containing 112lbs of gun powder across its crupper. He was almost through before the alarm was given. Whereupon perhaps 1,000 horsemen (some sources say only 600) galloped for Lille and safely reached their destination, 'but not one half of them carried in their powder with them,'[85] noted Parker. As for the remainder, Mérode-Westerloo paints a graphic if grisly picture of their fate:

Our men siezed their arms and opened fire; this made several sparks to set fire to some of the enemy's powder-bags; in an instant several hundred of them were hurled into the air amidst a terryfying explosion which shook the earth ... (The rest) turned about and made for Douai. As their powder-bags were made of linen and not leather, several sprang leaks, leaving a trail of powder along the road behind them. As they rode their horse-shoes made the sparks fly up which set fire to the powder-trail and this in turn ignited the sacks, blowing up a number of men and horses with an infernal din. It was a horrible spectacle to see the remains of men and horses, whose legs, arms and torsoes even had been flung into the trees. [86]

More successful reinforcement attempts were carried out at Casale (1697) and Turin (1706).

If direct intervention could not guarantee the interdiction of a besieger's supplies, recourse might be made to flooding when circumstances were favourable. Thus the French opened the sluices at Furnes and let in the sea in the autumn of 1708 in an attempt to place an impassable innundation across the roads leading south from Ostend. They even brought up galleys from Dunkirk to dominate the obstacle thus created, and the Allied garrison of the little town of Leffinghe, situated on a small rise above the floods, had to fight a series of stiff fights with enemy shipping and gun-boats before it finally succumbed to a surprise assault on the night of 24 October, launched whilst the garrison was joyously but immoderately carousing to celebrate the news of the surrender of the city of Lille that same day. However, Marlborough called up the Royal Navy to drive off the galleys, whilst special carts with high-wheels were constructed to keep a minimum of stores moving over the less deeply flooded roads. As a result, 1,700 barrels of powder were brought over and sent on to Lille during the first fortnight in October.

If both direct confrontation and interdiction failed to raise the siege, the relieving commander had one more card to play: namely the creation of a major diversion by means of a sudden descent on some important and distant enemy town or fortress, which, it might be hoped, would induce the besieger to draw off a large part of his army to deal with the new threat. On two occasions the French used sudden descents against Brussels, capital of the Spanish Netherlands, in order to disrupt crucial sieges elsewhere – namely in an attempt to save Namur in August 1695, and in the hope of saving the citadel of Lille in November 1708. Both attempts proved abortive, although terrible damage was wrought by Marshal Villeroi and the Elector of Bavaria respectively by indiscriminate bombardment of the city on each occasion. Indeed on the first occasion the whole Grande Place was burnt down. But such operations as these were often measures of desperation, and neither cited instance seriously affected the issue at the point of crisis. True, William III moved part of his army to join Vaudemont near Waterloo, but Villeroi dared not attack the strongly-posted Allied army. Marlborough, on the other hand, simply descended on the Scheldt at five places in a synchronized assault in the early morning of 26 November, surprised all the dozing French garrisons, and thereafter created such a threat to the Elector's line of retreat that he forthwith abandoned all his guns and 800 wounded before Brussels and fled for the safety of Mons. Two weeks later Boufflers surrendered the citadel of Lille. [87]

The capture of the covered way, the making of the breach and other operations
It is now time to return from this consideration of ancillary operations

surrounding an important siege to a description of the climacteric events at the siege itself.

By the time the Third Parallel was nearing completion, the saps should have been pushed far enough forward to begin to menace the *démi-lunes*. Similarly, a number of mortar and *pierrier* batteries would have been constructed to the left and right of the main trenches, whilst the cannon batteries established near the Second Parallel (St Rémy advised five) began to batter breaches in the *démi-lunes* and curtain-walls. Vauban believed that cannon sited further back in the first days of open trenches were largely a waste of time as the range was too extreme. This view is supported by Allied experience before both Namur and Lille, where early positions had to be moved forward after futile powder-consuming bombardments did the garrison little harm. The placing of batteries was a skilled art, for besides bringing heavy breaching fire to bear on the immediate objective, other guns had to engage all neighbouring enemy positions in attempts to neutralize the defender's cross-fire.

The construction of batteries, for both cannon and mortars, is minutely described by both St Rémy and Vauban, who differ only on points of detail. An eight gun 24-pdr battery required a space frontage of 60 paces (flanks excluded); the depth of its parapet had to be about 18 feet if enemy shot was to be kept out, and the individual gun embrasures were to be two feet wide on the inner edge and nine feet on the outer. It was desirable that such a position should be completed in 12 hours, and to do this the services of 110 pioneers and workmen working in hourly shifts were required, whilst a further 45 busied themselves preparing fascines. A battery of this size needed 390 nine-foot by nine-inch fascines for the front parapet besides 160 12-foot ones for the embrasures. Large numbers of gabbions were often incorporated in the earthern walls, and 800 smaller fascines were needed for the flanks; in all 1,840 six-foot picquets would be driven into the earth.[88] Solid timber platforms would then be laid and ready-use and reserve magazines, amply provided with overhead cover, would be established to the rear. Finally, the guns would be moved in.

Mortar battery construction was much the same, except that there were no embrasures. Vauban laid it down that each mortar needed a space 10 feet by 12, the platform sloping four inches towards the rear, and stipulated an interval of 15 feet between each mortar. The mortar-bed was to rest on a platform of massive beams with loose three-inch planks laid across the top. Their use, he adds is *not* against the houses of the town, 'which contributes nothing to the capture of the place, and the damage one does thereby in the long run turns out to the besieger's loss,'[89] but against the interior of the garrison's defence works.

Supported by solid shot, bomb and shell, the sappers and workmen dug their way onto the glacis creating a number of traverses (or sap-heads), often six. The time had now come to attempt to take the covered way and counterscarp. This was either done by a *coup de main*, or by further digging. For the former, Vauban suggested the massing of between eight and 10 companies of grenadiers, supported by the guard battalions of the Third Parallel and further fusiliers as necessary. After lining the trenches three deep, on a given signal (usually the cessation of the special bombardment laid on in advance) the troops clambered out of the trenches and made with all speed for their objective, entering it from all sides. Such storming efforts were not invariably successful. When Eugene attempted to storm the counterscarp at Lille on 7 September at the head of no less than 15,000 men, he only made minor gains for a loss of 3,000 casualties. A renewed assault exactly two weeks later made a little more progress, but at a cost of 1,000 killed and wounded, the latter including Eugene himself. Yet Vauban was convinced that if the storm was properly prepared and timed the foe should have already been induced to abandon the position.[90]

By 'properly prepared' Vauban meant the construction of sap-heads to a distance of 84 feet from the covered way (maximum grenade range), whereupon the trenches forked left and right following the line of the defences. Behind these positions, *Cavaliers* would be built, four-stepped entrenchments rising out of the ground to a height that could overlook – and sweep with musketry – the enemy posts protecting the covered way and counterscarp. This should induce the foe to abandon such an exposed position; as often as not he would blow his mines as 'the signal he does retreat', whereupon the grenadiers were immediately to occupy the craters and vacated positions, taking workmen with them well supplied with gabbions to commence immediately making the posts defensible against any 'interior' sortie attempt. At the same time, parties of picked men would be searching for enemy mine galleries to nip out the fuses and render them harmless whilst the foe hastily extemporised internal defences.

Next, covered by a hurricane of fire, the big breaching guns would be moved up overnight to their final position – namely onto the very edge of the counterscarp itself. Truly massive battery positions were needed to ensure their security. Then, all being ready, these pieces would fire at point-blank range, day and night, against the angle of the *démi-lune* or bastion wall ahead. St Rémy advocated the establishment of three such batteries, two holding ten, and one eight 32- or 24-pdr cannon, and firing at the target from three sides. Vauban held that two batteries would suffice. Service at such batteries could be costly in life and limb, so as usual cash incentives were offered to reinforce the men's courage. At the siege of Valence (October 1696), each 24-pdr cost the French Crown 300 francs for placing in the counterscarp battery, and a further 30 francs a day for operation. The sums dispensed for similar services with the mortars were 100 and 16 francs respectively.[91] Three guns in each 'flanking' battery were to engage the neighbouring enemy bastions; the rest concentrated their fire on the breach.

In St Rémy's opinion, two days of steady bombardment would suffice to create a 'practicable'* breach wide enough for 30 men to advance abreast. In these 48 hours, the 22 cannon engaged in breaching fire might have let off up to 2,200 shots.

Meanwhile the sappers would be cutting a passage through the counterscarp down towards the ditch-bottom of the *démi-lune*. If the ditch was wet, vast quantities of fascines and other bridging materials would have to be heaved into

---

*A breach was deemed 'practicable' when sufficient stonework and earth had been eroded into the ditch to enable an assaulting soldier to climb up it with ease, using both hands to wield his weapons.

place, but whenever possible dams would have already been established to block or divert any flow of water.

Then, when all was ready, a storming-party led by a 'forlorn hope' of volunteers, would assault the breach and endeavour to take possession of the positions on the *démi-lune*. Foot by foot the defenders would be killed or forced out, any gains being immediately consolidated by work-parties constructing new defences, heedless of danger.

The fire of the guns would then be switched to the walls of the main bastion beyond, and once the same procedures had been completed as were required for a *démi-lune* would be followed. Then, once the town had been stormed or surrendered, the identical sequence of operations had often to be mounted against the citadel.

Stormings of breaches could be very costly in terms of human life, as is illustrated by the notorious attack on the Terra-Nova breach at Namur on 30 August 1695. Two thousand Allied grenadiers and twice as many fusiliers stormed forward in six columns to cover the 800 yards dividing them from the main breach. First they were met by two French sorties – from the castle and Fort Coehoorn* – which effectually routed or halted the two outermost columns. The other formations however swept on led by Lord Cutts, the Comte de Riviera and the Duke of Holstein-Ploen, and for fearful loss they succeeded in becoming masters of the counterscarp, the covered way and took Fort La Cachette. The total cost was at least 2,000 casualties; the results were only local gains. Some contemporaries lavished praise on this operation. Le Peletier de Souzy, for instance, described it as *'un prodige de valeur'*;[92] Vauban's more critical assessment will be recorded in the next chapter.

Members of storming parties obviously ran great risks. Robert Parker participated in at least three important stormings. In the first (Athlone, 1691), he came to regret his zeal in volunteering for special duties.

> Here I had a narrow escape of my life, a stone which had been thrown from the top of the castle as I passed under, fell on my shoulder, the effects of which I feel to this day on every change of weather. This indeed I deserved for being so foolhardy as to put myself on this command when it was not my turn; but it was a warning to me ever after. It is an old maxim that he who goes so far as he is commanded is a good man, but he who goes further is a fool.[93]

Four years later he shared in the Terra-Nova attack mentioned above, receiving a ball through his shoulder which put him 'thirty weeks under cure'.[94] Then, in 1702, he accompanied Lord Cutts, in the storming of Fort St Michael at Venloo. Lord Cutts nicknamed 'the Salamander' on account of his charmed life and many wounds – told the storming party that if they took the covered way with ease, they were to exploit the success to the uttermost. 'We all thought these were very rash orders, contrary both to the rules of war, and the design of the thing,' reminisced the Irishman.

About four in the afternoon the signal was given, and according to our orders

*Named after its builder in 1692; in 1695, Coehoorn had to retake his own fortifications.

we rushed up to the covert-way; the enemy gave us one scattering fire only, and away they ran. We jumped into the covert-way, and ran after them. They made to a ravelin, which covered the curtain of the fort, in which were a Captain and 60 men. We seeing them get into the ravelin, pursued them, got in with them, and soon put most of them to the sword. They that escaped us, fled over a small wooden bridge, that led over the moat to the fort; and here like madmen without fear or wit, we pursued them over that tottering bridge, exposed to the fire of the great and small shot of the body of the fort. However, we got over the fausse-braye, where we had nothing for it, but to take the fort or die. They that fled before us climbed up by the long grass,* that grew out of the fort, so we climbed after them. Here we were hardput to it, to pull out the palisades, which pointed down upon us from the parapet; and was it not for the great surprise and consternation of those within, we could never have surmounted this very point. But as soon as they saw us at this work, they quitted the rampart, and retired down to the parade in the body of the fort, where they laid down their arms, and cried for quarter, which was readily granted them.[95]

Besides providing a graphic description of an attack pressed home, this passage illustrates what the seizure of a fleeting opportunity could achieve, saving days of digging and other routine preparations. Even Vauban, for all his dislike of rash assaults, laid down details for what he termed 'an accelerated attack' for use when the enemy defences were feeble or the garrison very weak. In such cases, the troops, organized into successive waves as shown, would storm from the *places d'armes* and attempt a direct storming of the target, taking up to two days of alternative action and rest to complete their task.[96] In this way the Turks instantly stormed an under-garrisoned Belgrade on 8 October 1690, capitalizing on their massive superiority of force – 50,000 against 5,000.

It would in any case be erroneous to believe that every siege went through *all* the stages described in recent pages. The cases we have cited, Namur and Lille, were really full-scale affairs, involving almost every refinement of siegecraft in both attack and defence. The great majority of sieges were far less complicated. Thus in 1690, at the siege of Cork, an attacking party made use of normal drainage ditches 'and other places convenient' for shelter to prevent a sally whilst the big guns were brought up,[97] rather than digging regular positions. On other occasions (as at Alicante already cited), special circumstances of siting or terrain would determine the form of attack. And in long wars like the Spanish Succession struggle, when the combatants became war-weary as the years dragged on, many of the niceties of siege-warfare were abandoned for more direct means on both the Allied and French side. Temperamental characteristics could induce a Coehoorn or a Villars to lose patience with full-scale sieges, and attempt *coups de main*. However, in the wars of the Polish and Austrian Succession, there was a return to the full Vauban concepts as practised in the Nine Years' War and earlier struggles of the preceding century.

*See p. 240 above.

The surrender of a town and fortress

No subject better illustrates the general seventeenth and eighteenth century prejudice in favour of 'the rules of war' than the conventions that surrounded the negotiation and conclusion of capitulations of towns and fortresses. All aspects were governed by complex formalities that were rarely ignored, save in times of great war exhaustion when irritability and mutual accusations of war crimes could poison the atmosphere.

We have already had occasion to mention Louis XIV's instructions to his military governors issued in 1705 concerning the duration of a satisfactory defence, but in some respects this did not accurately reflect the feelings of the day. It was widely felt, for instance, that a garrison that held out for a minimum of 48 days had done its duty, and was entitled to negotiate thereafter with the besieger for the best obtainable terms if there were no indications of a serious relief attempt being mounted in the immediate future. Similarly, once a practicable breach had been battered through the *main* defences of a city or fortress, and once the besieger had made himself master of the covered way and its environs and was thus in a position to attempt a general storming, many governors considered themselves fully entitled to beat the *chamade* and seek a parley with no more ado.

Although general stormings were not unknown (and we must distinguish carefully between 'general' and 'local' stormings, the latter being used as we have seen to capture the covered way), they were on the whole uncommon. The main reasons why garrisons did not defend their positions to the last man were humanitarian and logical rather than purely military. The horror of military excess prevalent at this time was one good reason – due to both the difficulty of replacing severe losses of one's own army and to moral considerations engendered by the onset of the Age of Reason. There was no doubt that a general storm could prove extraordinarily expensive in human life if the defender was determined; we have already seen how costly simple 'local' assaults proved at both Namur and Lille. Consequently any besieging army forced by the irrational obduracy of a garrison to sustain the losses of a general assault considered itself entitled, if ultimately successful in the attempt, to wreak havoc against both life and property, military and civil, in revenge. No quarter would be afforded the garrison, and the townsfolk would often be subjected to murder, despoliation and rape, whilst the property was looted and burnt. However much this 'compensation' might commend itself to certain sections of the blood-thirsty rank and file, rendered furious by the loss of comrades and lusting after women and plunder, it was rarely regarded as desirable by their masters, who wished to take possession of towns and fortresses as intact as possible for both military, economic and political reasons.* A pile of smoking ruins covering the corpses of a butchered population could not be easily rendered defensible against an enemy counter-attack, offered no economic or logistical aid for the continuation of the

---

*The harsh fate meted out to Badajoz by Wellington's army in 1812 after its costly storm was an example of the influence of folk-memory within the army. Most of the garrison survived – it was the hapless 'occupied' Spanish population that suffered three days of excess.

war, and would certainly be valueless as a pawn in any peace negotiations. In the
bitter Wars of Religion of the sixteenth and seventeenth centuries such towns as
Leyden, Magdeburg and Drogheda had received abrupt and brutal treatment,
ostensibly in the name of a Catholic or Calvinist deity, but such frightful
incidents became rarer in the decades that followed the Peace of Westphalia.
There were exceptions of course: the practically continuous Habsburg-Ottoman
struggles hold instances of atrocity and counter-atrocity, and the two deliberate
French rapes of the Palatinate, and Marlborough's devastation of Bavaria in
July 1704, show that the prosecution of warfare against the civil population
could still be as cruel and brutal as formerly, but the widespread contemporary
outcry these dark deeds evoked and the bitterness of the resultant propaganda
wars show that governments and influential societies of the time regarded such
excesses as unjustifiable.

Normally, however, military moderation was the rule. A besieger, as we have
seen, often sent in a formal, even polite, invitation to surrender at the outset of
the investment, and repeated it from time to time in increasingly stricter terms as
the operation proceeded. A final summons would be despatched when the main
breach was ready and the trenches and approaches completed – and this time
was to be regarded seriously, but as often as not the defending commander would
forestall his besieger by hoisting a white flag and requesting the opening of talks
with no further delay.

Once the offer had been made – and accepted – teams of negotiators would
meet to discuss the basis for a capitulation under cover of a general cease-fire. It
was often customary for the defenders to present a list of conditions acceptable to
them, which the besieger would reject or adjust individually according to his
mood. This would depend upon such considerations as the losses he had already
sustained, how much he needed the town without further ado, and the general
reputation of the garrison as clean fighters or otherwise. Often a besieger could
afford to be generous. The garrison might be permitted to evacuate their
positions with all the honours of war, marching out with drums beating, colours
flying, matches burning, bayonets fixed, and accompanied by their personal
baggage and a couple of symbolic cannon, and thereafter be escorted to an
agreed point or fortress after which they would be free to resume hostilities.
Sometimes a period of parole was insisted upon, at least for the officers. In the
case of a large town such as Lille, the town was often surrendered first. Thus in
September 1708, Marshal Boufflers agreed to surrender the city in return for the
free evacuation of his casualties to Douai, and freedom to withdraw his
remaining men into the citadel. At the other end of the scale, however, the
besieger might insist on nothing less than that the officers and garrison should
surrender all their arms and possessions and become prisoners-of-war. On other
occasions, when an army did not wish to burden itself with numerous other rank
prisoners to guard (although a proportion could often be induced to change
sides), the garrison might be disarmed and then allowed out 'with their hands in
their pockets' – the waist-bands of their breeches having been cut and
(sometimes) their shoes removed – to wander homewards as best they might.

Acceptable terms might take some time to be agreed, and the besieger could resort to threats, bluster or even temporary recommencement of operations to induce his opponent into a more 'reasonable' frame of mind. Thus at Namur in 1692 Louis XIV threatened a heavy communal fine for each day the city continued to hold out. At Bouchain, in 1711, Marlborough twice broke off negotiations and resumed a merciless bombardment until he induced de Ravignau to surrender unconditionally. After the Battle of Belgrade in 1717, and the devastating explosion of a Turkish magazine, it was comparatively easy to reach agreed terms. One or two of the articles of surrender – as proposed and amended – are worth citing here:

Article I: A complete cessation of hostilities to be observed during the capitulation.
Imperialist observation: 'We are not accustomed to act contrary to convention.'
Article II: All forts, munitions and artillery will be handed over by the garrison.
Imperialist observation: 'It is well known that what is due to a victor should be handed over to the victor.'
Article III: In return for the proper handing-over of the fortress and all munitions, the garrison will be permitted to withdraw freely with their wives and children, arms and baggage, drums beating and flags flying; the same condition to apply to any inhabitants who may wish to leave at the same time ... and also all ex-slaves who actually embraced the Mohammedan faith before the siege ...'
Imperialist observation: 'This is agreed provided that all slaves made during the present war, all prisoners of war and all deserters, are handed over.'

Other terms centred around the assistance the Imperialists were to provide the evacuating garrison. The Turks requested 1,000 carts to carry off their effects; the victors stipulated only 300. Escorts and protection were to be provided as far as the Iron Gate Pass for those Turks proceeding by water; as far as Moravia for the land party; the final Article decided when the time lapse before the agreement became operative. The Turks argued for an evacuation eight days after the signature of the final draft; the Imperialists insisted on a delay of only four days, and that a gate and its neighbouring fortifications were to be handed over at once, together with hostages (Article IX).

The agreement was signed by General de Brokhausen on behalf of Eugene on 18 August 1717, and immediately ratified by the Prince.

'Yesterday we solemnly sung a *Te Deum* in the Grand Vizier's tent', recorded an anonymous eye-witness on the 20th, 'for the victory over the common foe on the 16th of this month ... We have begun to fill in our lines of contravallation, and our grenadiers have taken possession of a gate of Belgrade, and the exterior walls. The Turkish garrison must leave on the 22nd to be escorted part by boat to Fietislavia, the rest by land to Nissa.'[98]

It was not unknown, in the highly-charged emotional atmosphere surrounding many such occasions, for both sides to make allegations concerning the other side's non-observance of the agreed terms. De Ravignau, for example, accused Marlborough of renegading on an agreement allegedly made in his name by a

Colonel Pagnies, to the effect that the French might evacuate with the full honours of war. True or false, the Duke's critics made maximum use of the allegation to blacken his character. A more celebrated contention of broken faith occurred during the previous war. On the grounds that the French had marched away several English battalions into captivity after the surrender of Dixmude and Deynse – despite a formal promise of free evacuation – the Allies took their revenge after the recapture of Namur by refusing to allow Marshal Boufflers to accompany his troops. An eye-witness account – by an unknown hand – survives in the British Museum, which also imparts something of the atmosphere of righteous indignation which surrounded this incident:

> We have a Marshal of France down by the market place – a fact that has excited a great outcry, but it is high time for us to demonstrate that we are not always to be made the dupes. We recall the capitulation of Heidelberg, and all the tricks and chicanery over the terms and cartels, and most of all we remember the capitulation of Dixmude and Deynse . . . It is (in revenge) for the execution of that capitulation that we hold the Marshal. Some while after he passed before the King, the Elector and the Landgrave, M. Dijkveldt went up to him, followed by several officers and M. d'Etang with four *Gardes du Corps* who surrounded him . . . M. Dijkveldt begged him to go aside a trifle as he had something to impart, but he replied three times that he was marching at the head of the garrison so that he could not comply, and that he could impart anything he desired there and then. My Lord Portland then approached and besought him also, so that he at last sent off an aide de camp to the Elector to complain that we were breaking the convention in respect of his person. Seeing that it was all to no avail, he drew aside, biting his lip. He demanded with heat to know if it was thus that we treated a man of his rank, one of the first men in all France, who was more important than we knew, and he claimed that all Europe would cry out against the affront now being made to him, and that the Allies would be able to boast with cause that if was the first advantage they had ever gained over him, for never before had a Marshal of France been seen in the breach, personally repelling an assault, as all the world would bear witness.

> M. Dijkveldt replied that the King was distressed to have been brought to this extremity, that he was only countenancing it because he was forced to it, and that he realized he would have to justify his action to all Europe. However he must not consider it a personal affront for all men acknowledged his bravery, and he could rest easy on that score as 100,000 men had been witnesses. Nevertheless, it was not the moment for him to indulge in idle threats. All these replies he made to each of the Marshal's bravados, who was by this time verily spitting fire and brimstone. He went on that we were generous enough to offer him the chance of leaving on parole providing he would send back our troops (i.e. the garrisons of Dixmude etc.). This he refused, saying that he could not undertake a thing that was not in his power. And so he is still here in Namur without guards, the town being his prison. [95]

This demonstration of Allied firmness soon had the desired effects: the imprisoned battalions were repatriated and the Marshal secured his liberty.

*   *   *

Such, then were the main forms and conventions of siege warfare. Small wonder if kings and commanders lavished rewards on their engineers-in-chief who brought such complex operations to a successful conclusion. Louis XIV gave Vauban a gift of 40,000 crowns for capturing Namur in 1692; on other occasions he awarded him captured cannon and wide estates. William III lavished promotions and honours on the modest Coehoorn after his recovery of the same fortress for the Allies. The canny Marlborough – as befitted his character – was less lavish with money, and indeed blighted the careers of Du Mey and De Pinto for their proven incapacity in the early stages of the siege of Lille. But the Duke's favourite engineer, Colonel John Armstrong, the hero of Bouchain, received the distinction of being represented alongside the Duke in no less than three of the Blenheim tapestries woven to commemorate his victories and triumphs. Armstrong eventually became a Lieutenant-General and a Fellow of the Royal Society.

16

The age of the great engineers

Until the seventeenth century kings and governments had mostly relied upon the assistance of non-military engineers for both the design of their fortifications and the planning of their sieges. At first sight, some of these experts belonged to the most unlikely professions. Several of the greatest artists of the Renaissance and Reformation devoted part of their time to the consideration of such military problems – including Michaelangelo, Leonardo da Vinci and Albrecht Dürer. It is even more surprising to find men of the cloth featuring prominently in lists of military engineers, but both Abbé Dufay and Donato Rosetti, Canon of Livorno, produced treatises of some note in their day. Taking these backgrounds into account, it becomes rather less strange that so many military engineers at the close of the seventeenth century were still civilians rather than professional soldiers.

Nevertheless, the greatest engineers of the age emerged from the ranks of the armies of their respective countries. They were three in number, namely the French Marshal, Sebastien le Prestre de Vauban (1633–1707), the only engineer of the seventeenth century to attain the highest military rank, the Dutch expert Menno van Coehoorn (1641–1704), and the Saxon George Rimpler (1612–83). The last named merits inclusion in this list despite his premature death at the siege of Vienna as his work was the basis of what became known as 'the German School', although this was far less famous than the other two, and some scholars indeed query its independent existence. Each of these men wielded much influence during their lives and after their deaths, inspiring groups of followers and imitators.

The *doyen* of these three was indubitably Vauban, whose skill and fame became legendary. Indeed his ability approached genius, for his interests embraced the whole military field and also took in government and national economics. Even the acid St Simon could hardly fault this paragon's character.

> For valour, bounty and probity, despite a rough and brutal exterior, (he) was without question the finest man of his century where sieges and fortifications were concerned, and also in the realm of handling men, whilst a further outstanding characteristic was his simplicity. [100]

His reputation as an engineer has probably never been surpassed. 'A town besieged by Vauban is a town taken; a town defended by Vauban is a town held' ran the seventeenth century adage. Estimates of his total constructions vary considerably. M. de Fontenelle of the *Académie Royal des Sciences* in Vauban's funeral oration claimed that the Marshal 'renovated 300 old fortresses and built 33 new; he conducted 53 sieges ... (and) took part in 140 spirited actions.' Voltaire declared that he 'regulated' 150 major towns and fortresses, but Sir Reginald Blomfield was able to identify with certainty only 92, admitting his list to be very incomplete.[101] The point is largely academic for Vauban's contribution was enormous by any standard.

It is perhaps surprising to record that, for all his influence, Vauban was not a great innovator; he was far more the perfector and developer of other men's ideas – at least where defensive engineering was concerned. The two predecessors who contributed most to the formulation of his ideas were Blaise François, Comte de Pagan (1604–53) and the Jesuit, le R. P. Georges Fournier (fl. 1647), and he freely acknowledged his debt to their work and to the great Italian School. As for his own contribution, Vauban has been much exposed to both fellow-engineers and authors, who have stridently proclaimed ideas to be his which he would have been the first to disown. His successors, for instance, attempted to rationalize his concepts into 'three orders' of fortification; the 'first' comprised a basically simple series of defences of the kind that has been described above; the 'second' replaced the angle bastions with small bastioned towers, added a second ditch, and placed large bastions in detached positions before the rampart; the 'third' modified the design of *tenailles* (low defences protecting walls), and added a quickset hedge along the top of the escarpment and along the *démi-lunes,* each of which was further defended by a ravelin or redoubt built in rear. Such systematization was, however, anathema to Vauban, who always deplored a doctrinaire approach. 'The art of fortification does not consist of rules or systems,' he wrote, 'but solely of good sense and experience.'

This statement notwithstanding, it is justifiable to assert that four broad principles or concepts underlay most of Vauban's constructive work. The first was to tailor any fortress design to the configuration of the ground, making the most of any local natural advantages. During his career he built fortresses on mountains for Louvois, including Mont Louis in the Pyrenees, Briançon on the River Dumerc and Château Queyras to crown a rock 4,000 feet above sea level (1692). For Colbert, he renovated such coastal fortresses as Dunkirk on the Channel and Concarneau in Brittany. To defend the critical north-eastern frontiers facing towards the Rhine, he constructed or renovated the famous triple line of fortresses amidst the plains and rivers of French Flanders. In each and every case the design was unique. Second, in every design he paid the greatest attention to producing the maximum possible output of defensive firepower; it was axiomatic that every approach to a fortress, and every part of its defences, should be covered by converging patterns of fire, both cannon and musketry. Third, he advocated defence in depth, designing successive rings of outworks and fortifications to push back the enemy batteries to maximum range from their main target – the bastion-trace. Fourth, he planned to permit

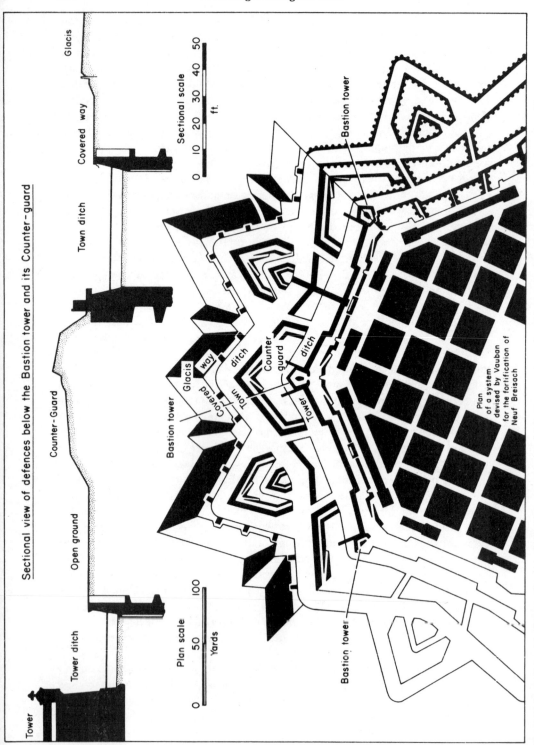

Sectional view of defences below the Bastion tower and its Counter-guard

Glacis

Covered way

Town ditch

Counter-Guard

Open ground

Tower ditch

Tower

Sectional scale

0   10   20   30   40   50

ft.

Plan scale

0   50   100

Yards

Bastion tower

Glacis

Covered way

Town ditch

Counter guard

Tower ditch

Bastion tower

Bastion tower

Plan
of a system
devised by Vauban
for the fortification of
Neuf Breisach

governors and garrisons to conduct a reasonably active defence by providing sally-ports and bridges for sorties to hold up the progress of the besiegers' works. To these four principles, present in all his work, he added in certain cases a fifth: he pointed out the advantages of building large fortified encampments capable of holding a field army adjacent to fortresses and experimented with the use of detached forts placed well beyond the regular defences. This he did, for instance, at Toulon (1692); and he ascribed the loss of Namur to the Allies in 1695 to the failure to make similar provision there.

Where the design of bastions was concerned, Vauban preferred an obtuse angle for the two faces in order to gain additional width for the gun platform and a greater command over the glacis. His defensive schemes became increasingly complex as they were pushed further and further out into the surrounding countryside. This tendency is well typified by one of his masterpieces, his self-confessed *'fille ainée dans la fortification'*, the city and citadel of Lille (refortified between 1668 and 1674). The citadel was his particular pride, a perfect pentagon enclosing a 180 yard parade ground besides a church, barracks and governor's lodging and stabling. It was perhaps merciful that he died the year before his *'reine des citadelles'* fell to the Allies after a Homeric siege in 1708. Even today, three centuries after its construction, the citadel of Lille retains most of its original features and remains an impressive monument to his work.

The development of *tours bastionées* was perhaps his most important contribution to fortress design. These were strong towers several storeys high enclosing gun platforms provided with flues to clear the powder-smoke. This speciality figured largely in the masterpiece of his later work, namely Neuf-Breisach on the Rhine. Its basic trace was octagonal, and every detail was recorded by one of Vauban's successors, Forest de Bélidor. Its internal diameter was 600 yards, each of the eight sides (bastions included) measured 360 yards, the curtain-walls stretching for 250 fathoms. These were 10 feet 2 inches thick at the base, tapering to five feet at glacis-level, sustained from within by 15 foot buttresses of stone and brick around which were packed enormous quantities of earth to form a total thickness of 18 feet at the summit. At the angles stood the *tours bastionées*, with outer faces measuring 17 feet 5 inches and with flanks 35 feet wide. The walls of these towers were 13 feet thick at the foot tapering to 8 feet at the top; they were flat-roofed, provided with a parapet, and stood two storeys high. Beyond the main trace lay extensive outworks in successive series, making a defensive zone some 380 yards deep. Access to this imposing fortress (see illustration and plan) was over drawbridges and a hinged bridge worked by counterweights, and through petard-proof gates some 10 feet wide, 13 feet high and 4 feet thick, some of which were dropped into position from above after the fashion of a mediaeval portcullis.[102]

So much for an outline of Vauban's work as a defensive engineer. His contribution to the active prosecution of siege warfare was even more notable. As before, much of his work consisted in perfecting and regularizing the ideas of earlier men, but it seems certain that he was the originator of one important innovation, namely the parallel-trench (or *places d'armes*) system. This has been described above but its main advantages may be recapitulated here – the provision of good cover for the attackers at 600, 400 and 200 yards from the ditch (thus reducing casualties), and the ability to mount several 'attacks' (as the forward-going approach trenches were called), in order to confuse the defence as to the point of greatest peril. This system was first used before Maastricht in 1673, and 19 years later it proved its value again (as on numerous other occasions) in reducing Fort Coehoorn at Namur. For the rest, Vauban taught that fortresses should be taken more by the shovel than the sword, and he deplored premature assaults as likely to result in needless loss of life. Yet so effective were his methods that the average time taken to bring sieges to satisfactory conclusions was *reduced* considerably in his day although some were very lengthy.

These aspects of Vauban's work soon gained international currency, and formed the basis for many other schools of military engineers. His ideas were disseminated partly by word of mouth – as numbers of his pupils were driven abroad and into the armies of France's foes by the religious intolerance of Louis XIV (1685) and the economies imposed in 1697 – and increasingly through the medium of printed publication. As an author, Vauban poses something of an enigma. Although he was indubitably a prolific writer of papers on many subjects for the French government, he steadfastly denied the validity of the many published works on fortification attributed to him which appeared during his lifetime – particularly abroad.* Many of these earlier volumes were indeed fabrications – but eventually three works of which he was indubitably the author became public, namely *Traité de l'attaque des places* (1704), *Traité de la defense des places* (c.1706), and *Traité des mines* (1707). In their original form – the first versions were probably written in the 1670s – these works were highly-classified documents, intended for the eyes of French marshals and generals only, but in an age of notoriously lax security it was not long before more or less complete versions appeared in the bookshops of Paris and the Hague, in due course running into many editions in several languages. Some of these included new material added by other hands. Thus the French 1779 edition of *L'attaque des places* includes a chapter devoted to the attack of bastion-towers which, as the engineer and mathematician M. le Blond pointed out in a footnote, is certainly not Vauban's work as the measures described break several of his cardinal rules for placing batteries.[103] Care therefore has to be taken in examining these publications, but as some copies of his original writings have survived in the *Depôt de la Guerre* it is possible to gain a reasonably accurate picture.

Much of Vauban's lasting significance was due to the work of his pupils and successors. His immediate lieutenants included many outstanding men who tended to be obscured by their greater chief, including Clément, Mesgrigni, Dupy-Vauban, Richerand and de Valory, to cite but a few.† Perhaps the most

---

*For example: *La Manière de fortification de M. de Vauban*, published in Amsterdam (1689) and in London (1691 and 1693).

†A fuller list is given in A. Allent, *Histoire du Corps Impérial du Genie* (1805), chapters XIV and XV.

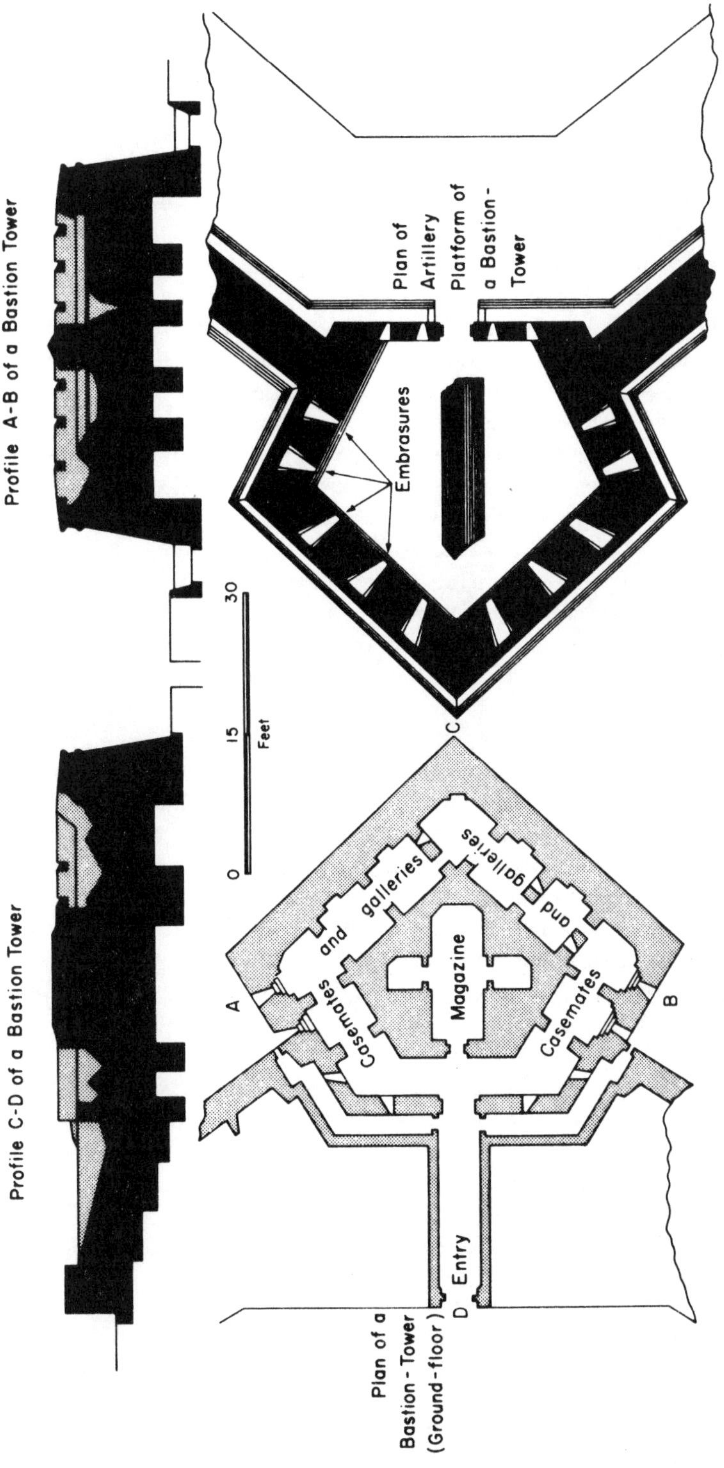

Detail of a Bastion Tower
(after the Vauban System)

Profile A-B of a Bastion Tower

Profile C-D of a Bastion Tower

Plan of Artillery Platform of a Bastion-Tower

Embrasures

30

15

0

Feet

Casemates and galleries

Magazine

Casemates and galleries

A

B

Plan of a Bastion-Tower (Ground-floor)

D Entry

important disciple of the next generation was Bernard Forest de Bélidor (1693–1761) whose learned treatises (*Le bombardier français* (1731), *Le traité des fortifications* (1735) and above all *La science des ingénieurs* (1739), incorporate many of the Marshal's concepts in the greatest detail. Bélidor accurately described the root of Vauban's greatness when he wrote '*il a pu descendre à l'examen d'une infinité des petits sujets.*'[104] Genius has been described as an infinite capacity for taking pains – and this attribute Vauban undoubtedly possessed in generous measure; yet he never lost sight of the priorities. Rather ironically he died in disgrace for criticizing the governmental organization of France.

The Marshal's influence spread throughout the world and persisted for many years after his death. In Russia, for instance, Peter the Great selected one of Vauban's pupils to design the Fortress of St Peter and St Paul to protect his new capital, whilst the future Field-Marshal Münnich absorbed many of Vauban's concepts during a year spent at Strasbourg (fortified by the master in 1681) as a French engineer (1700–1), and consistently applied what he had learnt throughout a long career serving a succession of tsars and tsarinas.

Within France itself, of course, his influence was all-pervasive. For once it was not a case of a prophet being without honour in his own country. Indeed, his ideas were possibly over-applied by generation after generation, becoming embalmed and partially distorted in the process. Not even engineers of the calibre of Marc René de Montelambert, nor the mathematician le Blond dared break away from his teachings. Shortly before the French revolution another notable expert, Chasseloup de Laubat, was moved to remark wryly that 'to attempt novelties in fortification is to write oneself down as ignorant,'[105] although in fact he did introduce important modifications of design. This notwithstanding, Vauban's bastion-defence remained the standard design of *la génie* until at least as late as 1870. Even then, indeed, the last was not heard of Vauban's fortifications. In 1914, the fortress of Maubeuge – virtually unchanged since Vauban's day – defied von Kluck's army from 25 August until 7 September, despite the advantages of modern howitzers and heavy guns. As for Le Quesnoy, it had to be stormed by infantry of Byng's Third Army in November 1918:

> The enemy refused to surrender . . . A forlorn hope of New Zealanders then approached with scaling ladders in the good old style and swarmed up the walls. There was only one ladder and three successive walls, but in some miraculous fashion the whole of the 4th New Zealand Battalion reached the top of the parapet with the loss of one man.
>
> On seeing that they had reached the rampart, the German commander at last hoisted the white flag.[106]

It would seem that Vauban and his disciples built well.

This is not to assert, however, that the French School enjoyed a monopoly of the arts and sciences of fortification. In Vauban's own lifetime the most outstanding rival was Baron Menno van Coehoorn, the 'Dutch Vauban' also known (with good reason) as 'the fighting engineer'. His son wrote the following description of his appearance and character:

> He was well made and of tall height: he had a martial air; he was a man of spirit and judgement, speaking little, but well and justly, civil to everyone, even the most junior soldier; as brave as one could be, and with the greatest *sang-froid* imaginable when under fire ... He was so disinterested (in self-advancement) that he neglected the fortunes of his family, so that he left them scarcely enough to live on.[107]

Coehoorn had seen much service at sieges and battles as an infantry officer and part-time engineer between 1657 and 1688 before he became well-known. At the siege of Bonn (1688) he was so disgusted by the way it was being conducted that he made formal remonstrations to the Elector of Brandenburg, and as a result his advice was adopted – successfully. Four years later he was sent to improve the fortifications of Namur at the behest of William III. His subsequent defence of 'Fort Coehoorn' – despite its unsuccessful conclusion – finally consolidated his reputation. Vauban himself sought a meeting with the wounded prisoner. His exchange was soon arranged, and as a newly-promoted Major-General he conducted the successful defence of Liège (1693), and two years later helped capture Huy. In 1695 he also had the opportunity to avenge his earlier setback when he was appointed to direct the Allied siege of Namur, which he brought to a successful though expensive conclusion. In recognition of this service he was appointed a Lieutenant-General and Director-General of Fortifications for the United Provinces. By this time he was a famous figure, called 'Father Coehoorn' by the troops, and after the Peace of Ryswick King Louis XIV vainly attempted to buy him into the French service. Instead he spent much time visiting and improving the Dutch frontier fortresses, earning thereby the Governorship of Dutch Flanders (1701) to add to his other dignities.

In the early years of the Spanish Succession struggle he was deeply concerned with the Allied capture of Kaiserwerth, Venlo, Ruremonde and Liège. What proved to be his last success was the siege of Bonn in 1702, which fell to the Allies after only 10 days of open trenches thanks to the heavy bombardment Coehoorn contrived to bring down about the ears of the garrison. This achievement gave rise to a verse likening the feat to the fall of Jericho:

> *Tout le monde fait un suprement miracle*
> *De ce que Jericho vit abatue ses murs*
> *Au seul son des trompettes; mais Je suis bier sûr*
> *Qu'une* Corne de Vache *(ô le grand spectacle!)*
> *Ne fit autrefois tant que de nos jours*
> *Quand de Bonn elle abat les murs et les tours.**[108]

*A rough translation: *'Everyone hailed it as a supreme miracle*
                            'When they saw the walls of Jericho fall
                            'At the sole sound of the trumpets; but I'm sure
                            'That a Cow's Horn (O, what a spectacle!)
                            'Did just as much in our days
                            'When at Bonn it brought down the walls and the towers.'

The following spring the ageing 'Father Coehoorn' suffered a severe stroke through over-exertion whilst leading the repulse of a French raid in mid-winter. He had recovered enough to be visited by Marlborough several times in early 1704, 'where were made all the dispositions for that campaign which had such glorious and happy consequences', but he was in fact dead (17 March) before Marlborough set out on his famous march to the Danube. He was widely mourned. Marlborough wrote to the deceased's son:

> I was most afflicted to learn today through your letter of the death of your Father, whose loss must be regretted by all those who have the least interest for the good of the State and the common cause in general. [109]

Coehoorn's integrity was questioned after his death by his enemy Paymaster-General Hop, who accused him of misappropriating 80,000 livres of secret service funds; whatever the truth of this charge which was never proved, the Baron only left some 50,000 crowns to his descendants.

Coehoorn's ideas varied in several important respects from those of his great adversary, Vauban. In basic design, he favoured the pentagon and 'royal hexagon', and advocated the use of outlying detached bastions beyond the trace. He laid special emphasis on fire: 'the strength of a fortress entirely depends on a constant fire from the flanks', and to increase this he advised the siting of a pair of demi-bastions along each curtain wall. For the rest, he was a great advocate of simplicity of design, scrapping the complex system of ravelins, half-moons, horn- and crown-works so dear to the French school as 'such needless stuff'. [110]

His preferred methods for taking enemy fortresses were even further away from Vauban. He taught the use of direct rather than indirect measures – looking for short-cuts at whatever cost in lives was necessary. He was greatly in favour of stormings, and these were performed at his behest at both Namur (1695) and Liège (1702). On the former occasion over 2,000 men were made casualties in two hours on 30 August. At the Terra Nova breach the Royal Regiment of Foot of Ireland alone lost 27 officers and 271 other rank casualties – including Robert Parker who was 'thirty weeks under cure' thereafter. [111] Such blood-letting horrified the humane Vauban, who modified his earlier good opinion of Coehoorn:

> I have served at 45 sieges or very near, and have taken part in all of them. I have also studied about six times as many. But never have I heard of anything like this or even approaching it in regard to such gross errors of commission . . . As for the beauty of the action, I find it too senseless to be estimable. [112]

It was a valid observation: Vauban had captured Namur three years earlier for a mere 300 casualties.

Coehoorn's second innovation was the invention of a lightweight trench mortar that was given his name. He may have invented this weapon as early as 1673 when he was serving as a grenadier officer in the trenches before Maastricht. Basically it was a grenade-thrower, and when used in large numbers (as at Bonn in 1703) could produce a hail of fire around a garrison's ears. The coehoorn mortar was adopted by the British army, a royal warrant dated

20 November 1708, mentions the provision of 60 'Coehoorn Mortars' for an expedition, and the weapon was certainly still in use in 1740. General Oglethorpe, for instance, used 20 against the Spanish fort of St Augustine in Florida; the Spaniards dubbed them *cuernos de vaca*.[113]

Coehoorn wrote several treatises which enjoyed some considerable fame, especially in Great Britain. In 1705, for example, Thomas Savary, Gentleman, produced a translation of *The New Method of Fortification translated from the original Dutch of the late famous Engineer, Menno, Baron van Coehoorn*. All in all, the Baron proved a worthy descendant of the great school of Dutch engineers which had flourished in the late 1500s in the days of Maurice of Nassau and William the Silent.

The third 'school' – that based on the work of George Rimpler – needs only a passing mention. Rimpler's book, *Fortification with Central Bastion* (1673) argued in favour of a polygonal trace with a central gun platform. His successors in the German School, the Sturm family (father and son – both civilians) and the capable Prussian, Landsberg the Younger (1670–1746), similarly distrusted the conventional bastion trace on account of the potential vulnerability of the corner bastions, and advised instead a polygonal *enceinte* guarded by *canonières* and *tenailles* in their stead. For the most part, however the German school degenerated as the 18th century progressed, adopting the standard of geometrical perfection as represented by the star-trace. As a result fortifications tended to be designed only to one pattern, regardless of the terrain; in other words formalisation of both design and method increasingly became the bane of the century.

No other country produced a reputable school of its own during our period, although there was no lack of highly competent field engineers in England, Sweden, Russia or Turkey. None, however, produced much originality of thought or method, but relied on adapting the concepts of Vauban, Coehoorn or Rimpler to their own requirements. Perhaps Great Britain's insular position and Sweden's general inaccessibility (and lack of an inspired opponent in the particular field we are discussing), account for their relative unoriginality in the arts of defensive engineering. However the former was fortunate to be able to call on the services of such men as the Richards brothers, Holcroft Blood and Colonel John Armstrong. The British proved very capable of directing sieges in Flanders under Marlborough – with the aid of their allies the Dutch we should add – and for that matter proved adept at designing smaller fortresses as typified by Fort George in the Scottish Highlands. They owned much, however, to Huguenot and Dutch masters. As for Russia, until the accession of Peter the Great her overall military development remained stunted, and thereafter her embryonic engineering services relied basically on imported foreigners such as Münnich, who based all his work on French models. Where the Ottoman Turks were concerned, their engineers represented the most modern branch of their even more out-dated forces. Their sappers, many of them renegade Christians or Bosnian slaves, had gained considerable experience from their close contact with Dutch and English experts during the Cretan War of 1664–69,[114] and until the great failures at Vienna in 1683 (as besiegers), and at Belgrade in 1717 (as besieged), they bore a well-earned reputation of being second to none as practitioners of the complementary forms of siege warfare. In both attack and defence they specialized in mining and 'perpetual storms' designed to wear down the resistance of their foes – as all too often was achieved.

Gradually, as the years passed, the governments of Europe came to recognize the need for providing their young engineer apprentices with formal instruction in the art before sending them into the field. Thus in Russia, the influential Münnich founded two engineering academies at St Petersburg and Moscow (*c.*1728) capable of training some 700 pupils between them. In England, after the failure to establish an earlier institution in 1721, the Royal Military Academy at Woolwich (originally an establishment mainly for gunners although some potential engineers were included from the start, and all studied a common syllabus including fortification),* was opened in 1741.[115] Earlier French experiments in the same direction based on the Paris Arsenal largely petered out after a few years despite the repeated pleas of Vauban for a college, and it was not until 1748 that Louis xv created the first permanent School of Engineering at Mezières. Prussia – in other respects well ahead of the rest of the field in respect of military academies – tended to be slower than most in this instance.

For the most part, therefore, it is true to assert that for much of the period covered by this history, the great majority of young engineers learnt their trade 'at the cannon's mouth' or in the status of apprentices at the feet of the great masters and their lieutenants. Whatever such methods of instruction may have lacked in terms of academic finesse was more than made up for by the value of personal experience and direct inspiration.

---

*Until 1759 the British Corps of Engineers *per se* comprised only warrant officers, and all young officers, on first commissioning, joined the Royal Regiment of Artillery. Only after 1761 were engineer officers directly commissioned as such.

References

PART ONE: *The Horse*

(1). Cited by J. Ambert, *Esquisses historiques . . . de l'armée française* (Brussels: 1840), p. 172.

(2). *La Correspondance de Napoleon Ier*, (Paris: 1870), Vol. XXXI, p. 426 note four.

(3). Cited by G. B. Turner, *A History of Military Affairs in Western Society* (New York: 1953), p. 23.

(4). See C. Walton, *The British Standing Army, 1660–1700* (London: 1894), p. 708; R. E. Scouller, *The Armies of Queen Anne* (O.U.P.: 1966), p. 251 and L. Cooper, *British Regular Cavalry* (London: 1965), p. 77.

(5). Add Ms 9724, f. 149 (Br. Mus.).

(6). M. le Blond, *Elemens de Tactique* (Paris: 1758), p. 217–8.

(7). G. Bodart, *Militar – Historisches 1618–1907, Kriegs-Lexicon* (Dresden: 1908), p. 810.

(8). Le Marechal de Puységur, *Art de la Guerre* (Paris: 1748), Vol. II, p. 150.

(9). Le Blond, *op.cit.*, pp. 218–20, quoting Marshal de Saxe.

(10). General Weygand, *L'Armée Française* (Paris: 1938), p. 180 *et seq.*, and Add Ms 32,750, f.233 (Br. Mus.).

(11). Godin Leffcovitch, p. 38, cited by G. T. Denison, *A History of Cavalary* (London: 1913), 2nd Edn., p. 249.

(12). W. H. Greenly – 'The Cavalry of Frederick the Great', article in the USI Journal, Vol. III (1909), p. 1302.

(13). See M. de Guignard, *L'École de Mars* (Paris: 1725), Vol. I, Book III, pp. 381–456 for a full description.

(14). *ibid.*, p. 561.

(15). See Ambert, *op.cit.*, p. 124 and *Historical Records of the British Army* – the 6th Regiment of Dragoon Guards (London: 1836), p. 25.

(16). Quoted in Ambert, *op.cit.*, p. 184.

(17). G. T. Denison, *A History of Cavalry* (London: 1913), 2nd Edn., p. 236.

(18). J. Laver, *British Military Uniforms* (London: 1948), pp. 10–11.

(19). Mérode-Westerloo, *op.cit.*, (Chandler Edn.), p. 276.

(20). *A Military Dictionary . . . by an Officer who served several years abroad* (London: 1702), entry under DR.

(21). R. de Montecuculi, *Mémoires, ou principes de l'art militaire* (trans. Paris: 1712), p. 228.

(22). Ivanhoff, p. 27, cited by Denison, *op.cit.*, p. 248.

(23). *A List of what forces his Ma'tie thinks necessary* . . . dated 1690 – King William's Chest, SP/8/8, f. 6 (P.R.O.).

(24). K.W.C. SP/8/13, f. 98 (P.R.O.).

(25). Ivanhoff, *op.cit.*, p. 15.

(26). Marshal de Saxe, *Mes Rêveries* (Paris: 1757), p. 56. A useful shortened version, edited by Brig.-Gen. T. Philips, was published at Harrisburg: 1944.

(27). Establishments, War Office 24/41, 45, 46 and 47 (P.R.O.); subsistence rates are laid down in the 1704 Mutiny Act, (*Annae* 3 and 4 cap. 5).

(28). Scouller, *op.cit.*, p. 95.

(29). Ambert, *op.cit.*, p. 200.

(30). Ivanhoff, *op.cit.*, p. 38.

(31). Ambert, *op.cit.*, p. 200.

(32). R. P. Daniel, *Histoire de la Milice Française . . . (Paris: 1721)*.

(33). J. C. Horsley, *Tales of an Old Campaigner* (London: 1904), p. 159.

(34). *Correspondence of Lord Raby with Cadogan* Strafford Papers, Add Ms 22196 letter dated 17 August 1706 (Br. Mus.).

(35). See Count Marsigli, *l'État Militaire de l'Empire Ottoman* (Amsterdam: 1752).

(36). Horsley, *op.cit.*, p. 415.

(37). Le Blond, *op.cit.*, p. 45.

(38). Ests. WO 24/23 (25/4/1700) & /75 (24/6/1708) & /38 (for 1705). P.R.O. See also comprehensive tables in Scouller, *op.cit.*, Appendix E.

(39). Guignard, *op.cit.*, Vol. I, p. 406–7.

(40). *ibid.*, p. 424.

(41). *ibid.*, p. 382.

(42). Puységur, *op.cit.*, Vol. I, p. 53 *et seq.*

(43). Davenant Mss, Vol. VIII (Add Ms 474f. 13 & 15 (Br. Mus.); and (for 1738) Add Mss 19,036, f. 1.

(44). Le Blond, *op.cit.*, p. 49; and Add Mss 19,036, f. 1 (Br. Mus.).

(45). F. G. Bengtson, *Charles XII* (London: 1960), p. 241–2.

(46). KWC SP/8/15, f. 67, 73 etc. (P.R.O.).

(47). KWC SP/8/8, f. 36 (P.R.O.).

(48). *idem* (for 1690) and Stowe Add Ms 481, f. 24 (for 1693), (Br. Mus.).

(49). Edward d'Auvergne, *History of the Campagne in Flanders . . . 1693*, p. 42.

(50). Scouller, *op.cit.*, Appendix E and list of sources, p. 373.

(51). Van Raa, *Het Stets Legers* (The Hague: 1950), Deel VIII, p. 219–20.

(52). Stowe Papers, Add Ms 470, ff. 4309 (Br. Mus.).

(53). Brigadier-General Wm. Kane, *The Campaigns of King William and Queen Anne* (London: 1745), p. 110.

(54). 'Regulations for Outposts' etc. in *Orders and Regulations for the Horse* (The Hague: 1691) P.R.O.

(55). Le Blond, *op.cit.*, pp. 187–208.

(56). Cited by Walton, *op.cit.*, p. 522.

(57). Saxe, *op.cit.*, Vol. I, p. 166.

(58). Duparq, Vol. II, p. 211, cited by Denison, *op.cit.*, p. 227.

(59). Daniel, *op.cit.*, cited by Ambert, p. 200.

(60). Lt. General Feuquières, *Mémoires*, Vol. III, p. 16.

(61). Blathwayt Mss, Add Ms 9723, f. 7 (Br. Mus.).

(62). Liskenne et Sauvan, *Bibliothèque Historique et Militaire* (Paris: 1844), Vol. IV, p. 648–9, citing Feuquières.

(63). Mérode-Westerloo, *op.cit.*, (Chandler Edn.), p. 233.

(64). W. S. Churchill, *Marlborough, His Life and Times* (London: 1947), Book I, p. 775.

(65). Kane, *op.cit.*, p. 110.

(66). Denison, *op.cit.*, p. 238.

(67). Parker, *op.cit.*, (Chandler Edn.), p. 81.

(68). J. J. G. Pelet and F. E. de Vault, *Documents relatifs à la Guerre de Succession en Espagne* (Paris: 1840), Vol. IV, p. 575.

(69). Mérode-Westerloo, *op.cit.*, (Chandler edn.), p. 268.

(70). Captain Robert Parker, *Memoirs of the Most Remarkable Military Transactions* etc. (Dublin: 1746) republished in an edited form by D. G. Chandler in *Two Soldiers of Marlborough's Day* (London: 1968), p. 134.

(71). Comte de Mérode-Westerloo, *Mémoires* (Brussels: 1840), republished in an edited and translated form by D. G. Chandler (as above), p. 325.

(72). Information supplied by the Historical Section of the Swedish General Staff.

(73). Denison, *op.cit.*, p. 244.

(74). Horsley, *op.cit.*, pt9.

(75). Saxe, *op.cit.*, Vol. I, p. 116.

(76). *ibid.*, Vol. I, p. 147.

(77). Ambert, *op.cit.*, p. 185.

(78). Greenly, *op.cit.*, p. 1302–3.

(79). Cited by Greenly, *ibid.*, p. 1323.

PART TWO: *The Foot*

(1). J. Ambert, *Esquisses historiques de l'Armée Française* (Brussels: 1840), p. 69.

(2). For 1727: Add Mss 32750, f. 233; For 1738: Add Mss 19036, f. 1; For 1748: Add Mss 35893, f. 148 (Br. Mus.), and E. Dussieux, *L'Armée en France*, Vol. II, p. 318.

(3). For 1689: KWC SP/8/5, f. 12 (P.R.O.); for 1696: SP/8/16, f. 56 (P.R.O.).

(4). Commons Journals, Vol. XVI; Establishments, WO/24/25 and WO/24/49 (P.R.O.).

(5). Het van Raa, *Het Statsches Leger*, Deel VII, p. 220.

(6). G. Craig, *The Politics of the Prussian Army* (Oxford: 1955), p. 8.

(7). M. le Blond, *Elemens de Tactique* (Paris: 1758), p. 26, citing Montecuccoli.

(8). Mérode-Westerloo, *Mémoires* (Chandler Edn. London: 1968), p. 150.

(9). WO/26/11, f. 272 (P.R.O.).

(10). De Guignard, *L'Ecole de Mars* (Paris: 1725), *Tome* I, p. 674.

(11). *ibid.*, cited by Rüstow, Vol. II, p. 104.

(12). See bibliography for a list of books by officers and other ranks of this period.

(13). J. F. C. Fuller, *British Light Infantry in the 18th Century* (London: 1925), p. 45.

(14). Col. J. B. Malleson, *Laudon* (London: 1884), p. 27.

(15). Anon, *A Short History of the Highland Regiments* (London: 1743).

(16). J-M. de la Colonie, *Chronicles of an Old Campaigner*, *op.cit.*, p. 415 and Marsigli, *op.cit.*, Bk. I, Ch. 14 and Bk. II, p. 197 *passim*.

(17). George Story, *An Impartial Relation of the War in Ireland* (London: 1693).

(18). St Rémy, *Memorial de l'Artillerie* (Paris: 1693), *Tome* II, p. 124.

(19). P. Young & J. Adair, *From Hastings to Culloden* (London: 1964), p. 209.

(20). Robert Parker, (Chandler Edn., London: 1968), p. 89.

(21). Luxembourg's despatch cited in de Beaurain, *Histoire militaire de Flandres* (Paris: 1755), *Tome* I, p. 206.
(22). Cited by H. L. Blackmore, *British Military Firearms 1650–1856* (London: 1961), p. 106.
(23). KWC SP/8/6, f. 66 (P.R.O.).
(24). Harl. Mss 745–63 (Br. Mus.).
(25). Louis-Napoléon Bonaparte et Col. Favé, *Études sur l'artillerie française* (Paris: 1863), Book II, p. 12.
(26). See H. L. Blackmore's book, *op.cit.*, for the best account of the weapon's development.
(27). Edward Wagner, *Cut and Thrust Weapons* (London: 1967), pp. 247 & 294; and L. Mouillard, *Les Régiments sous Louis XV* (Paris: 1882), p. 36–7.
(28). *Maréchal* de Saxe, *Rêveries on the Art of War* (ed. T. R. Philips, Harrisburg: 1944), p. 51.
(29). Puységur, *op.cit.*, p. 56, and Held, *op.cit.*, p. 54.
(30). Gen. Hugh Mackay, *Memoirs, Letters and a Short Relation* (Edinburgh: 1873), p. 52.
(31). Cited by H. L. Blackmore, *op.cit.*, p. 42.
(32). Saxe, *op.cit.*, p. 43.
(33). Harl. Mss 6844 (Br. Mus.) and F. Grosse, *Military Antiquities* (London: 1786), Vol. II, p. 9.
(34). See *Handbuch der Uniformkunde* (Hamburg: 1966) by Profs. R. & H. Knotel and H. Sieg.
(35). Mérode-Westerloo, *op.cit.*, p. 175.
(36). F. Grosse, *op.cit.*, Vol. II, p. 12; Treasury Papers 1/11 (P.R.O.) for 1708 entries.
(37). L. Mouillard, *Les Régiments de Louis XV* (Paris: 1882), pp. 37–8.
(38). Colonie, *op.cit.*, p. 305 (for Ramillies) and *ibid.*, p. 185 (for Schellenberg).
(39). SP/Mil/41/3 (P.R.O.) cited by Scouller, *op.cit.*, p. 80.
(40). Parker, *op.cit.*, p. 131(n).
(41). *ibid.*, p. 88(n).
(42). Ambert, *op.cit.*, p. 70 (for 1660) and Mouillard, *op.cit.*, p. 44–5.
(43). Puységur, *op.cit.*, *Tome* I, pp. 56–7; Le Blond, *op.cit.*, Book I, p. 28 *et seq.*
(44). Add Mss 4747, f. 15 (Br. Mus.).
(45). O. Groehle, *Die Kriege Friedrichs II* (Berlin: 1966), p. 227.
(46). Dalton, *op.cit.*, Vol. V. p. xxx, and Murray, *op.cit.*, Vol II, p. 441.
(47). Guignard, *op.cit.*, pp. 507–8 & 638.
(48). Stowe Mss 481, f. 38 (Br. Mus.), & Scouller, *op.cit.*, p. 378.
(49). J. R. Hutchinson, *The Romance of a Regiment* (London: 1898), p. 108.
(50). *Military Exercises, 1730* (edited by S. J. Gooding, Ontario: 1962) *passim.*
(51). Marquis de Santa-Cruz, *Réflexions Militaires, Tome* III, p. 85.
(52). Puységur, *op.cit.*, *Tome* I, pp. 137–8.
(53). Folard, *Commentaire sur Polybe*, Vol. II, p. 286.
(54). Saxe, *op.cit.*, p. 28.
(55). Friedrich de Grosse, *Militärische Schriften* (ed. Gen. von Taysen) (Berlin: 1893), p. 204.
(56). General Richard Kane, *Discipline for a Regiment of Foot upon action* ... (London: 1745), pp. 116–7.
(57). *ibid.*, p. 115.
(58). Le Mercure, September 1698, p. 175.
(59). Walton, *op.cit.*, p. 526.

(60). Puységur, *op cit.*, Vol. I, p. 57 *et. seq.*

(61). R. de Montecuculi, *Memoirs* (Paris: 1712), p. 223.

(62). Add Mss 9723, f. 7 (Br. Mus.).

(63). W. Sawle, *An Impartial Relation of the late Campaign in Flanders* (London: 1691), p. 8.

(64). KWC SP/8/5 f. 95 (or 44 or 124).

(65). *Maréchal de Catinat, Memoires et correspondance* (Paris: 1819), Vol. II, p. 237.

(66). J. Colin, *L'Infanterie au XVIIIième Siècle* (Paris: 1907), p. 29.

(67). J. Demoriet, *Le Major Parfait* (1683), (in Harl. Ms 4655), p. 43.

(68). Le Blond, *op.cit.*, pp. 405–6.

(69). Add Mss 21506, f. 98 (Br. Mus.).

(70). L. Weaver, *The Story of the Royal Scots* (London: n.d.), p. 13, citing Harte, *Life of Gustavus Adolphus.*

(71). Kane, *op.cit.*, pp. 109–37.

(72). Parker, (Chandler Edn.), *op.cit.*, pp. 88–9.

(73). Anon, *The Exercise for the Horse, Dragoons and Foot Forces* – G.II.R. (London: 1739), 2nd Edn, p. 77.

(74). Stowe Mss 444, f. 13 (Br. Mus.).

(75). Lucien Mouillard, *op.cit.*, p. 236, & Favé, *op.cit.*, Vol. IV, p. 245.

(76). Kane, *op.cit.*, p. 123.

(77). *Ibid.*, p. 128.

(78). Parker, (Chandler Edn.), *op.cit.*, p. 80.

(79). Le Blond, *op.cit.*, pp. 403–4, citing the *Ordonnance* of 6 May 1755.

(80). Ambert, *op.cit.*, p. 71.

(81). M. de Chevert, *Essai Générale de Tactique* (Paris: n.d.), Ch. 6 *passim.*

(82). Quoted by Camon, *op.cit.*, p. 37.

(83). F. M. A. de Voltaire, *La Siècle de Louis XV*, (Paris: 1826) tome 728 of the 'complete works', p. 157.

(84). English Historical Review, Vol. XII, p. 523.

(85). Grimoard, *op.cit.*, III, p. 182.

(86). *Correspondance de Louis XV et du Maréchal de Noailles*, ed. C. Rousset (1869), Vol. I, p. 123.

(87). Chequers Court Mss (1900).

(88). *Gentleman's Magazine*, 1743, p. 386.

(89). Col. Lloyd, *op.cit.*, p. 148.

(90). Stowe Mss (Br. Mus.), quoted by Lloyd, p. 150.

(91). General Stenbock's *Instructions*, dated Wäxjö, 24 January 1710; Smorgen *Regulations*, dated 5 March 1708. See also F. G. Bengtsson, *Charles XII* (London: 1960), pp. 85-90. '

(92). M. Jähns: *Geschichte der Kriegswissenschaften* (Berlin: 1889–91), Vol. III, p. 1664.

(93). O. Groehler, *op.cit.*, p. 227.

(94). M. de Rostaing, *L'Expérience des batailles de la Guerre de 1733 et 1741*, cited by Le Blond, *op.cit.*, p. 412.

(95). *Kriege Friedrichs*, Vol. I, p. 409.

(96). Folard, *Traité de la Colonne*, p. 18 in Chabot, *Abrégé des commentaires de Folard* (Paris: 1754), Tome I, p. 335.

(97). Saxe, *op.cit.*, p. 18.

(98). Preface to Saxe, *op.cit.*

(99). *op.cit.*, p. 11.

288 References, Sources and Bibliography

(100). *ibid.*, pp. 32–3.

(100). *ibid.*, pp. 32–3.
(101). Daniel, *op.cit.*
(102). Saxe, *op.cit.*, p. 34.
(104). *ibid.*, p. 103.
(105). *ibid.*, p. 23, (1877 Edn.).
(106). *ibid.*, p. 68.
(106). *ibid.*, p. 19.

PART THREE: *The Artillery*

(1). *Correspondance de Napoléon Iier*, Vol. XXX, p. 447.
(2). P. Daniel, *Histoire de la Milice Française* (Paris: 1721), Vol. II, Bk. XIII, p. 521.
(3). Sir G. Murray, *Marlborough's Letters and Despatches* (London: 1845), Vol. IV, p. 144.
(4). Sgt. J. Millner, *A Compendious Journal ... 1702–13* (Londonderry: 1733), pp. vii & 364.
(5). *Correspondance op cit.*, Vol. XXVI, p. 458 and Vol. XXXI, p. 328.
(6). Napoleon III, cited by F. Duncan, *History of the Royal Regiment of Artillery* (London: 1874), 2 vols, title page.
(7). Stowe Mss 444, ff. 8–12 (Br. Mus.) and *Archives de l'Artillerie*, carton 3/b/101.
(8). Capt. R. Parker, *Memoirs ...*, ed. D. G. Chandler, (London: 1968), p. 67.
(9). Stowe 444, entry under 25 August 1692 (the diary of Col. J. Richards).
(10). Brig. P. Young & J. Adair, *From Hastings to Culloden* (London: 1964), p. 210.
(11). Comte de Mérode-Westerloo, *Mémoires*, ed. D. G. Chandler, (London: 1968), p. 172.
(12). Le Blond, *Elemens de Tactique* (Paris: 1758), p. 220.
(13). Surirey de St Rémy, *Mémoires de l'Artillerie* (ed. Amsterdam; 1702), Vol. II, pp. 228–9.
(14). Le Blond, *op.cit.*, p. 220.
(15). By 1805, France possessed 21,938 cannon, howitzers and mortars for use in land operations. See D. G. Chandler, *The Campaigns of Napoleon* (New York; 1966), p. 357.
(16). Add Mss 32,750, f. 233 (for 1727) & *ibid.*, 25,893, f. 148 (for 1748), Br. Mus.
(17). Col. Cleaveland, *Notes on the Early History of the Royal Regiment of Artillery* (London: n.d.), pp. 192–4.
(18). *ibid.*, p. 169.
(19). Olaf Groehler, *Die Kriege Friedrich II* (Berlin: 1966), pp. 25, 45, 56–8.
(20). Daniel, *op.cit.*, Vol. II, p. 521, & A. Forbes, *History of the Army Ordnance Services* (London: 1929), Vol. I, p. 7.
(21). Ordnance Warrants WO/55/536 (P.R.O.); James II's amendments are cited in Cleaveland, *op.cit.*, pp. 83–91; repromulgations are to be found in WO/55/342 f. 16 (William III) –/342, f. 291 (Anne), and under 30 July 1715 and 17 June 1727 (for Georges I & II).
(22). See St. Rémy, *op.cit.*, Vol. I, Pt. I, pp. 41–54.
(23). St Rémy, *op.cit.*, Vol. I, Pt. 1 *passim*, & Daniel, *op.cit.*, Vol. II, p. 521 *et seq.*
(24). Napoleon III & Col. Favé, *Etudes sur le passé et l'avenir de l'Artillerie* (Paris: 1863), Vol. IV, p. 10.
(25). Daniel, *op.cit.*, Vol. II, p. 521 & Livre XIV, Ch. 10 *passim*.
(26). See Clode, *The Military Forces of the Crown* (London: 1869), Vol. II, p. 186.

(27). WO 47/17, entry under date stated.
(28). Clode, *op.cit.*, Vol. II, pp. 204–5.
(29). Duncan, *op.cit.*, Vol. I, p. 22.
(30). E. Picard & L. Jouan, *l'Artillierie Française au 18 ième Siècle* (Paris: 1906), p. 4.
(31). See Daniel, *op.cit.*, Vol. II, Book XIII, pp. 521–616.
(32). *ibid.*, p. 539.
(33). Picard & Jouan, *op.cit.*, pp. 3, 5, 9, & 11.
(34). J. W. Fortescue, *Historical and Military Essays* (London: 1928), pp. 177–8.
(35). WO/55/421, Nos. 23, 24 (P.R.O.) & Stowe Mss 444, ff. 13–22 (Br. Mus.).
(36). WO/55/424, Nos. 6 & 36.
(37). Cleaveland, *op.cit.*, pp. 185–234 under relevant entries.
(38). See *Occasional Papers*, R. A. Institute, Vol. I, p. 380 *et seq.* for period 1743–8.
(39). Based upon Cleaveland, *op.cit.*, pp. 185–234 & *Occasional Papers* as above.
(40). WO/47/17, f. 157 *et.seq.*
(41). *Occasional Papers, op.cit.*, Vol. I, p. 382.
(42). WO/55/536, Warrant of 25 July 1683 and subsequent amendments. (P.R.O.).
(43). Cleaveland, *op.cit.*, p. 51.
(44). Stowe 459, Diary of J. Richards, 1697–99 (Br. Mus.).
(45). Duncan, *op.cit.*, p. 113.
(46). WO/55/424 f. 20, (P.R.O.).
(47). *ibid.*, f. 23; Stowe 444, f. 14(b); Duncan, *op.cit.*, p. 92, (Albert Borgard's Journal).
(48). Stowe 444, ff. 13–22 (Br. Mus.).
(49). WO/55/424, ff. 36, 40, 46 & 48. (P.R.O.).
(50). Cleaveland, pp. 126–7; Het van Raa, Band VII, pp. 383–5.
(51). St Rémy, *op.cit.*, Vol. II, pp. 229–30.
(52). Stowe 444, ff. 13–22, (Br. Mus.).
(53). *Archives de l'Artillerie*, Carton 3/b/101, cited by Jouan, *op.cit.*, pp. 60–1.
(54). WO/47/18, f. 429, dated 14 March 1695–6.
(55). Treas./1/84, f. 35, & Clode, *op.cit.*, Vol. II, pp. 668 *et seq.*
(56). Stowe 444, f. 9 (Br.Mus.).
(57). St Rémy, *op.cit.*, Vol. II, p. 263.
(58). Picard & Jouan, *op.cit.*, p. 49.
(59). *ibid.*, pp. 53 & 60.
(60). *ibid.*, pp. 44–46.
(61). Mérode-Westerloo, *op.cit.*, p. 167.
(62). Daniel, *op.cit.*, Vol. II, Livre XIV, Ch. 10, p. 724.
(63). J. H. Owen *War at Sea under Queen Anne* (Cambridge: 1938), p. 30.
(64). Daniel, *op.cit.*, Vol. II, Ch. 10 *passim.*
(65). St Rémy, *op.cit.*, Vol. I, p. 212.
(66). Cited by A. Manucy *Artillery through the Ages* (Washington: 1955), p. 65.
(67). Anon., *An Impartial Account of ye Campagne of 1689* (London: 1690), p. 17.
(68). Stowe 444, f. 16 (Br. Mus.).
(69). M. de la Vallière the Younger *Mémoire touchant le superiorité des pièces d'artillerie longues et solides* Archives de l'Artillerie, Carton 4(b), f. 14.
(70). See Picard & Jouan, *op.cit.*, pp. 63–4.
(71). St Rémy, *op.cit.*, Vol. I, p. 257.
(72). Picard & Jouan, *op.cit.*, p. 67.
(73). Colin, *op.cit.*, p. 60, *et seq.*
(74). Gibb & Bowen, *Islamic Society and the West* (Oxford: 1950), Vol. I, p. 187 &

A. de Juchereau, *Histoire de l'Empire Ottoman depuis 1792* (Paris: 1844), Vol. I, p. 472.

(75). Stowe 458, entries under 25 April and 18 May, 1693 (Br. Mus.).

(76). Strafford Papers, Sloane 3392, dated 20 Sept. 1703 (Br. Mus.).

(77). Parker, *op.cit.*, p. 31.

(78). Stowe 471, ff. 52–3 (Br. Mus.).

(79). King William's Chest, SP/8/13, f. 93, (P.R.O.).

(80). Calendar of State Papers (Domestic), 1689–90, p. 347.

(81). WO/47/18, f. 431 (P.R.O.).

(82). See D. G. Chandler, *The Campaigns of Napoleon* (New York: 1966), p. 266.

(83). Stowe 444, entries as dated.

(84). Parker, *op.cit.*, p. 57.

(85). M. de Saxe, cited by Picard & Jouan, *op.cit.*, p. 111.

(86). A. Pernot, *Aperçu historique sur le service des transports militaires* (Paris: 1894), p. 63.

(87). St Rémy, *op.cit.*, Vol. II, pp. 224–31.

(88). Stowe 444, ff. 23–4.

(89). Cited by Picard & Jouan, *op.cit.*, p. 115.

(90). J. Colin, *Les Campagnes de Maréchal de Saxe* (Paris: 1901–6), Vol. I, p. 112.

(91). Stowe 458, entry as dated (Br. Mus.).

(92). Mérode-Westerloo, *op.cit.*, p. 167.

(93). See C. Walton, *History of the English Standing Army, 1660–1700* (London: 1894), p. 133.

(94). Stowe 444, entry under 5 July 1692 (Br. Mus.).

(95). Walton, *op.cit.*, pp. 198–9.

(96). Stowe 444, entry under 26 July 1692 (Br. Mus.).

(97). St Rémy, *op.cit.*, Vol. II, pp. 232–40.

(98). Stowe 444 ff. 23–4 (Br. Mus.).

(99). Hardy de Périni, *Batailles Françaises*, Vol. V (1672–1700), p. 118.

(100). St Rémy, *op.cit.*, Vol. III, Ch. VI, pp. 276–7.

(101). Stowe 444, entry under 3 August (Br. Mus.).

(102). St Rémy, *op.cit.*, Vol. I, pp. 101–3.

(103). Victor Hugo, *'1793'* (Paris: 1854) & C. S. Forester, *The Happy Return* (London: 1948), pp. 122–3.

(104). Col. C. Field, *Echoes of Old Wars* (London: n.d.), p. 78.

(105). Mérode-Westerloo, *op.cit.*, p. 168.

(106). *Letters of the First Lord Orkney*, English Historical Review, 1904, p. 315.

(107). Lt. A. W. Wilson, *The Story of the Gun* (Woolwich: 1944), p. 29.

(108). St Rémy, *op.cit.*, Vol. II, p. 263.

(109). Stowe 444, entry under 16 June, 1693 (Br. Mus.).

(110). Brunet, *Histoire de l'Artillerie* (Paris: 1842), Vol. II, p. 317.

(111). Archives de l'Artillerie, Cartons 2(b) & 2(c); and see Picard & Jouan, p. 115.

(112). Revue d'Histoire, *La campagne de 1745*, March 1905, p. 467.

(113). Wilson, *op.cit.*, p. 29.

(114). *ibid.*, p. 30.

PART FOUR: *Military Engineering*

(1). Sir R. Blomfield, *Sebastien le Prestre de Vauban* (London: 1938), p. 130.

(2). Sir G. Murray, *The Marlborough Despatches* (London: 1845), Vol. I, p. 246.

(3). *ibid.*, Vol. IV, p. 237 and Vol. V, p. 503.

(4). Maurice de Saxe, *Reveries on the Art of War* (T. R. Phillips Edn.) (Harrisburg: 1944), p. 89.

(5). J. W. de Sypersteyn, *Het Leven van Menno Baron van Coehoorn* (Leeuwarden: 1860), p. 53.

(6). Ordnance Warrant WO/55/536 (1683). (P.R.O.).

(7). Cleaveland, *op.cit.*, pp. 139 and 154.

(8). See Ambert, *op.cit.*, pp. 227–9.

(9). Major-General W. Porter, *History of the Corps of Royal Engineers* (London: 1889), Vol. I, p. 59.

(10). Sypersteyn, *op.cit.*, p. 8, and Dalton, *op.cit.*, Vol. III, p. 41, f.n. 8.

(11). Ambert, *op.cit.*, p. 227.

(12). Sypersteyn, *op.cit.*, p. 32.

(13). Parker, *op.cit.* (Chandler Edn.), p. 110.

(14). M. de Vauban, *Traité de l'Attaque des Places* (Paris: 1779 Edn.), p. 51.

(15). Blomfield, *op.cit.*, p. 97.

(16). A. Allent, *Histoire du Corps Impérial du Genie* (Paris: 1805), p. 362.

(17). Blomfield, *op.cit.*, p. 160–1.

(18). Letter to Louvois dated 23 Oct. 1688 – cited by Allent, *op.cit.*, p. 218 and Blomfield, p. 97; also Murray, *op.cit.*, Vol. II, p. 312.

(19). Blomfield, *op.cit.*, p. 99 and Allent, *op.cit.*, p. 218.

(20). Royal Warrant of 14 March, 1740, cited in Cleaveland, *op.cit.*, pp. 223–4.

(21). Cleaveland, *op.cit.*, pp. 135–8 (for 1716) and pp. 196–7 (for 1717).

(22). Père Daniel, *op.cit.*, Vol. II, Book XIII, p. 544 and Allent, p. 360.

(23). C. Falls, *Great Military Battles* (London: 1964), p. 12.

(24). Het van Raa, *op.cit.*, Deel VIII, p. 384.

(25). Vauban, *l'Attaque*, *op.cit.*, p. 7.

(26). Murray, *op.cit.*, Vol. V, pp. 441–2.

(27). Horsley, *op.cit.*, p.425.

(28). Dartmouth Papers, Hist. Mss. Commission, p. 61, and Murray, *op.cit.*, Vol. IV, p. 274.

(29). Ordnance Minutes WO/47/22 (P.R.O.).

(30). Stowe 444, f. 6 (Br. Mus.).

(31). F. Ley, *Le Maréchal de Münnich et la Russie au XVIIIe Siècle* (Paris: 1959), p. 38.

(32). St Rémy, *op.cit.*, Vol. II, p. 224.

(33). C. Dalton, *George I's Army* (London: 1912), Vol. II, p. 14.

(34). *House of Commons Journal*, 7 February, 1734.

(35). Favé, *op.cit.*, p. 60.

(36). Stowe 444, f. 3 (Br. Mus.).

(37). Parker, *op.cit.*, (Chandler Edn.), p. 33.

(38). Cleaveland, *op.cit.*, p. 161.

(39). Sbornik, *Recueil de la Societé d'Histoire Russe* (St Petersburg, 1867–1917), Vol. CI, p. 517.

(40). Mérode-Westerloo, *op.cit.*, (Chandler Edn.), pp. 147 and 194.

(41). F. Ley, *op.cit.*, p. 63.

(42). See W. S. Churchill, *Marlborough*, *op.cit.*, Book II, Ch. 25 *passim*.

(43). Based upon information drawn from G. Bodart, *op.cit.*, pp. 603–4.

(44). The Earl of Orrery, *The Arte of Warre* (London: 1677), p. 15.

(45). Ambert, *op.cit.*, p. 228.

(46). de Saxe, *Rêveries, op.cit.*, p. 121.

(47). Daniel Defoe, *An Enquiry upon Projects* (London: 1697), p. 135.

(48). Tho. Savery, *The New Method of Fortification translated from the Original Dutch, of the late famous Engineer, Menno, Baron van Coehoorn* (London: 1705), p. ii.

(49). Vauban, *l'Attaque, op.cit.*, p. 30.

(50). Parker, *op.cit.*, (Chandler Edn.), pp. 22–3.

(51). Vauban, *l'Attaque, op.cit.*, p. 1.

(52). William III, *Correspondentie*, 2nd Series, Vol. III, pp. 348–9.

(55). St Rémy, *op.cit.*, Vol. II, Ch. V *passim*.

(54). De Beaurain, *Histoire Militaire de Flandres* (Paris: 1755), Vol. I, p. 63.

(55). Cleaveland, *op.cit.*, pp. 129–31.

(56). *ibid.*, p. 224.

(57). Stowe 444, f. 5 (Br. Mus.).

(58). Vauban, *Traité de la Défense des Places* (Paris: 1779 Edn.), pp. 45–101 & tables p. 128.

(59). State Papers 8/11/f. 48 (in Dutch), (P.R.O.).

(60). *Archief van A. Heinsius*, Vol. II, p. 34.

(61). Reprinted in Vauban, *La Defense* etc, pp. 301–3.

(62). *ibid.*, pp. 51–4.

(63). Tho. Lediard, *History of John, Duke of Marlborough* (London: 1736), Vol. II, p. 304.

(64). Capt. George Carleton, *Memoirs* (London: 1812), p. 29-30.

(65). Add Mss 21493, No. 2 (Br. Mus.).

(66). *Archives du Dépôt de la Guerre*, Vol. 2081, No. 327 (Cited in Pelet, *op.cit.*, p. 413).

(67). Parker, (1747 Edn.), p. 30.

(68). St Rémy, *op.cit.*, Vol. IV, Pt. IV, p. 245 *et seq.*

(69). Murray, *op.cit.*, Vol. IV, p. 177.

(70). Stowe Mss 459, entry under 14 November 1697 (Br. Mus.).

(71). Manucy, *op.cit.*, p. 53.

(72). Vauban, *l'Attaque, op.cit.*, pp. 107–10.

(73). St Rémy, *op.cit.*, Vol. I, p. 217, *et seq.*

(74). Blondel (the Elder) cited in St Rémy, *op.cit.*, Vol. I, p. 257.

(75). *ibid.*, Vol. I, p. 250 *et seq.*; for the Austrian mortar see *Das Herresgeschichtliche Museum in Wien* (Gräz-Koln: 1960), p. 39.

(76). Vauban, *l'Attaque, op.cit.*, p. 74.

(77). State Papers (Foreign), Military Expeditions, Vol. I, p. 72, (P.R.O.).

(78). Vauban, *l'Attaque, op.cit.*, pp. 87 and 94.

(79). St Rémy, *op.cit.*, Vol. II, p. 150.

(80). Lediard, *op.cit.*, Vol. II, p. 482.

(81). Daniel Defoe, *The Life and Adventures of Mother Ross* (intro. by Sir J. Fortescue) (London: 1929), p. 128.

(82). Stowe 475, f. 129b (Br. Mus.).

(83). *ibid.*, f. 133.

(84). A. Parnell, *The War of the Succession in Spain* (London: 1905), pp. 258–66.

(85). Parker, *op.cit.*, (Chandler Edn.), p. 80.

(86). Mérode-Westerloo, *op.cit.*, (Chandler Edn.), p. 207.

(87). See Lediard, *op.cit.*, Vol. II, for best account of the operations about Lille.

(88). St Rémy, *op.cit.*, Vol. I, Part Two, p. 212; this authority also gives details for both larger and smaller batteries.

(89). Vauban, *l'Attaque, op.cit.*, p. 119.

(90). *ibid.*, p. 127.

(91). St Rémy, *op.cit.*, Vol. I, Part Two, p. 213.

(92). Blomfield, *op.cit.*, p. 17.

(93). Parker, 1746 Edn., p. 34.

(94). *ibid.*, p. 56.

(95). Parker, (Chandler Edn.), pp. 22–3.

(96). Vauban, *A Manual of Siegecraft and Fortification* (trans. of the 1668 Edn. by G. R. Rothrock) (Michigan U.P.: 1968), pp. 97–104.

(97). *The Diary of Wm. Cramond*, Add Mss 29878, dated 25 September 1690 (O.S.) (Br. Mus.).

(98). Stowe Mss 230, f. 241 *et seq.*, (Br. Mus.).

(99). Add Mss 81695, ff. 167–8 (in French), (Br. Mus.).

(100). Quoted by Blomfield, *op.cit.*, p. 174.

(101). *ibid.*, p. 205-6, and Voltaire, *La Siècle de Louis XIV* (recent edn. Paris: 1966), Vol. I, p. 120.

(102). Belidor, *La Sciences des Ingenieurs* . . . (Paris: 1729).

(103). Vauban, *l'Attaque, op.cit.*, p. 209.

(104). Quoted by Blomfield, *op.cit.*, p. 52.

(105). Quoted in the *Encyclopaedia Brittanica*.

(106). Sir A. Conan Doyle, *British Campaigns in France and Flanders* (London: 1926), p. 146.

(107). Sypersteyn, *op.cit.*, p. 59.

(108). *ibid.*, p. 45.

(109). Murray, *op.cit.*, Vol. I, p. 247.

(110). Tho. Svary, *op.cit.*, p. iii.

(111). Parker, *op.cit.*, (Chandler Edn.), p. 7.

(112). Col. P. Lazard, *Vauban, 1633–1707* (Paris: 1934), p. 267 and *Mémoires de Feuquières, op.cit.*, Vol. IV, pp. 209–10.

(115). Maucy, *op.cit.*, p. 60.

(114). See *The New Cambridge Modern History*, Vol. VI, p. 743, f.n.

(115). Brigadier Sir John Smyth VC, *Sandhurst* (London: 1961), pp. 27–32.

Sources and Bibliography

1 MANUSCRIPT SOURCES

a *British Museum*
Additional Mss.
230, 444, 458, 459 and 470–481 (Stowe Mss)
745–763 (Harleyan Mss). 3392 (Sloane Mss)
4655, 4747 (Davenant Mss)
9723, 9724 (Blathwayt Mss)
19036, 21493, 21506, and 22196 (Stafford Papers)
25893, 29878 (Diary of Wm. Cramond)
32750, 35893, 81695.

b *Public Records Office*
Calendar of State Papers (Domestic) 1689–90
State Papers 8–5, –6, –8, –13, –15, –16 (King William's Chest)
Ordnance Warrants, WO/55, /536, and WO/47/22
State Papers (Military), 41/3
State Papers 8/11
State Papers (Foreign) Military Expeditions, Vol. I
Treasury Papers 1/11, 1/84
War Office Papers 24/23, /25, /38, /41, /45, /46, /47, /75
War Office Papers 26/11
War Office Papers 47/17, /18
War Office Papers 55/421, /424, /536
Regulations for Outposts etc; Orders and Regulations for Light Horse (The Hague
    1691)

c *Château de Vincennes*
Archives de l'Artillerie, Cartons 2/b, 2/c; 3/b/101; 4/b (Vallière the Younger)
Archives du Dépôt de la Guerre, vols 1552, 1554, 1651, 1836, 2081.

d *Historical Manuscripts Commission*
Atholl Papers (1891)
Buccleuch Papers (1903)
Bath Papers (1904)
Chequers Court Mss (1900)

Dartmouth Papers (Report XI, 1887)
Northumberland Papers (1872)
Portland Papers (1930)
Spencer Papers (1871)

e *Elsewhere*
Archief van A. Heinsius (The Hague)
Occasional Papers, R. A. Institute (Woolwich)
Blenheim Palace Papers
Apthorpe Papers

2 PRINTED BIBLIOGRAPHIES AND MILITARY ENCYCLOPAEDIAS

Bodart, G., *Militär-historisches Kriegs-Lexicon 1618–1905*, (Vienna & Leipzig: 1908)
Delbruck, H., *Geschichte der Kriegskunst*, Vols. 1 & 2 (Berlin: 1900 *et seq.*)
Dupuy and Dupuy, *The Encyclopaedia of Military History*, (London: 1970)
Eggenberger, D., *A Dictionary of Battles*, (London: 1967)
Harbottle, T. B., *A Dictionary of Battles*, (London: 1905)
Jähns M., *Geschichte der Kriegswissenschaften*, 3 vols. (Berlin: 1889–91)
Pohler, J., *Bibliotheca historico-militaris*, Vol. 1 (Munich: 1890)

3 PRINTED DOCUMENTARY SOURCES

Correspondance de Napoléon Iier, vols. xxvi, xxx, xxxi, (Paris: 1870 *et seq.*)
Dalton C., *Army Lists and Commission Registers*, 6 vols., (London: 1898–1904)
Eugene, Prince, *Feldzüge des Prinz Eugen von Savoyen*, 1st & 2nd Series, (Vienna: 1876–92)
Journals of the House of Commons, (London, various dates)
Murray Sir G. (Editor), *The Letters and Dispatches of John Churchill*, 5 vols., (London: 1845)
Pelet J. & Vault F. le, *Mémoires militaires relatifs à la succession d'Espagne sous Louis XIV*, 11 vols. & atlas, (Paris: 1836–42)
Raa J. W. van, *Het Staatsche Leger (1702–15)*, Part VIII, 22 vols., (The Hague: 1953–9)
Van 'T Hoff B., *The Correspondence 1701–11 of John Churchill and Anthonie Heinsius*, (The Hague: 1891)
William III, King, *Correspondentie*, (2nd series), vol. 3, (London: 1843)

4 GENERAL WORKS

Boudet, J., *The Ancient Art of Warfare*, 2 vols., (Paris: 1966, London: 1969)
Chandler, D., *The Art of Warfare on Land*, (London: 1974)
Fisher, H. A. L., *A History of Europe*, (London: 1943)
Hamley, E. D. B., *Operations of War*, 7th Edition, (Edinburgh: 1923)
Matloff, M., (Editor), *American Military History*, (Washington: 1969)
Montgomery, B. L., *A History of Warfare*, (London: 1968)
Preston, Wise and Werner, *Men in Arms*, (London: 1956)

Spaulding, Nickerson and Wright, *Warfare*, (London: 1925)
Weygand, General, *L'Armée Francaise*, (Paris: 1938)
Young, P. & Lawford J., *History of the British Army*, (London: 1970)

5 CONTEMPORARY PUBLISHED WORKS AND MEMOIRS

Anon. *An Impartial Account of the Campagne of 1689*, (London: 1690), probably by W. Sawle
Anon. *The Exercise for the Horse, Dragoons and Foot Forces,G.II. R,*(London: 1739)
Auvergne, E. d', *History of the Campagne in Flanders . . . 1693*, (London: 1694)
Belidor, M. de, *La Science des Ingenieurs dans la conduite des travaux de fortification*, (Paris: 1729)
Carleton, Capt. George, *Memoirs*, (London: 1925)
Catinat, Maréchal de, *Mémoires et Correspondance*, (Paris: 1819)
Chevert, M. de., *Essai Générale de Tactique*, (Paris: n.d.)
Defoe, D., *An Enquiry upon Projects*, (London: 1697)
–, *The Life and Adventures of Mother Ross*, (ed. Sir J. Fortescue), (London: 1929)
Demorinet, J., *Le Major Parfait*, (n.p.: 1683)
Feuquières, Lt. Général A. M. de Pas, Marquis de, *Mémoires*, (Paris: 1775)
Folard, le Chevalier de., *Commentaire sur Polybe*, (Paris: 1754)
–, *Traité de la Colonne*, (Paris: 1754)
Friedrich de Grosse, *Militärische Schriften*, (ed. Gen. von Taysen), (Berlin: 1893)
Gooding, S. J. (ed.), *The Military Exercise 1730*, (Ontario: 1962)
Guignard, M. de., *L'Ecole de Mars*, 2 vols, (Paris: 1725)
Horsley, J. C. (ed.), *The Chronicles of an Old Campaigner (J–M de la Colonie)*, (London: 1904)
Kane, R., *The Campaigns of King William and Queen Anne*, (London: 1745)
–, *Discipline for a Regiment of Foot upon Action . . .*, (London: 1745)
Le Blond, M., *Elémens de Tactique*, (Paris: 1758)
Lediard, T., *Life of John, Duke of Marlborough*, 3 vols, (London: 1736)
Mackay, H., *Memoirs, Letters and a Short Relation*, (Edinburgh: 1873)
Marsigli, Count, *L'État militaire de l'Empire Ottoman*, (Amsterdam: 1752)
Mérode-Westerloo, Comte de, *Mémoires*, 2 vols, (Brussels: 1840)
–, *Memoirs*, (abridged version, ed. & trs., D. G. Chandler), (London: 1968)
Military Dictionary, by an Officer . . ., (London: 1702)
Montecuculi, R. de, *Mémoires, ou principes de l'art militaire*, (Paris: 1712)
Parker, Capt. Robert, *Memories of the Most Memorable Military Transactions*, (Dublin: 1746)
–, *ibid*, (abridged version, ed. D. G. Chandler), (London: 1968)
Puységur, Marechal J. F. de, *L'Art de la Guerre . . .*, 2 vols, (Paris: 1748)
St Rémy, S. de, *Memorial de l'Artillerie*, 2 vols, (Paris: 1693; Amsterdam: 1702)
St Simon, Duc de, *Mémoires*, 40 vols, (Paris: 1881–1907)
Santa-Cruz, Marquis de, *Réflexions Militaires*, 4 vols, (Paris: n.d.)
Savery, T., *The New Method of Fortification . . . of the late famous Engineer, Menno, Baron van Coehoorn*, (London: 1705)
Sawle, W., *An Impartial Relation of the late Campagne in Flanders*, (London: 1691)
Saxe, Maréchal de, *Rêveries on the Art of War*, (ed. T. R. Philips), (Harrisburg: 1944)
–, *Mes Rêveries*, (Paris: 1757)
Smorgen, Regulations of, (Stockholm: 1708)

Stenbock, General, *Instructions*, (Wäxjö: 1710)
Story, G., *An Impartial Relation of the War in Ireland*, (London: 1693)
Vauban, S. le P., *Traité de l'Attaque des Places*, (edition, Paris: 1779)
–, *Traité de la Défense des Places*, (edition, Paris: 1779)
–, *On Mines*, (edition, London: 1792)
–, *Project d'une Dîme Royale*, (Paris: 1707)
–, *A Manual of Siegecraft and Fortification*, (new edn. of the 1668 version ed. G. R. Rothrock), (Michigan: 1968)
Voltaire, F. M. A. de, *La Siècle de Louis XIV*, (edition, Paris: 1929)
–, *La Siècle de Louis XV*, (Paris: 1826)
Villars, C. L. H., Duc de, *Mémoires*, (ed. by de Vogüé), (Paris: 1887)

6 PUBLISHED SECONDARY AUTHORITIES

Allent, A., *Histoire du Corps Impérial du Genie*, (Paris: 1805)
Ambert, J., *Equisses Historiques de l'Armee Française*, (Brussels: 1840)
Anon., *A Short History of the Highland Regiments*, (London: 1743)
Arneth, A., *Prinz Eugen von Savoyen*, 3 vols, (Vienna: 1858–64)
Ashley, M., *Marlborough*, (London: 1939)
Atkinson, C. T., *Marlborough and the Rise of the British Army*, (London: 1924)
Barnett, C., *A History of the British Army*, (London: 1970)
–, *Marlborough*, (London: 1974)
Baxter, S. B., *William III*, (London: 1966)
Beaurain, J. de, *Histoire Militaire de Flandres*, 2 vols, (Paris: 1755)
Belloc, H., *The Tactics and Strategy of the Great Duke of Marlborough*, (London: 1933)
Bengtsson, F. G. *Life of Charles XII, King of Sweden*, (London: 1960)
Blackmore, H. L., *British Military Firearms, 1650–1856*, (London: 1961)
Blomfield, Sir R., *Sebastien le Prestre de Vauban*, (London: 1938)
Bonaparte, Louis-Napoléon, & Favé, Col., *Études sur le passé et l'avenir de l'Artillerie*, (Paris: 1863)
Boulanger, J., *Le Grand Siècle*, (Paris: 1949)
Brunet, J., *Histoire de l'Artillerie*, (Paris: 1842)
Burton, I. F., *The Captain-General*, (London: 1968)
Cambridge Modern History, the New, vols 6 & 7, (London: 1970 & 1964)
Cannon, R., *Historical Records of the British Army*, vol 18, (London: 1835)
Chandler, D. G., *The Campaigns of Napoleon*, (London: 1967)
–, (ed.), *Two Soldiers of Marlborough's Wars: Robert Parker and the Comte de Mérode-Westerloo*, (London: 1968)
–, *Marlborough as Military Commander*, (London: 1973)
Churchill, Sir W. S., *Marlborough, his Life and Times*, 4 vols, (London: 1933–8)
–, *History of the English Speaking Peoples*, vol 2, (London: 1956)
Clark, Sir G. N., *The Seventeenth Century*, (Oxford: 1947)
Cleaveland, Col., *Notes on the Early History of the Royal Regiment of Artillery*, (London: n.d.)
Clode, C. M., *The Military Forces of the Crown*, (London: 1869)
Colin, J., *L'Infanterie au XVIIIième siècle*, (Paris: 1907)
–, *Les Campagnes du Maréchal de Saxe*, 5 vols, (Paris: 1901–6)
Conan Doyle, Sir A., *British Campaigns in France and Flanders*, (London: 1920)

Coxe, Archdeacon W. C., *Memoirs of John, Duke of Marlborough,* 6 vols, (London: 1820)

Dalton, C., *George I's Army,* 2 vols, (London: 1912)

Daniel, R. P., *Histoire de la Milice Française,* 2 vols, (Paris: 1721)

Denison, G. T., *A History of Cavalry,* (London: 1913)

Duffy, C. F., *Fire and Stone* (London: 1975).

Duncan, F., *History of the Royal Regiment of Artillery,* 2 vols, (London: 1874)

Dussieux, E., *L'Armée en France,* (Paris: n.d.)

Falls, Capt. C., *The Art of War,* (London: 1960)

–,(ed.), *Great Military Battles,* (London: 1964)

Forbes, A., *History of the Army Ordnance Services,* 2 vols, (London: 1929)

Fortescue, Sir J. W., *A History of the British Army,* vol 1, (London: 1899)

Fuller, J. F. C., *British Light Infantry in the 18th Century,* (London: 1925)

–, *The Decisive Battles of the Western World,* 3 vols, (London: 1953–5)

–, *The Conduct of War 1618–1960,* (London: 1961)

Gibbs & Bowen, *Islamic Society and the West,* 2 vols, (London: 1950)

Groehler, O., *Die Kriege Friedrichs II,* (Berlin: 1966)

Grosse, F., *Military Antiquities,* 2 vols, (London: 1786)

Hatton, R. M., *Charles XII,* (London: 1968)

Henderson, N. P., *Prince Eugen of Savoy,* (London: 1964)

Hill, C., *The Century of Revolution, 1603–1713,* (London: 1967)

Hutchinson, J. R., *The Romance of a Regiment,* (London: 1898)

Juchereau, A. de, *Histoire de l'Empire Ottoman . . .,* (Paris: 1844)

Kamen, H., *The War of Succession in Spain,* (London: 1969)

Klopp, O., *Der Fall des Hauses Stuart,* 14 vols, (Vienna: 1875–8)

Knotel, R. H., and Sieg, H., *Handbuch der Uniformkunde,* (Hamburg: 1966)

Laver, J., *British Military Uniforms,* (London: 1948)

Lazard, Col. P., *Vauban, 1633–1707,* (London: 1934)

Ley, F., *Le Maréchal de Münnich et la Russie au XVIIIième siècle,* (Paris: 1959)

Malleson, J. B., *Loudon,* (London: 1884)

Manucy, A., *Artillery Through the Ages,* (Washington: 1955)

Mouillard L., *Les Régiments de Louis XV,* (Paris: 1882)

Ogg, D., *Europe in the 17th Century,* (London: 1948)

Parnell, A., *The War of Succession in Spain,* (London: 1905)

Perine, H. de, *Batailles Françaises,* vol 5, (Paris: n.d.)

Pernot, A., *Aperçu historique sur la service des transports militaires,* (Paris: 1894)

Picard, E. & Jouan, L., *L'Artillerie Française au 18ième siècle,* (Paris: 1906)

Quimby, R. S., *The Background of Napoleonic Warfare,* (New York: 1957)

Rostaing, M. de, *L'Exposé des batailles de la Guerre, 1733–48,* (Paris: n.d.)

Rousset, C., *Histoire de Louvois,* 4 vols, (Paris: 1862–3)

–, *Correspondance de Louis XIV et du Maréchal de Noailles,* (Paris: 1889)

Sbornik, M. de, *Recueil de la Société d'Histoire Russe,* vol CI, (St Petersburg: 1867–1917)

Scouller, R. E., *The Armies of Queen Anne,* (Oxford: 1966)

Smyth, Sir J., *The Story of Sandhurst,* (London: 1963)

Sypersteyn, J. W. de, *Het Leven van Menno van Coehoorn,* (Leewarden: 1860)

Taylor, Sir F., *The Wars of Marlborough 1702–09,* (Oxford: 1921)

Trevelyan, Sir G. M., *England in the Reign of Queen Anne,* 3 vols, (London: 1930–4)

Turner, G. B., *A History of Military Affairs in Western Society,* (New York: 1953)

Wace, A., *The Marlborough Tapestries at Blenheim Palace,* (London: 1968)

Wagner, E., *Cut and Thrust Weapons*, (London: 1967)

Walton, C., *The British Standing Army, 1660–1700*, (London: 1894)

Weaver, L., *The Story of the Royal Scots*, (London: n.d.)

Wilson, A. W., *The Story of the Gun*, (Woolwich: 1944)

Wolseley, Field-Marshal G. J., *Life of Marlborough to the Accession of Queen Anne*, 2 vols, (London: 1894)

Young, D. and Adair, J. E., *From Hastings to Culloden*, (London: 1964)

Young, P., *The British Army, 1642–1970*, (London: 1967)

Note: Sources used in the introduction to this volume will be found cited in full in the relevant footnotes.

General appendices

NOTES

1. This section is organized as follows:–
   Appendix One – List of major wars, 1688–1745, and summary of engagements.
   Appendix Two – List of major land engagements, and capitulations in the field.
   Appendix Three – List of sieges and capitulations of field forces inside towns.
   Appendix Four – Dates of specimen sieges.
2. *Dating:* New Style dates used throughout; in some cases authorities differ on exact dates of sieges etc; the ones given here are the most probable.
3. *Categories:* All engagements are rated from A to D depending on *total* casualties:–
   A – over 30,000 (land)   B – over 20,000
   C – over 10,000 (land)   D – under 10,000
       Other types of military activity are categorized as follows:
   S+ – siege which succeeded (see *Result* column for details); S^{++} – siege abandoned.
   S(cap) – capitulation of a field force within the town as well as the garrison.

Bav. – Bavarians	*P'mont.* – Piedmontese
Eng. (or *Br.*) – English (or British)	*Pruss.* – Prussians
Fr. – French	*Russ.* – Russians
Hung. – Hungarians	*Sax.* – Saxons
Imp. – Imperialists	*Span.* – Spaniards
Ital. – Italians	*Tur.* – Turks

5. *Casualties:* those under a) represent the successful side; under b) the losers.
   When authorities differ on details, the figures given are the most probable.
   n.d. reveals that no reliable details are available. All figures quoted are to be regarded as only approximate.

APPENDIX ONE

MAJOR WARS 1688–1745 AND SUMMARY OF ENGAGEMENTS ANALYSED BELOW

Dates*		Title	Total Battles A – C	Other land actions	Sieges	Caps. in Field
1.	(1682)–1699	Austro-Turkish War	3	3	2	–
2.	1688–1697	Nine Years' War (or War of Augsburg)	4	5	6	–
3.	1700–1721	Great Northern War	4	16	3	2
4.	1701–1714	War of the Spanish Succession	9	27	25	–
5.	1703–1711	Hungarian Revolt	–	7	–	1
6.	1710–1712	Russo-Turkish War	1	–	–	1
7.	1715	Scottish Rebellion	–	1	–	–
8.	1716–1718	Austro-Venetian War against the Turks	2	2	3	–
9.	1718–1720	War of the Quadruple Alliance against Spain	–	2	1	–
10.	1737–1738	War of the Polish Succession	1	4	2	1
11.	1736–1739	Austro-Russian War against the Turks	1	4	4	–
12.	1740–(1748)	War of the Austrian Succession	5	11	7[+]	–
13.	1741–1742	Russo-Swedish War	–	1	1	–
14.	1745–(1746)	Scottish Rebellion	–	3	–	–

* Dates given in parenthesis indicate periods not within the limits of this volume.

APPENDIX TWO

MAJOR LAND BATTLES AND CAPITULATIONS

Name	Date	War	Category	Contestants a)	Contestants b)	Casualties a)	Casualties b)	Result
Derbend	1688 5 September	1	D	a) Baden: 12,000 Imperialists	b) Pasha of Bosnia: 15,000 Turks	a) 200	b) 7,000 (incl. 2,000 Pws.)	Imp. victory.
Nissa	24 September	1	C	a) Baden: 17,000 Imperialists	b) Redschid Pasha: 40,000 Turks	a) 400	b) 10,000 (& 30 guns)	Imp. victory.
Fleurus	1690 1 July	2	B	a) Luxembourg: 50,000 French	b) Waldeck: 38,000 Imp. & Allies	a) 6,000	b) 19,000 (& 49 guns)	Fr. victory.
The Boyne	11 July	2	D	a) William III: 35,000 Anglo-Dutch	b) James II: 23,000 Irish & French	a) 2,000	b) 1,500	Eng. victory.
Staffarda	18 August	2	D	a) Catinat: 12,000 French	b) Victor Amadeus: 18,000 P'ment	a) 2,000	b) 4,000 (incl. 1,200 Pws. & 11 guns)	Fr. victory.
Aughrim	1691 22 July	2	D	a) Ginckel: 18,000 Anglo-Dutch	b) Saint-Just: 25,000 Irish & French	a) 2,700	b) 4,400 (& 6 guns)	Eng. victory.
Szlankamen	19 August	1	B	a) Baden: 50,000 Imperialists (56 Bns. & 116 Sqns.)	b) Mustapha Köprili: 100,000 Turks (70,000 Inf, 30,000 Cav., 154 guns)	a) 8,000	b) 20,000 (& 154 guns)	Imp. triumph.
Leuze	19 September	2	D	a) Luxembourg: 4,000 French	b) Waldeck: 12,000 Dutch & Allies	a) 700	b) 1,900 (incl. 1,400 Pws.)	Fr. victory.
Steenkirk	3 August	2	B	a) Luxembourg: 57,000 French	b) William III: 70,000 Allies	a) 7,000 (& 8 guns)	b) 8,000 (incl. 1,400 Pws. & 10 guns)	French success.
Landen	1693 29 July	2	B	a) Luxembourg: 80,000 French (98 Bns, 201 Sqns., 71 guns)	b) William III: 50,000 Allies	a) 9,000	b) 14,000 (& 84 guns)	French victory.
Marsaglia	4 October	2	C	a) Catinat: 40,000 French	b) Victor Amadeus: 36,000 P'mont	a) 3,000	b) 11,000 (incl. 2,000 Pws. & 24 guns)	Fr. victory.
Toroella	1694 27 May	2	D	a) de Noailles: 26,000 French	b) Escalona: 20,000 Spaniards	a) 1,300	b) 5,700 (incl. 2,200 Pws.)	Fr. victory.
Lugos	1695 20 September	1	D	a) Mustapha II: 50,000 Turks	b) Veterani: 8,000 Imp.	a) n.d.	b) 5,000	Turk. victory.
Olaschin	1696 26 August	1	D	a) Mustapha II: 60,000 Turks	b) Augustus II of Saxony: 50,000 Imp.	a) 4,000	b) n.d.	Turk. victory.
Zenta	1697 11 September	1	A	a) Eugene: 50,000 Imperialists (51 Bns, 112 Sqns., 60 guns)	b) Elmas Mohammed: 100,000 Turks (60,000 Inf, 40,000 Cav., 200 guns)	a) 2,100	b) 30,000 (& 45 guns)	Imp. triumph.
Narva	1700 30 November	3	B	a) Charles XII: 10,000 Swedes (21 Bns, 48 Sqns., 37 guns)	b) Croy: 40,000 Russ. & Allies plus 20,000 irregulars	a) 2,000	b) 20,000 (& 179 guns)	Swedish triumph.
Carpi	1701 9 July	4	D	a) Eugene: 22,000 Imperialists	b) Villeroi: 38,000 French & Italians	a) 100	b) 500 (incl. 150 Pws)	Imp. success.
Riga	18 July	3	D	a) Charles XII: 8,000 Swedes	b) Steinau: 20,000 Russians & Allies	a) 1,200	b) 2,800 (& 26 guns)	Swedish vic.
Chiari	1 September	4	D	a) Eugene: 22,000 Imperialists	b) Villeroi: 38,000 French & Allies	a) 200	b) 3,800 (incl. 200 Pws)	Imp. victory.
Kasaritsch	16 September	3	D	a) Schippenbach: 6,000 Swedes	b) Scheremetjew: 8,000 Russians	a) 800	b) 1,000	Swedish vic.
Erestfer	1702 9 January	3	D	a) Scheremetjew: 12,000 Russians	b) Schippenbach: 5,000 Swedes	a) 1,200	b) 1,800 (incl. 400 Pws & 4 guns)	Russian vic.
Cremona	1 February	4	D	a) Crénant: 10,000 Fr. & Span.	b) Eugene: 8,000 Imperialists	a) 1,500	b) 1,200 (incl. 400 Pws)	French vic.
Nimwegen	11 June	4	D	a) Burgundy: 25,000 French	b) Ginckel: 23,000 Dutch	a) 200	b) 700 (incl. 300 Pws)	French success.

Name	Date	War	Category	Contestants a)	Contestants b)	Casualties a)	Casualties b)	Result
Kletschow	1702 19 July	3	D	a) Charles XII: 17,000 Swedes	b) Steinau: 22,000 Saxons & Poles	a) 1,100	b) 3,900 (incl. 1,900 Pws)	Swedish vic.
Hummelshof	29 July	3	D	a) Scheremetjew: 15,000 Russians	b) Schlippenbach: 4,000 Swedes	a) 1,400	b) 1,600 (incl. 400 Pws)	Russian vic.
Santa Vittoria	26 July	4	D	a) Vendôme: 4,000 French	b) Visconti: 2,800 Imperialists	a) 200	b) 1,000 (incl. 400 Pws)	French vic.
Luzzara	15 August	4	D	a) Eugene: 25,000 Imperialists	b) Vendôme: 30,000 French	a) 2,700	b) 3,500	Stalemate.
Friedlingen	14 October	4	D	a) Villars: 17,000 French	b) Baden: 14,000 Imperialists	a) 2,700	b) 2,900	French success.
Siegbardin	1703 11 March	4	D	a) Elector of Bavaria: 12,000 Bav.	b) Schlick: 10,000 Imperialists	a) 500	b) 2,500	Bavarian suc.
Schagarin	27 March	3	D	a) Lewenhaupt: 1,300 Swedes	b) Oginski: 8,700 Russians	a) 200	b) 3,000	Swedish suc.
Stollhofen Lines	19–25 April	4	Passage	a) Baden: 24,000 Imperialists	b) Villars: 35,000 French	a) 200	b) 2,700	Imp. success.
Pultusk	1 May.	3	D	a) Charles XII: 2,000 Swedes	b) Steinau: 12,000 Saxons & Poles	a) 600	b) 2,000	Swedish suc.
Steckene	27 June	4	D	a) Sparr: 7,000 Dutch	b) Hessey: 2,500 French & Spanish	a) 1,300	b) 700	Costly Dutch success.
Eckenren	30 June	4	D	a) Boufflers: 19,000 Fr. & Sp.	b) Opdam: 15,000 Dutch & Allies	a) 2,300	b) 3,300 (incl. 800 Pws & 48 guns)	French vic.
Höchstädt	20 September	4	D	a) Elector of Bavaria & Villars:— 23,000 Fr. & Bav.	b) Styrum: 18,000 Imperialists	a) 1,500	b) 4,500 (& 37 guns)	Fr-Bav. suc.
Speyer	15 November	4	C	a) Tallard: 8,000 French	b) Hesse-Cassel: 20,000 Imperialists	a) 4,000	b) 6,000 (incl. 2,000 Pws & 23 guns)	French vic.
Castelnuovo	1704 11 January	4	D	a) Vendôme: 10,000 Fr. & Sp.	b) Solari: 4,000 Spaniards	a) 1,500	b) 900 (incl. 900 Pws)	French success.
Eisenstadt	20 March	5	D	a) Heister: 4,400 Imperialists	b) Károlyi: 10,000 Hungarians	a) n.d.	b) 2,000	Imp. success.
Schmöllnitz	28 May.	5	D	a) Bercséni: 10,000 Hungarians	b) Ritschau: 2,400 Imperialists	a) 400	b) 1,600 (& 4 guns)	Rebel success.
Raab	13 June	5	D	a) Heister: 3,600 Imperialists	b) Forgach: 7,400 Hungarians	a) 200	b) 2,800 (incl. 2,000 Pws & 6 guns)	Imp. success.
Schellenberg	2 July	4	C	a) Marlborough: 25,000 Allies	b) d'Arco: 11,000 French & Bavarians	a) 6,000	b) 4,000 (& 16 guns)	Allied success.
Blenheim	13 August	4	A	a) Marlborough: 52,000 Allies (65 Bns., 160 Sqns., 60 guns)	b) Tallard: 56,000 French & Bavarians (79 Bns, 140 Sqn., 90 guns)	a) 12,000	b) 34,000 (incl. 14,000 Pws & 72 guns)	Allied victory.
Pata	8 October	5	D	a) Bussy-Rabutin: 3,000 Imp.	b) Cassus: 12,000 Hungarians	a) 100	b) 4,000	Imp. victory.
Punitz	7 November	3	D	a) Schulenburg: 6,500 Russ. & Sax.	b) Charles XII: 9,000 Swedes	a) 1,000	b) 2,000	Saxons escaped.
Tyrnau	26 December	5	D	a) Heister: 7,000 Imperialists	b) Rákóczi: 20,000 Hungarians	a) 500	b) 2,000 (& 30 guns)	Imp. success.
Elixhem	1705 18 July	4	Passage and D	a) Marlborough: 14,000 Anglo-Dutch	b) Caraman: 15,000 French & Bavarians	a) 200	b) 2,000 (& 18 guns)	Allied success.
Gemauerthof	27 February	3	D	a) Lewenhaupt: 7,000 Swedes	b) Scheremetjew: 20,000 Russians	a) 1,000	b) 5,000	Swedish vic.
Cassano	16 August	4	D	a) Vendôme: 22,000 Fr. & Sp.	b) Eugene: 24,000 Imperialists	a) 3,000	b) 4,500 (inc. 500 Pws & 7 guns)	French success.
Zsibó	11 November	5	D	a) Herbeville: 13,000 Imp.	b) Rákóczi: 24,000 Hungarians	a) 600	b) 6,000 (& 28 guns)	Imp. success.

(Appendix 2 Cont.)

Name	Date	War	Category	Contestants a)	Contestants b)	Casualties a)	Casualties b)	Result
Fraustadt	1706 13 February	3	C	a) Rhenskjold: 12,000 Swedes	b) Schulenburg: 18,000 Saxons & Allies	a) 2,000	b) 13,000 (inc. 8,000 Pws & 31 guns)	Swedish triumph.
Calcinate	19 April	4	D	a) Vendôme: 41,000 Fr. & Sp.	b) Reventlow: 19,000 Imp. & Prussians	a) 500	b) 3,000 (& 6 guns)	French victory.
Ramillies	23 May	4	C	a) Marlborough: 62,000 Allies (74 Bns., 123 Sqns., 120 guns)	b) Villeroi: 60,000 Fr., Span., & Bav. (70 Bns, 132 Sqns., 70 guns)	a) 3,600	b) 18,000 (inc. 6,000 Pws & 54 guns)	Allied triumph.
Turin	7 September	4	C	a) Eugene: 30,000 Imperialists (plus 5,000 militia)	b) Burgundy: 60,000 Fr., Span. & Bv. (only 17,000 engaged)	a) 3,000	b) 9,000 (inc. 6,000 Pws & 213 guns)	Imp. success.
Castiglione	9 September	4	D	a) Medavi: 15,000 French	b) Hesse-Cassel: 10,000 Imperialists	a) 1,000	b) 4,000 (inc. 2,500 Pws & 20 guns)	French success.
Kalisch	29 October	3	D	a) Menshikoff: 36,000 Russ. & Sax.	b) Mardefeld: 12,000 Swedes	a) 1,000	b) 4,000 (inc. 2,600 Pws)	Russian vic.
Almanza	1707 25 April	4	C	a) Berwick: 30,000 Fr. & Span. (72 Bns., 77 Sqns., 40 guns)	b) Galway: 15,000 Allies (25 Bns, 77 Sqns., 30 guns)	a) 2,000	b) 7,000 (inc. 3,000 Pws & 24 guns)	Fr.-Spanish victory.
Lines of Stollhofen	22 May	4	Passage	a) Villars: 30,000 French	b) Bayreuth: 20,000 Imperialists	a) n.d.	b) n.d.	French success.
Oudenarde	1708 11 July	4	B	a) Marlborough: 80,000 Allies (85 Bns, 150 Sqns., 110 guns)	b) Vendôme & Burgundy: 80,000 Fr. & Span. (90 Bns, 170 Sqns.)	a) 4,000	b) 15,000 (inc. 8,250 Pws & 25 guns)	Allied victory.
Golontschin	12 July	3	D	a) Charles XII: 7,000 Swedes	b) Repnin: 33,000 Russians	a) 1,600	b) 1,500 (inc. 600 Pws & 24 guns)	Swedish suc.
Trentschin	4 August	5	D	a) Heister: 10,000 Imperialists	b) Rácóczi: 16,000 Hungarians	a) 500	b) 6,500 (inc. 500 Pws & 14 guns)	Imp. success.
Dobroje	11 September	3	D	a) Charles XII: 12,000 Swedes	b) Galitzin: 6,000 Russians	a) 2,000	b) 3,000	Swedish vic.
Wynendael	28 September	4	D	a) Webb: 11,000 Allies	b) La Motte: 22,000 French	a) 1,000	b) 3,000 (inc. 500 Pws & 19 guns)	British suc.
Propoisk	9 October	3	C	a) Menshikov: 17,000 Russians	b) Lewenhaupt: 13,000 Swedes	a) 4,000	b) 6,000 (inc. 1,000 Pws & 17 guns)	Russian vic.
Hondschoote	14 November	4	D	a) Monroux: 3,000 French	b) Katten: 1,200 Prussians	a) 200	b) 1,200 (inc. 1,000 Pws)	French success.
Poltava	1709 9 July	3	C	a) Tsar Peter I: 80,000 Russians (58 Bns, 70 Sqns., 100 guns)	b) Charles XII: 21,500 Swedes (18 Regts, 12 Sqns., 4 guns)	a) 1,300	b) 9,600 (inc. 2,800 Pws & 4 guns)	Russian vic.
Perewolotscha	28 July	3	Cap.	a) Menschikov: 40,000 Russians	b) Lewenhaupt: 14,000 Swedes	a) nil	b) 14,000 Pws	Result of Poltava.
Rumersheim	26 August	4	D	a) Du Bourg: 6,000 French	b) Mercy: 7,000 Imperialists	a) 400	b) 2,600 & 4 guns	French success.
Malplaquet	11 September	4	A	a) Marlborough: 110,000 Allies (128 Bns., 253 Sqns., 100 guns)	b) Villars: 80,000 French (96 Bns, 180 Sqns., 60 guns)	a) 24,000	b) 12,000 (inc. 3,000 Pws & 16 guns)	Costly Allied success.
Helsingborg	1710 10 March	3	D	a) Steenbock: 14,000 Swedes	b) Rantzau: 11,000 Danes	a) 3,000	b) 6,000 (inc. 2,000 Pws)	Swedish vic.
Almenara	27 July	4	D	a) Stahremburg: 24,000 Allies	b) Villadarias: 22,000 Fr. & Span.	a) 400	b) 1,800 (inc. 300 Pws)	Allied vic.
Saragossa	1710 20 August	4	C	a) Stahremburg: 22,000 Allies	b) De Bay: 20,000 French & Spanish	a) 1,600	b) 10,000 (inc. 5,000 Pws & 36 guns)	Allied vic.

Name	Date	War	Category	Contestants a)	Contestants b)	Casualties a)	Casualties b)	Result
Brihuega	9 December	4	D	a) Vendôme: 12,000 Fr. & Sp.	b) Stanhope: 4,000 Allies	a) 1,500	b) 4,000 (inc. 3,400 Pws)	Franco-Span. victory.
Villaviciosa	10 December	4	D	a) Vendôme: 21,000 Fr. & Sp.	b) Stahremberg: 13,600 Allies	a) 4,000	b) 5,000 (inc. 2,000 Pws & 22 guns)	Franco-Span. victory.
Nagy-Majteny	1711 1 May	5	Cap.	a) Pálffy: 6,000 Imperialists	b) Karslyi: 10,000 Hungarians	a) nil	b) 10,000 Pws	Amnesty and truce.
Faltschin-on-the-Pruth	24 July	6	C & Cap.	a) Mehmet Pasha: 260,000 Turks (140,000 Inf., 100,000 Cav.)	b) Tsar Peter I: 40,000 Russians (33,000 Inf, 7,000 Cav., 122 guns)	a) 7,000	b) 3,000 (inc. 900 Pws)	Turkish vic.
Lines of Ne Plus Ultra	5/6 August	4	Passage	a) Marlborough: 85,000 Allies	b) Villars: 90,000	a) n.d.	b) n.d.	Allied manoeuvre suc.
Tortosa	25 October	4	D	a) Glines: 3,000 Spaniards	b) Wetzel: 2,000 Imperialists	a) n.d.	b) 1,500 (inc. 600 Pws)	Spanish suc.
Denain	1712 24 July	4	D	a) Villars: 24,000 French	b) Eugene & Albemarle: 10,000 Allies	a) 2,100	b) 6,400 (inc. 4,100 Pws & 12 guns)	French vic.
Gadebusch	30 December	3	D	a) Steenbock: 14,000 Swedes	b) Scholten: 12,000 Danes	a) 1,700	b) 6,000 (inc. 2,000 Pws & 13 guns)	Swedish vic.
Tonning	1715 16 May	3	Cap.	a) Frederick IV: 40,000 Danes & Rus.	b) Steenbock: 10,000 Swedes	a) nil	b) 10,000 Pws	Danish suc.
Rügen	2 March	3	D	a) Anhalt-Dessau: 22,000 Pr.	b) Amfeldt: 5,000 Swedes	a) 500	b) 2,500	Pr.-Sax. vic.
Storkyro	2 March	3	D	a) Apraxim: 18,000 Russo-Ven.	b) Amfeldt: 5,000 Swedes	a) 500	b) 3,000	Russian vic.
Sheriffmuir	13 November	7	D	a) Argyle: 3,300 Lowland Scots	b) Mar: 10,000 Jacobites	a) n.d.	b) n.d.	Drawn battle.
Carlowitz	1716 2 August	8	F	a) Kurd Pasha: 10,000 Turks	b) Pálffy: 3,000 Austrians	a) 1,000	b) 700	Turkish suc.
Peterwardein	5 August	8	C	a) Eugene: 63,000 Imperialists	b) Damad Ali Pasha: 60,000 Turks	a) 4,500	b) 6,000	Imperial vic.
Kissoda	23 September	8	D	a) Eugene: 16,000 Imperialists	b) Mustafa Pasha: 70,000 Turks.	a) n.d.	b) 4,000	Imperial vic.
Belgrade	1717 16 August	8	B	a) Eugene: 50,000 Imperialists (52 Bns, 180 Sqns, guns n.d.)	b) Chalil Pasha: 150,000 Turks (80,000 Cav., 70,000 Inf.)	a) 5,400	b) 20,000 (inc. 5,000 Pws & 131 guns)	Great Imperial victory.
Milazzo	1718 15 October	9	D	a) Lede: 9,300 Spaniards	b) Caraffa: 6,000 Imperialists	a) 1,700 (inc. 200 Pws)	b) 1,800 (inc. 300 Pws)	Spanish suc.
Francaville	1719 20 June	9	D	a) Lede: 29,000 Spaniards	b) Mercy: 21,000 Imperialists	a) 2,000	b) 3,100	Spanish suc.
Bitonto	1734 25 May	10	D	a) Montemar: 16,000 Spaniards	b) Pignatelli: 6,200 Imperialists	a) 800	b) 1,000	Spanish suc.
Bari	26 May	10	Cap.	a) Montemar: 15,000 Spaniards	b) Pignatelli: 4,095 Imperialists	a) nil	b) 4,000 Pws	Officers released on parole.
Colorno	5 June	10	D	a) Maillebois: n.d. Fr. & Sard.	b) Wurtemberg: Imperialists – n.d.	a) 700	b) 5,550	Narrow French success.
Parma	29 June	10	C	a) Coigny: 53,000 Fr. & Sard.	b) Mercy: 37,000 Imperialists	a) 4,000	b) 6,000	Fr.-Sard. vic.
San Bendetto	15 September	10	C	a) Konigsegg: 20,000 Imperialists	b) Broglie: 40,000 Fr. & Sard.	a) 900	b) 7,100	Imperial vic.
Guastalla	19 September	10	D	a) Charles-Emmanuel: 40,000 Fr. & Sard.	b) Konigsegg: 27,000 Imperialists	a) 6,000 (inc. 100 Pws)	b) 5,800 (inc. 100 Pws)	Fr.-Sard. suc.

(Appendix 2 cont.)

Name	Date	War	Category	Contestants a)	Contestants b)	Casualties a)	Casualties b)	Result
Ostrovica	1737 22 July	11	D	a) Travnik: 5,000 Turks	b) Raunach: 4,500 Austrians	a) n.d.	b) 700	Austrians scattered.
Kornia	1738 3 July	11	D	a) Konigsegg: 40,000 Austrians	b) Mohammed Pasha: 17,000 Turks	a) 1,300	b) 2,000	Austrian suc.
Mehadia III	13 July	11	D	a) Philippi: 10,000 Austrians	b) Mohammed Pasha: 20,000 Turks	a) 1,000	b) 5,000	Austrian suc.
Grocka	23 July	11	C	a) Elmas Mohammed: 80,000 Turks	b) Wallis: 40,000 Austrians	a) 8,000	b) 5,600 (inc. 400 Pws)	Turkish vic.
Stawutschene	28 August	11	D	a) Münnich: 30,000 Russians	b) Weli Pasha: 100,000 Turks	a) 100	b) 2,000 (& 48 guns)	Russian suc.
Mollwitz	1741 10 April	12	D	a) Frederick II: 23,400 Prussians	b) Neippberg: 16,600 Austrians	a) 4,600 (inc. 700 Pws)	b) 4,500 (inc. 1,500 Pws & 7 guns)	Prussian suc.
Wilmanstrand	3 September	13	D	a) Lascy: 10,000 Russians	b) Wrangel: 5,000 Swedes	a) 3,000	b) 4,000 (inc. 1,500 Pws & 24 guns)	Russian suc.
Scharding	1742 17 January	12	D	a) Schönreith: 4,000 Austrians	b) Tonnig: 7,000 Bavarians	a) 1,000	b) 650 (inc. 500 Pws)	Austrian suc.
Chotusiz	17 May	12	C	a) Frederick II: 28,000 Prussians (33 Bns, 70 Sqns, 80 guns)	b) Lothringen: 28,000 Austrians (36 Bns, 92 Sqns, 40 guns)	a) 5,000 (inc. 800 Pws)	b) 6,300 (inc. 3,300 Pws & 16 guns)	Prussian vic.
Campo Santo	1743 8 February	12	D	a) Gages: 13,000 Spaniards	b) Traun: 11,000 Austro-Sard.	a) 4,000 (inc. 800Pws)	b) 2,000 (inc. 400 Pws & 4 guns)	Spanish suc.
Dettingen	27 June	12	D	a) George II: 35,000 Allies (42 Bns, 31 Sqns., 98 guns)	b) Noailles: 26,000 French (49 Bns, 44 Sqns., 56 guns)	a) 2,500 (inc. 450 Pws & 1 gun)	b) 4,000 (inc. 1,200 Pws)	Allied suc.
Velletri I	1744 17 June	12	D	a) Gages: 5,000 Spaniards	b) Pestaluzzi: 1,000 Austrians	a) n.d.	b) 1,000 (& 5 guns)	Spanish suc.
Weissembourg	5 July	12	D	a) Coigny: 40,000 Fr. & Bav.	b) Nácesdy: 10,000 Austrians	a) 1,800 (inc. 300 Pws)	b) 1,100 (inc. 450 Pws)	Fr.-Bav. suc.
Bellino	17-19 July	12	D	a) de Givry: 24,000 Fr. & Span.	b) Du Verger: 6,000 Sardinians	a) 3,000	b) 1,500 (inc. 400 Pws)	Initial Aust. success repulsed.
Velletri II	11 August	12	D	a) Gages: 24,000 Span. & Neap.	b) Lobkovitch: 16,000 Austrians	a) 3,500 (inc. 2,100 Pws)	b) 1,500 (inc. 88 Pws)	Fr. & Span. suc.
Coni	30 September	12	D	a) Conti: 26,000 Fr. & Span.	b) Charles-Emmanuel III: 25,000 Austro-Sard.	a) 4,000	b) 4,500 (inc. 900 Pws & 3 guns)	Fr. & Span. suc.
Pfaffenhofen	1745 15 April	12	D	a) Batthyani: 10,000 Austrians	b) de Ségur: 7,000 Fr. & Bav.	a) 800	b) 2,400 (& 9 guns)	Austrian suc.
Fontenoy	11 May	12	C	a) de Saxe: 60,000 French (69 Bns, 119 Sqns., 70 guns)	b) Cumberland: 50,000 Allies (51 Bns, 90 Sqns., 101 guns)	a) 6,000 (inc. 400 Pws)	b) 12,000 (inc. 3,000 Pws)	French vic.
Hohenfriedberg	4 June	12	B	a) Frederick II: 58,500 Prussians (69 Bns, 151 Sqns., 192 guns)	b) Lothringen: 58,700 Austro-Saxons (61 Bns, 164 Sqns., 122 guns)	a) 4,800	b) 13,730 (inc. 5,080 Pws & 66 guns)	Prussian vic.
Bassignano	27 September	12	D	a) Gages: 50,000 Fr. & Span.	b) Charles Emmanuel III: 30,000 Austro-Sard.	a) 1,000	b) 2,500 (inc. 1,500 Pws & 12 guns)	Fr. & Span. suc.
Soor	30 September	12	C	a) Frederick II: 22,500 Prussians (49 Bns, 132 Sqns., 98 guns)	b) Lothringen: 39,300 Austro-Saxons (49 Bns, 132 Sqns, 98 guns)	a) 4,000 (inc. 300 Pws)	b) 7,500 (inc. 3,000 Pws & 19 guns)	Prussian vic.
Prestonpans	1 October	14	D	a) Charles Edward: 2,450 Highlanders	b) Cope: 2,200 Anglo-Hanoverians	a) 110	b) 1,800 (inc. 1,500 Pws)	Jacobite vic.

Name	Date	War	Category	Contestants a)	Contestants b)	Casualties a)	Casualties b)	Result
Hennersdorf	23 November	12	D	a) Rochow: 8,500 Prussians	b) Buchner: 5,500 Saxons	a) 120	b) 1,400 (inc. 900 Pws & 4 guns)	Prussian suc.
Kesselsdorf	15 December	12	C	a) Anhalt-Dessau: 30,000 Prussians (35 Bns., 93 Sqns., 33 guns)	b) Rutowski: 31,000 Austro-Saxons (47 Bns., 63 Sqns., 42 guns)	a) 5,100	b) 10,500 (inc. 6,700 Pws & 40 guns)	Prussian vic.
Falkirk	1746 17 January	14	D	a) Lord George Murray: 8,000 Highlanders	b) Hawley: 8,000 Anglo-Hanoverians	a) 150	b) 800 (inc. 400 Pws)	Jacobite success.
Culloden	16 April	14	D	a) Cumberland: 9,000 Anglo-Hanoverians	b) Charles-Edward: 5,400 Highlanders	a) 300	b) 1,560 (inc. 558 Pws)	British victory.

APPENDIX THREE

SELECTED SIEGES 1688-1745

Name	Date	War	Category	Contestants a)	Contestants b)	Casualties a)	Casualties b)	Results
Belgrade	1688 11 Aug. – 6 Sept.	1	S+	a) Elector of Bavaria: 53,000 Imp. (& 65 guns)	b) Ibrahim Pasha: 8,300 Turks (& 86 guns)	a) 1,300	b) 8,300 inc. 1,300 Pws & 86 guns	Imperialist success.
Mainz	1689 16 July – 8 Sept.	2	S+	a) Lothringen: 60,000 Imperialists	b) d'Huxelles: 8,000 French	a) 5,000	b) 2,200	5,800 French allowed free evacuation.
Nissa	1690 16 Aug. – 8 Sept.	1	S+	a) Mustafa Köprili: 60,000 Turks.	b) Stahrenberg: 4,000 Imp.	a) n.d.	b) n.d.	Imp. garrison allowed to march to Belgrade.
Mons	1691 15 Mar. – 10 Apr.	2	S+	a) Vauban: 92,000 French (& 90 guns)	b) Allied garrison: 4,800	a) n.d.	b) 4,800	Allied garrison made Pws.
Namur	1692 26 May – 1 July	2	S+	a) Vauban: 46,000 French (& 127 guns)	b) Barbançon: 8,300 Spaniards	a) 3,000	b) 8,300 (inc. 43,000 Pws)	French success.
Namur	1695 1 July – 5 Sept.	2	S+	a) William III: 80,000 Allies (& 200 guns)	b) Boufflers: 13,000 French	a) 18,000	b) 13,000 (inc. 5,000 Pws)	Great Allied success.
Ath	1697 15 May – 5 June	2	S+	a) Catinat: 52,000 French	b) Allied garrison: 3,700	a) 200	b) 3,700 inc. 3,200 Pws & 32 guns	Successful French storming.
Barcelona	6 June – 10 Aug.	2	S+	a) Vendôme: 32,000 Fr. (supported by d'Estrées fleet)	b) Spanish garrison: 16,000	a) 10,000	b) 12,000 (inc. 5,000 Pws & 36 guns)	French success.
Riga	1700 27 Feb. – 1 Oct.	3	S++	a) Dahlberg: 6,000 Swedes (garr.)	b) Augustus II: 20,000 Saxons & Poles	a) n.d.	b) n.d.	Saxons forced to abandon siege.
Luttich	1702 13 June – 17 Oct.	4	S+	a) Marlborough: 40,000 Allies	b) Tilly: 8,000 French-Spaniards	a) n.d.	b) 3,000	Garrison evacuates to Antwerp on capitulation.
Guastalla	29 Aug. – 9 Sept.	4	S+	a) Vendôme: 33,000 Fr. & Span.	b) Solari: 2,200 Imperialists	a) n.d.	b) 2,200 Pws	Garrison made Pws despite agreed terms.
Ruremonde	29 Sept. – 7 Oct.	4	S+	a) Marlborough: 25,000 Allies	b) Hornes: 2,400 French	a) 60	b) 40–50	Garrison evacuates to Louvain on capitulation.
Bonn	1703 27 Apr. – 15 May	4	S+	a) Marlborough: 40,000 Allies	b) d'Alègre: 3,600 French	a) 600	b) 860	Garrison evacuates to Luxembourg on terms.
Landau	1704 9 Sept. – 7 Oct.	4	S+	a) Baden: 30,000 Imperialists	b) Laubanie: 5,000 French	a) 5,000	b) 3,500 (inc. 500 sick)	1,500 French allowed free evacuation.
Trarbach	4 Nov. – 20 Dec.	4	S+	a) Hesse-Cassel: 20,000 Allies	b) French garrison: 600	a) 1,000	b) 600 (inc. 350 Pws)	French made Pws.
Verrua	1704/1705 14 Nov. – 9 Apr.	4	S+	a) Vendôme: 30,000 Fr. & Span.	b) Fresen: 7,250 P'mont.-Imps.	a) 12,000	b) 7,000 (mostly Pws)	French success: relief attempt fought off.
Gibraltar	21 Oct. – 30 Apr.	4	S+	a) Hesse-Darmstadt: 4,000 English (supported by Leake's fleet)	b) Villadarias: 20,000 Fr. & Span. (& Tessé)	a) n.d.	b) 12,000	Siege abandoned.
Barcelona	1705 18 Sept. – 6 Oct.	4	S+	a) Peterborough: 11,000 Sp. & Eng. (supported by a flotilla)	b) Velasco: 5,800 Spaniards	a) n.d.	b) 5,000 (mostly Pws)	Garrison made Pws.
Badajoz	4 – 17 Oct.	4	S++	a) Puebla: 1,000 Span. (garr.)	b) Galway: 22,000 Anglo. & Port.	a) n.d.	b) 1,000	Siege abandoned on Tessé's approach.

Name	Date	War	Category	Contestants a)	Contestants b)	Casualties a)	Casualties b)	Results
Ostend	1706 19 June – 9 July	4	S+	a) Marlborough: 20,000 Allies	b) La Motte: 5,000 Fr. & Span.	a) 1,600 (sailors inc.)	b) 800	4,800 allowed to march out; Spaniards join Allied cause.
Menin	22 July – 22 Aug.	4	S+	a) Marlborough: 30,000 Allies	b) Caraman: 5,500 Fr. & Span.	a) 2,620	b) 1,101	4,400 allowed to march out to Douai on capitulation.
Dendermonde	27 Aug. – 9 Sept.	4	S+	a) Marlborough: 6,000 Allies	b) de Valée: 4,000 French	a) n.d.	b) 4,000 (mostly Pws)	Garrison made Pws by Allies.
Turin	2 June – 7 Sept.	4	S++	a) Daun: 10,500 Imp. & P'mont (Garr. relieved by Eugene's army)	b) La Feuillade: 36,000 Fr. & Span.	a) 3,000 (inc. 2,000 deserters)	b) 14,000	Siege abandoned by French after Eugene's victory (qv).
Toulon	1707 14 July – 22 Aug.	4	S++	a) St-Pater: 9,000 (supported by Tessé's army)	b) Eugene: 38,000 P'mont-Imp. (supported by English fleet)	a) n.d.	b) 10,000	Allies abandon siege.
Lerida	13 Sept. – 11 Nov.	4	S+	a) Orleans: 30,000 Fr. & Span.	b) Hesse-Darmstadt: 2,500 Allies	a) n.d.	b) 1,000	1,500 Allies allowed free evacuation on capitulation.
Lille	1708 12 Aug. – 10 Dec.	4	S+	a) Eugene: 35,000 Allies (& guns) (covered by Marlborough's army of 75,000)	b) Boufflers: 16,000 French	a) 16,000	b) 7,000	9,000 French allowed free evacuation to Douai.
Pultava	1709 1 May – 8 July	3	S++	a) Russian garrison: 4,000 (relieved by Peter I's army)	b) Charles XII: 16,000 Swedes	a) n.d.	b) n.d.	Swedes abandon siege after battle (qv).
Tournai	27 June – 3 Sept.	4	S+	a) Marlborough: 40,000 Allies	b) Surville: 7,000 French	a) 5,400	b) 3,900 (inc. 700 sick)	3,100 French repatriated after exchange.
Douai	1710 23 Apr. – 25 June	4	S+	a) Marlborough: 60,000 Allies	b) Albergotti: 8,000 French	a) 8,000	b) 2,860	5,000 French allowed free evacuation to Cambrai.
Bouchain	1711 9 Aug. – 14 Sept.	4	S+	a) Marlborough: 30,000 Allies	b) de Ravignau: 5,000 French	a) 4,800	b) 5,000 (inc. 2,500 Pws)	French garrison made Pws.
Landrecies	1712 17 July – 2 Aug.	4	S++	a) Du Barail: 5,000 French (supported by Villars' army)	b) Anhalt-Dessau: 20,000 Allies (supported by Eugene's army)	a) n.d.	b) n.d.	Siege abandoned on Villar's approach.
Bouchain	1 – 19 Oct.	4	S+	a) Villars: 20,000 French	b) Gravenstein: 2,000 Allies	a) 400	b) 2,000 (inc. 1,600 Pws)	Allied garrison made Pws.
Gerona	1712/1713 1 Nov. – 3 Jan.	4	S++	a) Brancas: 4,000 Spaniards (supported by Berwick's army)	b) Wetzel: 9,000 Imperialists (supported by Stahrenberg's army)	a) n.d.	b) n.d.	Spaniards abandon siege.
Landau	1713 11 June – 20 Aug.	4	S+	a) de Bezons: 20,000 French (supported by Villars' army of 90,000)	b) Wurttemberg: 7,000 Spaniards	a) 10,000	b) 7,000 (inc. 5,000 Pws)	Costly French success.
Barcelona	1713/1714 July – 12 Sept.	4	S+	a) Philip V: 30,000 Spanish (supported by Berwick's army)	b) Garrison: 16,000 Spanish rebels	a) 20,000	b) 6,000	Siege ended by amnesty.
Stralsund	1715 9 Aug. – 22 Dec.	3	S+	a) Anhalt-Dessau: 70,000 Pruss., Sax. & Poles	b) Charles XII: 12,000 Swedes	a) 10,000	b) 12,000 (inc. 6,000 Pws)	Russian success.
Corfu	1716 25 July – 20 Aug.	8	S++	a) Schulenburg: 6,000 Venetians	b) Mustafa Pasha: 70,000 Turks	a) n.d.	b) n.d.	Turks abandon siege.
Temesvar	1 Sept. – 14 Oct.	8	S++	a) Eugene: 45,000 Austrians	b) Mustafa Pasha: 18,000 Turks	a) 4,500	b) 3,000 (& 156 guns)	12,000 Turks allowed free evacuation.
Belgrade	1717 29 June – 18 Aug.	8	S+	a) Eugene: 100,000 Imp. (& 200 guns)	b) Mustafa Pasha: 30,000 Turks (& 300 guns)	a) 20,000	b) 5,000 (& 300 guns)	Great Imperialist success.
Messina	1719 20 July – 20 Sept.	9	S+	a) Mercy: 18,000 Imperialists	b) Spinola: 4,000 Spaniards	a) 5,200	b) 900 (& 160 guns)	3,100 Spaniards allowed free evacuation.

(Appendix 3 cont.)

Name	Date	War	Category	Contestants a)	Contestants b)	Casualties a)	Casualties b)	Results
Novara	1734 1 – 7 January	10	S+	a) Coigny: 13,000 Fr. & Sard.	b) Imperialist garrison: 1,300	a) n.d.	b) n.d.	French-Sardinian success.
Philippsburg	24 May – 27 July	10	S+	a) Berwick: 117,000 French	b) Wittgenau: 4,500 Imperialists	a) 10,000	b) 1,000 (& 124 guns)	3,500 Imperialists allowed free evacuation.
Oczakov	1737 12 July	11	Storm	a) Münnich: 60,000 Russians	b) Java Pasha: 22,000 Turks	a) 4,000	b) 22,000 (inc. 3,000 Pws & 100 guns)	3,000 Turks joined Russia.
Banjaluka	25 July – 4 Aug.	11	S++	a) Turkish garrison: 5,000	b) Saschen-Hildburghausen: 13,000 Austrians	a) n.d.	b) 1,000	Turks abandon siege.
Orsova	1738 12 May – 10 July	11	S++	a) Kehrenberg: 2,000 Austrians	b) Mohammed Pasha: 20,000 Turks	a) n.d.	b) n.d.	Turks abandon siege.
Choczin	29 August	11	Capitul.	a) Münnich: 30,000 Russians	b) Turkish garrison: 1,000 Turks	a) n.d.	b) 1,000 Pws	Russian success.
Helsingfors	1742 4 September	13	Capitul.	a) 60,000 Russians	b) du Bousquet: 15,000 Swedes	a) n.d.	b) n.d.	Negotiated surrender.
Prague	27 July – 28 Dec.	12	S+	a) Lobkowitz: 44-60,000 Aust.	b) Belle-Isle: 26,000 French (inc. 6,000 sick)	a) n.d.	b) 2,800 mostly Pws	4,200 marched out.
Prague	1744 6 – 16 Sept.	12	S+	a) Frederick II: 80,000 Prussians	b) Harsch: 14,900 Austrians	a) 500	b) 14,900 (inc. 13,500 Pws & 116 guns)	Austrian garrison made Pws.
Freiburg	17 Sept. – 30 Nov.	12	S+	a) Coigny: 30,000 French	b) Damnitz: 7,000 Prussians	a) 16,000	b) 7,000 (inc. 4,800 Pws & 250 guns)	French success.
Louisburg	1745 25 Apr. – 17 June	12	S+	a) Pepperell: 6,000 Anglo-Canadians	b) French-Canadian garrison: 3,000	a) n.d.	b) n.d.	French garrison allowed to sail to Brest.
Tournai	25 Apr. – 19 June	12	S+	a) de Saxe: 75,000 French	b) Brakel: 6,000 Dutch (inc. 5,000 sick)	a) n.d.	b) n.d.	Dutch allowed free evacuation.
Ostend	8 – 24 August	12	S+	a) de Saxe: 50,000 French	b) Chanclos: 4,000 Allies	a) 2,000	b) 4,000 (inc. 3,400 Pws)	Garrison made Pws.
Kosel	27 Aug. – 5 Sept.	12	S+	a) Nassau: 20,000 Prussians	b) Flandrini: 2,300 Austrians	a) n.d.	b) 2,300 Pws & 52 guns	Prussian success.

APPENDIX FOUR

	Namur 1695	*Lille 1708*	*Bouchain 1711*	*Belgrade 1717*
Investment	1 July	13 August	9 August	29 June
Lines completed	10 July	21 August	23 August	22 July
Trenches opened	11 July	22 August	23 August	16 July
Outworks taken	24 July	21 September	11 September	11 August
Town capitulation arranged	4 August	23 October	*and of citadel* 12 September	*and of citadel* 17 August
Town evacuated by garrison	6 August	26 October	*and citadel* 14 September	*and citadel* 22 August
Citadel isolated	28 August	26 October		
Outworks taken	30 August	–		
Citadel breached	1 September	–		
Final capitulation arranged	5 September	8 December		
Garrison marches out		11 December		

Index